EXPANDING HUMANITY'S

Vision of God

EXPANDING HUMANITY'S
Vision of God

NEW THOUGHTS ON
SCIENCE AND RELIGION

Edited by

ROBERT L. HERRMANN

Templeton Foundation Press
Philadelphia and London

Templeton Foundation Press
Five Radnor Corporate Center, Suite 120
100 Matsonford Road
Radnor, Pennsylvania 19087

Designed and typeset by Nesbitt Graphics, Inc.

Most of the chapters in this book were originally published in other formats: as journal articles, sections of books, sermons, and the like. As a result, the chapters of this book contain a variety of spelling, capitalization, and usage styles, particularly for scientific and religious terms.

Library of Congress Cataloging-in-Publication Data

Expanding humanity's vision of God : new thoughts on science and religion / edited by Robert L. Herrmann.
      p. cm.
  Includes bibliographical references.
  ISBN 1-890151-50-5 (pbk. : alk. paper)
  1. Religion and science.   I. Herrmann, Robert., 1928-

  BL240.2.E893   2001
  291.1'75—dc21   2001027018
                                                          CIP

Printed in the United States of America

01   02   03   04   05   06   10 9 8 7 6 5 4 3 2 1

CONTENTS

PREFACE

This book is a collection of essays and sermons that were awarded prizes in a recent award program of the John Templeton Foundation. The program was announced in December 1998 and concluded on April 1, 2000. Over this period, three hundred entries were received and thirty-five were awarded prizes totaling $233,000.

Guidelines offered examples of the kinds of essays and sermons the program was seeking, emphasizing the importance of the science-religion dialogue. Program leaders pointed out that Sir John Templeton is deeply committed to fostering an expanded vision of God that is informed by recent discoveries of science about the nature of the universe and the place of humans in our world. He believes the stage is set for keen and creative minds to launch out on a new exploration of theology, respectful of our great religious heritage, but focusing on the new visions and new possibilities that have come to us through the momentous scientific discoveries of the twentieth century.

The target audience for this program included theologians, ministers, priests, rabbis, imams, leaders of other faith traditions, scientists, educators, policymakers, artists, writers, and others who are respected for their religious thinking and who represent a diversity of religious traditions. Because of this diversity, the essays and sermons chosen for this book display rich, varied, and often expansive visions, many of which resonate with one of our original contest questions, "Can we have a more comprehensive, more exploratory, more humble theology?" There is also considerable cultural diversity, with authors from Germany, Israel, India, Iran, and Australia.

The book is divided into three parts. In the first, "Contemporary Science Raising Theological Questions," thirteen chapters address the many fascinating questions raised by physicists about quantum theory, by cosmologists about our enormous universe, and by biologists about our evolutionary past and future and the new theological challenge of artificial intelligence. For example, Günter Thomas draws many parallels between the "new creation" of the Bible and complexity theory in contemporary science, while Pirooz Fatoorchi addresses the scientific understanding of the creation of the universe from an Islamic perspective. Richard Rice discusses the tensions many scientists with religious beliefs face in the course of their work and the ways in which these tensions may be ameliorated. Brian Edgar focuses on the theological implications of developing medical technologies that may extend human life beyond its current life span, while Kuruvilla Pandikattu tackles the implications for religion if humans were to become immortal. Peter Heltzel concludes Part I by making connections between human attempts to create artificial intelligence and God's creation of the universe and everything in it.

In "New Visions of Theology," six chapters stretch our thinking about God into new frameworks by joining theology with quantum indeterminacy, by perceiving nature as sacred, and by a synthesis of science with Jewish and Eastern philosophies. Michael King, for example, discusses the devotional and cerebral aspects of Western and Eastern religions and the ways in which these two qualities have affected, and may continue to affect, scientific inquiry around the world. Rami Shapiro presents a kabbalistic "map" that will allow us to unify our sciences, both material and spiritual, while presenting an idea of God that incorporates and transcends them both.

In "Historical and Philosophical Perspectives on the Science-Religion Dialogue," the tone is more searching. The five authors look somewhat less optimistically at the future of science-theology interaction, taking into account the unfulfilled promises of the past and the limitations of our own humanity. Roger Shinn explores our historical and theological understanding of nature and the ecological ramifications. David Mehl uses the context of Reformation Sunday to encourage a new reformation between science and religion, a reformation marked by humility and common sense. And Theodore Roszak rounds out the book by analyzing humanity's place in the universe in keeping with the evidence suggested by the "new cosmology."

While the contributors to this volume approach the science-religion dialogue from varying perspectives, each writes with the attitude that theologians and scientists can, indeed must, communicate with each other—questioning, researching, informing—in an effort to bring greater understanding to all of us.

Eleven additional winning papers in the contest, which are not included in this book, can be viewed on the Templeton Foundation's Web site, www.templeton.org.

Robert L. Herrmann

PART I

CONTEMPORARY SCIENCE RAISING
Theological Questions

CHAPTER 1

Knowledge of the Unseen: A New Vision for Science and Religion Dialogue

HYUNG S. CHOI

Dr. Hyung S. Choi is the director of the Canyon Institute for Advanced Studies where he leads interdisciplinary research on fundamental areas of knowledge. He is professor of mathematical physics and philosophy of science at Grand Canyon University, Phoenix, Arizona. He is also a recipient of a number of awards for his teaching and research, including the Templeton Foundation's essay award on Humility Theology and the Quality and Excellence in Teaching Award from the Center for Theology and the Natural Sciences.

Professor Choi received his Ph.D. in theoretical physics at the Graduate Center of CUNY. He also holds a master of divinity from Princeton Theological Seminary and a master of philosophy from the Graduate Center of CUNY. Dr. Choi was a Witherspoon Postdoctoral Fellow at the Center for Theology and the Natural Sciences in Berkeley for two years before he took his current job.

Science, in the last century, has found strange aspects of the physical world that seemed quite different from what classical physics had taught us.[1] In hindsight, it is an irony that while modernity in its positivistic spirit started out with the notion that the reality perceived by our senses is the only knowable reality there is, we now end up with the idea that the true nature of physical reality is quite different from what we experience through our senses. The legend of the tangibility of matter, or what may be called "the matter myth," which served as the basis for the certainty of knowledge, was lost.[2] Here, within science, was raised the problem of reality (an ontological problem), issues of the limits of human knowledge (an epistemological problem), and the problem of testability (a methodological problem). Relativity and quantum physics, which serve as the pillars of contemporary science, and more recently chaos theory, are now presenting us with a radically new physical view of the world in which positivistic, deterministic, materialistic philosophies no longer have secure places. They present us with deeper, greater, and more mysterious aspects of nature. Scientists now proceed to the area that traditionally belonged to metaphysics, discussing the possibility of the ultimate reality of the universe, the origin and finality of the cosmos, the problem of consciousness, and the like. The natural sciences, as they touch upon the edge of objectivity and empirical testability, raise many questions about the world to which science itself cannot provide definite answers within its limited framework. In these frontiers of science, our metaphors are running out and our common sense often breaks down. We have to wrestle with the limits of our knowledge, logic, and rationality. Here in science the fundamental epistemic problems are naturally raised as they were in religion and theology in earlier centuries.

We now start to take seriously, especially in fundamental physics and cosmology, the things that are not seen. As recent developments in theoretical physics and cosmology witness, as speculative as they may be, some theories quite beyond what can be directly measured by physical apparatus are possible and are indeed commonplace. It not only raises a possibility for the epistemology of the unseen in general, but also makes its ontological discussion feasible.

The Unseen in Science-and-Theology Discussion

An important area that has been largely neglected in the recent science-and-religion discussion is the issue of the unseen. Exploring the knowledge of the possible rich texture of the unseen—the "physical" or otherwise—should be a part of our endeavor to restore what we have lost from the treasury of human ideas. Science can benefit from this creative imagination, and theology will be able to address again a fuller view of the world.

There is a significant epistemological and methodological parallel between scientific and theological claims concerning the unseen. The claims of the unseen in both disciplines are often inferred from the seen. Of course, the inferential nature of science has been known since the time of Aristotle. However, during the last few centuries, the discussion of the unseen in religion has been severely limited because of the positivistic epistemology that suspects anything that does not fit in the grand narrative of the matter myth.

A partial justification of the discussion of the unseen in science and theology comes from various limit theorems that we have discovered in science during the last century. These include Heisenberg's uncertainty principle, event horizons, and possible singularities of the universe. In mathematics, we have found equally fundamental limits, such as Gödel's incompleteness theorem, Turing's incomputability theorem, Chatin's theorem for unprovability of algorithmic randomness, and the unpredictability in deterministic chaos systems.

At first, it looks as if these theorems impose permanent barriers to human knowledge. However, careful examination tells us that many of these theorems and principles have to do with the limits of our epistemic ability as we investigate things from within specific systems. This means that if we view these theorems and principles in a different way, then they can be seen as the windows that open up our minds to the things that are beyond the confinements of the system. For example, Heisenberg's principle has led us to a new vision of microscopic realities beyond the visible and tangible macroscopic apparatus. D'Espagnat therefore aptly described quantum mechanics as a "window to the unseen."[3] The limit of the speed of light also leads us to the recognition that there are regions of the universe that are hidden from our observation. Gödel's and Turing's results may imply that there are more things that the human mind can do than what perfect machines can execute.[4] This may point to a possibility that the human mind might possess a power to reflect on something beyond what is a mechanical process of nature. The study of chaos systems illustrates the fact that there may be certain orders in this world beyond our predictive power. In some sense, the limit principles and theorems free us from the bondage of small mental frameworks as they point to greater systems that lie beyond themselves.

As we think further on the issues of the unseen in science-religion discussions, it is useful to examine some analogous issues we have in theoretical physics. We have many theories that deal either with the things that are partially unobservable or with the things that are, even in principle, unobservable. Among the examples are the ideas of David Bohm's "hidden variables," the theory of "beables" by J. S. Bell, various interpretations of quantum physics, quantum cosmological models near the Planck scale, and higher-dimensional theories presented by superstring theory and M-theory. There has also been a spectrum of the unseen with different degrees, from those which have closer connections to the observable to those which have more remote connections and finally to those which seem to have no testable connection. Of course,

direct application of these ideas to the unseen in religious discourse is
not likely, considering that there exists a considerable linguistic and
characteristic gulf in between them. However, these examples in
physics provide us with very useful metaphors and analogies as well
as important cautions against naïve conclusions and extrapolations in
science-and-theology discussions.

Contemporary physics has shown clearly how counterintuitive
nature can be as we step out from the scale of ordinary experiences.
This posits a clear caution against a premature and dogmatic talk about
God in terms of our ordinary logic and rationality. Von Neumann's impossibility proof for hidden variable theories is a good example of the
mistakes of this type. As J. S. Bell later found out, Von Neumann used a
well-established theorem in statistics to categorically refute hidden variable theories. This theorem, which was completely valid in classical statistics, turned out to be inapplicable to Bohm's counterintuitive nonlocal theory. The idea of gauge symmetry is another highly mathematical
abstraction which plays a central and essential role in theoretical particle physics.[5] Though it appears at the heart of many fundamental physical processes and has made particle physics tremendously successful, its
ontological interpretations so far have not been the subject of a serious
discussion in the physics community.

Bell's theorem on a local hidden variable theory teaches us another important lesson in our discussions of the unseen. Until the publication of Bell's theorem, physicists had taken freedom in imagining the
ontological status of the quantum world and thought that one's choice
between local hidden variable theories and the Copenhagen interpretation would be just a matter of personal taste. However, it turned out
that in certain cases one's choice in this "metaphysics" made a difference in physics by resulting in different experimental outcomes. Hence,
the alleged "metaphysics" of yesterday has become the "physics" of today. Certainly this illustrates vividly that our epistemic limits provide
the freedom for metaphysical construction but at the same time that
theories beyond the observable may be constrained by the structures of
the observable.

In hindsight, the epistemic limits that we have encountered in
physics and mathematics in the twentieth century should not have
been so surprising. They came as surprises because we wrongly believed
that, in the spirit of scientism, science may be extended indefinitely and
our logic and mathematics are certain. At the dawn of quantum
physics, Heisenberg saw clearly the problem that is inherent in all scientific investigations. He understood that "what we observe is not nature

itself, but nature exposed to our method of questioning."[6] We have limits due to our methodology, predetermined scopes, sensory-perceptive assumption, logic and rational ability, mathematical languages and metaphors, and our limited experimental tools, among other things.[7] Most of these limits stem from the fact that we are not the wholly other in our relationship with the things that we want to investigate. All investigations of a subject matter from within are inherently limited.

These limits exhibit two important characteristics. First, they are epistemological, not ontological. In other words, definite knowledge is not available not because there is nothing to learn but because our ability is limited. Hence, there is no reason to suppose that any ontological discontinuity exists at these epistemic limits. Second, these epistemic limits are usually limits, incompleteness, and uncertainties, not epistemic impossibilities. Our knowledge beyond these limits may be partially available either because partial investigations are possible or because these limits usually do not come all at the same time. In our science-and-religion discussion, the epistemic limits on our side naturally allow for the possibility of one-directional knowledge transfer— that is, there exists the possibility of divine revelation from the other side even though we do not have much control over how the information may be transferred to us.

The "Natural" and the "Supernatural"

Across these limits in fundamental investigations of the world, no inherent ontological distinction exists between the seen and the unseen, and between the "speakable and unspeakable," as J. S. Bell put it.[8] In light of this epistemology of the unseen in science, we must rethink terms such as "natural" and "supernatural." We can no longer identify what we can observe as natural things nor can we equate what we cannot observe with supernatural ones. What then is the criterion for this ontological demarcation? Is it not just an imaginative mental category that we inherited from the prejudice of modernity? When we talk about "nature," are we talking about the totality of things that exist? The affirmative answer to this question requires a radical revision of our conceptual categories, for there is no way of distinguishing the "natural" and the "supernatural."

There is a further issue—nature, as we know it, contains phenomenon of consciousness as its part. Given that the most immediate human experience is our conscious experience and that nature at its most

fundamental level is neither tangible nor separable—as quantum mechanics tells us—can we then define nature as material existence? What
then is "material"? For the distinction between the natural and the supernatural to be meaningful at all, there must be a way to distinguish
them. Historically, the term "supernatural" is known to have been
coined by Thomas Aquinas as he tried to reconcile Aristotelian naturalistic philosophy with Christian theism. Later in the seventeenth century, as mechanical philosophy became very popular among scientists
and philosophers, the idea of nature acquired a different sense.
Mechanical philosophy had sought to explain all natural phenomena in
terms of matter and motion. The natural then effectively became mechanical. As pursuit of certain knowledge continued through the
Enlightenment, whatever was not "natural" became unqualified as an
object of knowledge, and subsequently acquired a sense of being unreal.

In light of our contemporary understanding of the world, the sharp
demarcation between "natural" and "supernatural" is not tenable since
we can no longer subscribe to the hard naturalism that is based on the
mechanical notion of matter. One can still subscribe to soft naturalism,
which allows for the possibility of reality beyond what is material.
However, we then need to redefine what we mean by nature and naturalism. My contention is that the distinction between "natural" and "supernatural" should now be discarded as an unjustified and unfruitful category that stems from modern prejudice. The only valid demarcation may
be the distinction between the seen (observable) and the unseen (unobservable) as they can be readily distinguished by our epistemic limits.

We now see science as our active mental and physical engagement
with nature. Even as we strive to be as "objective" as possible using various objectification processes in science, quantum mechanics clearly
demonstrates that there is no purely objective way of knowing nature.
No fundamental knowing processes are either totally objective or totally subjective, but are interactive. Here, both in science and religion,
we see epistemological parallels such as our active participation, epistemic limitations, possible ontological continuity, and communal dis-
cernment. Depending upon what should be considered as data for religious or theological knowledge, we can have some methodological
parallels between science and theology as well.[9] This presents an interesting possibility for the unity of knowledge of the seen and the unseen
on a deeper level. Abner Shimony, a philosopher of science and a quantum physicist, for example, suggested the possibility of constructing an
integrated epistemology based on his naturalistic metaphysics. One of

his points of departure is the idea that science and metaphysics should mesh and complement each other unless convincing reasons are given why it should fail.[10]

Willem Drees's *Religion, Science, and Naturalism* offers a naturalistic approach to theology with the premise that "the natural order is the whole of reality that we know of and interact with; no supernatural or spiritual realm distinct from the natural world shows up within our natural world, not even in the mental life of humans," while leaving a room for religion in that "we have a sense of gratitude and wonder with respect to the reality to which we belong."[11] As one can see from Drees's case, ontological presuppositions often preclude the possibility of certain types of knowledge since ontology informs epistemology. Ideas concerning "how the world is" tell us something about "what can be known about the world." It seems inconsistent that Drees precludes the unseen, while physics, which he regards as the best description of fundamental aspects of nature, takes the unseen seriously.

Since ontology informs epistemology and vice versa, it is important to consider some ontological models that include the realm of the unseen. The case of David Bohm serves as a great example for this.[12] Bohm explicitly constructed a model for the unobservable or "hidden" physical reality. But he did not stop at nonlocal hidden variable theories for quantum physics. He went on to construct a metaphysical system that is consistent with his own hidden variable theory.[13] His discussion on the "implicate" and "explicate" orders provides us with a concrete example of how one might bridge the gulf between theories of the unseen in physics and theories of the unseen in traditional metaphysics. In his metaphysics, the "explicate" order in which we experience the world is the enfolding or manifestation of what is actually lying in a deeper dimension that he called the "implicate" order. There is no discontinuity between these two, though we can only experience what has been enfolded unto us. Bohm's metaphysics was not presented just as an analogy or metaphor; it was meant to be a description of the single seamless reality that would encompass both the visible and the invisible.

Another promising possibility for the description of the unseen that goes beyond physical experience is using the concept of higher dimension. Ever since Plato's famous allegory of the cave, people have thought about the possibility that there may be a radically new way of looking at the true nature of the world. In science, this new vision of the world was introduced by Riemann in the nineteenth century and again by Einstein in the early twentieth century and has revolutionized our understanding of the natural world. Some leading theologians and philosophers such as Karl Heim, Paul Tillich, and Huston Smith have alluded to this new way of thinking about the world and have pointed out that this "dimensional" metaphor or model can be very useful in dealing with many religious enigmas and problems.[14] Though Kant has persuaded the modern mind that human thoughts are categorically limited within three-dimensional space and one-dimensional time, the theoretical physics community today talks about the possibility that we may be living in a real, higher-dimensional spacetime, containing perhaps ten or eleven dimensions. Currently we do not know whether these theories can ever be put to the test, but physicists are working hard to come up with some predictable results in a low energy limit.

This dimensional framework expands our imaginative horizons immensely. The model can provide a heuristic framework in which we can talk about immanence and transcendence at the same time since it is possible for different dimensions to possess different properties. For example, a spatial dimension possesses entirely different characteristics than that of the time dimension but they can be seamlessly combined to form a unity. For Tillich, human spirituality signifies "openness" to the greater reality beyond the physical one and this spiritual dimension of humanity is what makes humans distinctive. Karl Rahner also contends that the human being essentially experiences itself as a transcendental being, as spirit beyond the realm of ordinary space and time. Karl Heim suggested that this dimensional metaphor would preserve both distinction and unity between the spiritual and the physical.

The Unseen and Divine Action

This dimensional model can represent a dynamic relationship between the seen and the unseen. The Greek fathers, such as St. Basil, talked about God's logos operating in the creation of divine *energia* or "energy," which flows toward all creation. This divine "energy" represents manifesting grace in contrast to the unknowable divine essence.[15] This echoes Paul's assertion that invisible qualities of God have been made visible in creation. In this model, such religious concepts as revelation may be treated in a natural way since it is possible to consider one-directional information flow from a higher dimension to a lower one. A lower dimension does not have access to a higher dimension (which therefore imposes epistemological limits) but they together form a continuum of reality (which therefore preserves ontological continuity). In this vision, we do not even need to look for "openness" or "room" in the "physical" order to avoid the problem of "suspension" or "violation" of natural laws. Divine action can simply be understood as higher-order laws working seamlessly with lower-order laws.

Even in the naturalistic framework, the openness of natural order is quite obvious from the fact that all our scientific laws are constructed a posteriori. No law, deterministic or not, closes the possibility of the existence of other laws—just as the perfectly deterministic Newtonian laws of mechanics do not exclude the possibility of the other perfectly deterministic laws of electromagnetism prescribed by Maxwell's equations. If electromagnetism had not been known to humanity, the lifting of a massive object by magnetic field without mechanical support would have been considered a "violation" of the natural order. However, for those who have known the laws of electromagnetism, the lifting event neither violated nor suspended the Newtonian laws. Newtonian laws were working perfectly as well all along. The idea that deterministic laws necessarily imply the causally closed universe is simply misguided.

On the road of science we have experienced many turns and surprises. Today theoretical physicists are considering the possibility that these Newtonian and Maxwellian laws, along with other laws of physics, may be just different manifestations of a single law on a deeper level for which we might not have a tool for direct investigation. Usually deeper or more general laws tender surprising phenomena, as we have experienced in twentieth-century physics. Phenomena such as lasers, superconductivity, Bose-Einstein condensation, and Einstein-Podolsky-Rosen effects were completely foreign and impossible in classical physics.

I am not here promoting "anything goes" in nature. On the contrary, in the spirit of true science, I am suggesting the serious consideration of the unseen—that our current limited vision should not blind us to the possibility of the greater reality that we have not yet seen or known.

This new heuristic framework, which departs radically from the framework of modernity, can be a fruitful ground for theological reflections. Of course, I have no reason to suppose that any model that has been developed in science or mathematics is sufficiently adequate in describing the reality that may lie beyond the accessible empirical or rational order. However, as our experience and knowledge of the world increases, we admit happily that all we can do in science and theology is to try to find a better and ever more adequate language that may enable us to describe in some limited way the things that may ultimately be indescribable. As we expand our minds' horizons, we also expand our understanding of God, for we know God is the ultimate reality—far greater than any human imagination of the unseen.

NOTES

1. The development is well described in John Wheeler, *At Home in the Universe* (Woodbury, NY: American Institute of Physics, 1994). See the collection of works by the American Physical Society, *More Things in Heaven and Earth: A Celebration of Physics at the Millennium,* ed. Benjamin Bederson, (New York: Springer-Verlag, 1999). For more philosophical discussions, see J. Hilgevoord, ed., *Physics and Our View of the World* (Cambridge: Cambridge University Press, 1994).

2. See for example, Paul Davies and John Gribbin, *The Matter Myth* (New York: Simon & Schuster, 1992).

3. Bernard D'Espagnat, *Reality and the Physicist: Knowledge, Duration, and the Quantum World* (Cambridge University Press, 1989).

4. Roger Penrose, *Shadows of the Mind* (Oxford: Oxford University Press, 1994).

5. Effectiveness of mathematical abstraction in modern physics is recognized by David Hilbert, James Clerk Maxwell, Albert Einstein, and Alfred North Whitehead, and continually has impressed many mathematicians and physicists. See Morris Klein, *Mathematics and the Search for Knowledge* (Oxford: Oxford University Press, 1985).

6. Werner Heisenberg, *Physics and Philosophy* (New York: Harper & Row, 1958).

7. John D. Barrow, *Impossibility: The Limits of Science and the Science of Limits* (Oxford: Oxford University Press, 1998).

8. J. S. Bell, *Speakable and Unspeakable in Quantum Mechanics* (Cambridge: Cambridge University Press, 1993).

9. See the works in Russell, Stoeger, and Coyne, eds., *Physics and Philosophy and Theology* (Vatican City State: Vatican Observatory, 1988) and Mark Richardson and Wesley Wildman, eds., *Religion & Science: History, Method, Dialogue* (New York: Routledge, 1996).

10. Abner Shimony, *Scientific Method and Epistemology* and *Natural Science and Metaphysics,* vols. 1 and 2 of *Search for a Naturalistic Worldview* (Cambridge: Cambridge University Press, 1993).

11. Willem Drees, *Religion, Science, and Naturalism* (Cambridge: Cambridge University Press, 1996).

12. Alfred N. Whitehead also rigorously integrated his scientific theory with metaphysics. However, since many theological works were done already on his metaphysics, I will not deal with it here.

13. David Bohm, *Wholeness and the Implicate Order* (London: Routledge & Kegan Paul, 1980); D. Bohm and B. J. Hiley, *The Undivided Universe* (London: Routledge, 1993).

14. See Karl Heim, *God Transcendent* (London: Nisbet and Co., 1935); Paul Tillich, *Systematic Theology*, vol. 3 (University of Chicago, 1963); Huston Smith, *Forgotten Truth: Primordial Tradition* (San Francisco: HarperCollins, 1976).

15. Vladimir Lossky, *The Mystical Theology of the Eastern Church* (Crestwood, NY: St. Vladimir's Seminary Press, 1986).

Republished with permission from *Perspectives on Science and Christian Faith,* vol. 53, no. 2, The American Scientific Affiliation, Ipswich, MA.

CHAPTER 2

The Strangely Relational World of Quantum Mechanics

CATHERINE H. CROUCH

Catherine H. Crouch is an experimental physicist at Harvard University studying silicon microtextures formed with high-energy laser pulses. She thanks William K. Wootters of Williams College and N. T. Wright of Westminster Cathedral, London, for invaluable discussions. A full version of this article with footnotes is available at *www.regenerator.com*.

In the popular imagination, Albert Einstein represents the ultimate physics genius—when people want to personify the stunning role that physics has played in the development of the modern world, they turn to the bushy-haired German Jew whom *Time* named "Man of the Century." But while Einstein is rightly celebrated for his association with relativity, one of the two major innovations in twentieth-century physics, it's less well known that he vehemently opposed the other theory that rocked the twentieth-century scientific world—quantum mechanics. The brainchild of several of Einstein's contemporaries, quantum mechanics makes mind-bending predictions such as simultaneous causes and effects, particles that seem to be in more than one place at the same time, and an unsettling randomness at the heart of the universe.

Albert Einstein was convinced it couldn't be the whole story, largely for the same kinds of philosophical and aesthetic reasons that caused an earlier world to reject Copernicus's idea that the earth was not the center of the universe. The story of why Einstein, along with other less well-known physicists, violently opposed certain aspects of quantum theory—and why they were probably wrong—has many parallels for Christians who want to make judgments about, or draw theological conclusions from, the ever-changing world of basic science.

And surprisingly, in recent years the theory that reportedly caused Einstein to protest, "God does not play dice [with the universe]," not only has turned out to be right, but may be remarkably congruent with Christian convictions. Call it the quantum leap of faith.

Outside of the physics world, the theory of relativity has much more name recognition than quantum mechanics. Not that either is widely understood, of course; relativity is often assumed to be the scientific justification for the ideological relativism now popular in coffeehouses and dorm rooms everywhere. On the contrary, relativity was actually developed to preserve certain absolutes—namely, to demonstrate that the laws of physics apply regardless of whether the person observing them is moving or at rest, and regardless of the speed of the observer's motion. Under Einstein's brilliant tutelage, physicists realized that the physical universe is governed by underlying laws that are not dependent on human perspective. Certain uncomfortable issues left unexplained by previously known physics became entirely comprehensible with the application of Einstein's theories, leading to an understanding of the universe that was in one sense less random and more coherent than had ever been achieved before.

Quantum mechanics (qm), while not directly contradicting the theory of general relativity, did appear to turn its beautiful rationality on its head. In qm, most physical events are described not in terms of definite outcomes but in terms of probabilities. Previous physical theories, such as Sir Isaac Newton's tremendously successful theory of universal gravitation, were deterministic: if we knew an object's initial properties and a few basic laws, we could predict with mathematical confidence exactly how that object would behave. Their universe was orderly, rational, and predictable—the kind of universe a modern Westerner might happily embrace.

The only problem was that when classical physics, which works so well at describing many phenomena, was applied to certain fundamental questions like the underlying structure of atoms, something was clearly missing. In fact, experimental evidence obtained by Lord Ernest Rutherford at the beginning of the twentieth century, indicating that atoms were made up of a core nucleus surrounded by electrons, simply could not be understood classically. If the classical picture were all there was to it, atoms should immediately collapse in a burst of radiation.

Quantum mechanics was proposed, in a remarkable instance of scientific synchronicity, out of the concerted work of several physicists in the 1920s. The new theory was a terrific success at solving some of the mysteries that had bedeviled classical theorists, at least at the level of providing a mathematical apparatus whose predictions fit the experimental data exceedingly well.

In the qm world, physical objects have not well-defined properties but probabilities of having properties. Take the location of any given particle—qm is stubbornly unwilling to tell you where each electron in your body's roughly billion billion billion (10^{27}) atoms is right now. Chances are, they're all pretty much where you think they are, but there is a real (though extraordinarily small) chance that right now, at least one of your electrons "is" outside of your personal space. In fact, qm refuses to commit to where the electron is, preferring instead to say merely that at any given time, that electron has a certain probability of being in a certain place. This idea—that chance, rather than definite predictability, describes the behavior of the universe—prompted Einstein's uneasy comment about God playing dice.

But the trouble with qm goes well beyond randomness. In 1935, Einstein, together with two colleagues (Boris Podolsky and Nathan Rosen), identified a consequence of qm that at best seemed paradoxical and, at worst, flew in the face of conventional ideas about cause and effect. In certain situations, a measurement made on one particle (known as an epr measurement, for Einstein, Podolsky, and Rosen) appears to affect instantly the properties of another particle, no matter how far apart the two particles are. This seemed to directly violate one of the cherished ideas of relativity, namely that nothing can travel faster than the speed of light. One consequence of this cosmic speed limit is that interactions between particles, such as the electric attraction between positive and negative charged particles, do not happen instantly if the particles involved are separated by some distance; it takes time for the field that mediates the attraction to travel between the two particles. For Einstein, Podolsky, and Rosen, the apparently instantaneous effect of an event in one place on a particle elsewhere was strong evidence that something was rotten in qm's picture of the universe.

It took many decades for the technology of experimental physics to catch up with the epr challenge. But in the past decade physicists have performed many experiments to determine whether the epr paradox in fact is reflected in reality. The outcomes of these experiments indicate that, indeed, nature is as bizarre as qm tells us, confirming Einstein's worst fears. Physicists such as Stephen Hawking of Cambridge University (who followed Sir Isaac Newton over three hundred years later in a prominent professorship of mathematical physics) have heralded these results as indicating that God does indeed "play dice" with the universe—if there is a God, this God cannot be purposeful or act deliberately in the world, since the randomness and irrationality of quantum mechanics demonstrate that no one, even God, can foresee the future, much less exert control over it.

So it's not surprising that when they think about physics at all, many thoughtful Christians are tempted to bury their heads in the post-modern sand. Surely Einstein was right to resist the idea of a God who is little more than a cosmic gambler, wondering where his electrons are today. The situation is not made easier by qm's manifest success at driving scientific and technological progress in physics, chemistry, biology, and computer science (quantum computing, which depends on some of qm's more bizarre features, is coming eventually to a chip near you). Like medieval theologians confronting the uncomfortable evidence that Copernicus's theory simply worked better than Ptolemy's, biblically informed people may wonder if cosmos is giving way to chaos.

In truth, though, it's not so simple. First, the world of classical physics was hardly friendly to the biblical picture of a personal God involved with his creation. In a world of billiard balls bouncing off one another with immutable mathematical precision, the idea that God (or, indeed, free wills of any sort) could intervene in the process seemed increasingly incredible. The French scientist Laplace reportedly said, when asked by Napoleon what role God played in his cosmology, "Sire, I have had no need of that hypothesis." For orthodox Christianity, those were certainly not the good old days.

But second, there is a big difference between a physical theory— the equations and predictions of qm—and its interpretation—the conclusions we draw from the equations about reality itself. Since the development of qm, physicists and philosophers of science have argued with one another about what it actually means. Does the probabilistic nature of quantum mechanics imply that randomness is a fundamental quality of our universe? While the orthodox interpretation (known as the "Copenhagen interpretation" for the home of Niels Bohr, one of its main advocates) insists that the behavior of particles really has a random quality, others hold that the world only appears to be governed by chance—we simply have not found the laws that would divulge its underlying purposefulness. Such metaphysical questions are not answered by the theory of qm itself.

Since curiosity is a required characteristic for a physicist, and since most physicists do not observe disciplinary boundaries to their curiosity, a number of theoretical physicists have ventured to the very edges of their turf to speculate about the meaning of qm. Out of their speculations, a number of different interpretations have emerged. One deserves particular attention from those who believe in a Creator. Sometimes known as the "Ithaca Interpretation of Quantum Mechanics" because it was devised by N. David Mermin of Cornell University in Ithaca, New York, this interpretation, surprisingly, makes contact with some of the most fundamental Christian beliefs about God and creation.

Mermin's central idea is simple: The basic elements of physical reality are not individual objects but relationships between what we perceive to be individual objects. (To use Mermin's more technical terminology, correlations between the properties of individual objects, rather than the "correlata," the properties of the individual objects themselves, are the basic constituents of a physical theory.) Individual objects as such most certainly exist. However, if we insist on knowing the properties of individual objects rather than the properties of relationships between objects, our efforts are doomed to appear paradoxical and incoherent. Physics, it turns out, is not about probing the properties of smaller and smaller billiard balls (electrons, quarks, or neutrinos)—it is about the properties of the relations between those objects, which indeed derive their identity from their relations. The primacy of objects gives way to the primacy of relationships.

It is beyond the scope of this essay to explain the technical argument that can be made after taking this interpretive step. But essentially, Mermin's approach eliminates qm's apparent violations of cause and effect. If we consider the relationships to be fundamental, rather than individual objects, then the outcomes of epr measurements are no longer paradoxical but follow naturally from what is known about the relationships between the objects involved. The universe is rational, Mermin suggests, because it is relational.

Christian readers of Mermin suddenly find themselves in familiar territory. For any deeply Christian account of the creation seems bound to have a relational quality. From the enigmatic "us" in Genesis 1:26 to the fully formed descriptions of the Trinity in the creeds, Christian thought posits a relationality in God himself. And the universe exists, Jewish and Christian theologians have long asserted, in continuous, ongoing, dynamic, loving relation to God. (In a suggestion that has particular resonance with qm's emphasis on the role of the observer, the eighteenth-century philosopher Berkeley went so far as to say that the reality of the universe comes from God continually regarding it.)

Under Mermin's interpretation, at least, qm turns out to be as much an ally as a foe to the Christian understanding of the world, and some of its most "irrational" elements actually compel a more relational rationality.

Does all of this prove anything? Not really. For one thing, Mermin's interpretation is just that—an interpretation, probably not subject to experimental verification in the way a true scientific hypothesis would be. Even if it is ultimately persuasive because of the elegant way it solves several knotty puzzles, a picture of a fundamentally relational cosmos does not by itself lead us very close to the Christian picture of a God who is Creator, Redeemer, and Sustainer of creation. Many other theological and philosophical options are compatible with Mermin's interpretation, including notably the "panentheism" of Charles Hartshorne and process theologians, which falls well short of the biblical witness to God.

Similarly, the probabilistic nature of qm has been taken by Hawking as proof positive that the universe lacks purpose and design; yet others, such as the British physicist and Anglican priest John Polkinghorne, see an opening for divine and human free will that had been excluded from previous models of the cosmos. Indeed, Polkinghorne points out that in certain kinds of complex physical systems, although the outcomes of microscopic events are governed by probability, the behavior of the system as a whole proceeds within certain boundaries. This could serve as an analogy for how the cosmos as a whole could be working out the purposes of God while permitting freedom of choice to individuals and the possibility of random determination of atomic events. Most, if not all of the time, several different theologies are consistent with the same evidence.

This is hardly surprising if the Gospel of John is to be trusted in its claim that "no one has ever seen God. It is God the only Son, who is close to the Father's heart, who has made him known" (John 1:18). Or if Genesis is to be believed when it describes God making humanity in his own image. Or if the whole of Scripture does indeed, as it claims, make God's character clear precisely through his interactions (his relations!) with human beings, especially Israel and the Church. Compared to these sources, the creation as a whole is a minor witness. It was made by God and thus reflects some of his qualities, just as a sculpture tells viewers something about the sculptor. But simply seeing an exhibition of sculpture does not give a complete picture of who the sculptor is, whereas reading the sculptor's letters to her family, meeting her children, and especially meeting the sculptor herself, tell much more.

So, like every other scientific discovery, qm (which itself is subject to being superseded by a more adequate theory, just as classical physics was) tells us something, but not enough, about God. It is fascinating to speculate, though, on how Einstein might have responded to the dramatic experimental confirmations of qm, that theory he found so un-palatable, near the close of the twentieth century. Would he have given up, with Stephen Hawking, and concluded that God was a cosmic gambler after all? Or would he have begun to suspect that far from playing dice, God was more intimately and personally involved in the world than classical physics ever imagined?

This chapter was originally published in *Re: generation quarterly* 6.1 (spring 2000).

CHAPTER 3

Physics and Faith: The Luminous Web

BARBARA BROWN TAYLOR

Barbara Brown Taylor is an Episcopal priest in the diocese of Atlanta. Ordained in 1983, she served parishes in Georgia for fifteen years before assuming her current post as Butman Professor of Religion and Philosophy at Piedmont College in Demorest, Georgia. She is the author of nine books, including *God in Pain: Teaching Sermons on Suffering*, and *The Luminous Web: Essays on Science and Religion*.

Before anyone enters the strange universe of quantum physics, it is necessary to recognize "the word problem." Since this largely unseen world defies common sense and refuses to behave like the visible world in which we hit tennis balls and drive cars, our usual ways of describing reality leave a great deal to be desired. The language of physics is math, not English, and those who cannot do the math should be wary of thinking they understand quantum mechanics. "Language evolved to help people get around on earth," writes George Johnson, "not down inside atoms."[1]

No one has ever seen a quark, for instance. These particles within particles were invented by Murray Gell-Mann in 1961 because he needed them to make one of his theories work. The word itself alludes to a line from James Joyce ("Three quarks for Muster Mark") in *Finnegan's Wake*.[2] According to Gell-Mann, quarks exhibit such things as "flavor" and "color." There are "up" and "down" quarks. There were once "truth" and "beauty" quarks as well, but according to my friend Louis Jensen "this was a little much for the physics community so they changed 'beauty' and 'truth' to 'bottom' and 'up'." But a quark remains a theoretical construct, leading Niels Bohr to say that "we must be clear, when it comes to atoms, language can be used only as in poetry."[3]

Bohr's point is that our language is not adequate to describe things we cannot see, much less understand. The best we can do is to create images that give us some handle on how those things act. Thus physics is less concerned with what nature *is* than with what can be *said* about nature.

Bohr might as well have been talking about religion. (Once, when the astronomer Allen Sandage was overheard talking in a restaurant, he was mistaken for a minister.[4]) As a preacher, I spend most of my life pressed up against the limits of language. I do not have the foggiest idea who God really is. I am not even sure I want to know, since any such knowledge would by definition blow all my existing circuits. Still, it is my business to say what I can, so I too seek images for what can never be said, using words such as "up," "down," "beauty," and "truth." I remain clear, as Bohr said, that when it comes to God, language can be used only as in poetry.

Meanwhile, science has made some curious word choices of its own. Although Einstein is best known for his two theories of relativity, neither of them asserts relativity in any ordinary sense. In his special theory of relativity, Einstein declared that central aspects of nature are anything *but* relative. Natural laws remain constant regardless of motion, and the speed of light is an absolute for all observers whatever their frame of reference. In his general theory of relativity, Einstein described the way gravity molds space-time. "Einstein could have called his accomplishments the Special Theory of a Cosmic Absolute and the General Theory of Gravitational Absolute," writes Gregg Easterbrook. "How might twentieth-century thought have developed," he goes on to ask, "if its preeminent scientific mind had chosen to favor the word 'absolute' instead of 'relativity'?"[5]

Likewise, chaos theory does not offer scientific proof of utter chaos in the cosmos. On the contrary, it describes laws of complexity that actually place boundaries on chaos. Meanwhile, word choices such as "relativity" and "chaos" support public perception that science has overthrown meaning. And since meaning is the domain of religion, this raises the question of competing worldviews, which is very much an issue in the dialogue between science and religion.

We human beings tend to base our worldviews on the prevailing physics of the day. While I have heard the argument made the other way around, it seems true to me that our government, our schools, our economies, and our churches all reflect our understanding of how the world works, and when that understanding changes—as it is changing right now—all of those institutions are up for revision. If you are familiar with Margaret Wheatley's work, then you know that her insights into the new science have changed the way some organizations are being managed in this country. If you are an educator, then you know that new theories about how the mind works have changed the way you do your job. As someone invested in the body of Christ, I am vitally interested in what changes may be up for the church as well.

While the Bible has no overt interest in cosmology apart from God's sovereignty over it, the basic concept seems to be that of a three-tiered universe, with a flat earth supported by pillars below and capped by the round dome of the heavens above. The waters above the heavens explained why the sky is blue, and the waters below the earth went down into the abyss. As early as five hundred years before Christ, the Greeks had figured out that this could not be so. If the earth were flat, then why did it cast a round shadow on the moon during a lunar eclipse? Eudoxus of Cnidos was the first to put forward a planetary theory based entirely on spherical motions.[6] Aristotle's adoption of it, with a round earth sitting at the center of the universe, made it the cosmology to be reckoned with for some two thousand years.

While Rome was too busy conquering the world to care very much what was going on in the sky, Christianity was focused on the world after this one. As Saint Ambrose put it in the fourth century, "To discuss the nature and position of the earth does not help us in our hope of the life to come." A little before him, Tertullian had sighed, "For us, curiosity is no longer necessary."[7] Before they could say, "Wait! We take it back!" their words had become prophetic. The Dark Ages descended on Europe and science guttered out like a lamp deprived of oil.

While scholars such as Thomas Aquinas continued to think in the dark, it was almost a thousand years before there was a renaissance of learning in Europe. With the invention of the printing press, intellectual classics that had lain dormant for centuries suddenly became both available and affordable. A Pole named Mikolai Kopernik could not get enough of them. He read his way from Cracow to Bologna and back again, returning home with volumes of Aristotle, Euclid, Archimedes, and Ptolemy in his luggage. He also came home with the name most us know him by—Copernicus—the man who changed our vision of the universe.

Through his observation of the seasons and his reading of the classics, Copernicus believed that the sun, not the earth, belonged at the center of things. He also guessed what trouble that swap might cause, which was why he delayed publication of his work until his death was imminent. Although the church was undergoing its own revolution at the time, both Protestants and Catholics agreed on Copernicus. "Who will venture to place the authority of Copernicus above that of the Holy

Spirit?" John Calvin howled out loud, while Martin Luther simply called the man a fool.[8]

Some fifty years later, when Galileo Galilei surveyed the heavens through the telescope he had made, he concluded that Copernicus had been right. After a high-handed campaign to convert the pope to his cosmology, Galileo was ordered to appear before the Inquisition, where he was reminded that the issue was not scientific merit but obedience. In his defense, Galileo quoted the words of Cardinal Baronio, who said, "The Bible tells us how to go to heaven, not how the heavens go."[9]

His inquisitors were not impressed. On June 22, 1633, when he was seventy years old, Galileo got down on his knees in the great hall of a Dominican convent in Rome and read the renunciation they had written for him.

> Wishing to remove from the minds of your Eminences and of every true Christian this vehement suspicion justly cast upon me, with sincere heart and unfeigned faith I do abjure, damn, and detest the said errors and heresies, and generally each and every other error, heresy, and sect contrary to the Holy Church; and I do swear for the future that I shall never again speak or assert, orally or in writing, such things as might bring me under similar suspicion.[10]

Galileo spent the last eight years of his life under house arrest in his villa outside Florence. While his daughter read him the seven daily psalms of penitence that were part of his sentence, the old man sat by the window, where he could watch the planets through his telescope.

In 1611, the King James translation of the Bible was published with a note to readers that creation had occurred on the evening before the twenty-third of October in the year of 4004 B.C.E. In 1616, the Catholic Church banned all books that suggested the earth moved at all. But the scientific revolution could not be stopped. It gathered momentum through the seventeenth century, fired by the work of a British mathematician and natural philosopher named Isaac Newton.

With the publication of his book *Principia*, which was published in 1687, Newton planted the seeds of a new worldview. In it, he laid down the laws of celestial dynamics. Reducing them to four simple algebraic formulas, he revealed a solar system that worked like a vast machine. The machine, he said, was made of parts—some of them as small as an atom and others as huge as the sun—but they all obeyed the same laws. In this way, he not only vindicated Galileo but also unseated Aristotle, who believed that the heavens and the earth were governed by different laws.

Apparently Newton never meant to unseat God too. At the end of his book he wrote that "this most beautiful system of the sun, planets and comets could only proceed from the counsel and dominion of an intelligent and powerful Being."[11] He could not explain where the laws came from unless they came from God, in other words, but the laws themselves left very little for a deity to do. God may have designed the machine and thumped it into motion, but once the thing got moving it seemed to do just fine all by itself. As far as the universe was concerned, God's job was most like that of a night watchman: someone who dozed in a lawn chair while the stars spun in their courses overhead.

On the whole, human beings were so charmed by the illusion of control Newton's metaphor offered that we began to see ourselves as machines too. Believing that Newton told us the truth about how the world works, we model our nations, our economies, our families, and ourselves on atomistic principles. You are you and I am I. If each of us will do our parts, then the big machine should keep on humming. If a part breaks down, it can always be removed, cleaned, fixed, and replaced. There is no mystery to a machine, after all. According to Newton's instruction manual, it is perfectly predictable. If something stops working, any reasonably competent mechanic should be able to locate the defective part and set things right again.

While Christianity resisted this metaphor for a while, the illusion of control proved too hard to pass up. Theology became increasingly specialized and systematized. Our "God view" came to resemble our worldview. In many places, it is still possible to hear God described as a being who behaves almost as predictably as Newton's universe. Pull this lever and a reward will drop. Do not touch that red button, however, or all hell will break loose. In this clockwork universe, the spiritual quest is reduced to learning the rules in order to minimize personal loss (avoid hell) and maximize personal gain (achieve salvation).

The emphasis on individual welfare is no mistake, either. It goes with the Newtonian worldview, in which the atom is the basic building block of the cosmos. In the physical universe, even something as huge as the sun is made up of tiny atoms, which is why it behaves the same way they do. All big things can be broken down into small things, and it is those small things—those single units of indivisible matter—that count. No whole creation is more than the sum of its parts. To understand the whole, all you have to do is understand the parts.

When this model is transposed to the human universe, the individual human being becomes the atom—the single unit of social matter that is the basic building block for all social groupings. Once again, all big things can be broken down into small things. Nations, communities, churches, and families are all reducible to the individuals who make them up. If a child acts out, take the child to a counselor. Fix the child, without ever inquiring into the health of the family. If a poor woman sells crack to feed her children, send the woman to jail. Punish the woman, without ever asking about the society in which she lives.

In this clockwork universe, the way to keep the whole thing running is to focus on the parts. If one of them breaks down, then repair it. If it cannot be repaired, then replace it. There is nothing wrong with the whole that cannot be fixed by tinkering with the parts. There is no such thing as the whole. The individual is the fundamental unit of reality.

Recently I spent a couple of days at a Benedictine monastery in California. It was a gorgeous place, with a courtyard full of fragrant orange trees and a retreat house full of antiques. When I first came through the door, one of the brothers glided up to me and said, "I know what you're thinking: 'If this is poverty, I can't wait to see chastity!'"

Four times a day, a bell rang in the courtyard. As soon as it did, the brothers stopped whatever they were doing, put clean white robes on over their work clothes, and met in the chapel to pray. The rest of us were welcome to join them, but our presence was not required. If we did not show up then they would pray for us, as they prayed for everyone else in the world—for those who were present along with those who were absent, for those who were inclined toward God along with those who were not, for those who were in great need of prayer along with those who were not aware they needed anything at all.

Prayer was their job, and they took it seriously. They prayed like men who were shoveling coal into the basement furnace of some great edifice. They did not seem to care whether anyone upstairs knew who they were or what they were doing. Their job was to keep the fire going so that people stayed warm, and they poured all their energy into doing just that.

In their presence, I realized how atomistic many prayers are. So many of us pray chiefly as individuals. We confess our own sins, give thanks for our own blessings, ask God to address our own concerns. Even those with voluminous prayer lists can feel as if they are working alone, racing through the dark with their petitions like a midnight mail carrier.

Twentieth-century theology bears the marks of the Newtonian worldview, both in terms of its faith in reason and its urge to compartmentalize. Over the past hundred years or so, the study of theology has been divided up into parts that require prefixes: biblical, historical, systematic, practical, feminist, womanist, liberation, and so forth. Similarly, most seminary curricula are divided into four separate areas of study with courses taught by professors who are rarely caught in each other's classrooms. While everyone agrees how important it is for students to synthesize all this learning, they may have a hard time finding anyone on campus who can show them by example how this is done. While most parish ministers still function as general practitioners, they receive the lion's share of their training from theological specialists.

In most places, clinical pastoral education is part of that training. Seminary students are packed off to hospitals, community mental health centers, or residential treatment programs where they learn the basics of Freudian theory along with certain helpful psychotherapeutic techniques. Later, when they put this knowledge to use in their churches, they will find that it works well enough with individual parishioners but offers little insight into the complex life of communities. Why? Because Freud's worldview was that of Newton and Descartes, in which individual parts bump up against each other, project their mental stuff all over each other, and react.

Perhaps this is why so many large churches resemble corporations, complete with departments, ranked staff members, and organizational charts. Even in churches with congregational polities, the pictures tend to look like pyramids, with straight lines of power that run from top to bottom. At one parish I served, I was determined to discover an alternative and finally came up with a chart that looked more like a zinnia.

At the center of five concentric circles was the Holy Spirit. Emanating from that was a circle for the lay and ordained leaders of the church, with tendrils that reached into the next circle, where all the functioning committees of the church were found. That circle in turn reached into the larger circle of the entire membership of the church, and that circle opened onto the world beyond the church.

The first time I put that chart on the table with my lay leaders, I might as well have lit some incense and begun the meeting with a round of chanting "OM." The corporate types were appalled. They wanted lines of authority, not spheres of influence. They wanted to know who was responsible for what and where the buck stopped.

Where was the top of this thing, anyway? What do you mean there is not a top, only a center? And why all the porousness between one circle and the next? Why can't the finance committee just do its job without revisiting the mission of the church? Isn't that the mission committee's job?

I could not blame them. I liked straight lines myself, especially when my goal is getting from point A to point B. The problem was that I never could eke one single straight line out of parish ministry. For years, I would pull out my compass in the morning, plot a straight course to my goal for the day, and find myself six miles off the path by noon. It was all those *people* who fouled things up. Over and over again, they would show up without appointments to talk about their unhappiness with the church cleaning woman, or a new idea they had for Sunday school, or their fear of losing their middle daughter to drugs. Never once did any of them ask to see the church organizational chart first, to be sure I was the right person to talk to about these things.

Parish life was just as fluid at the community level. I learned never to predict the outcome of any meeting. The ones I thought would produce mushroom clouds often turned out to be wildly creative, while the ones I expected to be uneventful lasted the longest of all. There was simply no telling what would happen, especially when people listened to each other. One person would say something and the whole atmosphere in the room would change. A decision that had seemed inevitable was suddenly open to question. I often wished there were some way to track what happened in a room when individuals started acting as a community. The very air would become lighter. People would say eloquent things that surprised even them, leading other people to change the positions they had been devoted to one moment before.

Eventually I got the message that parish ministry was not and would never be about getting from point A to point B for me. It was not a journey with a beginning and an end. It was more like a dance, with a lot of wide-open space to be explored. To spend my time trying to arrive at a particular point on the dance floor would have been to waste the music.[12] A much more promising prospect was to learn how my different partners moved, and to swap as many dance steps with them as I could.

In other words, there is another way to conceive of our life together. There is another way to conceive of our life in God, too, but it requires a different worldview—not a clockwork universe in which individuals function as discreet springs and gears, but one that looks more like a luminous web, in which the whole is far more than the parts.

In this universe, there is no such thing as an individual apart from his or her relationships. Every interaction—between people and people, between people and things, between things and things—changes the face of history. Reality is not a well-oiled machine that behaves in logical, predetermined ways. Instead, it is an ever-unfolding process that defies precise prediction. In it, order and chaos are not enemies but fraternal twins. Creation depends on both of them. Together they shape life.

If this sounds like religious language, it is not. It is language inspired by quantum physics, which has caused a revolution in the way we see our world. There is nothing wrong with Newton's old model, as far as it goes. The problem is that Newton believed the atom was indivisible—that it was the smallest possible particle in existence. Now we know there are even tinier bits of matter at the subatomic level, which do not operate the way Newton said they should. While his rules still work in the world we can see, there is another, very different set of rules at work in the world that *makes up* the world we can see.

My own introduction to the new science came five years ago, when I attended a clergy leadership conference at which Fred Burnham spoke. An Episcopal priest with a doctorate in the history of science from Johns Hopkins, Burnham is dedicated to holding peace talks between science and religion. As a believer in God, he cannot keep scientific truth and religious truth in separate boxes. He was there to talk to us about chaos theory, and in particular about how the science of complexity might be useful to us as parish leaders. While I had read some classical physics and math before that, no one had ever suggested that it had anything to do with my life in the church.

When I entered the room, Burnham was pecking at the keyboard of a computer. The machine sat in the front of the blackboard on a low desk. The screen remained blank as the group assembled. Then Burnham greeted us, pressed "Enter," and turned his back on the computer screen as he delivered his lecture. At the beginning there was nothing but one thin green line snaking its way around the interior of the screen. First it made something that looked like a lopsided figure eight and then it doubled back on itself—roughly, not exactly—as if a young child had tried to trace the design twice.

Burnham was apparently oblivious to what was going on behind him. From time to time, so was I. I did not know one thing about chaos theory. I had always assumed I was incapable of understanding it, but as Burnham introduced us to fractals, complexity, and non-linear equations, I had what I can only call a religious experience. Jumping from the science to the meaning I made of it, I understood why my life would not run along straight lines. I understood why my ten-year plans never work. And rather than feeling miserable about those things, I began to glimpse a deeper level of physical reality at which my life was behaving exactly as it should.

By calling this a religious experience, what I meant is that I experienced salvation in it. I was rescued from my atomistic understanding of myself in ministry, in which I was the mechanic and my parish the machine I was supposed to run. The new science gave me metaphors for my life in community, which had far more chaos in it than Stephen Covey would deem acceptable but which was also embraced by a boundary I can only call love.

If I had been a better student of the Bible, none of this should have been news to me. But I am also a student of the culture, which is still hooked on the mechanical model of reality. In Burnham's classroom, I discovered another worldview that dissolved that dotted line down the middle of me. Both my reason and my faith were challenged by what I was seeing in front of me. Science seemed to be speaking to my spirit. As I watched the image on the computer screen develop into a design shaped like a butterfly, I thought, "This is *math*. No one ever told me math could be beautiful." When Burnham finally named the design—"a strange attractor"—and explained that it was a visual representation of the mathematical "magnet" that pulled randomness into some semblance of order, I knew I had found a window on the universe that would occupy me for some time to come.

If you have ever seen the design a free-swinging pendulum traces in sand, then you have seen an attractor at work. Since I am not a scientist, I am not always sure what I am looking at, nor do I have the theoretical background to discern all the implications of a particular phenomenon. But as a preacher (which is to say a roving reporter of life on the planet) I reserve the right to make meaning out of what I see. This drives some of my scientific friends crazy. They try to help me understand that science is not in the business of making meaning, and that the minute I wring metaphors out of scientific phenomena I have left the realm of fact for fiction. One critic has even warned me that as a nonscientist reading science I am in great peril: "Anyone who does not enter the sheepfold by the gate but climbs in by another way can be in a lot of trouble." I know it is so, but that knowledge does not seem to help me apply the brakes. As a believer in one God, I think everything is connected to everything else. What is exciting to me is that believers in science are beginning to think the same thing—not the God part but the connection part.

Early in the twentieth century, at the Institute for Advanced Study in Princeton, Albert Einstein and his colleagues Boris Podolsky and Nathan Rosen tried to undermine quantum theory with something now known as EPR experiment (for *E*instein, *P*odolsky, and *R*osen). According to quantum theory, a subatomic particle that decays into two particles becomes a set of "twins"—a single system with two parts, spinning in opposite directions. No one knows which one is spinning "up" and which is spinning "down" until a measurement is made, but according to the laws of physics they must always balance each other.

So far so good. Now imagine those two particles flying apart—one of them heading around the dark side of the moon while the other lingers in the laboratory above the nimbus of Einstein's hair. If Einstein could nab that one and reverse its spin, he theorized, then the other particle would have to reverse itself too—even if it were light years away. According to the laws of quantum physics, this is exactly what would happen. Because the two particles were in a state of "quantum entanglement" (Erwin Schrödinger's phrase[13]), they would behave in complementary ways no matter how far apart they were. Since this eerie idea violated Einstein's own theory of special relativity—he called it "spooky action at a distance"—he concluded that quantum theory was wrong.[14]

Unhappily for him, subsequent experiments proved him wrong instead. Once two particles have interacted with each other, they remain related regardless of their physical distance from one another. In some sense, they stay in contact through space and time, although the point does not seem to be that they are using some kind of faster-than-light communication. The much more confounding point seems to be that they do not behave as two separate particles, but one.

In scientific language, they must be considered a single non-separable object. Researchers think it has something to do with field theory—fields being invisible, non-material structures that may turn out to be the basic substance of the universe. You know about gravitational fields and electromagnetic fields. If you stand under a high power wire and hold a fluorescent light bulb in the air, there is a good chance it will light up, because you are standing in a power field. Well, imagine another kind of field that knits the whole cosmos together, so that a shiver in the Milky Way gives us a shiver right here, faster than the speed of light.

The science stops there, but my imagination goes on. I think about the mother who sits bolt upright in her bed in the middle of the night, "knowing" something has happened to her child. I think about the

strange communication between twins, who may end up making similar choices in their lives even though they have been separated from
birth. The meaning I make out of the EPR paradox is that such phenomena occur because the two are not really two but one. Each one
"knows" what the other is doing not because they happen to be psychic
but because they belong to the unbroken wholeness of the universe.

Consider Paul's metaphor of the church as Christ's body. As different as we are and as many functions as we serve, we are far more than
a collection of parts. We may act that way sometimes, with the left side
pulling against the right and the feet refusing to take a step until the
hands have apologized, but there are also times when we clearly participate in some form of community—or better yet, communion—that
translates us into the mind of Christ. The more in tune we are, the better we respond. This is not something that only happens to us person by
person but something that happens to all of us at once. There is no explanation for it in terms of cause and effect. This head of ours, this guiding mind, does not speak into a tape recorder or send directions by fax,
but plenty of us have experienced the presence as real.

In quantum physics, such mysterious action-at-a-distance is
known as non-locality, but it is only one of the phenomena that have
changed the scientific landscape. Another is Heisenberg's uncertainty
principle, which asserts that it is not possible to know both where a particle is and where it is going. The closer you come to determining its location, the further you go from determining its momentum. If you
change your tactics, and focus on its momentum, you will no longer be
able to say where it is. In between your measurements, it exists as probability wave—a combination of all the possible ways it could go—which
all remain possible until you focus on it. When you take your measurement, the wave collapses. It assumes an actual value, but only because
you asked it to.

One analogy might be the strobe light under which some of us
danced in the sixties. We were in constant motion in the darkness—
hands in the air, heads thrown back—some of us with our eyes closed
and others searching the crowd for a friend. It was a tableau that
changed every second, with infinite possibilities. When the strobe came
on, the probability wave collapsed. The light took our measure and we
were captured in time, like a moving picture frozen on a single frame.
An observer looking at that frame might say, "There is a woman who
dances without moving her feet," to which the woman might say, "No,
that is just how you happened to catch me at the moment. Take the
measurement again and the picture will be different."

With quantum theory, there are no dancers, only the pictures. In a tenet of the new science that tries the most philosophical mind, a thing cannot even be said to be one thing or another until someone interrupts it to find out what it is. Plus, the interruption itself has to be taken into account. The moment you set up a scientific experiment, you become one of the dancers. The light you shine on a particle so that you can see it carries its own momentum, which bumps into the particle and changes its heading. You cannot observe the phenomenon without entering into relationship with it, and the relationship changes the equation.

Some physicists object that Heisenberg's uncertainty principle is a theoretical result. It is possible mathematically but not experimentally, since an electron exists more as a "spread" than a distinct entity. Strictly speaking, this means that an electron lacks the basic hallmarks of existence. "From the quantum angle," Paul Davies explains, "an electron is not simply an electron. Shifting energy patterns shimmer around it, financing the unpredictable appearance of photons, protons, mesons, and even other electrons. In short, all the paraphernalia of the subatomic world latches on to an electron like an intangible, evanescent cloak, a shroud of ghostly bees swarming around the central hive."[15] That is what makes it generally impossible to measure. It is not a discrete individual, but part of a complex network of relationships.

If you are feeling a little disoriented right now, let me assure you that you are in very good company. The people who discovered all this stuff were a little dazed by it too. Werner Heisenberg, the originator of the uncertainty principle, remembers late-night discussions with Niels Bohr that ended almost in despair. Recalling one of them, Heisenberg wrote, "When at the end of the discussion I went alone for a walk in the neighboring park, I repeated to myself again and again the question: Can nature possibly be so absurd as it seemed to us in these atomic experiments?[16]

Bohr himself said, "Anyone who is not shocked by quantum theory has not understood it." Erwin Schrödinger, a fellow physicist, was even more blunt than that. "I don't like it," he said, "and I'm sorry I ever had anything to do with it."[17]

The reasons for their dismay are manifold. In the first place, the physical world seems to obey two different sets of rules. At the macro level of trees and rocks, Newtonian mechanics work just fine. A tree can be said to have a definite position in space and time, and a rock dropped from a window will fall at a predictable rate to a predictable spot on the ground. Everything in this world happens for a reason and can be explained in terms of cause and effect.

At the micro level of quantum particles, however, these rules no longer apply. A photon may be said to be both particle and wave. If you know where an electron is you cannot, by definition, know where it is going. If you know where it is going, you cannot know where it is. Furthermore, you cannot know any of these things without interacting with them, which means that you will never know how they behave when you are not watching.

While quantum mechanics is set up so that it works at the macro level, using it on that large scale would be like measuring the distance between Chicago and New York with a six-inch ruler. Meanwhile, Newtonian mechanics is so unwieldy at the micro level that employing it there would be akin to doing brain surgery with a bulldozer.[18] For all practical purposes, each level requires its own set of rules. Those of us who live in the macro world may well wonder how the big, visible objects in our world can behave differently from the tiny, invisible stuff of which they are made—where two things may act as one, and one as two.

The new science requires a radical change in how we conceive the world. It is no longer possible to see it as a collection of autonomous parts, as Newton did, existing separately while interacting. The deeper revelation is one of undivided wholeness, in which the observer is not separable from what is observed. Or, in Heisenberg's words, "the common division of the world into subject and object, inner world and outer world, body and soul is no longer adequate."[19]

Is this physics or theology, science or religion? At the very least, it is poetry. As far back as the thirteenth century, the Sufi poet Jelaluddin Rumi wrote, "You think because you understand *one* you must also understand *two*, because one and one make two. But you must also understand *and*."

For John Polkinghorne, who was a mathematical physicist at Cambridge before he became an Anglican priest, the "and" between science and religion is their common search for truth. In a slim volume called *Quarks, Chaos and Christianity,* he makes some startling connections between the discoveries of physics and the articles of faith. Our experience of light as both particle and wave may give us a way to express our experience of Jesus as both human and divine, he says. Ask a human-like question and you get a human-like answer. Ask a divine-like question and you get a divine-like answer. As different as they may be, both languages are necessary. The deep truth is not either but both.[20]

Likewise, says Polkinghorne, the simple act of boiling water gives us a parable of what scientists call a "phase change." At 100 degrees

Centigrade a very small amount of water becomes a very large amount of steam as H_2O moves from the liquid regime to the gaseous one. While the liquid and the gas behave in different ways, they remain the same substance. The laws of nature have not changed; only their consequences have. When Polkinghorne considers the mystery of Christ's death and resurrection, what he sees is a phase change. Jesus was the first puff of steam in a new regime, which some of us call the kingdom of God. As a physicist, Polkinghorne knows that a new regime is accompanied by new phenomena. In Jesus' case, those phenomena include the boiling up of death into everlasting life.[21]

One of the most interesting and controversial theoretical physicists in print is David Bohm, who died in 1992. Working in the area of relativistic quantum field theory pioneered by Paul Dirac, Bohm caught a glimpse of reality in which the universe neither occupies space and time nor contains many different things. Rather, he said, it behaves more like one interwoven thing that takes time and space seriously but not too seriously—perhaps by treating them as idioms that the universe finds necessary in order to communicate itself to observers.[22]

While he said that as a scientist, I heard him as a theologian, and began to wonder if the universe might have a "memory" that pre-dates the big bang. Back before that explosion triggered the expansion of time and space, there was that egg of the universe in which all places were one place and all things were one thing. I would call it the garden of Eden, only the beauty of the garden lay in its diversity. The beauty of this earlier reality was its unity, its total coherence. Mind, matter, and time were not yet different. They were all floating in the same yolk. Then the universe was born and the one became many. Quantum particles became planets, galaxies, clusters, and superclusters. Atoms became blue-green algae, toads, palm trees, and swans. Space became here or there, as time became then or now.

But what if deep down in the being of these many things remains the memory of their being one, which makes them behave in ways that torture scientists? Space and time are not separable. Light is both particle and wave. A particle way over there responds instantly to a particle way over here, as if the two were not two but one.

What if our mental torture only comes about because we insist on conceiving reality as many when it is truly and deeply one? All appearances to the contrary, "the universe remains as it was in the beginning, when all places were one place, all times one time, and all things the same thing."[23] Explaining Bohm's work, Timothy Ferris suggests that "the universe began as a hyperdimensional bubble of space, all but four of the dimensions of which compacted to form what we today call sub-atomic particles. Those particles look to us like zillions of individual things, but that is merely their appearance in the four dimensions of spacetime. In hyperspace they could very well be *one* thing—could, therefore, be not only connected but identical."[24]

Once, when the physicists John Wheeler and Richard Feynman were discussing string theory, Wheeler said, "Feynman, I know why all electrons have the same charge and the same mass."

"Why?" Feynman asked.

"Because they are all of the same electron!" Wheeler replied.

The writer of Ephesians put it like this, "There is one body and one Spirit . . . one Lord, one faith, one baptism, one God and Father of all, who is above all and through all and in all" (4:4–6). We have made much of the "above all" in Christian theology, placing God at the top of the organizational chart of the universe and ourselves, as God's deputies, right below. But what about the "through all and in all" part of the equation? In a world like ours, which even the new science calls a web of relationship, there is no place to stand apart from and above the rest of creation. Only in the most abstract sense can we assert our sovereignty over blue-green algae, toads, palm trees, and swans. Our dominion, such as it is, lies in the privilege of our consciousness. We among all the others have been given the job of keeping covenant. We among all the others have been given the privilege of knowing whom to thank. Meanwhile, we live in covenant with every living creature of all flesh, and our survival depends on our responsiveness to that fact.

In Sunday school, I learned to think of God as a very old white-bearded man on a throne, who stood above creation and occasionally stirred it with a stick. When I am dreaming quantum dreams, what I see is an infinite web of relationship, flung across the vastness of space like a luminous net. It is made of energy, not thread. As I look, I can see light moving through it as a pulse moves through veins. What I see "out there" is no different from what I feel inside. There is a living hum that might be coming from my neurons but might just as well be coming from the furnace of the stars. When I look up at them there is a small commotion in my bones, as the ashes of dead stars that house my mar-row rise up like metal filings toward the magnet of their living kin.

Where am I in this picture? I am all over the place. I am up there, down here, inside my skin and out. I am large compared to a virus and small compared to the sun, with a life that is permeable to them both. Am I alone? How could I ever be alone? I am part of a web that is pure relationship, with energy available to me that has been around since the universe was born.

Where is God in this picture? God is all over the place. God up there, down here, inside my skin and out. God is the web, the energy, the space, the light—not captured in them, as if any of those concepts were more real than what unites them—but revealed in that singular, vast net of relationship that animates everything that is.

At this point in my thinking, it is not enough for me to proclaim that God is responsible for all this unity. Instead, I want to proclaim that God *is* the unity—the very energy, the very intelligence, the very elegance and passion that make it all go. This is the God who is not somewhere but everywhere, the God who may be prayed to in all directions at once. This is also the God beyond all directions, who will still be here (wherever "here" means) when the universe either dissipates into dust or swallows itself up again. Paul Tillich's name for this divine reality was "the ground for all being." The only thing I can think of that is better than that is the name God revealed to Moses: "I Am Who I Am."

This shift in my image of God is so radical that calling God "she" seems minor by comparison. It is not a matter of my sudden conversion to pantheism (of which I am often accused), since that belief system makes no provision for a God beyond creation. But I do plead guilty to pan*en*theism, which understands God to be both transcendent and immanent. As Joseph Campbell once asked, what if the universe is not merely the product of God but also the manifestation of God—a "eucharistic planet" on which we have been invited to live?

"I Am Who I Am" does not sound to me like the self-identification of a deity who stands over reality and sometimes stirs it with a stick. Instead, it sounds like the singular utterance of the only One who ever was, is, or shall be, in whom everything else abides. For the moment, we see through a glass darkly. We live in the illusion that we are all separate "I ams." When the fog finally clears, we shall know there is only One.

NOTES

1. "The Unspeakable Things That Particles Do," *The New York Times* (July 27, 1997), 5.
2. Johnson, *Fire in the Mind* (New York: Alfred A. Knopf, 1995), 52.
3. Ibid., 146.

4. Richard Elliott Friedman, *The Disappearance of God* (Boston: Little, Brown, 1995), 222.
5. "Science Sees The Light," *The New Republic* (October 12, 1998), 28.
6. John North, *The Norton History of Astronomy and Cosmology* (New York: W. W. Norton, 1995), 67.
7. Timothy Ferris, *Coming of Age in the Milky Way* (New York: Simon & Schuster, 1998), 42.
8. Ibid., 67.
9. Kenneth L. Woodward, "How The Heavens Go," *Newsweek* (July 20, 1998), 52.
10. Ferris, *Coming of Age in the Milky Way*, 100.
11. Ibid., 121.
12. My thanks to Alan Watts for this image from his lecture "Coincidence of Opposites" in volume I of "The Tao of Philosophy" audiocassette series, produced in 1973 by the Electronic University (Box 2309, San Anselmo, CA 94979).
13. Alain Aspect, "Bell's inequality test: more ideal than ever," *Nature* (March 18, 1999), 189.
14. Ferris, *The Whole Shebang*, 277.
15. Paul Davies, *God and the New Physics* (New York: Simon & Schuster, 1983), 162–163.
16. Margaret J. Wheatley, *Leadership and the New Science* (San Francisco: Berrett-Koehler, 1992), 4.
17. Ibid., 31.
18. My thanks to Dr. Louis K. Jensen for these metaphors.
19. Davies, *God and the New Physics*, 112.
20. John Polkinghorne, *Quarks, Chaos and Christianity* (New York: Crossroad, 1997), 112.
21. Ibid., 82–83.
22. Ferris, *The Whole Shebang*, 283.
23. Ibid., 284.
24. Ibid., 287.

An earlier version of this chapter was originally published in *The Christian Century*, June 2–9, 1999, pp. 612–619 and the revision appeared in chapter 3 of *The Luminous Web: Essays on Science and Religion*, by Barbara Brown Taylor, published by Cowley Publications, 2000.

CHAPTER 4

From Physics to Metaphysics:
The Changing Face of Scientific Imagination

AVIHU ZAKAI AND AYVAL RAMATI

Dr. Zakai teaches in the Department of History and Department of American Studies at the Hebrew University of Jerusalem. Among his publications are *Exile and Kingdom: History and Apocalypse in the Puritan Migration to America; Europe and the New World: The Discovery and Conquest of America by European Powers in the 15th–17th Centuries; Theocracy in Massachusetts: Reformation and Separation in Early Puritan New England; History and Apocalypse: Religion and Historical Consciousness in Europe and America in the Early Modern Period.*

Dr. Ramati is a lecturer in the Department of History and History of Science at the Hebrew University of Jerusalem. She received her Ph.D. at UCLA in 1994 and is currently working on the final stages of a book manuscript on her most recent topic of research, science and spirituality in the works of Newton and Leibniz.

Since the scientific revolution of the seventeenth century, scientists have sought new knowledge in a relatively straightforward, traditional manner. Experiments would be performed, hypothesis tested, and science would slowly and gradually progress as new data accumulated. Every now and then, of course, a sudden, great leap would occur, which would unveil some significant and unexpected new discovery. Today, however, there are some scientific fields in which the frontiers have been pushed so far forward that scientists have found themselves asking questions that have always been considered to be metaphysical, not scientific, in nature. It no longer seems possible in physics to do research without confronting questions once thought to be metaphysical—is it meaningful to speak of time before the creation of the universe? Did the universe have a beginning? What exactly is the logical status of "other universes" if these universes cannot be observed? Is it

41

meaningful to speak of what cannot be observed? For that matter, what meaning should we attach to the existence of extra dimensions of "superstring theory" that are compacted so minutely that they can never be observed?

All these questions relate essentially to the growing rift in modern scientific thought between theory and experiment. For example, the best theoretical physicists today are preoccupied with theories that are extremely difficult to test experimentally, such as the "superstring theory," which has never yielded a direct testable prediction. In their reaction to such an important "metaphysical turn" in current scientific thought, Nobel Prize-winning physicist Sheldon Glashow and his Harvard university colleague Paul Ginsparg have likened "superstring theory" to medieval theology: "Contemplation of superstrings," they write, "may evolve into activity . . . to be conducted at schools of divinity by future equivalents of medieval theologians. For the first time since the Dark Ages, we can see how our noble [scientific] search may end, with faith replacing science once again" (Richard Morris, *The Edges of Science*, 1990).

The shift from physics to metaphysics is one of the most common features of the modern scientific imagination. Instead of the scientific revolution's disenchantment of the world, which constituted a reaction to medieval theological teleology of a sacred structure of order inherent in the fabric of the universe, modern science rather tends again to the re-enchantment of the world of nature. Holistic considerations, which cannot be tested or proved, begin to dominate the horizon of scientific imagination and determine the edges of science. Acknowledging their growing inability to explain the unimaginable complexity of world phenomena through mere physical principles, scientists are no longer content with the results of experiments and rather seek after an overarching, holistic framework, according to which the phenomenon of the world may be better explained and understood. For example, although physicists cannot observe quarks or gluons, these entities have nonetheless become elements of the model of subatomic reality because they lead to predictions that scientists can measure. There is a growing tendency among scientists to tolerate "hyperspace" and "superstring" theories, despite the fact that seven of the spatial dimensions of supergravity and six of the dimensions of superstrings (where the one-dimensional strings reside) are hidden and curled up in spaces much smaller than the size of the proton and so are invisible.

The profound difficulties modern scientific thought has encountered lead to the growing understanding that the solution to the mystery of the essential nature of reality ought to be understood in terms of a higher realm of reality—metaphysics—which as yet cannot be an object to our senses or to our most sophisticated scientific instruments. Paradoxically, then, the tremendous advance of science leads rather to a quest after higher, metaphysical considerations that may provide better understanding of the mystery of reality. Such reasoning is evident by the increased crossing of the boundaries from physics to metaphysics in the scientific community. And nowhere is this shift more evident than in the scientific imagination.

To understand the profound transformation apparent in the modern scientific imagination, it is necessary to place it in the wider ideological, philosophical, and historical context of scientific thought, most specifically in light of the shift from the medieval imagination to the scientific revolution, as well as the change between the seventeenth century and modern scientific thought. The scientific and philosophical revolution of the seventeenth century led to the destruction of the Cosmos, that is, the disappearance of the medieval conception of the world as a finite, closed, and hierarchically ordered whole (in which the hierarchy of value determined the hierarchy and structure of being, rising from the dark, heavy, and imperfect earth to the higher and higher perfection of the stars and heavenly spheres), and its replacement by the indefinite and even infinite universe bound together by the identity of its fundamental components and laws, in which all these components are placed on the same level of being (Alexander Koyré, *From the Closed World to the Infinite Universe*, 1958).

The scientific revolution inaugurated a radical change in the conception of nature and matter. Before the seventeenth century, scientific imagination was based in part on Aristotelian physics, according to which the world had within it principles and powers of development. Natural things changed as a result of their inherent tendency to embody more perfectly the rational form of the essence that defined them. Aristotle's natural world is a world of inherent tendencies, continual transformations, and teleological development; nature is an organic being achieving maturity through self-development. During the thirteenth century, Thomas Aquinas produced a majestic synthesis of Aristotelian natural philosophy and Christian theology that became a prominent form of Christian scientific imagination throughout the medieval period. The essence of Thomas's synthesis was to interpret Aristotle's principles inherent in nature as powers instilled there by God, which He used in his providential work. God *cooperated* with natural powers in a way that respected their integrity while accomplishing his purposes.

The shift from the medieval to the scientific revolution imagination is particularly apparent in regard to the rise of mechanical philosophy during the seventeenth century, the doctrine that all natural phenomena can be explained by matter and its motion, the regularity of
which can be expressed in the form of natural laws, ideally formulated
in mathematical terms. In medieval scientific imagination nature revealed God's symbolic presence, and was seen as a system of symbols,
or signatures of its Creator. During the seventeenth century some leading figures maintained that nature contributes nothing to divine providence because it lacks any integrity and power of its own. Matter is passive and does not possess any inherent qualities or intrinsic powers. It
was no longer considered as capable of any power or purpose apart
from the hand of God. The seventeenth-century scientific imagination
thus constructed a new conception of the nature of reality, in contrast
to the medieval conception of the "great chain of being," which revealed God's symbolic presence in creation. Nature, as a result, lost integrity and was deprived of any teleological development of its own.
The scientific revolution therefore led to the disenchantment of the
world.

The mechanical, scientific worldview of the seventeenth century
rested on a single, fundamental assumption—*matter is passive.* It possesses no active, internal forces of its own. Matter in the seventeenth
century possessed only the passive qualities of size, shape, and impene-
trability. Change therefore did not result from the operation of internal
principles and powers, as in Aristotelian natural philosophy; instead,
the laws of impact and the new principle of inertia explained motion. In
short, the seventeenth-century science replaced Aristotle's conception
of nature as an organic being by the view of nature as a huge machine
whose parts undertook various movements in response to other parts
doing the same thing. Mechanical philosophy thus became the hall-
mark of the scientific revolution. In the absence of internal principles
and inherent qualities governing change, external laws controlled material bodies. Since matter is totally passive, it is God who imposes natural laws on the world. The mechanization of the natural world was a
profound revolution; a new conception emerged of what was real in
the world. Particles of matter in motion defined the new reality. The
real world was that which could be described in mechanical terms. In
such scientific thought, evidently, the concept of nature was radically
transformed.

An important consequence of the mechanical view of the universe
was the discarding of considerations based on value-concepts, such as

perfection, harmony, meaning and aim, or the medieval concept of the "great chain of being," and finally the utter devalorization of being, the divorce of the world of value and the world of fact. Instead, the seventeenth-century scientific imagination constructed a new concept of the nature of reality, a new vision of nature as homogeneous and nonhierarchical. With the appearance of the mechanical notion of a one-dimensional and homogeneous reality, the "testimony" of nature became more and more problematic, as did the very notion of divine immanence and activity in the created order. Moreover, since seventeenth-century scientific language emptied nature of any intrinsic meanings and qualities of its own, natural phenomena no longer seemed to symbolize and reflect each other and that which is beyond them; the symbolic-allegorical perception of nature as a network of mutual references was discarded. In sum, the medieval sense of God's symbolic presence in his creation, and the sense of a universe replete with transcendent meanings and hints, had to recede if not to give way entirely to the postulates of univocation and homogeneity of the scientific revolution.

The twentieth-century scientific imagination seems to be leading back from science to metaphysics by constructing impressive dimensions of reality and new infinite universes, which are hidden from our senses and can be understood only in mathematical, metaphysical terms, as in "superstring," "quantum," and "hyperspace" theories. Thus where in medieval thought God was the source of all beings and the foundation of all structure of order in the universe, he is now displaced by the power of mathematics, which illuminates the possible existence of worlds and universes that lie beyond the material, physical world of everyday life and experience. The profound transformation in scientific imagination from physics to metaphysics did not occur all at once. It is based upon three major and well-defined stages. The first occurred during the scientific revolution, which excluded metaphysical discussions and equivocal qualities, replacing them with a quantified, univocal matter. The next stage saw the expansion of abstract mathematical languages in many new areas, such as chemistry, biology, and also the social sciences. Today we are facing a new, or third, phase in the transformation of the scientific imagination from physics to a mathematical metaphysics, in which scientists tend to rely more and more on mathematical formulations that have no experimental results. The new mathematical vocabulary—including the tenth dimension of "hyperspace," which according to Michio Kaku is far beyond our current technological abilities to explore or deduce from an extremely nonsensible logic

(*Hyperspace: A Scientific Odyssey Through Parallel Universes, Time Warps, and the Tenth Dimension,* 1994)—cannot be verified by any present experimental results. In this stage, scientists are coming to tolerate "hyperspace" and "superstring" theories, as well as models of infinite universes, which have been not actualized by experimental proofs. However abstract and metaphysical some twentieth-century mathematical languages may be, they are not based upon private subjective experience and should not be confused with other imaginative vocabularies, such as mystical experiences of higher dimensions or artistic descriptions of reality. Instead, these vocabularies are cultivated within a well-defined mathematical community, which allows metaphysics to flourish as a precise intersubjective discourse capable of exploring what lies beyond experimental results.

As science advanced and expanded its experimental apparatus, it conquered more and more material domains that had been unknown and traditionally considered as untidy and irrelevant in the scientific imagination of the seventeenth century. With the growing success of the experimental method during the next two centuries, it became more and more apparent that the simplicity and stability of Newtonian atoms no longer fitted the experimental results. A more sophisticated mathematical imagination was needed to capture the complexity and entanglement of differing levels of material organizations, which went on being discovered as time passed. The expansion of mathematics in the next three centuries did not remain in the studies of mathematicians but infiltrated into almost all scientific fields, thus transforming intuitive concepts, such as matter, energy, space, time, and infinity. To the degree that the understanding of nature is demonstrated by the ability to describe and predict the behavior of physical systems, physics and mathematics had made astounding progress by the end of the nineteenth century. By then, highly abstract mathematical fields had been introduced into physics to keep up with the growing elusiveness of matter. Yet the more the experiments with fields became interactive, interrogative, and penetrating, the more elusive matter proved to be. To compensate for the growing complexity of matter, major epistemological transformations occurred in the scientific and mathematical imagination during the twentieth century.

At the beginning of the century, Einstein's mathematical formulations of special and general relativity profoundly modified Newtonian abstractions of space, time, matter, and energy. In addition, the penetrating and interactive gaze of quantum physics completely shook the foundations of classical matter. The deeper and more invading the measurement, the more elusive and spirit-like materiality became. At the subatomic level, quantum matter became an elusive wave-like and particle-like being. In order to move beyond the realm of classical physics, quantum physicists had to give up the paradigm of a detached observer and an independent reality. More far-reaching speculative conclusions regarding the meaning of the quantum void have been expressed in the more popular literature. For example, Fritjof Capra's *The Tao of Physics* (1975) and Gary Zukav's *The Dancing Wu Li Masters* (1979) stressed the close parallels between quantum physics and oriental mysticism.

To capture the increasing elusiveness of subatomic duality, the linkage between the large and the small and the whole and its parts, physicists can no longer employ the seventeenth-century mathematical imagination, which found univocal, homogeneous, stable, controllable, and predictable material billiard balls. The mathematical vocabularies of quantum physics combined with special and general relativity have become a reflection of our own expanding scientific consciousness. Francis Bacon in his "Fourth Aphorism" predicted what was to come when he said that "the universe is not to be narrowed down to the limits of the understanding . . . but the understanding must be stretched and enlarged to fill in the image of the universe as it is discovered." The gradual evolution in the complexity of the scientific imagination (which continuously urges for simplicity) goes with a gradual shift from anthropocentric affinities to more objective and mathematical perspectives. Or, in A. N. Whitehead's terms, "all science as it grows towards perfection becomes mathematical in its ideas" (*Science and the Modern World*, 1953). This can be seen in the highly abstract contemporary theories of QED (Quantum Electrodynamics), Weinberg Salam theory, and QCD (Quantum Chromodynamics). All these theories are fascinated by the behavior of spontaneous symmetry breaking. Indeed, during the second half of the twentieth century, physicists had created a language in which the most fundamental constituents and symmetries of the world cannot be directly observed. Physicists may talk consistently about forces in terms of the preservation of symmetry, but in order to do so they have to be careful in their choice of systems that preserve this symmetry. Physicists cannot observe quarks or gluons, but these entities have, nonetheless, become elements of the subatomic reality because they lead to predictions that scientists can measure.

The shift from physics to metaphysics as evident in twentieth-century science is based ultimately upon mathematical languages that have paved the way for new metaphysical nonsensual experiences.

Indeed, according to theoretical physicist Paul Davies (*God and the New Physics*, 1982), twentieth-century mathematical scientific languages have given us much more interesting and precise answers on the nature of creation and reality than any traditional theological discussion has ever produced. Yet, as the physician Lewis Thomas writes, "The greatest of all the accomplishments of twentieth-century science has been the discovery of human ignorance" ("Debating the Unknowable," *Atlantic Monthly*, 1981). This is indeed the essence of the "metaphysical turn" in modern scientific imagination: the growing understanding that the solution to the mystery of the essential nature of reality ought to be understood in terms of a higher realm of reality—metaphysics—which as yet cannot be an object to our senses or to our most sophisticated scientific instruments. Such an important recognition may force us to reconsider once again the notion of divine immanence and activity in the created order: namely, it may reinforce the sense of God's symbolic presence in his creation, and the sense of a universe replete with transcendent meanings and hints. And this may provide in the future rich and imaginative solutions in the scientific imagination about the nature of divine activity and the essential nature of reality, or the relationship between the order of grace and the order of creation.

REFERENCES

Alexander, H. G. *The Leibniz-Clarke Correspondence* (Manchester: Manchester University Press, 1956).

Barrow, John D., and Joseph Silk. *The Origin of the Universe* (New York: Basic Books, 1994).

Bohm, David. *Wholeness and the Implicate Order* (New York: Routledge and Kegan Paul, 1980).

Boyle, Robert. *An Essay Containing a Requisite Digression, Concerning Those That Would Exclude Deity from Intermeddling with Matter*, 1663, in *Selected Philosophical Papers of Robert Boyle*, ed. with an Introduction, M. A. Stewart (Indianapolis: Hackett, 1991).

———. *About the Excellency and Grounds of the Mechanical Hypothesis*, 1674, in *Selected Philosophical Papers of Robert Boyle*, ed. with an Introduction, M. A. Stewart (Indianapolis: Hackett, 1991).

Brockman, John. *The Third Culture* (New York: Simon and Schuster, 1995).

Brooks, John H. *Science and Religion: Some Historical Perspectives* (Cambridge: Cambridge University Press, 1991).

Burtt, Edwin A. *The Metaphysical Foundations of Modern Physical Science: A Historical and Critical Essay* (London: Routledge and Kegan Paul, 1967 [1924]).

Capra, Fritjof. *The Tao of Physics* (London: BBC Publications, 1977).
————. *The Turning Point* (New York, Simon and Schuster, 1982).
Cassirer, Ernst. *The Philosophy of the Enlightenment* (Boston: Beacon Press, 1955 [1951]).
Cohen, Bernard. *The Birth of a New Physics* (New York: Norton, 1985).
————. *Revolution in Science* (Cambridge, Mass.: Harvard University Press, 1985).
Cole, K. C. *Sympathetic Vibrations: Reflections on Physics as a Way of Life* (New York: Bantam, 1985).
Crease, Robert, and Charles Mann. *The Second Creation: Makers of the Revolution in 20th-Century Physics* (New York: Macmillan, 1986).
Davies, Paul. *God and the New Physics* (New York: Simon and Schuster, 1983).
————. *Superforce* (New York: Simon and Schuster, 1984).
————. *The Forces of Nature* (Cambridge: Cambridge University Press, 1986).
————. *The Mind of God* (London: Penguin, 1994).
Deason, Gary B. "Reformation Theology and the Mechanistic Conception of Nature," in *God and Nature: Historical Essays on the Encounter between Christianity and Science,* ed. Lindberg, David C., and Ronald L. Numbers (Berkeley: University of California Press, 1986).
Dyson, Freeman. *Disturbing the Universe* (New York: Harper and Row, 1979).
————. *Infinite in All Directions* (New York: HarperCollins, 1988).
Eddington, Arthur. *The Philosophy of Physical Science* (Ann Arbor: University of Michigan Press, 1958).
Feynman, Richard. "The Development of the Space-Time View of Quantum Mechanics," *Science* 153 (1966).
————. *QED: The Strange Story of Light and Matter* (Princeton: Princeton University Press, 1985).
Fine, Arthur. *The Shaky Game: Einstein Realism and the Quantum Theory* (Chicago: University of Chicago Press, 1986).
Freudenthal, Gideon. *Atom and Individual in the Age of Newton: On the Genesis of the Mechanistic World View* (Dordrecht: D. Reidel, 1986).
Funkenstein, Amos. *Theology and the Scientific Imagination from the Middle Ages to the Seventeenth Century* (Princeton: Princeton University Press, 1986).
Gal-Or, Benjamin. *Cosmological Physics and Philosophy* (New York: Springer-Verlag, 1981).
Gascoigne, John. "From Bentley to the Victorians: The Rise and the Fall of British Newtonian Natural Theology," *Science in Context* 2, no. 2 (autumn 1988).
————. *Cambridge in the Age of the Enlightenment: Science, Religion, and Politics from the Restoration to the French Revolution* (Cambridge: Cambridge University Press, 1989).
Gell-Mann, Murray. *The Quark and the Jaguar* (New York: W. H. Freeman, 1994).
Gilson, Etienne. *The Spirit of Medieval Philosophy,* trans. A. H. C. Downes (New York: Scribner, 1936).
————. *The Philosophy of St. Thomas Aquinas,* trans. Edward Bullough (New York: Dorset Press, 1972 [1924]).
Gregory, Bruce. *Inventing Reality: Physics as a Language* (New York: Wiley Science Editions, 1988).
Hawkins, Stephen. *A Brief History of Time* (London: Bantam, 1988).

Heidegger, Martin. *What Is a Thing?* (Chicago: Henry Regency Co., 1967).

————. "Modern Science, Metaphysics, and Mathematics," in Martin Heidegger, *Basic Writings,* ed. David F. Krell (New York: HarperCollins, 1993), pp. 271–305.

Heisenberg, Werner. *Physics and Beyond: Encounters and Conversations* (New York: Harper and Row, 1971).

Hofstadter, D. R. *Gödel, Escher, Bach: An Eternal Golden Braid* (New York: Basic Books, 1979).

Holton, Gerald. *Introduction to Concepts and Theories in Physical Science* (Princeton: Princeton University Press, 1985).

————. *Thematic Origins of Scientific Thought: Kepler to Einstein* (Cambridge, Mass.: Harvard University Press, 1988).

Issar, Arie S. *From Primeval Chaos to Infinite Intelligence* (Aldershot: Avebury, 1995).

Jacob, Francois. *The Logic of Life: A History of Heredity* (New York: Vintage Books, 1976).

Jacob, Margaret C. *The Cultural Meaning of the Scientific Revolution* (New York: Knopf, 1988).

————. and Teeter, Betty J. *Newton and the Culture of Newtonianism* (Atlantic Highlands, N. J.: Humanities Press, 1995).

Kaku, Michio. *Introduction to Superstrings* (New York: Springer-Verlag, 1988).

————. *Hyperspace: A Scientific Odyssey through Parallel Universes, Time Warps, and the Tenth Dimension* (New York: Oxford University Press, 1994).

Kargon, Robert H. *Atomism in England from Hariot to Newton* (Oxford: Clarendon Press, 1966).

Kauffman, Stuart A. *Origins of Order: Self-Organization and Selection in Evolution* (New York: Oxford University Press, 1993).

Kline, Morris. *Mathematics and the Search for Knowledge* (New York: Oxford University Press, 1985).

Koyré, Alexander. *From the Closed World to the Infinite Universe* (Magnolia, Mass.: Peter Smith Publisher, 1983).

Lange, Frederick A. *The History of Materialism and Criticism of Its Present Importance* (New York: Harcourt, Brace, 1925).

Lindberg, David C., and Ronald L. Numbers, eds. *God and Nature: Historical Essays on the Encounter between Christianity and Science* (Berkeley: University of California Press, 1986), p. 186.

Mayr, Otto. *Authority, Liberty, and Automatic Machine in Early Modern Europe* (Baltimore: Johns Hopkins University Press, 1986).

Morris, Richard. *The Edges of Science* (New York: Prentice Hall, 1990).

Newton, Sir Isaac. *Sir Isaac Newton's Mathematical Principles of Natural Philosophy and His System of the World,* ed. Florian Cajori, 2 vols. (Berkeley: University of California Press, 1962).

Pagels, Heinz. *The Cosmic Code: Quantum Physics as the Language of Nature* (New York: Simon and Schuster, 1982).

————. *Perfect Symmetry: The Search for the Beginning of Time* (New York: Simon and Schuster, 1985).

Penrose, Roger. *The Emperor's New Mind* (Oxford: Oxford University Press, 1989).

Prigogine, Ilya, and Isabelle Stengers. *Order Out of Chaos* (New York: Bantam, 1984).

Sarasohn, Lisa T. *Gassendi's Ethics: Freedom in a Mechanistic Universe* (Ithaca: Cornell University Press, 1996).

Smolin, Lee. *The Life of the Cosmos: A New View of Cosmology, Particle Physics, and the Meaning of Quantum Physics* (New York: Crown, 1995).

Stephen, Sir Leslie. *History of English Thought in the Eighteenth Century,* 2 vols. (New York: Harbinger, 1962 [1876]).

Thomas, Lewis. "Debating the Unknowable," *Atlantic Monthly* (1981).

Westfall, Richard S. *Force in Newton Physics: The Science of Dynamics in the Seventeenth Century* (London: Macdonald, 1971).

———. *The Construction of Modern Science: Mechanisms and Mechanics* (Cambridge: Cambridge University Press, 1977 [1971]).

Wheeler, J. A. *Genesis and Observership* (Princeton University: John Henry Laboratories, 1976).

Whitehead, A. N. *Science and the Modern World* (Cambridge: Cambridge University Press, 1953).

Weinberg, Steven. *The First Three Minutes: A Modern View of the Origin of the Universe* (New York: Basic Books, 1977).

———. *Dreams of a Final Theory* (London: Vintage, 1995).

Zohar, Dana. *The Quantum Self* (London: HarperCollins, 1991).

Zukav, Gary. *The Dancing Wu Li Masters* (New York: Morrow, 1979).

CHAPTER 5

Complexity in Systematic Theology: The Case of the Christian Concept of "New Creation" in the Dialogue with Science

GÜNTER THOMAS

Dr. Thomas is a professor of theology at Heidelberg University in Germany. He holds a Th.M. in theology from Princeton University, a Ph.D. in theology from Heidelberg University, and a Ph.D. in sociology from Tübingen University. He is the author of several books and articles on theology and science, theology and culture, and the theory of religion.

Introduction[1]

Times are changing. When in 1967 the second volume of the *Encyclopedia of Philosophy* came out, there was no article on "complexity" included, but the seventh volume carried an article by the philosopher of science Mary Hesse on "simplicity," which ended with remarks on Ockham's razor.[2] Simplicity was the crucial issue at that time. The negative result also holds true for the large Italian *Encyclopedia Filosophia* from 1957, which offers only a lemma on "complicatio." As a matter of fact, times *are* changing. In 1976, the sociologist (sic!) Niklas Luhmann wrote an article on complexity for the "Historisches Wörterbuch der Philosophie" (thirteen volumes including an index).[3] In 1998 followed the "Encyclopédie Philosophique Universelle," and the new Routledge Encyclopedia of Philosophy, which also carries an article on computational complexity.

Within a rather short period of time, the term complexity became a central conceptual metaphor in quite a number of academic discourses.[4] However, the proliferation of the use of the concept and even the development of a science of complexity does not coincide with a common conceptual outline, something that did not change since

Niklas Luhmann's complaint about insufficient definitional rigor and a rather loose use of the concept in various disciplines. Besides some noteworthy exceptions, so far the concept of complexity has not yet really reached mainline continental and especially German theology. However, times might change, even in theology.

Complexity is a strictly self-referential concept Whoever talks about complexity faces it in two ways: Complexity on the level of the observed "reality" and on the level of the discourse. It is my contention that the concept of complexity is able to clarify theological work in at least three ways, which will structure the following paper:

1. In order to gain conceptual clarity, I will start with remarks regarding the background of the *concept of complexity* I am going to use in the subsequent presentation on theology's own complexity.
2. In a second step I try to show how the notion of complexity can illuminate the multi-referential nature of the craft of systematic theology. Different types of systematic theology can be reconstructed as specific reductions of complexity in the task of doing theology. These reductions of complexity present different types of "openness through closure." Here I would like to talk about *operational* or *external complexity* on the level of theological discourse.
3. After talking *about* theology I will move on to *doing* theology and not jump immediately into the dialogue with complexity in science. More specifically, I would like to elaborate to a certain extent the Judeo-Christian concept of "new creation." I would like to indicate what kind of complexity theology faces if it takes seriously the claim to talk about God on the basis of the pluri-form and heterogeneous biblical witnesses. This type of complexity I label *internal complexity on the subject level.*
4. In the final section I will turn back to the interaction between theology and sciences and ask what concepts could be useful to communicate the "novelty" of the new creation to other non-theological discourses.

Complexity in Systems Theory

The concept of complexity is used in a variety of quite diverse academic discourses ranging from ecology to theoretical physics and to macroeconomics. In order to map the field I would like to divide it into at least three loosely connected spheres. Besides some attempts to develop a rather general mathematical theory of complexity, there are those other disciplines in which complexity is tied to debates about chaotic and non-linear systems in the physical sciences, to issues in chemistry and in biology. In the third sphere complexity is part of general systems theory, which is used in psychology, in political sciences, and primarily in sociology. In this case the systems under observation are social, psychological, and cultural systems.[5] Without any doubt, there is much overlap between the three spheres and in all of them complexity is strongly bound to the basic idea of self-organization.[6] However, instead of transferring complexity theory from the natural sciences to theology,[7] I want to turn first to complexity in systems theory, which was developed by the sociologist and social philosopher Niklas Luhmann over the past three decades.[8]

Luhmann analyzes self-organized and autopoietically operating systems that exercise a considerable degree of "autonomy" as well as creative adjustment to their environment. The term complexity denotes the fact that not all elements in a given unity can be connected at the same time. Since not all relations can be actualized in a given moment, complexity implies selectivity. To distinguish elements from relations is fundamental to complexity, since it is the basis for the observation of selectivity. To assess complexity, it is necessary to observe two situations: one with more, one with less selective interconnectedness. Since the number of relations is growing exponentially with the elements, the operations of selective actualization of relations always imply horizons of further possibilities. Whatever is, could be different. There are always more possibilities than actualizations. The selective establishment of relations, as one side of complexity, always reveals contingency: contingency from previous states and operations, the simultaneity of other possibilities, and the question of future possibilities of substitution. Therefore, complex systems have an immanent history, conditioned by their own history of selections.[9]

Complexity is, strictly speaking, not an operational term but always a concept used in observations (including self-observations) and descriptions. Complexity is not available from within its own operation. Complexity describes something that can only be distinguished from something else, that is actually introduced by the distinction that is carried with the concept itself.

But what is the distinction drawn by this concept? According to Luhmann, "complexity is the difference between complete and selective connecting,"[10] that is to say the unity of the difference between both. Complexity is a concept that refers to a specific type of description that utilizes this distinction.

Complexity can be seen in a given system or in its environment. However, only the complexity in systems is organized or structured complexity. To observe complexity we need a system that observes the world from its own perspective, taking the world to be the unity of the difference between the system and its environment. The observation of complexity depends on the observation undertaken by systems that are based on "meaning" ("Sinn").[11] In case the self-observation of complexity is reintroduced into the system, various forms of hypercomplexity can develop.

We should keep in mind that we face a paradox. The complexity of the environment of a given system or its internal complexity is neither determined nor created by the observed system and its own observation. The given system can only react to this complexity, even though this complexity "exists" only as a result of the observation of this system by another system.

The difference between system and environment is characterized by a steep drop of complexity: the border between environment and system consists of a limitation of possibilities. To be more precise, the possible relations inside the system are always selectively limited in relation to the complexity in the environment. The structuring of complexity inside the system takes place in light of a specific environment and this reduction of complexity has to preserve some compatibility with its environment. Reduction of complexity means that the structure of the relations between the elements of a system, an environment, or a whole world is reconstructed with a smaller number of relations. Therefore, the reduction and the preservation of complexity are two sides of the same observation. At the basis of such reductions are structures that enable the selective preservation of a realm of possibilities. Hence, the degree of internal complexity in a given system depends on such structures. The level of complexity might change in a system, depending on its size and the complexity of its environment. The increase of complexity in systems A, B, and C at the same time increases the complexity of the system X that observes the systems A, B, and C. Its environment becomes more complex, something with far-reaching consequences in theology as a social system. We have to keep in mind that there is neither a strict causal relation between environment and the system, nor an abstract autonomy. As a result, even small changes in the environment might lead to rather far-reaching consequences in the system, or, due to its autopoietic self-reproduction, the system might be almost "immune" to changes in its environment.

When the complexity of a system increases drastically, it can, based on internal differentiation, establish subsystems with their own autopoietical "freedom." As a consequence, there is some relation between the accepted degree of complexity and the form of differentiation in a system or society. The internal differentiation of academic disciplines is a telling example. The second type of reaction to increasing complexity is the temporalization of complexity. What cannot be related at the same time is related sequentially. This takes time, but it enables more relations to be actualized. Language is a good example of this process.

Observing Theology—Multi-referential Discourse and Typified Complexity

If theology enters the interdisciplinary discourse on complexity, it faces a double challenge or what Luhmann might call "hypercomplexity." Theology not only observes complexity but discovers, by means of self-observation, that it itself is "subjected" to complexity. Any way of dealing with complexity without including the observer in the field of the observed entities would be too simplistic and naive. Niklas Luhmann's theory of complexity was primarily developed for social systems based on meaning and operating on the basis of communication, that is to say, systems that undertake self-observation and face such hypercomplexity. Among the currently discussed theories of complexity it is most suited to uncover complexity within theology's own discourse.

Systematic theology can be described out of many perspectives. Sociological, philosophical, and psychological descriptions as well as philosophy of science perspectives are possible.[12] For the current purpose I would like to engage in theological self-observation or self-description and describe it theologically:[13] It is the critical reflection on the church's communication about the triune God in terms of its preaching, teaching, and action, based on the biblical witnesses, adjusted to its own specific time, and in favor of further understanding of God.[14] In short, systematic theology is a peculiar type of second-order communication about religious communication.[15] While this is a kind of standard description, we might ask: What can be seen, if the theological self-observation is geared toward complexity?

Systematic theology emerges out of selective relations between the interaction of many elements. Without any doubt, theology has to take into account confessional contexts, the tradition of the churches, as well as the biblical texts together with their exegetical analysis. At the same time it relates to its own theological past in order to maintain coherence and it develops perspectives on other confessions (ecumenical context) as well as other religions (context of religious pluralism). In doing that, theology has to address questions and problems that come up in the experience of the church as well as in the wider culture. Theology is always a public task, and for this reason the Chicago theologian David Tracy asserted that theology is expected to address at least three "publics." Theology should address the church, the academic public, and the general culture.[16] In all of these three spheres, theology encounters different styles of reasoning and rationality.

Yet, this picture of three public spheres drawn by David Tracy is still not differentiated and fine-tuned enough, since the three publics are in turn complex and diversified. They have a complex internal structure. Regarding the church as a public arena, we need to differentiate the lay people who theology should somehow address, the classical Protestant who prefers to stay close to his local parish, the future ministers who need to be academically educated, and finally the discourse which characterizes decision makers in the institutional settings. Neither is the more general cultural public uniform. Academic theological reflection mostly targets the highly literate culture at the expense of the more popular culture and rarely takes up the challenges stemming from our culture's saturation by mass media. Finally, the academic public does not just consist of colleagues from the department of literature as you might think reading Tracy. Philosophy, not just philosophy of religion, is a crucial reference point and also the sciences have to be taken into account, that is, in treating issues of creation and cosmology. Psychology and sociology want to be considered for theological issues relating to psychological or sociological processes, that is, in the talk about Christian identity, conversion, or the church. Finally, historical studies and philosophy of history justly are at the basis of much theological construction.

The relations to these academic discourses have at least three dimensions. Theology encounters, analyses, and criticizes *their* perspective on those subject matters that are at issue: creation, church, history, and so on. In addition, theology faces their perspective on the task of theology. Lastly, within such engagements, theology searches for forms of thought to articulate its own content, express its own subject matter, and make intelligible its knowledge to a given culture whose common sense as a cultural system is very much influenced by the sciences. As any religious utterance has to use ordinary language, theological reflection has to employ conceptual tools that originate not all in its own conceptual space.

Already this short sketch makes visible the complexity of the task of theology. No finite theologian and no research team can establish a complete and simultaneous network of relations between all elements, given the non-determinate relationship between theology and its cultural environment. This makes every theology inevitably a humble enterprise.

In former times, theology could explicate its beliefs by utilizing the grammar and the vocabulary of a widely accepted metaphysical system, which claimed to lay out the basis of all reflection. The times of such nice "package deals" or metaphysical consensus are over. The *increase* of complexity of other social systems in the environment of theology (i.e., natural sciences, political science, arts, mass media, etc.) inescapably *increases* the complexity inside theology, if theology wants to stay somehow attuned to its environment and wants to avoid a fundamentalist "flight to an insular existence." If theology relates to other academic discourses, it has to do it in more or less limited ways—parochial dialogues—in quite specific attempts at "limited translation." However, as Luhmann's complexity theory has shown, the construction of distinct, ordered, and focused theological projects of dialogue with other discourses such as the sciences is based not just on establishing new relations, but is inevitably rooted in the systematic interruption of other instances of interconnectedness. These types of theological ventures, which are directed toward specific relational patterns, are still all an internal description, even if one distinguishing indicator of one project over against others may be the extent to which it can take up specific *external* perspectives on theology or non-theological bodies of knowledge.[17]

Without reduction of complexity, there is no distinct theology. Theology, as a multi-referential endeavor, has to be selective. Yet, any attempts at reducing complexity can go too far. As a result, the system can lose contact with its environment or can endanger its own self-reproduction. Given this pressure for contingent and risky selectivity, I would like to suggest that different types of reduction of theological complexity result in different types of theology, such as more philosophical theology, hermeneutical theology, biblical theology, and so on.[18] Or, the other way around, various theologies represent different types of reduction of complexity. However, without further qualification, this could lead to the false impressions that all reductions of complexity can be treated equally and that all relations as well as elements are equal. Treating all relational patterns as equal overlooks the central insight that theological reflection has a kind of gravitational center, often called "scripture-principle,"[19] which provides any type of theology with the necessary degree of complexity. The internal complexity of scripture is a safeguard against oversimplification within theology.

What does it mean? Well, not just for first-order theological discourse such as preaching, but even for second-order reflection, the library of biblical texts provides the primary source for theological imagination. The texts provide the guiding distinctions in theological talk about God, the world, and human beings. In turning to biblical texts, systematic theology takes into account historical research and is critically and constructively explicating, unfolding, and evaluating dense symbolic nets or clusters found in the library of biblical texts. Some interpreters might speak of root metaphors, which cannot be translated completely in conceptual language but can be unfolded in such language. Such a return to biblical texts favors a "second naïveté" and does not represent a return to naive precritical readings. Yet over against a "thinning out" of theology in metaphysical and philosophical theologies, such biblical theology provides the thick and rich texture for other types of theology, which can be realized through a temporalization of theological complexity, that is to say an oscillation between the evaluation of biblical texts and a rather conceptual and constructive way of doing systematic theology.[20] Such a temporalization of complexity can never escape selectivity either. Yet its texture provides the rich distinctions that have to be taken into account to a certain extent in dialogues between theology and science. On the one hand, this texture guards against oversimplification of Christian theology, and, on the other hand, this theological endeavor makes apparent the *indispensably* reductionistic side of any meaningful dialogue.

Yet, difference comes before unity; openness requires operational closure. In the following sections of the paper I will examine one specific theological symbol: new creation. At the same time, I will provide an example of temporalized complexity within the systematic theological discourse. In order to take up the guiding distinctions I will turn to the thick texture of biblical texts, move on to systematic reflections, and eventually shift to some remarks on the dialogue with science. Hence, "closure" will lead to "openness."

New Creation Seen Through Exemplary Biblical Texts

The theological conception of a new creation runs like a Wittgensteinian cord through both the Hebrew and Christian Bibles. Even though the term itself—"new creation"—appears only in a small number of texts, the "cord" consists of a multiplicity of threads that can be found in many traditions and are entwined. The new creation is one perspective on God's redemptive and saving action and at the same time one dimension of the final, eschatological work of God.[21] Why is the concept of a new creation so interesting for the dialogue between religion and science? I think for four reasons:

1. In theology, we have to move beyond the split between natural and cultural processes that is manifest in the separation of creation and new creation, which means theology needs to recover the dimension of creation in the economy of salvation.

2. New creation is a theological symbol that is linked to a large number of other theological topics such as Christ, the resurrection, the foundation of the church, the work of the Spirit, and so on. In short, it is very tightly woven into the fabric of theology.

3. New creation reintroduces complexity in a too-simplified theological account of creation and God's action, since creation, theologically speaking, is neither complete nor unqualified. Furthermore, the concept of new creation asks for additional distinctions and qualifications in our talk about *creatio continua* and *providentia.*

4. The symbol or concept of new creation inserts further complexity in the dialogue between science and religion, which many times uses the concept of "creation" as an interface or shared ground for dialogue.[22]

By turning to a "theological theology" more self-referentially oriented toward the biblical traditions, complexity does not decrease.[23] A more biblical orientation in theology is no flight to false simplicity. Rather, the other way around. It is my contention that in systematic theology we need to turn to biblical texts, to reintroduce a little bit more complexity into our theological reasoning. For this reason, in the following section I will not outline a traditional or contemporary systematic-theological position on the issue of new creation. Instead, I want briefly to introduce three texts, which inform the theological talk about new creation.

The first text is part of the apostle Paul's correspondence with the church in Corinth, which he himself founded. It dates back to about

54–56 C.E. The passage is taken out of an argumentation, in which
Paul describes his ministry of reconciliation. This text is important, as it
is one of the few places in which the conceptual term "new creation"
appears.[24]

2 Corinthians 5:14–21

14 For the love of Christ urges us on, because we are convinced
that one has died for all; Therefore all have died.

15 And he died for all, so that those who live might live no
longer for themselves, but for him who died and was raised
for them.

16 From now on, therefore, we regard no one from a human
point of view; even though we once knew Christ from a human point of view, we know him no longer in that way.

17 So if anyone is in Christ, there is a new creation: everything
old has passed away; see, everything has become new!

18 All this is from God, who has reconciled us to himself
through Christ and has given us the ministry of reconciliation;

19 that is, in Christ God was reconciling the world to himself,
not counting their trespasses against them, and entrusting
the message of reconciliation to us.

20 So we are ambassadors for Christ, since God is making his
appeal through us; we entreat you on behalf of Christ, be
reconciled to God.

21 For our sake he made him to be sin who knew no sin, so that
in him we might become the righteousness of God.

The conceptual space in which Paul talks about new creation is
Jesus Christ, specifically what happened for all people through his life,
death, and resurrection.[25] The death of Christ was an event of true love
that opened up a new future for man. The event of Christ's resurrection
is adequately understood only if it is seen as the future of all humankind. Why? Paul applies a typology of the original being, similar to the
first and second Adam scheme, in which the resurrected Christ is the
new humankind in whom every human being can participate in the
new creation.[26] Without any doubt, in this text, new creation is a rather
anthropocentric concept. New creation denotes a new existence characterized by love.[27] The newly created people define themselves through
Christ and communicate this perspective to each other, since like

Christ, this is the way they know and perceive each other.[28] For Paul, new creation is the fundamental term expressing the idea that through Christ man belongs to the new creation, that is to say, he is saved from death. Hence, "new creation" is a key term of Paul's theological anthropology, yet at the same time "new creation" already points beyond a merely "new creature."[29] The Gospels do not define man through the past, but by means of a future that appeared in Christ. However, for human beings, new creation is a strictly relational term: it "exists" only in Christ. Since Christ, not all of creation and not all human beings are newly created. But as a dynamic reality, the new creation wants to be communicated and spread by the ambassadors for Christ. Yet, in Christ, the new creation is not a future, not just a possibility; it is a present actual reality, creating a perspective in which "everything has become new!" It is worth mentioning that God's Spirit is not alluded to by Paul, neither is baptism, at least not explicitly. Taken on its own, this passage could lead to the conclusion that in new creation matter just does not matter.

This picture changes if we move on to another text, taken out of Paul's letter to the church in Rome. The relation between creation and new creation is an important stream within the whole letter. How can human beings achieve knowledge of God if they misread the book of creation and misuse the Torah? How can human beings be liberated from the power of sin and death? The eighth chapter describes the situation in which man no longer quarrels with himself and with God. Only the life guided by the Spirit of God can correspond to the Torah and God's will.

Romans 8:14–30

14 For all who are led by the Spirit of God are children of God.
15 For you did not receive a spirit of slavery to fall back into fear, but you have received a spirit of adoption. When we cry, "Abba! Father!"
16 it is that very spirit bearing witness of God,
17 and if children, then heirs, heirs of God and joint heirs with Christ—if, in fact, we suffer with him so that we may also be glorified with him.
18 I consider that the sufferings of this present time are not worth comparing with the glory about to be revealed to us.
19 For the creation waits with eager longing for the revealing of the children of God;

20 for the creation was subjected to futility, not of its own will
but by the will of the one who subjected it, in hope

21 that the creation itself will be set free from its bondage to decay and will obtain the freedom of the glory of the children
of God.

22 We know that the whole creation has been groaning in labor
pains until now;

23 and not only the creation, but we ourselves, who have the
first fruits of the Spirit, groan inwardly while we wait for
adoption, the redemption of the bodies.

24 For in hope we were saved. Now hope that is seen is not
hope. For who hopes for what is seen?

25 But if we hope for what we do not see, we wait for it with
patience.

26 Likewise the Spirit helps us in our weakness; for we do not
know how to pray as we ought, but that very Spirit intercedes with sighs too deep for words.

27 And God, who searches the heart, knows what is the mind
of the Spirit, because the Spirit intercedes for the saints according to the will of God.

28 We know that all things work together for good for those
who love God, who are called according to his purpose.

29 For those whom he foreknew he also predestined to be con-
formed to the image of his Son, in order that he might be the
firstborn within a large family.

30 And those whom he predestined he also called; and those
whom he called he also justified; and those whom he justified he also glorified.

This is a much debated text, which uses metaphorical and mytho-
logical language at numerous places.[30] The consummation of the believers is at the same time the liberation of the whole creation of the power
of futility.[31] But the final redemption of the believers is seen over against
the pain and the suffering in the current situation. This suffering of the
believers indicates that the future glory is still hidden. The final consummation consists of a final revelation that makes apparent and visible that
they are children of the risen Christ. Out of this tension between the actual, current situation and the final consummation, Paul develops his
view of an eschatological crisis. The suffering of those who are liberated
to be sons and daughters of God makes them representatives of the suffering creation and representatives of creation's future consummation.

The fate of the creation and the fate of humankind are intertwined. Paul uses anthropocentric images and personifies the creation so that she can suffer, hope, and long for liberation. Subjected to futility, creation is not any more creation as it was in the beginning. That means that theology has to deal with a creation in the process of corruption and brokenness. Therefore, we cannot simply equate the theological concept of creation with nature. Nature is creation with the mark of a deep rupture, with the fate of futility, regardless of God's ongoing nurturing, saving, and preserving. However, this nature is not yet what it could be and will be. Theologically speaking, creation can only be conceptualized within the framework of a dynamic ontology. On the one side, Paul does not enter cosmological speculation. On the other side, he does not content himself with the renewal of the human, that is, Christian subjects. Within the frame of anthropomorphic reasoning, he transcends anthropocentric thinking, because Christian hope wants to be shared hope. The cosmological dimension is a necessary implication of the Christ event.

The transforming power of this process is God's creative Spirit. As creative principle of life (in the creation) and new life (resurrection), he takes over the finitude, weakness, and suffering of the whole "old creation." The Spirit is so deeply immersed in this process that he works inside human beings. The coming of the Spirit is the beginning of the whole creation's consummation. By dwelling inside the believers, God comes to his creation. In spite of everything, there is a sharp divide between the "now" full of suffering and the final consummation.

I began by mentioning the apocalyptical background of some of Paul's writings. However, there is one crucial difference to classical apocalyptic thought: Namely, the new world does not come after the total destruction of the old, as can be found in other texts.

A last remark on Romans 8. The new creation conceptualized as final consummation is anchored in the cross and resurrection of Jesus Christ. Further, it is brought about by God's Spirit, transforming, renewing the creation. Any theistic conception of God cannot describe, given this implicit but nevertheless deep trinitarian structure of the new creation, this process. To put the point the other way around, only a trinitarian thinking of God can introduce sufficient complexity in God's dynamic relation to the world.

Let me now briefly turn to a third text, written or edited about three hundred years before Christ. It was worked out by the so-called Third Isaiah, the final editing group that completed what we today know as the biblical book of Isaiah.[32] It is a very subtle composition and a wonderful exercise of what, in the current academic jargon, is called intertextuality. As a matter of fact, it is an ancient hypertext, since almost every phrase is an allusion to other texts known by the writers as well as the readers.

Isaiah 65:17–25

17 For I am about to create new heavens and a new earth; the former things shall not be remembered or come to mind.

18 But be glad and rejoice forever in what I am creating; for I am about to create Jerusalem as a joy and its people as a delight.

19 I will rejoice in Jerusalem and delight in my people; no more shall the sound of weeping be heard in it, or the cry of distress.

20 No more shall there be in it an infant that lives but a few days,or an old person who does not live out a lifetime; for one who dies at a hundred years will be considered a youth, and one who fails short of a hundred will be considered accursed.

21 They shall build houses and inhabit them; they shall plant vineyards and eat their fruit.

22 They shall not build and another inhabit; they shall not plant and another eat; for like the days of a tree shall the days of my people be, and my chosen shall long enjoy the work of their hands.

23 They shall not labor in vain, or bear children for calamity; for they shall be offspring blessed by the LORD—and their descendants as well.

24 Before they call I will answer, while they are yet speaking I will hear.

25 The wolf and the lamb shall feed together, the lion shall eat straw like the ox; but the serpent—its food shall be dust! They shall not hurt or destroy on all my holy mountain, says the LORD.

If we look at this text, the new creation is a multi-dimensional process. It starts with the cosmic dimension, pointing to the fullness and completeness of creation, heavens *and* earth. This cosmological approach has a divine dimension, since it implies a heightened and intensified presence and closeness of God in the city (19) and as persons

(24). In addition to this cosmological dimension, we can see a transformation of the social and cultural identity of the city. "As cosmic as the newness to come is, it is also as specific as Jerusalem."[33] The most advanced and yet very ambivalent cultural invention of ancient times is not dissolved, but renewed into a treasured city.[34] But there is also a biographical, personal dimension to this process. Everyone can live his or her full life, which will not be destroyed by illness, wars, or political turmoil. The house and the vineyard are symbols of the rich and settled, that is to say, the blessed life. The future will be without the risk of destruction and death. The dimension of personal-biological life is captured in verse 23, since to labor in vain is one of the most stark experiences of futility that is possible, the paradox of the death of one's own life in one's life. Since offspring are the visible, public, and sensuous sign of God's blessing, to labor in vain clearly signifies the total absence of God's blessing to his creature seen as in creaturely creativity.

Finally, we reach the natural dimension in verse 25, that refers to Isaiah 11:6–8 and several other texts.[35] What is the point of this romantic picture, in the English world called the "peaceable Kingdom," in German the "eschatologischer Tierfrieden"? Four points, relevant to our theme, may be highlighted:

1. Wild animals such as the wolf, lion, cobra, viper, and bear are all deadly animals and this life-threatening force in the non-domesticated environment will disappear.[36]
2. The separation between the chaotic and death-laden wild nature and the peaceful and domesticated nature of sheep, ox, and cow will disappear.[37]
3. Most importantly, when the lion will eat straw, life will no longer be sustained at the cost of life. The philosopher Alfred North Whitehead's phrase "life is robbery" will not hold true any more.[38]
4. When the serpent will eat just dust, the forces of destruction, temptation, sin, and death will no longer exert any power.

To sum up, we get a picture of the new creation as God's action in those places and in those circumstances where life is threatened, future is endangered, and the so-called natural resources of the powers of regeneration are exempt. Even the signs of God's blessing, labor and offspring, have turned out to increase the situation of objective futility. This perceptive account of the forces of destruction goes beyond the human world into the realm of biological animal life untouched by human cultivation, domestication, and domination.

Unfortunately, I have to break up the evaluation of biblical texts. There are a number of texts that would need to be evaluated for our topic that would introduce further themes and further complexity. For instance, I have to leave untouched any explication of the connection between creation, illness, and healing in the New Testament, as well as any notion of creativity in the parables of Jesus. A full account of new creation would also need a careful reading of the New Testament witnesses to the cross and bodily resurrection of Jesus Christ as well as the visions of a new Jerusalem in the Book of Revelation. Hopefully, even these three texts briefly examined above can provide some insight into the complexity of theology's subject matter, if systematic theology allows the biblical texts to interfere with its own construction.

What comes out is a rather complex picture of a multi-dimensional process in terms of time, authorship, and subject matter of the new creation. When does it take place? Who brings it about? Are we as humans involved in it? What levels and dimensions of reality are going to be changed? Here the systematic theologian, on the operational level of doing "theological theology," faces the task of establishing necessarily selective relations within the web of interconnections, that is to say, the task of the reduction of the internal complexity in theology.

Creatio Viatorum—*Systematic Reflections on New Creation*

The notion of "new creation" is central to an understanding of the Christ-event, the life of the church, and for the shape of Christian hope. However, the biblical texts don't provide a totally unified and coherent scheme and—for many good reasons—cannot replace the constructive theological task of developing a contemporary understanding of "new creation." Again, theological complexity needs to be "temporalized." Not all possible relations can be actualized simultaneously. For the present purpose, I have to restrain myself to a few remarks and a quite narrow perspective on "new creation."

Thinking about new creation, we are forced to draw a distinction between the old and the new creation. This distinction makes it impossible to equate the scientific concept of nature with the theological concept of creation.[39] The Christian view on nature requires the differentiation of different perspectives and the perception of different realities.

Any attempt to undercut this distinction oversimplifies the Christian perspective on reality by a too far-reaching reduction of complexity.[40]

Within the "event" of the new creation it seems helpful to distinguish between three dimensions or coordinates: the temporal, the social, and the factual. In terms of the *temporal* dimension it is a widely held theological consensus that the risen Jesus Christ is the beginning of the new creation and Christians participate "in Christ" (2 Cor. 5:17). The beginning of this reality will find its fulfillment and end in a "new heaven and earth." Regarding the *social* dimension, Christ is, as the "new Adam," the first risen from the dead. He is the beginning of a process in which the Christians as well as the "people called" get involved in the praxis of love, justice, and reconciliation. The social horizon of this socio-cultural process is the total inclusion of all human beings.[41] The *factual* dimension indicates the "depth" or scope of this process of renewal and concerns the simple question, "What is renewed in this process?" Is the *creatio nova* a social-cultural and psychological process leading to a new self-understanding and the new identity of believers as justified sinners? Is the renewal limited to human beings or does it transcend the personal and social reality into the realm of "nature"? If the latter is the case, we might ask ourselves whether this is brought about exclusively through a renewed relationship between human beings and the natural world[42] or also through new creative acts of God within nature. Already the brief evaluation of biblical traditions in the section above suggested that the new creation encompasses multiple levels of reality. It affects a multiplicity of "realities" within the cosmic unity of heaven and earth.[43] Certainly, the new creation has the personal dimension of the individual believer, a social dimension in the formation of redemptive and healing communities, as well as a cultural dimension influencing and transforming deep-seated patterns and other socio-cultural systems ranging from politics to the arts. Yet there is not just in Isaiah 65 but also in several other texts a growing sensitivity to life-destructive and chaotic forces and constellations in "nature" that are overcome in what is perceived as the final "eschatological" acts of God. The destruction of animal life by other animals and the destruction of human life through fatal illness are prominent examples.[44] The new creation has cosmic dimensions and reaches out to all spheres of life, natural processes included.[45] Insofar as it encompasses all spheres of life, it responds not just to human sin, but to chaotic forces beyond human agency.[46]

One might speculate on what could be the rationality behind the new creation of heaven(s). First, the inclusion of heaven denotes a totality of the cosmos. In addition a "new heaven" might be required because God's presence in the world experiences deep changes. But what is of central importance is the renewal of heaven as a created reality, which marks a fundamental change in the realm of possibilities and transcultural realities.[47] The whole created unity consisting of heaven and earth, comprising realities as well as possibilities, needs to be renewed.

However, even if theology includes such a strong notion of cosmic transformation, we are left with a crucial question that arises from the *connection* of the temporal (when?) and the factual dimensions (what?) of new creation. What is included in it and when does it take place? While many theologians maintain the idea that with the resurrection of Jesus Christ from the dead "the future of the new creation of all things already began in the midst of this dying and vanishing world," they would reserve the cosmic transformation for some distant "eschatological" time or even time beyond time.[48] However, if the resurrection is the beginning, the multi-dimensional process of renewal must not be reserved for some distant future—even though the final consummation of the new creation is not yet realized. In the past, part of the reason the transformation of the cosmos could not be seen as a *present reality* was the idea of a closed universe without novelty, chance, or "freedom." As a consequence, nature and history were strictly juxtaposed. In more recent times, the focus on the "stable" laws of physics and chemistry did not encourage the idea of a present transformation of "heaven and earth." Instead of restricting the new creation to a last state "beyond time," I would like to put forward a different view, by borrowing a term from ecclesiology. Between the resurrection and the final "kingdom of God" the church is not *ecclesia triumphans* but *ecclesia viatorum*. As *ecclesia viatorum* the church has not yet reached its fulfillment, but it is already on its way. In a similar vein, since the resurrection of Jesus Christ, the whole creation (heaven and earth as well as nature and culture) has become a *creatio viatorum* on its way to the final completion and transformation. As a *creatio viatorum* creation is characterized by a temporary simultaneity of the old and the new. In so-called natural as well as cultural processes the power and source of renewal is God's Spirit. As the spiritual gifts renewing the communion of faith stem from the concurrence of the work of the Holy Spirit and human creativity, so too, God's renewing work toward a new creation might well make use of creativity in natural processes. In addition, if we take the Eucharist as the paradigm and center of the new creation in the life of the church, we can see how the renewing work is a) linked to the natural as well as cultural order of the old creation and b) is parochial, local, and hence has, metaphorically speaking, a grainy structure. The renewing work is universal, but not in the sense of taking place at every point in space and time. There is no equal distribution of the renewing spirit in creation. Even though in between the resurrection and the final consummation God is "at work," the transformation is not a seamless and continuous or evolutionary development toward the final perfection.

If we look back at the brief theological characterization of the new creation, we can envisage a larger reorientation in terms of creation and eschatology. To include the "twisted force of evil entrenched" in our existence and the cosmic order, the picture of the transition from creation to new creation provides a strong argument for a rather specific relation between creation and new creation.[49] As Jürgen Moltmann pointed out, in our thinking about creation, we can look at creation in the light of redemption (1), or at redemption in the light of creation (2).[50] In the latter view, creation was basically perfect; it was disordered by human sin and eventually will be restituted by grace. The notion of a *restitutio ad integrum* provides the basic orientation, or a "paradise lost—paradise regained" pattern. Due to its strong anthropocentric view of redemption, this model, which is dominant in Western theology, leads quite frequently to a theological disregard of "nature."[51] According to the former view, the creation at the beginning is God's beginning of an unfolding history, which finds its final consummation and completion in the new creation. In the light of this final completion the first creation might be good but not yet perfect. This model is certainly more open to a transformation as well as an inclusion of "nature" into this process. If we ask the simple question, "What is the central 'problem' to which the new creation is responding to?" we see that the first model can incorporate the second with its emphasis on sin, but not the other way around.

To sum up this preliminary and very short exegetical and systematic sketch, I would like to describe at least some features of God's renewing work on creation *in between* resurrection and final consummation.[52]

1. New creation comes with a new closeness and a new presence of God in his creation, which cuts across a total theistic transcendence and a pan(en)theistic immanence of God and exceeds his providential presence.
2. It has a responsive character insofar as it responds to chaos, distress, loss, and death.

3. It breaks up the tragic "unity of life and death in favor of life"[53] and overcomes Whitehead's dictum "life is robbery." The continuation and enrichment of life does not take place at the cost of other life.

4. The renewal of the creation starts taking place locally and temporally, hence it has a kind of grainy structure. Yet the dynamic movement from the resurrection of Jesus of Nazareth to the final consumption is a move from the particular to the universal.

5. As *creatio viatorum*, creation is characterized by a simultaneity of old and new.

The claim that God will create a new heaven and earth certainly does not stand at the very center of Christian belief. Yet neither is it peripheral, since it is connected with many other elements of Christian thinking such as creation, Christology, pneumatology, and eschatology, to name just a few. If theology is not willing to give up any type of "realism," the claim of the renewal of heaven and earth implies a truth claim about an extralinguistic entity: the world. Neither the meaning nor the truth of this claim depend on an affirmation from the side of the sciences. It is already meaningful in the context of Christian liturgical practice and within the dense web of Christian discourse. Yet holding up the belief in the one creator, theology itself attempts to explicate the reality of this claim in relation to other discourses about the world.

An Intermediate Reflection—Temporalization of Theological Complexity and the Need to Return to the Dialogue with the Sciences

If we look back, we might ask ourselves whether science and theology should not be kept apart as much as possible. Both discourses should not become polluted, as the anthropologist Mary Douglas might say, by false exchange.[54] In addition, should not the biblical scholars and the systematic theologians stay away from any attempts to try to develop interfaces with other academic discourses, given the complexity of the subject matter with which they are already dealing? Are not such interfaces established at the high cost of severe and sometimes destructive oversimplifications of the religious symbol system, not to say of the scientific knowledge systems? Would it not be sensible to establish relationships only on the level of a social scientific meta-discourse regarding ways of reasoning, using models and paradigms and forms of thought, and not on the level of content?

Even though I argued earlier for a *temporary disconnection* of inter-relationships between systematic theology and other scientific discourses, at this point, as I mentioned already at the end of the last section, I have to say no wholeheartedly to such a radical split. Theology cannot eventually isolate itself and develop a purely "theological theology" as the sole type of reflection. Theology has to take the risk of *temporalizing theological complexity* and search for interfaces with other discourses, natural sciences included. Based on my example of new creation, I would like to put forward two arguments and add another clarifying remark on the task of "limited translations."

1. If theology holds up its own claims, that is to say, the claims that the transformation brought about by the new creation even includes the transformation of "nature," this subject matter forces it to enter into dialogue with discourses that correctly claim to be competent in these areas. Even if theological propositions are always propositions about the world, God, and the self, they always carry with them truth claims about "extra-linguistic entities," even though they are communicated and "verified" only in the discourse of a whole way of life in which eventually God himself takes care for the truth of our thoughts about him. Insofar as the "God-talk" about "new creation" is in some respect also talk about this world, the dialogues are unavoidable due to the issues on the level of subject matter, the "Sachebene."[55] Theology has to engage in attempts at "translating" its own claims into other relevant discourses. Avoiding such a task would not do justice to the depth and reach of the actions of the triune God. Theology is forced by these inner-theological reasons together with cultural demands to make itself intelligible by means of such limited attempts at translation.[56]

2. Quite obviously, there is no real autonomy on the operational and conceptual level of doing theology, that is to say on the level of constructing "theological theology." Even if theology wants to avoid such conflicts, theologians often take on board more general features of reality, formulated, among others, by science, and these assumptions quite often enter theology in the form of unrecognized assumptions as well as unevaluated "forms of thought."[57] For instance, when talking about the novelty of the new creation, Jürgen Moltmann assumes that novelty cannot emerge out of the multi-layered process of reality. It has to come through a future, which comes to us as *adventus,* seen over against

the future as *futurum*, which is completely conditioned by the past and present.[58] In addition, the newness of the new creation has to come as a complete novelty after the "end of this world." Without going into more detail, it is apparent that even Moltmann implicitly relies on a picture of a rather closed universe without novelty and real chance. This, however, has to be discussed and disputed in relation with the sciences, even though the background assumptions of theological reasoning can never be made completely conscious. Hence, Moltmann's considerations regarding the new creation make apparent that on its operational level, systematic theology always presupposes certain assumptions about the nature of the world or the cosmos, even if it wants to set itself apart from so-called cosmological discourses or only tacitly refers to so-called scientific knowledge.

For these two theological reasons, even "theological closure" leads inevitably to openness. Theology has to temporalize its own complexity through shifting patterns of various "types of theology" in order to discuss the novelty of the new creation on the level of personal, social, and eventually biological processes. At this point, complexity theory again enters into the picture.

3. My aim is not to strive for higher-order metaphysical explanations of general features of the natural world or of scientific theories that could be considered to be starting points for new attempts to formulate a natural theology. These interdisciplinary translations never intend to provide some sort of foundation for theological reasoning or theological truth claims. Instead of focusing on the shortcomings of scientific explanations and the "God of the gaps" or on the need to ground the rationality of religious discourse, the conversation I have in mind concentrates on what *can* be said in scientific theories and what *can* be said theologically on theology's own ground.[59] "Limited translations" come out of fields of creative resonance between disciplines. They imply a search for correlations between theological and scientific descriptions, and are somehow able to make intelligible theological concepts within other (social or natural) scientific frameworks and allow the perception of creative differences.[60] They neither replace scientific explanations nor do they require an actual lack of theory. Using the characterization of theology as *fides quaerens intellectum*, these translations can be seen as attempts to search non-theological means of *intellegere*, in addition to theology's own understanding of itself on its own terms.

The Process of New Creation in Dialogue with Complexity Theory in Science

To connect cosmology with eschatology is not a novelty. Numerous far-reaching suggestions have been put forth during this century, from the side of philosophy and theology as well as the natural sciences. They range from the suggestions of P. Teilhard de Chardin and Alfred N. Whitehead to more recent suggestions such as the physical eschatology of Frank Tipler.[61] At this point, I cannot engage in an evaluation of these suggestions for the issue at stake. In addition, I will quite consciously leave out eschatological questions concerning the issue of the final consummation[62] and concentrate on the problem of God's current and specific actions toward the new creation.[63] Furthermore, in doing that, I cannot dwell on contributions referring to quantum theory[64] as well as the whole complex of "top-down causality" and "whole-part relations" in order to conceptualize God's action in this world.[65]

Instead, I would like to engage in a tentative dialogue with recent developments in complexity theory.[66] These developments already have proved to be quite fruitful in conceptualizing a way to explore the ongoing creative relationship of God to his world.[67] However, compared to the past and current discussions, I see the need to add further complexity to the dialogues by differentiating the notion of creation into "creation" and "new creation."

What are the advantages in addressing complexity theory in dealing with new creation? I would like to name just three points of concern:

1. Complexity theory is concerned with diverse types of systems. In a similar way, if we look at the various levels that are part of the new creation, we are faced with many type-different as well as type-identical systems that constitute for each other multi-layered environments: persons, social entities, biological configurations, and so on. They all represent living systems with self-organized complexity.

2. Since complexity theory is dealing with systems that show high degrees of autopoietic self-reproduction, it might be able to cut across the strict division between "natural" and "cultural" processes, which is so influential in traditional treatments of "new creation."

3. While the dialogues centering on the "anthropic principle," regardless of its weak or its strong version, focus on general conditions of the universe that provide the right physical conditions for the emergence of intelligent life, which itself can observe this

process, the theory of complexity is geared toward specific, temporal, universal yet also local features of our world. The concept of a general design is still needed insofar as those processes within specific spheres of reality, which can be described by complexity theory, are still based on the general and universal laws of physics and chemistry. These laws belong to the universal features of the cosmos. Yet the theoretical position of the argument about design changed. Information-governed self-organization is a phenomenon that is local. These emerging local orders are on the one hand still part of the evolutionary history but on the other hand have their own stories of becoming. Instead of favoring a remote general designer of the cosmos, complexity theory calls for a rather "local" involvement of God.

In order to speak about the beginning of new creation we have to draw a distinction, that is to say, the distinction between God's ongoing preserving and providential action in regard to the "first creation" and God's renewing action as part of his new creation. Based on the biblical notion of new creation, I suggest that the events of its beginning are no longer characterized by the pursuit of life at the cost of other life.

Based on the philosopher Fred Dretske's[68] distinction between triggering and structuring causes, Niels H. Gregersen proposed a model for God acting "as structuring cause who continuously may wire and rewire the probability rates of self-organizing processes."[69] In such providential actions God is working through a change of the possibility spectrum or space of a given system, thereby not determining the course of events, but rather by constraining, opening up, or moving the possible courses of events. In doing this, "probability rates are raised for some pathways rather than for others."[70] This feature of being local and responsive to concrete configurations of information-governed autopoietical systems and corresponding possibilities in the environment of the respective system bears some close resonance to the events of the new creation sketched out above, at least "in between" the resurrection of Christ and the final consummation. Niels H. Gregersen calls this type of God's providential action "context-sensitive."[71] However, we have to keep in mind that, due to the thorough interconnectedness of complex systems, any change of the probability space of system A might also simultaneously change the spaces of the systems B, C, and D. Moreover, the change in A in favor of a strengthening of its autopoietical reproduction might deteriorate or even destroy the possibility spaces of D out of which D can choose or trigger the actual pathway of events. Precisely at this point, the issue of the "unity of life and death in favor of life" reappears. And at this point, I would like to ask whether it is conceivable within the conceptual context of complexity theory to think of a change of a possibility space that does not simultaneously destroy or limit other positive possibilities of alternative interconnected systems. Is it possible to speak of God as the one who provides new possibilities, opening up new possibility spaces that do not imply destruction on some other level of complexity or for some other system? Could not it be that the novelty of the new creation is the harmonious coordination of multiple autopoietical systems of the various levels of complexity—natural, biological, psychological, social—based on a non-destructive "coordination" of the various possibility spaces? The biblical notion of a renewal that includes the heaven as a realm of possibilities might point in such a direction. Moreover, the novelty of the new creation takes place in contexts of distress, destruction, and the endangerment of life by the brutal self-continuation of other life. At this point, hope and love as gifts of the Spirit may enter the possibility space as *structuring* causes. Is it conceivable to have such a change in the possibility spaces of the various type-different systems, even within the given laws of complexity, that one can talk about such a kind of novelty that justifies the use of the concept of "new creation"? These are just tentative questions that certainly require further exploration. These are not clear-cut solutions, admittedly, but pointers for research, in which theology might attempt to translate its own vocabulary into complexity theory and in which complexity theory might itself point to areas where there is some resonance that calls for translations between both discourses.

Retrospect and Prospect

Dealing with complexity is a complex task. Any discipline that enters into the debate about complexity in a reasonable way has to locate itself within its own field of investigation. In doing so, it becomes itself an object under observation, a case of complexity. For this reason, I introduced a concept of temporalized complexity that is well suited for the craft of doing theology in the medium of communication. In a second step I tried to show how various types of theology are emerging out of specific reductions of complexity, suggesting that theology has to develop specific forms of temporalized complexity leading to special types of theological discourse and create particular interfaces for the dialogue between science and theology. In a third step and a fourth step, I utilized a "closure" procedure, which led to a brief exercise in a more biblically oriented systematic theology. In this endeavor the complex rationality of biblical texts is allowed to engage with the constructive task of systematic theology. However, such a rather "theological theology" might momentarily lead to theological "closure" regarding the dialogue between theology and science. Yet, following the dynamic of "openness through closure," this approach *necessarily* leads, as I tried to show in the fifth step, to a new encounter with sciences, including one dealing with the problem of complexity. What seemed to be a theology less in contact with questions of science turned out to be just a moment in a process. For many reasons, "theological theology" on topics such as creation and new creation cannot detach itself from scientific discussions of cosmology. Hence, the distinction drawn between "closure" and "openness" turned out to be part of the indispensable temporalization of complexity within the theological discourse. The problem of complexity does not vanish, even if theology unfolds itself into what I would call "theological theology."

In the next step, which I conceived of as a search for "limited translations," I asked how those aspects of God's renewing action that take place already today within the "old creation" can fit into the picture of autopoietical processes, which seem to be able to explicate theological talk about providence. Can complexity theory help us to articulate the reality of the new creation? At this point, I could primarily raise tentative questions only and I am afraid the answers will be more complex, but that seems to be the fascinating challenge before us.

Embedded in the various steps of the presentation there is an argument about the methodological adjustments of the dialogues between science and theology. The necessary and, during the last decade, quite enriching interaction between science and theology becomes even more complex if rather specific notions such as "new creation" are introduced into the dialogue. This increasing complexity in the dialogue might include more creative tensions and call into question rather simple solutions that do not risk enough difference by practicing a too far-reaching reduction of the internal complexity of theological discourse. However, as we learn from science, the increased complexity might be an enrichment. If the dialogue proceeds to have the effect of reconfiguring the discourse, its complexity might be a step to new emerging and enriching encounters between theology and science. It could well be that what results from an increased complexity in this dialogue might reflect, in its own way, the reality of new creation, as fragmentary as are all searches for understanding.

NOTES

1. The following essay is based on a public lecture given at the University of Aarhus/Denmark on December 13, 1999. The lecture was part of a lecture series set up by the International Workshop on Concepts for the Analysis of Complex Systems in order to explore the notion of complexity in a variety of academic disciplines. The paper owes very much to an ongoing conversation with Niels Henrik Gregersen.

2. Hesse, Mary, "Simplicity," in: Edwards, Paul (ed.), *The Encyclopedia of Philosophy. Vol. 7* (New York: Macmillan, 1967), pp. 445–448.

3. Luhmann, Niklas, "Komplexität," in: Ritter, Joachim (ed.), *Historisches Wörterbuch der Philosophie. Vol. 4* (Darmstadt: Wissenschaftliche Buchgesellschaft, 1976), pp. 939–941.

4. And yet the concept of complexity is not a modern invention. For ancient and medieval roots, especially with reference to the mathematical theology of Nicolaus von Kues, see Luhmann, Niklas, "Haltlose Komplexität," in: idem, *Soziologische Aufklärung. Vol. 5. Konstruktivistische Perspektiven* (Opladen: Westdeutscher Verlag, 1990), pp. 59–75.

5. The differentiation between a "natural" and a "cultural" sphere should not be read as a renewal of the old division between nature and culture. But I do see (1) different degrees of mathematical formalization and quantification, (2) different types of self-observation and self-regulation within the systems, and (3) quite different types of paradoxes of observation, that is to say different types of participant observers in the observed. For instance, the philosophical problems resulting from the physical world's self-observation by means of physicists are not as deep as the ones resulting from society's self-observation by other social systems.

6. See, i.e., Eve, Raymond A. et al. (eds.), *Chaos, Complexity, and Sociology. Myths, Models, and Theories* (Thousand Oaks: Sage Publications, 1997); Coyne, George V. and Karl Schmitz-Moormann (eds.), *Origins, Time, and Complexity. Vols. 1 and 2* (Geneva: Labor et Fides, 1993); and Krapp, Holger and Thomas Wägenbaur (eds.), *Komplexität und Selbstorganisation. "Chaos" in den Natur-und Kulturwissenschaften* (München: Fink, 1997).

7. For a transfer from the natural sciences to theology see Coyne/Schmitz-Moormann, op. cit.

8. Niklas Luhmann certainly is the most influential social philosopher in Germany right now. He died in November of 1998. In the European context Luhmann is far more influential than Juergen Habermas, since his systems theory is applied in legal studies, literature, economics, paedagogics, theology, political theory. For a very early account of complexity see Luhmann, Niklas, *Vertrauen. Ein Mechanismus zur Reduktion sozialer Komplexität* (Stuttgart: Enke, 1973[2]; Orig. 1968); idem, "Komplexität," in: idem, *Soziologische Aufklärung. Vol. 2. Aufsätze zur Theorie der Gesellschaft* (Opladen: Westdeutscher Verlag, 1975), pp. 204–220; "Temporalisierung von Komplexität. Zur Semantik neuzeitlicher Zeitbegriffe," in: idem, *Gesellschaftsstruktur und Semantik. Studien zur Wissenssoziologie der modernen Gesellschaft. Vol. 1* (Frankfurt/M.: Suhrkamp, 1980), pp. 235–300; "Complexity and Meaning," in: idem, *Essays on Self-reference* (New York: Columbia University Press, 1999), pp. 80–85; *Soziale Systeme. Grundriß einer allgemeinen Theorie* (Frankfurt/M.: Suhrkamp, 1987), pp.

45–51; "Haltlose Komplexität," op. cit.; speziell für den Wissenschaftskontext siehe *Die Wissenschaft der Gesellschaft* (Frankfurt/M.: Suhrkamp, 1990), pp. 362–468.

9. Traditions self-evidently use relations that are well known, unquestioned, and do not need to be selected. See Luhmann, "Haltlose Komplexität," p. 68.

10. Luhmann, "Haltlose Komplexität," p. 62.

11. For an elaboration of Luhmann's specific use of meaning see Luhmann, *Soziale Systeme,* ch. 2.

12. For Luhmann's own sociological descriptions of Christian dogmatics see Luhmann, Niklas, *Funktion der Religion* (Frankfurt/M.: Suhrkamp, 1977), p. 126 and idem, *Die Religion der Gesellschaft,* unpublished manuscript, pp. 132–145.

13. To make things more complex, one has to keep in mind that all that is being done internally within theology can also be described from the outside in multiple ways. It can be described by means of literary studies (writing texts, based on the art of intertextuality), by means of sociology and especially of sociology of knowledge. If one uses the instruments of philosophy of science, one might see the construction of hypotheses, claims about reality, and open or more subtle referential claims, and so on. These external descriptions can be reintroduced as conceptual tools in the theological discourse.

14. Again, at this point we take departure from Luhmann, insofar as the system theoretician Luhmann himself defines systematic theology sociologically: "Unter Dogmatik verstehen wir im weitesten Sinne jene gedanklichen Konzepte, mit denen das Grundmaterial religiöser Erfahrung und situationsbezogener Interpretation gesichtet, fachlich bearbeitet, auf Fehler hin korrigiert und systematisiert wird" (Luhmann, *Funktion der Religion,* 126).

15. However, under close scrutiny, the concept of second order reflection runs into unsolvable difficulties. Insofar as the second order reflection wants to provide critique and orientation, it itself needs criteria or "guiding distinctions" for its "observation." At this point, theology cannot be just "talk about talk about God," but needs to become, in its own way, talk about God. For good reasons, F. D. Schleiermacher points out that dogmatic theology has to be "orthodox as well as heterodox," that is to say, it assumes a reconstructive as well as a constructive task and therefore requires divination. See Schleiermacher, F. D., *Kurze Darstellung des theologischen Studiums zum Behuf einleitender Vorlesungen (1830)* (Darmstadt: Wiss. Buchgesellschaft, 1982), pp. 77–80 (§202–§208). When K. Barth refers to the need to listen to the "Word of God," he actually addresses the same structural problem of combining reconstruction and creative construction.

16. See Tracy, David, *The Analogical Imagination. Christian Theology and the Culture of Pluralism* (New York: Crossroad, 1981), pp. 3–98.

17. The distinction between internal and external perspectives goes back to Schleiermacher's coordination of dogmatics and philosophical theology and can even be found in A. von Harnack's differentiation of a "theology from the inside" and "theology from the outside." See Schleiermacher, *Kurze Darstellung des theologischen Studiums,* and von Harnack, Adolf, *Die Entstehung der christlichen Theologie und des kirchlichen Dogmas* (Gotha: Leopold Klotz, 1927), pp. 54f. However, a full-blown external perspective developed inside a non-theological

discourse should not be confused with an internal theological self-description, a) by means of a selective reproduction of the outside perspective, or, b) by selectively using conceptual instruments from non-theological discourses. This seems slightly overlooked in Niels Henrik Gregersen's distinction between theology1 and theology2. See Gregersen, Niels Henrik, "Autopoiesis. Less than Self-constitution, More than Self-organization," in: *Zygon* 34 (1999): 117–138.

18. For an early differentiation of various forms of systematic theology see Schleiermacher, F. D., *Der Christliche Glaube* (Berlin: Walter de Gruyter, [1830] 1960), §27, 4, who distinguishes a more "biblical," a more "scientific" (*wissenschaftlich*) and finally a rather "symbolic" (confessional) dogmatic. All represent "internal" perspectives. Yet his own "scientific" (*wissenschaftliche*) dogmatic still presupposes a unified idea of science (*Wissenschaft*).

19. For a still lucid account see Kelsey, David H., *The Uses of Scripture in Recent Theology* (Philadelphia: Fortress Press, 1975).

20. For an illuminating account of the diverse (mis)understandings of biblical theology see Welker, Michael, "Biblische Theologie," in: *RGG 4th ed.* 1998, pp. 1549–1553.

21. For two more recent exegetical studies see Mell, Ulrich, *Neue Schöpfung. Eine traditionsgeschichtliche und exegetische Studie zu einem soteriologischen Grundsatz paulinischer Theologie* (Berlin/New York: Walter de Gruyter, 1989); Minear, Paul Sevier, *Christians and the New Creation. Genesis Motifs in the New Testament* (Louisville: Westminster John Knox Press, 1994).

22. McGrath, Alister E., *The Foundation of Dialogue in Science and Religion* (Oxford: Blackwell, 1998), pp. 36–80 provides a more recent example of this exclusive focus on creation.

23. The seemingly tautological term "theological theology" draws a distinction between more philosophical or sociological types of theological reasoning and more biblically oriented types that nevertheless formulate the gospel for the current culture and move beyond the mere "observation" of other theologies.

24. All of the following biblical passages are taken from the NRSV.

25. For the concept within Paul's thinking see Stuhlmacher, Peter, "Erwägungen zum ontologischen Charakter der *kain' ktisis* bei Paulus," in: *Evangelische Theologie* 27 (1967), 1–35.

26. That is, see Pate, C. Marvin, *Adam Christology as the Exegetical Substructure of 2 Corinthians 4:7–5:21* (Lanham/New York: University of America Press, 1991).

27. For a classical interpretation along this line see Bultmann, Rudolf, *Der zweite Brief an die Korinther* (KEK; Göttingen: Vandenhoeck and Ruprecht, 1976), pp. 158ff., and Barrett, Charles Kingsley, *A Commentary on the Second Epistle to the Corinthians* (BNTC; London: A. and C. Black, 1973), pp. 172ff.

28. For this reason, the extended exegetical debate about a more ecclesiological or a more topological interpretation of "in Christ" seems to be misplaced.

29. Barrett, op. cit., 173, and Furnish, Victor Paul, *II Corinthians* (AB; New York: Doubleday, 1984), p. 333.

30. See among many Wilckens, Ulrich, *Der Brief an die Römer. Bd. 2* (EKK; Neukirchen: Neukirchener Verlag, 1980), pp. 135–170; Käsemann, Ernst, *An die Römer* (HNT; Tübingen: J.C.B. Mohr, 1980⁴), pp. 217–237, and Fitzmyer, Joseph A., *Romans* (AB; New York: Doubleday, 1993), pp. 497–528.

31. The term *ktisis* for creation either refers to the whole non-human creation (Wilckens, op. cit., 153) or nature, including human beings (Käsemann, op. cit., 225).
32. For the historical background and literary structure see Oswalt, John N., *The Book of Isaiah. Chapters 40–66* (NIC; Eerdmans: Grand Rapids, 1998), pp. 3–19, for the text, 652–662; Brueggemann, Walter, *Isaiah 40–66* (Westminster Bible Companion; Louisville: Westminster John Knox Press, 1998), pp. 245–250; Westermann, Claus, *Isaiah 40–66. A Commentary* (OTL; Philadelphia: Westminster Press, 1969).
33. Brueggemann, op. cit., 246.
34. "This new infrastructure of the city will be marked by peace, justice, righteousness, and faithfulness" (Brueggemann, op. cit., 247).
35. Cf. Westermann, op. cit., 410.
36. For Oswalt, op. cit., 662, these animals "symbolize all the devouring, ravening, poisonous aspects of our world, both inside and outside human nature."
37. Rather typical yet too simplistic and anthropocentric, Oswalt, op. cit., p. 662 is stating: "Nature will no longer be our enemy, nor we its."
38. See Whitehead, Alfred North, *Process and Reality. An Essay on Cosmology* (corr. ed.; New York: Macmillan, 1978), p. 105.
39. The problem has quite a long tradition and imposes many difficulties on the theological side.
40. At this point it seems necessary to take issue with the proposal put forth by Philip Hefner. He embraces a biological concept of nature to such an extent that what can be translated as sin, that is to say "factors of trial and error and fallibility," becomes the "source of life and goodness." See Hefner, Philip, *The Human Factor. Evolution, Culture, and Religion* (Minneapolis: Fortress Press, 1993), pp. 137f., following Burhoe, Ralph, *Toward a Scientific Theology* (Belfast: Christian Journals Limited, 1981), pp. 65ff. The very methodological problem in Hefner's approach is that he places theology just on the plane of "interpretation and significance" provided by "elements that are derived from empirical study" and thereby effectively pulls back from cognitive claims deriving from the Christian tradition (Hefner, loc. cit., p. 31).
41. See Janowski, Christine J., *Allerlösung. Annäherungen an eine entdualisierte Eschatologie, 2 Vols.* (Neukirchen-Vluyn: Neukirchen 2000).
42. This is the pattern underlying the positions of Radford Ruether, Rosemary, *Gaia and God. An Ecofeminist Theology of Earth Healing* (San Francisco: Harper, 1992); McFague, Sally, *Super, Natural Christians. How We Should Love Nature* (Minneapolis: Fortress Press, 1997); Moltmann, Jürgen, *Gott in der Schöpfung. Ökologische Schöpfungslehre* (München: Kaiser, 1985). While Sally McFague emphasizes that "salvation is for all of creation," the salvation of nature only implies the salvation from destructive human interventions. "The Hope for a New Creation" does not involve hope for nature. Cf. McFague, Sally, *The Body of God. An Ecological Theology* (Minneapolis: Fortress, 1993), pp. 182, 198–202.
43. There is an important parallel that should be highlighted. Michael Welker shows by an analysis of Genesis 1 and 2 that the process of creation can be described as the build-up and preservation of relations of interdependency between various spheres and levels of created reality. These spheres comprise nature as well as culture. As creation includes culture, not just nature, so does

new creation include nature, not just culture. See Welker, Michael, *Schöpfung und Wirklichkeit* (Neukirchen-Vluyn: Neukirchener Verlag, 1995), ch. 1.

44. These concerns should not be brushed aside by statements like: "In nature death is not an enemy, but a friend of the life process" or "The consumer-consumed relation is an inevitable part of the biotic condition. Consequently the effort to escape from the ambiguity of killing other life in order to live is finally impossible" (Radford Ruether, loc. cit., pp. 53, 225). It could well be that the biblical traditions developed a differentiated sensitivity that should not be dismissed—even if it creates problems for contemporary theological reflection. Even though illness is a thoroughly social construction, it seems to be telling that the Gospels describe Jesus as healing. "The uniqueness of the miracles of the historical Jesus is that current acts of healing and exorcism are given an eschatological meaning. In these acts a new world begins" (Theissen, Gerd and Annette Merz, *Der historische Jesus*, 2nd ed. [Göttingen: Vandenhoeck and Ruprecht, 1997], p. 279, trans. G. Th.). The healing miracles point to the scope and depth of the new creation.

45. One might ask whether these spheres of life have some resonance with the emergent levels of reality that cannot be reduced to each other as described by Peacocke, Arthur, *Theology for a Scientific Age. Being and Becoming—Natural, Divine, and Human* (Minneapolis: Fortress Press, 1993), pp. 213–244, esp. 217. Cf. also Barbour, Ian, *Issues in Science and Religion* (Englewood Cliffs: Prentice-Hall, 1966), pp. 324–337, idem, *Religion in an Age of Science. The Gifford Lectures 1989–1991, Vol. 1* (San Francisco: Harper, 1990), pp. 165–172.

46. For a most recent elaboration of this dimension of creation cf. Löning, Karl and Erich Zenger, *Als Anfang schuf Gott. Biblische Schöpfungstheologien* (Düsseldorf: Patmos, 1997), pp. 17–78. A detailed exegetical lesson about "the vitality of evil and the fragility of creation" as well as "the survival of chaos after the victory of God" is provided from a Jewish perspective in Levenson, Jon D., *Creation and the Persistence of Evil. The Jewish Drama of Divine Omnipotence*, 2nd ed. (Princeton: Princeton University Press, 1988). While Levenson's proposal seems to be in danger of adopting an almost dualistic view, Anderson, Bernhard W., *Creation Versus Chaos* (Philadelphia: Fortress Press, 1987), might underestimate the persistence of destruction and evil. To avoid misunderstandings: The biblical notion of the unordered and the Greek notion of chaos cannot and should not be equated with modern conceptions of chaos in chaos theory.

47. For an elaboration of heaven, yet without taking into account the "new heaven," see Welker, Michael, *Schöpfung und Wirklichkeit* (Neukirchen-Vluyn: Neukirchener Verlag, 1995), ch. 3.

48. Moltmann, Jürgen, *Das Kommen Gottes. Christliche Eschatologie* (München: Kaiser, 1995), p. 156. Moltmann limits the term "new creation" to the cosmic dimension and contrasts the "temporal creation" with the second "eternal and 'deified' creation" (p. 291). For a similar view based on the sharp distinction between finite time and eternity, see, e.g., Link, Christian, *Die Spur des Namens. Wege zur Erkenntnis Gottes und zur Erfahrung der Schöpfung* (Neukirchen-Vluyn: Neukirchener Verlag, 1997), pp. 195–212.

49. Thomas F. Torrance mentions the need for the redemption of the cosmos as "the 're-ordering' of creation" in the context of the irreversibility of time in the

open-structured world of relativistic quantum theory and non-equilibrium thermodynamics. See Torrance, Thomas F., *The Christian Frame of Mind. Reason, Order, and Openness in Theology and Natural Science* (Colorado Springs: Helmers and Howard, 1989), pp. 102–105.

50. Moltmann, op. cit., 287ff.

51. For a lucid historical reconstruction see Santmire, H. Paul, *The Travail of Nature. The Ambiguous Ecological Promise of Christian Theology* (Minneapolis: Fortress Press, 1985). Santmire comes to the wider conclusion "that the presuppositions of the anthropocentric view of the biblical theology of nature are indeed formally similar to the spiritual motif of theological reflection about nature in the West" (p. 188). An analysis of recent Protestant approaches is provided by Hartlieb, Elisabeth, *Natur als Schöpfung* (Frankfurt/M.: Lang, 1996).

52. Without any doubt, a new conceptualization of the new creation calls for new differentiations between the notion of a) continuing creation, b) providence, and c) God's blessing of creatures. However, any attempt to describe anew these classical distinctions requires a detailed Trinitarian reconstruction as well as an answer to the question how the Christ-event transformed the work of the Spirit. At the moment, I can only openly point out that these new differentiations and clarifications have to be searched for.

53. This formula is borrowed form Eberhard Jüngel. In Jüngel's opinion, it is a characterization of love and eventually of God. See Jüngel, Eberhard, *Gott als Geheimis der Welt* (Tübingen: Mohr, 1982), pp. 434–446.

54. Douglas, Mary, *Purity and Danger. An Analysis of the Concepts of Pollution and Taboo* (London: Routledge, 1966).

55. On the theological side, such a dialogue starts with a complex stance: a) hope for unity (of reality), b) a recognition of difference (diverse perspectives, rationalities, and conceptual languages), and c) a search for translations and enrichments (reinforcing mutual understanding) through fields of resonance with other discourses. By emphasizing hope, difference, and the processual nature of the search for limited translations I admit being more skeptical regarding the project of a "new natural theology" than many of its proponents. See, e.g., Polkinghorne, John, *The Faith of a Physicist. Reflections of a Bottom-Up Thinker. The Gifford Lectures 1993–1994* (Princeton: Princeton University Press, 1994), esp. pp. 42ff. To start with hope *and* difference also seems to be more adequate than to start with a strong assertion of coherence as in the model advocated by Gregersen, Niels Henrik, "A Contextual Coherence Theory for the Science-Theology Dialogue," in: idem/von Huysteen, J. Wentzel (eds.), *Rethinking Theology and Science. Six Models for the Current Dialogue* (Grand Rapids: Eerdmans, 1998), pp. 181–231. The idea at the very core of the coherence theory is that "all knowledge is essentially of a piece" (p. 192 with reference to Nicholas Rescher). Instead I would prefer starting with difference and the more humble claim put forward in the model of internal realism, yet add to it the need for the search for coherence. Yet this need is also theologically grounded in the belief in the unity of the creator and is based on the hope in God's renewal of the whole creation. In Rescher's theory the unity of the "piece" cannot be any more than a regulative idea.

56. Given the complex nature of our culture and the plurality of our academic discourses, there is no single dialogue that brings theology into contact with "the

reality," with "the one modern rationality," with science (with a capital S), or with "the world." There is no single way to interact with all hierarchies of complexity and all emergent levels of reality, with all "worlds." For this reason, every attempt at translation is limited in scope. Over against Niels H. Gregersen's ("Theology in a Neo-Darwinian World," in: *Studia Theologica* 48 [1994], pp. 125–149) and Wentzel van Huyssteen's (*Duet or Duel. Theology and Science in a Postmodern World* [London: SCM Press, 1998], pp. 159ff.) model of theological "redescriptions" of scientifically conceptualized reality, the model of "limited translations" takes seriously the insight that we have our ontologies only in the medium and in relation to specific symbol systems, that is to say "languages." That the various languages talk about "the same reality" can only be affirmed by these languages and by means of translations, not by a confirmatory look at some undescribed (unconceptualized) reality. The concept of redescription also leaves open the door for two possible misunderstandings. First, that theological descriptions can only be redescriptions, without any "stand alone" truth claims including ontological claims; secondly, that theology can live without any form of explanation. For these reasons, I prefer in spite of far-reaching agreements with the model of theological "redescriptions" the notion of "limited translations."

57. For this reason, temporalized complexity in theology does not imply a simple unidirectional temporal sequence moving from biblical texts to dogmatics and eventually to dialogues with relevant sciences and humanities. Instead there is a circular process or a dynamic oscillation, which allows not many points of entry but asks for the co-emergence of the different types of theology.

58. See Moltmann, *Gott in der Schöpfung*, 143ff.; idem, *Das Kommen Gottes*, pp. 42–47, even though nine years earlier he had described creation as an "open system." See Moltmann, "Schöpfung als offenes System," in: idem, *Zukunft der Schöpfung* (München: Kaiser, 1977), pp. 123–139. This basic ontological assumption is one of the reasons that for Moltmann the "new creation" can only come at the end of times.

59. They are limited in a threefold sense: a) Due to the need to temporalize complexity they are limited in comparison to a "theological theology." b) They are limited insofar as they are not translations of whole languages of description. No translation can be complete. c) Every limited translation will also lead to the illumination of specific differences in the use and the construction of these languages. Nevertheless, this procedure wants to avoid a "strong" causal-explanatory approach as well as a very "weak" interpretive approach, in which theology excludes any type of explanation and just provides meaning to what is already known.

60. This striving for some kind of coherence or positive resonance coalesces with the notion of "consonance" as it was suggested in a paper by McMullin, Ernan, "How Should Cosmology Relate to Theology?" in: Peacocke, Arthur R. (ed.), *The Sciences and Theology in the Twentieth Century* (Notre Dame: University of Notre Dame Press, 1981), pp. 17–51.

61. Tipler, Frank J., "The Omega Point Theory. A Model of an Evolving God," in: Russell, Robert J., et al. (eds.), *Physics, Philosophy, and Theology. A Common Quest for Understanding* (Vatican City State: Vatican Observatory, 1988), pp. 313–331.

62. Cf. Polkinghorne, John and Michael Welker (eds.), *The End of the World and the Ends of God. Science and Theology on Eschatology* (Harrisburg: Trinity Press, 2000).

63. In terms of traditional dogmatic distinction the current actions of God concern his *creatio continua, providentia generalis, providentia specialis*—and, as we would like to emphasize, in certain respects the *creatio nova*.

64. See Russell, Robert J., "Quantum Physics in Philosophical and Theological Perspective," in: idem et al. (eds.), *Physics, Philosophy, and Theology. A Common Quest for Understanding* (Vatican City State: Vatican Observatory, 1988), pp. 343–374, and idem, "Theistic Evolution. Does God Really Act in Nature?" in: *CTNS Bulletin* 15 (1995): 19–32, esp. 23.

65. Peacocke, Arthur R., *Theology for a Scientific Age. Being and Becoming— Natural, Divine, and Human* (Minneapolis: Fortress Press, 1983), pp. 53–55, 157–160, and idem, "God's Interaction with the World. The Implications of Deterministic 'Chaos' and of Interconnected and Interdependent Complexity," in: Russell, Robert J., et al. (eds.), *Chaos and Complexity*, pp. 263–288, esp. 282ff; idem, "The Sound of Sheer Silence," in: Russell, Robert J., et al. (eds.), *Evolutionary and Molecular Biology. Scientific Perspectives on Divine Action* (Notre Dame: University of Notre Dame Press, 1999), pp. 314–319. I consider both approaches to be complementing rather than competing with a dialogue with complexity theory.

66. For a general introduction see the literature mentioned in the introduction as well as Luhmann's writings on complexity in social systems. For a recent theoretical proposal that gives an impression of the range of complexity theory see Bak, Per, *How Nature Works. The Science of Self-Organized Criticality* (Oxford: Oxford University Press, 1997). See also Kauffman, Stewart, *At Home in the Universe. The Search for Laws of Self-Organization and Complexity* (New York: Oxford University Press, 1995), and Cillier, Paul, *Complexity and Postmodernism. Understanding Complex Systems* (London: Routledge, 1998).

67. For such a theological reception of complexity theory see Gregersen, Niels Henrik, "The Idea of Creation and the Theory of Autopoietic Processes," in: *Zygon* 33 (1998): 333–367; idem, "Autopoiesis: Less than Self-Constitution, More than Self-Organization. Reply to Gilkey, McClelland and Deltete, and Brun," in: *Zygon* 34 (1999): 117–138. See also idem, "The Creation of Creativity. Theology and the Principles of Self-Organization," unpublished paper; idem, "Theology and the Sciences of Self-Organized Complexity," unpublished paper.

68. Dretske, Fred, "Mental Events as Structuring Causes of Behaviour," in: Heil, John and Alfred Mele (eds.), *Mental Causation* (Oxford: Clarendon, 1995), pp. 121–136.

69. Gregersen, "Theology and the Sciences of Self-Organized Complexity," p. 20f.

70. Gregersen, "The Idea of Creation and the Theory of Autopoietic Processes," p. 361.

71. See Gregersen, "Theology and the Sciences of Self-Organized Complexity," p. 17.

This chapter will be published in Kees van Kooten Nrekerk and Hans Buhl (eds.): *Complexity Science. The Humanities and Theology*, (fall 2001).

CHAPTER 6

Leaving Behind the God-of-the-Gaps: Towards a Theological Response to Scientific Limit Questions

CHRISTIAN BERG

Christian Berg holds degrees in physics from Würzburg University and in theology from Heidelberg University. He has conducted doctoral research at Princeton Theological Seminary and is a theological doctoral candidate at Heidelberg University. He is working in theology with Dr. Michael Welker at Heidelberg and with Dr. Michael Jischa at the Technical University of Clausthal in the field of technology assessment in sustainable development.

Limit Questions at the Interface between Science and Theology

Scientists Raise Limit Questions

Nowadays quite a number of scientists are concerned with questions going beyond the realm of their scientific work. Numerous books have been published in the last decades in which scientists have addressed issues going beyond their investigations as scientists, referring to questions of origins, to limit questions, or to questions about God. These are issues such as the "Physics of Immortality" (Tipler), the "Mind of God" (Davies), or the "Theory of Everything" (Hawking).[1] Apparently, scientific investigation leads to questions that cannot be answered from science itself. One will hardly find explicit religious statements in a scientific journal. That these questions are nevertheless relevant for a deeper understanding of reality, and that they are of importance not only for academic curiosity, but appeal to a broader public, can be seen by the fact that they are debated in popular, non-technical writings. The theses of Jacques Monod, Carl Sagan, Richard Dawkins, Frank Tipler,

Paul Davies, Stephen Hawking, or Stephen J. Gould have helped shape the public's (mis-?)understanding considerably at the interface between science and religion. Unfortunately, sometimes they have failed to make clear where their scientific investigations end and their metaphysical reflections start. Little theological expertise is necessary to realize that the latter are, at least on average, not as sophisticated by far as the former—to theology's cost. Is it, for instance, really true that "revealed theology is to natural theology as geocentric astronomy is to heliocentric astronomy" as Frank Tipler asserts (Tipler 1994: 338)? Is religion "now part of science" (1994: 339)? Is it true that "if we do discover a complete theory" that we then "would know the mind of God" (Hawking 1988: 175)? It should be unquestioned that there is a need for theological contributions to this debate. But how can theology properly contribute? I want to argue the following thesis:

- ❧ Theology needs to respond to the limit questions raised by scientists. On the one hand theology ought to take seriously how scientists themselves conceive the scientific endeavor. Theology ought to account for the autonomy of scientific explanations. On the other hand from both the scientists' and theologians' viewpoints a total separation of science and theology is unsatisfying.
- ❧ The autonomy of science prohibits theology from interfering with any kind of god-of-the-gaps. In order to provide both an autonomy of science and a place for sensible theological contribution to the interface between science and theology, one needs to know how a god-of-the-gaps has to be understood and why it ought to be avoided.
- ❧ Despite all the explanatory power science has achieved, it is nevertheless limited. Not even a "Theory of Everything" could explain literally everything. Several contingencies would remain unexplained even in a "Theory of Everything," simply because the scientific method is limited.
- ❧ Nevertheless, if we do seek an interpretation of *all* experience, we need to relate the scientific insights to the broader setting of life and look for explanations going beyond scientific methods. The Christian doctrine of creation offers a reasonable explanation for those questions that a scientific account of reality leaves open: the contingencies in the scientific description of reality correspond to the fact that the world is understood as being created by God's free and sovereign will. Today's physics (especially quantum mechanics and chaos theory) teaches us that we are living in environ-

ments that are inaccessible to science insofar as they are highly
contingent. Here is a legitimate place for theology to speak about
God's continuing creation and God's action *without* being in
danger of using a god-of-the-gaps. God works, as it were, at the
methodological limits of science. The striking feature about today's physics is that it reveals these limits in the midst of our physical reality as humans.

  ❧ Since scientific insights are not sufficient for a rational account of
all experience, they need to be related to the broader setting of
personal life.

Scientists Claim the Autonomy of Science

An apparently necessary condition for a proper and sustainable
theological contribution to those limit questions raised by scientists,
which can at least be tolerated (or even accepted) by them, would be to
account for the way scientists themselves conceive their scientific endeavor. Since the scientific description of reality does not explicitly refer
to any religious statements, the theoretical and cognitive description of
reality science provides is independent of religious intervention. That
seems to be one fundamental assumption shared by a vast majority of
scientists. The latest explicit proposal of this kind comes from Stephen J.
Gould (Gould 1999). One out of two "primary claims" of his principle of
NOMA—the Non-Overlapping Magisteria—is to attribute equal status
to both "magisteria" (58–59). Although he himself is not dedicated to a
specific religious tradition, he wants to acknowledge the importance of
religion "for any complete human life" (59). But Gould is also very concerned about the "independence of the magisteria" (1999: 63), because
only by means of this independence can "the false conflict between science and religion" (6) be avoided.

I do not think that such a separation of science and theology, such
a return to old dichotomies, can be the final goal of relating these disciplines.[2] I do think, however, that theology has to take seriously what I
assume to be a common denominator among (the vast majority of) scientists, namely, the independence of the causal explanations science
provides from any religious influence.[3] Scientists might (and do) differ
in their metaphysical and religious interpretations of scientific insights.
But most of them would presumably agree that religious assertions
must not enter the level of causal explanation of the world. This conviction is certainly shared by many theologians as well—at least in principle. The times are passed in which God easily entered the level of scien-

tific explanations as a hypothesis. Ours is rather a time of separation or independence into two separate realms of reality. Indeed, such a separation has had a long tradition in modernity and was revitalized under the influence of neo-orthodoxy, existentialism, and analytic philosophy (cf. Barbour 1998: 84–89).[4]

Is Total Independence Sufficient?

Yet can we remain content with a dichotomy of science and theology, with two watertight compartments of reality? Do we not have to move beyond the position of independence that has been prevailing in the twentieth century? "We cannot remain content with a plurality of unrelated languages if they are languages about the same world" states Ian Barbour (1998: 89). But why do we need to understand the world of science and the world of theology as "the same," why do we need to conceive reality as a unity? Let us just consider some arguments from the viewpoint of scientists and theologians respectively.

Coming from the scientist's viewpoint, on the one hand, I submit that the unity of reality is suggested by critical realism. Critical realism, the prevailing epistemological position among scientists,[5] asserts that science makes "tentative ontological claims" (Barbour 1974: 42) about reality. Scientists believe that their theories do refer in some way or another to reality, although these theories are always provisionary and revisable. This is not to be understood naïvely as if our theories were real *pictures* of reality (as in naïve realism), but still it is upheld that we do have at least some access to reality. I submit that this very concept of critical realism in science forbids a total separation of science and religion from the viewpoint of a *critical realist scientist.* For science leads us to acknowledge that humans are psychosomatic unities. Insights from diverse fields of the life sciences proved the strong correlation between psychic and somatic phenomena. A consequent critical realist approach, however, would imply that this psychosomatic unity in one way or another refers to the *real nature* of human beings. Different kinds of experience, for example, scientific or religious, are at least related via the experiencing subject; they cannot refer to two *totally separate* realities.[6] In other words, if we take critical realism in science seriously, the insights in our physical constitution suggest that we should not treat the scientific and the religious realms of life as totally distinct. The critical realism of scientists thus consequently suggests that we also take into consideration the broader setting of life and that we not build up a dichotomy between science and religion.[7] Moreover, one could also support this position from an evolutionary epistemological perspective, for the process of evolution was a "belief-gaining process" (van Huyssteen 1997: 151), that is, there are roots for our beliefs in evolutionary biology.

Coming from a theological view of reality, on the other hand, implies also some kind of unity of reality because of the unity of the Triune Creator. Since Christians believe the Triune God to be the Creator of heaven and earth, "of all that is, seen and unseen," ultimately reality has to be understood as one. This cognitive dimension of Christian faith, its truth claim about reality, is the reason that critical realism has been defended not only in science, but also in religion (Barbour 1974: 49–70) and theology (van Huyssteen 1997: 40–52). Theology too makes ontological claims and is not just providing helpful devices for coping with life. The critical realist theologian rejects "the claim that religious language provides only a useful system of symbols that can be action guiding and meaningful for the believer without being in any sense reality depicting in its cognitive claims . . ." (van Huyssteen 1997: 43).

Since both science and theology make thus tentative ontological claims about reality, there is need for relating both fields, if possible in a constructive dialogue. A first step towards such a dialogue can be seen in the limit questions raised by scientists.[8] However, theologians might hesitate to engage in this field despite the need for dialogue, in order not to slide back to some sort of god-of-the-gaps.

The God-of-the-Gaps—What It Is and Why It Ought Not to Be

Too often in history there have been conflicts between "science" and "theology." The ideas of Bruno, Galileo, Newton, and Darwin are just a few examples of what is seen by many as a conflict between either the church or theology and science. Bruno was burned, Galileo arrested, some of Newton's remarks induced the "god-of-the-gaps," Darwin's theory was strongly debated by theologians and has been repudiated by some of them. How can theology be sure not to provide another example of this sort without simply withdrawing from these issues? Especially since some current theological interpretations of scientific insights seem to come close to a god-of-the-gaps concept. John Polkinghorne, for example, speaks of "*intrinsic gaps*" in the bottom-up description of reality due to the indeterminacies of chaotic systems, and of humans as "people of the gaps" (1993: 237). Although he states that he is not implying an "unacceptable return to the God of the gaps, in the pejorative sense of the word" (ibid.), I doubt that it is helpful to use this phrase "god-of-the-gaps," which has been so strongly debated throughout the past centuries. Holmes Rolston, in his recent book, seeks a theological interpretation of modern evolutionary biology (Rolston 1999). He sees God as being a "countercurrent to entropy, a sort of biogravity that lures life upward" (364). He obviously mixes scientific terms (entropy) with terms suggesting an agent (lure). To answer the question of why life started on earth, Rolston refers to "divine coaching on occasions" (368).

In a situation in which many scientists—being critical of religious interference—address religious issues, theology needs to search for profound interpretations of scientific findings that are clearly repudiating the failures of past approaches, in this case the god-of-the-gaps. Since nobody could sensibly claim to believe in a god-of-the-gaps, because it is in a way the negation of a positive concept of God, one should be clear about such a concept and the underlying assumptions, in order to prevent it from sneaking in through the back door.

What Is a God-of-the-Gaps Concept?

J. H. Brooke speaks of a "god-of-the-gaps" concept "if statements about God are used to fill the gaps in scientific explanation" (Brooke 1991: 29). To assume that God would be able to fill the gaps in the scientific explanation of reality presupposes that God acts on the same level as the natural causes. Having rejected Thomistic theology and the Aristotelian theory of the four causes at the beginning of modern times, only the efficient causality *(causa efficiens)* remained as a matter of scientific interest (cf. Brooke 1991: 54–56).[9] In fact, this isolated interest in the *causa efficiens* was one of the reasons why the new scientific method has been so successful. No reference to any purpose, to any final cause *(causa finalis)* was accepted any more. From now on an explanation was solely seen in naming an efficient cause, that is, describing a certain phenomenon in terms of a general law and boundary conditions. Nevertheless, this sole concentration on the *causa efficiens* has ever been a pure methodological assumption, not an ontological claim (at least not by science as a discipline).[10] The scientific description of reality deliberately and methodologically dispenses with reference to God on the level of the efficient causal description of reality.[11] This implies that scientists know all they need to know *as scientists* if they are able to name all the causal factors leading to a certain event, if this event can be shown to be a special case of a broader natural law, and if they can build a consistent broader theory that embraces this natural law and co-heres with other laws. If everything is explained in terms of efficient causality, if the theory fits the data (or vice versa), and if predictions for future events are possible, they are content with the explanatory power of this theory. The only thing remaining to be done is to search for an even simpler theory, which could explain the same data with even fewer theoretical assumptions, and to search for a more comprehensive theory that includes more phenomena than the current theory.

Since this sole interest in the *causa efficiens* seems to exclude God from nature (God does not enter the level of scientific description of na-ture), time and again a place for God's action has been sought by refer-ring to God as some sort of explanation for *gaps* in the scientific account of the world.[12] The first famous example of referring to God instead of a scientific, efficient causal explanation was brought about by Newton. His theory of gravity could explain the planetary motions and provided a broader theoretical framework for the works of both Galileo and Kepler. But Newton could not explain why all planets orbit around the sun in the same direction. Therefore he explained this aesthetically pleasing scheme by appealing to God's initial design (Brooke 1991: 29). Of course such an explanation was soon be shown as shortsighted, since already Kant and Laplace could give a very sensible efficient causal explanation of this phenomenon with their nebular hypothesis. What Newton saw as divine intervention, which could not be further explained, was now shown to be just the possible result of an efficient causal explanation ("possible" as long as that theory was not proved). Therefore, when Laplace explained his nebular hypothesis to Napoleon and was asked by the emperor where he accounted for the Creator in his theory, his famous reply stated that he had no need of that hypoth-esis (cf. Barbour 1998: 35).

The scientific endeavor tries to explain all of reality *insofar* as it ex-hibits efficient causal qualities and can be viewed with scientific means. Science tries to account for the *whole* of reality *insofar* as it fits its means. There is *no realm or gap* in the scientific explanation that could not pos-sibly be explained sometime. This claim of science, to deal with all of re-ality exactly *insofar* as it can be dealt with by scientific means, has been enormously successful. Any attempt to put God's action on this level has been repudiated sooner or later. Hence one sees at the heart of a god-of-the-gaps an underlying relationship between science and theol-ogy, in which God's action is seen to be in competition with efficient causality. Whenever a god-of-the-gaps concept occurs, someone has tried to explain natural processes by God's intervention, has used God as a hypothesis in order to explain gaps *in the causal explanation* or to explain something "better" than without the God-hypothesis.

Why Is a God–of–the–Gaps to Be Avoided?

Why should theologians not try to engage in scientific theories showing how God acts in nature? Out of the many possible approaches to this question we shall list just a few arguments from the viewpoints of both scientists and theologians.

What objections can scientists have against a god-of-the-gaps? As we said, a god-of-the-gaps uses the God-hypothesis in order to explain phenomena on the level of an efficient causal explanation of reality. If there were such gaps, there would be phenomena that could be detected by our senses or scientific apparatus that have no explanation at all in terms of efficient causality. Even after thorough investigation there would be phenomena that remain unexplainable and mysterious, holes or gaps in the causal nexus. The causal explanation of the world would be incomplete. Yet this is at odds with all that the history of science has taught us. Surely there are unexplainable phenomena, but the physical reality seems to be extremely self-consistent and closed. How can we be so sure about that? Well, of crucial importance for physicists are certain conservation rules, for example, energy conservation. However, we simply do not see any violation to this, any "holes" where energy would enter our world out of nothing. The conservation of energy has proven to be very well validated.[13] From this alone scientists have very good reasons to assume that it is highly unlikely that they have accidentally missed the gaps the god-of-the-gaps would use. The history of science is therefore a fascinating story of filling explanatory gaps in the scientific account of the world. A god-of-the-gaps simply does not work in the long run. It never has worked. Every time scientists and theologians argued about God's role in nature and theologians explained natural phenomena in terms of God's action, theology was defeated sooner or later.

Moreover, the very notion of a natural law presupposes a self-contained causal nexus of the world. The assumption that something happens apart from natural laws endangers the very concept of the natural law itself. The theories of astrophysics for instance make sense only *insofar* as one presupposes the validity of the same laws in every point in space-time. All scientific research has to presuppose that all natural phenomena exhibit certain regularities. If this search for regularities were abandoned, there would be no difference between science and, let us say, collecting stamps.

If young-Earth creationists claim that God created fossils, distant galaxies, and the whole universe in such a way that they only *appear* to be old, one can just as well assume that God created the whole universe just ten minutes ago. Everything up to that moment would just be illusionary, including all of what we believe we had experienced until ten minutes ago. If one is willing to assume the possibility of the former (that God could arbitrarily intervene into the causal nexus), one can never exclude the possibility of the latter. This is not to say that it is literally impossible to claim that, but it does not go together with critical realism.

Furthermore, most physicists are thrilled and fascinated by the "beauty" of a mathematical description of reality (this holds, I submit, similarly for all scientists).[14] Consistency and coherence are major criteria for the validation of theories (cf. Barbour 1998: 113), and ever since the beginning of the scientific endeavor this search has been successful. Coming from the scientist's experience of this "beauty" of natural laws, the old deistic idea of the perfection of the divine laws still exerts some attraction. A dubious light would be cast on the Christian God if God's created lawful order has to be supplemented by direct divine intervention. Like a God who unfortunately forgot to account for certain phenomena and has to trespass on his own preserves.[15] This might sound like a rather soft, aesthetic argument. But the aesthetic intuition of scientists and their search for coherent and "beautiful" solutions for the description of natural phenomena has opened the door for new scientific insights and theories. The history of science as it appears to date has been a history of developing ever more comprehensive, more abstract, and more inclusive theories. As we know, "Occam's razor," stating that the fewer assumptions a scientific theory needs the better it is, has certainly proved to be a secure guide for developing theories.

Moreover, if occasionally a natural explanation were not even imaginable for certain phenomena, believing in God's intervention would literally be the only possible explanation. In other words, believing in God would be inevitable. Yet seeing God at work in this world is not possible by means of sense impressions or reasoning alone; it necessitates some kind of revelatory experience. Conceiving God's action requires God's revelation. However, precisely because God reveals Godself wherever and whenever *God* wants to be revealed, there could

not be a lawlike coercive principle or sensation that forces one to accept
an event as *God's* action. In other words, if God is revealed only where
God wants to be revealed, a revelatory experience is something that
cannot be understood as following with cogent necessity from any sensation. If literally no other explanation were possible, one would *have to*
acknowledge God's action. Interestingly enough, the Bible itself quite
often refers to events of God's action in a context where other explanations are not only possible but even mentioned. For instance, in John
12:28–29 it is said that there are different interpretations of a certain
phenomenon among the same people, which some interpret as thun-
der, others as an angel, while the writer himself conceives this as a
voice from heaven.

Finally, one could see God's self-limitation to preserve the created
order—including the natural laws—as being part of a kenotic understanding of God. That God bears the final consequences of the laws of
this world becomes apparent most clearly in the Cross. If God limits
Godself not to violate the dynamics and the laws of the human sphere
of God's creation, why should God choose not to preserve the (apparently less important but) even more consistent natural laws? In other
words, does a god-of-the-gaps reveal an underlying *theologia triumphans*?

"Theory of Everything"?

The history of science reveals a remarkable unification of theories. In
physics, for instance, already some one-and-a-half centuries ago the
forces of magnetic and electric fields could be described by one comprehensive theory of electromagnetic fields. Maxwell showed that magnetic forces, which had been known for centuries, and the electric
forces, which were discovered later, are in fact only two sides of the
same coin. The excitement such a discovery produced among physicists
can only be understood if one recalls Occam's principle of economy.
The theory of electromagnetism was only one step in an ongoing unification of theories. The forces of the electromagnetic field itself could
be shown more recently as a special case of an even more comprehensive theory, which includes the electromagnetic and the weak force
(Weinberg/Salam). Physicists are now trying to unify this theory with
the theory for the strong force to a Grand Unifying Theory (GUT). They
hope that finally there will be only one giant comprehensive theory including all other theories of physics, which might be called a "Theory of
Everything" (TOE). Hawking thinks "if we do discover a complete the-

ory," we could finally answer "why it is that we and the universe exist,"
then "we would know the mind of God" (Hawking 1988: 175). Indeed,
the scientific description of the world has to be conceived as one that is
aiming for a complete description of reality in terms of (efficient) causal
explanations. Physics in particular and science in general aim to explain
the *whole* of reality. On such a level any religious "explanations" cannot
be but disastrous. If science tries to explain the whole of reality, however, is there any room left to speak about God's action in the world?
Could science maybe one day answer each and every question?

Gödel's Theorem

Every scientific theory is constrained by the theories of lower levels of explanations: psychological explanations are constrained by biology, biology is constrained by chemistry, chemistry by physics, and the
like.[16] At the end of that chain, physics is constrained by mathematics.
This is important, because mathematics itself cannot be proven to be
self-consistent and complete. Certain parts of mathematics can, but not
mathematics as a whole. Euclidean geometry, for example, can be completely "axiomatized," which means that there is a *finite* stock of axioms
"from which all of the infinitely many truths of Greek geometry can be
derived" (Moore 1991: 172). Yet what holds in geometry does not hold
in other fields of mathematics. It does not hold, for example, in set theory as the mathematician Kurt Gödel showed. Gödel demonstrated that
no single base of statements suffices for proving *all* truths in set theory
(Moore 1991: 173).[17] Furthermore, it is generally impossible to prove
from within a given system that the axioms used for that system are
consistent (Davies 1992: 166). Hence one can never find a single theoretical system explaining all possibly true statements—not even in
mathematics. As Paul Davies puts it, "No rational system can be proved
both consistent and complete" (167). If this holds even in mathematics,
which constrains all other sciences, "then surely it is true for all
other forms of rational human reasoning too" (van Huyssteen 1998:
71). This implies that any TOE could not account for its own validity. If
consistency is accepted as a necessary condition for any description of
reality, there hence can never be a rational system that is complete at
the same time. Even from logical grounds, the concept of a TOE is limited in its explanatory power.[18] Therefore, even if a TOE will be found
one day, it will never *explain* reality *wholly*, for *any* scientific account
of reality is limited to those aspects of reality scientific methods can
deal with.

Contingencies

General Contingency and Intelligibility of the World

It is important to realize that scientific investigation necessarily makes two "regulative assumptions" about the quality of the world.[19] The world need not be at all, and it need not be orderly and intelligible (cf. Barbour 1998: 90). Every scientific endeavor has to presuppose these two characteristics of the world, because on the one hand, if the world were *not intelligible*, the very attempt to understand it would be senseless. It literally *could* not be understood. On the other hand, if the world were *not contingent* (but necessary), one would only need to know what is necessary to understand the world. Since all empirical reality is obviously not necessary, but changeable and variable, such a rationalism tends to neglect the importance of empirical data. So science takes both the intelligibility and the contingency of reality as regulative assumptions.

Surely these two regulative assumptions of science need not be *reflected* by scientists in order to keep the scientific enterprise going. Of course, one could simply say that these assumptions obviously work. However, since most scientists are critical realists, they assume that their explanations of the world have in some way or another to do with reality. But, as we saw, one could argue that critical realism should not be restricted to the scientific realm. Hence it would only be very consistent to reflect upon the regulative assumptions and apply some kind of critical realism for them as well. If one understands critical realism in such a way as a broader epistemological attitude towards different kinds of experiences,[20] that instrumentalist option ("it simply works") would not be a very satisfying answer. Simply stating "science works anyhow" is certainly true, but it is not a sufficient rational answer if one seeks an interpretation of different kinds of experiences, some of which go beyond science.

Different Types of Contingencies

Having a closer look at the contingency of the world, one can, according to Barbour, distinguish four different types of contingencies, as they appear from a scientist's viewpoint (Barbour 1998: 211–12). They point to limitations of any scientific account of the world. We shall list the four types and shall ask, in each case, whether or not that particular contingency is likely to be explained or resolved by future scientific research.

   i) Contingency of *laws*. Even a TOE would have to provide an answer to the question "why do we have 'our' set of natural laws?"

Maybe scientists can show someday how everything in the world behaves according to a TOE. Then we would still not know whether or not that TOE would include the *only* possible set of laws. A TOE itself cannot be proven to be necessary.

This contingency cannot be resolved, simply because, according to Gödel, it will never be possible to prove a consistent and complete description of reality—a TOE—to be right.

ii) Contingency of *boundary conditions*. Moreover, any physical description of concrete reality consists of two basic components: a general regularity or natural law and boundary conditions. Only through the use of the latter are scientists able to make predictions concerning concrete events. It is important to realize that no scientific theory itself accounts for these boundary conditions. The boundary conditions have to be added to the equations externally, either through measurement(s) or through another theory (which itself at some point has to measure boundary conditions). This is usually not a problem in normal science, but what about the initial conditions of the universe as a whole? Stephen Hawking and Jim Hartle try to avoid the need of boundary or initial conditions of the universe by trying to explain the universe without a definite origin in time (Hawking 1988: 136, 141). Hawking himself stresses that this hypothesis is just a "proposal" (1988: 136), so it is not at all clear by now whether or not that would be possible. Maybe Hawking's attempt will succeed and we will finally find a theory that can explain the initial conditions of the universe. In that case the contingency of initial conditions would at least partially be reduced to the contingency of laws.[21] But still, if we ever find a theory that embraces the initial conditions, we still would not be able—according to Paul Davies—to prove such a theory as right (Davies 1992: 90).

iii) However, even supposing Hawking's idea were true, he cannot answer the question: "What is it that breathes fire into the equations and makes a universe for them to describe?" (Hawking 1988: 174). For that there is anything at all and not nothing is really a thrilling question, which is expressed by the contingency of *existence*. Why has the world that is described by contingent laws not only remained possible but actually become real? "Why does the universe go to all the bother of existing?" (ibid.).

The sheer existence of something can never be proven to be necessary. Even if there were only *one* possible TOE (which is unlikely),[22] so that we would know that if there ever were a universe, it would have such and such qualities, we could never prove why this had to become real. This is simply beyond the structure of our natural laws: they always presuppose the existence of their object.

iv) Finally, the contingency of *events* refers to the fact that not only the general structure and existence of the universe as a whole, but also events *in* the universe are contingent. Currently the discussion focuses on basically *two sources* of such contingencies: quantum phenomena and chaotic systems. Most physicists at the moment do conceive quantum mechanical indeterminacy as an *intrinsic* ontological feature of nature, that is, a source of contingent events. The well-known question is whether or not there are "hidden variables" determining the outcome of (then only *apparently*) random quantum events (such as, for example, the decay of a certain atomic nucleus). To date most physicists doubt such an intrinsic determinism and maintain a probabilistic interpretation (cf. e.g., Polkinghorne 1989: 56–59).

There is still another source for the contingencies of events. Dynamic (chaotic) systems seem also to induce contingencies of events. The debate about the ontological status of chaotic indeterminacies and the relationship between the micro-world of quantum mechanics and the macro-world of deterministic chaotic systems is not yet decided (cf. Kellert 1993).[23] One possible interpretation does say that chaotic dynamics will indeed take the tiny indeterminacies of quantum-mechanical systems and stretch them into macroscopic variations (Kellert 1993: 73). In a way the chaotic system could function as a measurement apparatus for quantum systems by coupling with that system and amplifying unobservable micro-changes to macroscopic level (ibid.).

Although this link between micro- and macro-world is still debated, even opponents of a close link between micro-world and macro-world assume that chaotic systems do exhibit ontological indeterminacies. Polkinghorne, for instance, also claims an ontological indeterminacy for chaotic systems, despite the fact that he is critical about this amplifying of quantum mechanical indeterminacies (cf. Polkinghorne 1998: 48–75; Polkinghorne 1991: 34–48). Paul Davies considers this type of event even as an own (fifth) category of contingencies (1992: 169–70). Therefore, it does seem that we have two kinds of sources for contingent events, chaotic systems and quantum phenomena.

The question concerning possible future research has to be answered slightly differently concerning this last kind of contingency, for it is still a controversial one. In fact, if there ever is contingency of events, we can *never be sure* about it. In order to see this let us assume this interpretation were "true" in the sense that it would indeed be impossible to detect any regularity in random events. In that case we could never know for sure about this being true "ontological chance." It does not even exclude the possibility of a strict *deterministic* algorithm. This can be seen by the following example: Consider a sequence of random numbers such as 415926535 . . . Apparently, this sequence is randomly distributed. In fact, it satisfies all necessary conditions for random numbers.[24] Yet it is still perfectly determinate. For these are digits of pi, starting with the second digit after the decimal point.

What does that imply for our context? Well, if you did not know about the existence of pi, but would find a sequence of, let us say, the first thousand digits of pi; if you only knew statistics, but no trigonometry or geometry, it could happen that you would believe that this is just a sequence of random numbers. It could be that you would never realize that this sequence follows a well-defined algorithm. Similarly, if this is conceivable even in this simple example, one can never exclude some sort of regularity (or even a strict algorithm) underlying those events that appear to be accidental in nature.

Theological Interpretations

"Creation" as Explanation for Contingency and Intelligibility of the World

From a theological perspective the regulative assumptions of science, intelligibility, and contingency of the world are anything but vague and accidental, for they correspond to the Christian notion of creation. The Judeo-Christian notion of creation sees the order of the world as ultimately grounded in God's rationality (cf. Barbour 1998: 27–29). Torrance expresses this close link of the notion of creation and the concept of an orderly universe: "The doctrine of the One God, the Creator of all things visible and invisible, and the ultimate source of all order and rationality . . . gave rise to the conception of the universe as one harmonious system of things characterized by one pervasive if multi-variable order throughout. This rational unity of the cosmos . . . which is the correlate of Judeo-Christian monotheism, has ever since constituted one of the fundamental assumptions of all science: it is the ground of our confidence that wherever we may direct our inquiries we will find the universe accessible to rational investigation . . ." (2–3).

At the same time the world is not seen as necessary, since it was created through God's sovereign will. "This concept of contingent order, however, . . . is the direct product of the Christian understanding of the constitutive relation between God and the universe . . ." (ibid., 70). From a Christian viewpoint the contingency of the world reflects God's sovereignty. The world need not be at all and it need not be like it actually is. Rather, the world is the way it is because God wanted it this way.[25]

Of course, the fact that the Judeo-Christian concept of creation fits the regulative assumptions of science, and that it even contributed to the rise of science, does not prove its validity. Other "explanations" are possible—the simplest would be just to assume both as "given." But if one seeks comprehensive understanding of *all* reality, if one defends a critical realist approach not only for the strictly scientific realm, it does make perfect sense to look for a fitting counterpart at those points where science obviously faces an "inter"-face. The question then will be what "face" is on the other side.

Creatio Ex Nihilo

We can even go beyond the interpretation of the general contingency of the world and look out for more specific theological interpretations for each of the four types of contingencies mentioned above. As we said, science is not able to explain these contingencies. Shall we accept them just as "given"? Ian Barbour draws theological parallels to each of these contingencies (Barbour 1998: 212–14). He sees theological parallels for the contingency of *existence* and the contingency of *boundary conditions* in the *creatio ex nihilo,* the doctrine of the creation out of nothing. *Creatio ex nihilo* does not so much refer to an initial act, but expresses that the world is fundamentally dependent on God, who deliberately and freely chose to create the world as it is. That the world is, although it need not be, and that the boundary conditions of the universe made possible the development of life, are seen as grounding on God's deliberate and free choice to create a world that need not be (cf. also Torrance 1981: 3).

Now, is this theological interpretation of *creatio ex nihilo* an *explanation* for the contingencies of existence and of boundary conditions? Does theology offer her help to science? We saw that both the contingency of existence and the contingency of laws—to which, as we said, in the "worst case" the contingency of boundary conditions might be reduced—will never be solvable by science. Now one could either accept the contingencies as purely accidental, just as "given," or one could "reduce" these contingencies by referring to God. But is the reference to God, seen from a purely logical point of view, a helpful explanation? Is this a satisfying reduction of contingencies? For one could as well continue asking "who created God?" Like in the story told by Stephen Hawking about the woman who interrupted an astronomer's lecture declaring that the world is a flat plate resting on the back of a giant turtle. When the lecturer asked what the turtles rest upon, she replied, "But it's turtles all the way down!" (Hawking 1988: 1) I see no reason why the assumption to stop the regress within God would on logical grounds *alone* have *a priori* any more explanatory power than to accept the world as "given," as a result of "pure chance," or else. But the question is whether or not we remain content with pure, logical grounds. I doubt we can.

Hence I see two options. Either we continue asking "where does this law, this regularity and the like come from?" even "where does God come from?" or we stop this process at some point by reference to a God who needs no further explanation. Christians believe this as being the Triune God, who is revealed in Jesus Christ by the power of the Holy Spirit. The "knowledge" about the Triune God, however, does certainly not come from reason, but from God's revelation in Christ.

The Christian claim that God created the universe is not a "causal explanation," because the notion of causality in science comes to its limits if one considers the universe as a whole. For "causality" in the sense science uses it presupposes time (or time is the condition for the possibility of change and causality). However, if there were no time, the notion of causality could not be applied. A "supernatural creation cannot be a causative act in time, for the coming-to-being of time is part of what we are trying to explain. If God is invoked as an explanation for the physical universe, then this explanation cannot be in terms of familiar cause and effect" as it is stated by Paul Davies (1992: 58). For that reason the Christian claim that the universe is created does not compete with scientific theories (for it is not a *causal* explanation), but rather with different metaphysical claims about the structure of ultimate reality.

If one does seek a consistent and coherent explanation of the world and a satisfying interpretation of *all* experience, it will therefore be of crucial importance how reality as experienced in other realms of life fits into that explanatory scheme. I submit, seen from this perspective, that the Christian viewpoint has much more to offer than, let us say, an agnostic one.

Creatio Continua and God's Action

To be sure, the conclusion just made is a very important achievement, for it clearly shows the limitations of any scientific description of reality, and the legitimacy and explanatory power of a Christian view of reality. Nevertheless, that discussion remained on the level of presuppositions of the scientific enterprise and general conditions of the universe. What about any space for speaking about particular divine action and providence—without sliding back to a god-of-the-gaps? The theological doctrine of the *creatio continua* expresses God's continuing creative action in the world, God's creative and orderly power. For that reason Barbour relates this theological doctrine to the contingency of *laws* and the contingency of *events* named above (Barbour 1998: 213). Barbour sees the *creatio continua* as a theological expression of God's immanence and God's sustaining power. Since it is not at all a matter of course that the natural laws are continually valid, God is seen as the sustainer of the natural laws. Moreover, God is not only active as the "ground of being," but continually immanent in the process of the world and participating in it. We saw earlier that religious assertions must not be a substitute for causal explanations if a god-of-the-gaps should be avoided. However, what if the causal explanations that science seeks simply come to their *limit?* What if science itself could not provide a "*causal* explanation" for certain phenomena? We said that for the universe as a whole causality indeed faces its limits. Something similar holds concerning the contingency of events.

Quantum Mechanics

Before we give a theological interpretation of the contingencies of events, a preliminary remark is necessary: Besides the problems directly related to the god-of-the-gaps, one has to be aware that any theological interpretation of scientific insights can only be provisional (for certainly the scientific insights themselves are). Therefore it seems wise to interpret only relatively validated theories. At the same time, however, it is clear that theology has always been responding to culture, which includes nowadays especially science. I suppose there is nothing wrong with revising theological interpretations of concrete scientific results, as long as one makes clear that this interpretation is, of course, as provisionary as those results are.

Among the contingencies named above, obviously the contingency of events is of particular interest for considering God's action in the world. We said that the god-of-the-gaps implies God competing with natural efficient causality and with explanations science will possibly search for. Yet in the case of quantum events it seems that there simply *is no* causal explanation in the sense in which we usually use this phrase. According to the probabilistic interpretation of quantum mechanics, the quantum mechanical indeterminacies have "no cause" in the sense that there is no other physical entity determining the outcome of this event. This interpretation would state that there are no "hidden variables," no detectable parameters implicitly determining those events.

Now we have seen that one can never be sure about the real nature of "random" events. It might be that there is an underlying structure behind what appears to be random. That is conceivable even in the simple example given above (digits of pi), even in the realm of what physics already knows. So it is well conceivable that there is an underlying regularity behind the apparently random events of quantum mechanics that would never be detectable—maybe in principle. Hence one might very well see some kind of regularity due to God's action behind that which appears to be random. For this reason Robert Russell maintains: "If we interpret quantum physics in terms of ontological indeterminacy, we can conceive of God as *acting* in nature without violating the laws of nature, since according to these laws, nature provides a set of necessary causes, but this set is not sufficient to bring about the actual event" (Russell 1995: 23).

To refer to God in this context would not imply a god-of-the-gaps, *as long as one does not claim that this reference has any explanatory power on the level of the efficient causality.* As long as one wants to avoid any god-of-the-gaps, it must not make any difference for the scientific theories whether one accepts random events as pure chance or sees some kind of divine action behind them. Again, this interpretation must make no difference on the causal level. It must not only be undetectable, but it must also not hinder the search for causal explanations. Only if these premises are strictly provided can one interpret random events theologically without being in danger of a god-of-the-gaps. In other words: If science says "this is due to chance and nothing else," the Christian might claim that ultimately this is not "pure" chance, but is also related to God's will for this creation, for God is Lord of all that is. However, is it not possible that some day "hidden variables" will be found and that this interpretation will have to be revised? It is possible. Yet I do not think that this should make theologians refrain from giving any interpretation at all. Since, firstly, we can never be sure about the ontological status of chance, and secondly, this interpretation of quantum mechanics has been validated and is accepted by the majority of physicists, a tentative theological interpretation seems very legitimate. Otherwise theology would have to withdraw from any such interpretation at any time, because one can never be sure about the ontological status of random events.

Chaos Theory

Chaos theory reveals an exciting feature of nature that can lead to a shift of our perspective on the world. In classical mechanics the orderly was normal, irregularities exceptional. God's action was seen either in the supernatural or in the whole structure of natural laws. Quantum mechanics revealed an underlying indeterminacy that induces contingency into the world. Nevertheless, this has barely an influence on macroscopic events, because quantum mechanical phenomena appear, at least normally, only on the micro-level (for statistical reasons they are usually not relevant on a macroscopic level). Hence using exclusively this sort of contingency for speaking of God's action would thus be implicitly reductionist.[26] Chaotic systems, on the contrary, induce contingencies on the level of macroscopic events. Chaos theory reveals that we do not live in a world in which only the natural laws, actually or at least potentially known to us, dominate the process of the world. We rather live, as it were, on islands of order in an ocean of chaos. We are surrounded by contingencies built in the structure of the universe on very deep levels. As we said, any concrete description of events in nature entails both laws and boundary conditions. Now, chaos theory reveals the *crucial* importance of boundary conditions. Furthermore, any real physical system contains a *huge amount* of principally indeterminate, contingent boundary conditions.[27]

Of course, this is not to say that simply "anything goes." "A chaotic system is not totally 'chaotic' in the popular sense, corresponding to absolutely random behavior" (Polkinghorne 1998: 52). Yet it does point to the fragility of our world and to its sensitivity to boundary conditions. In addition, the boundary conditions are to quite an extent influenced by what can only be seen as due to *chance* from a scientific viewpoint. Therefore, having grasped that one can never exclude some pattern or regularity behind that which appears to be random, a further theological interpretation is still possible. Therefore, chaotic systems too have been interpreted as related to divine action and providence. Polkinghorne suggests that we conceive of God as giving information input in dynamical systems: "active information" to "exercise providential interaction with creation" (1998: 62). He draws on the effect that chaotic systems have numerous numbers of possible future states with the same energy (their phase space trajectories lead to different states but have the same energy).[28] "The 'choice' of path actually followed corresponds not to the result of some physically causal act (in the sense of an energy input) but rather to a 'selection' from options (in the sense of an information input)," which enables God to "influence his creation in a non-energetic way" (1991: 45). Even scholars whose interpretations differ from Polkinghorne's conceive of chaos theory as providing room for God's action. Nancey Murphy (1997: 348) argues that the "real value of chaos theory for an account of divine action is that it gives God a great deal of 'room' in which to effect specific outcomes without destroying our ability to believe in the natural causal order."[29]

To be sure, this process of providential action warrants a more technical and detailed discussion. Does God, for instance, *determine* the outcome of those events or just influence them (like the lure in process thought)? Certainly one has to account for the freedom of God's creation. It also needs to be discussed whether one has to understand God as working in *every* quantum event and/or chaotic event or only *occasionally*. Furthermore, future research will have to answer the question to what extent quantum mechanical systems influence macroscopic chaotic processes. However, whether or not the contingency of chaotic phenomena is related to quantum mechanics, quantum mechanics and chaos theory reveal our daily world as being highly contingent, to a high degree inaccessible to science—*in principle*. It thus provides legitimate room for a theological interpretation of these contingencies by referring to God's action and providence.

God's Action at the Limits?

Does all this imply that God's action is restricted to the limits? Does this lead to a remote designer or a God who is only responsible for the temporal or spatial limits of our universe? Not at all! *For it is not only the limits of time and space at which science comes to its limits.* The concept of *creatio continua*, which interprets the contingency of laws and events, expresses God's ongoing involvement in the world and God's sustaining power. Moreover, the contingencies of events induced through quantum mechanical indeterminacies and chaotic phenomena reveal that we are living in a world that is to a very high extent contingent and therefore not accessible to the scientific description of reality. These "limits" of science are therefore almost everywhere present in our physical world: in comparatively simple (chaotic) physical systems as well as in larger phenomena such as weather; in the sphere of biological systems and individuals as well as in the sphere of societies, stock markets, and the like. To say that God is working at the "limits" in the sense of this paper has to be understood solely methodologically, in order to distinguish God's action from the efficient causality science describes. The "limits" are limits of the *methods of science,* and have nothing to do with any limitation of God's action to a certain realm of nature (e.g., the Big Bang) or a limitation of God's power.[30] To "reduce" God's action to the limits in this way is to do nothing else but to take seriously the autonomy of science and the repudiation of any god-of-the-gaps, which is to be argued from both science and theology.

Outlook: Not Filling the "Gaps" but Crossing the "Gulf"

We more and more realize that even a TOE could not give a complete explanation of reality. To be sure, in principle there are no gaps *in* the scientific account that could be filled by theology. If theologians want to avoid any god-of-the-gaps, they have to make sure that they do not conceive of God as working on the level of efficient causality. Nevertheless, there remains, even on a cognitive level, a fundamental "gulf" between the scientific description of the world and an overall account of reality as it is experienced in "the broader and richer setting of personal life," to use a phrase from Polkinghorne (1996: xi). This "gulf" has nothing to do with any kind of "gap" referred to in the god-of-the-gaps. For a sufficient explanation of this broader setting of life, however, that "gulf" between science and "the rest of life" must be bridged. The need for crossing this gulf becomes apparent by the fact that scientists raise limit questions that science itself cannot answer. In raising these questions scientists have started building the bridge across the gulf, but they cannot finish it on their own. There is no way suggested by science itself as to how the framework of the scientific account of reality could fit into that "richer setting of personal life." This fit has to be evaluated apart from scientific reasoning. That is not to say that science would not work without this fit. However, it does say that the scientific insights are "floating" unless they are not related to other dimensions of life, unless they are grounded in life. Surely this need not be a theological or religious grounding. No cogent proof of theological truth claims will ever be possible. Yet in some way or another everybody who strives for a rational explanation of reality needs to consider *both* the scientific account *and* the realm of personal life. Both consistency of theoretical ideas themselves and consistency between theoretical insights and the sphere of life need to be established for a rational explanation of *all* experience. The question at issue is therefore not how God would work in the gap (for in principle there is no gap), but how our metaphysical and religious traditions can cross the gulf between the scientific *description* and our *holistic experience* of reality. How can theological reflections be linked to the bridge already partly built by the limit questions raised by scientists? Only if this gulf is bridged, only if the "floating" scientific insights are grounded, will an integrated interpretation of all experience be possible.

Paul Davies is aware of the fact that "we are barred from ultimate knowledge, from ultimate explanation" (1992: 231). If we wish to progress beyond science, he states, "we have to embrace a different concept of 'understanding' from that of rational explanation" (ibid.). He assumes the "mystical path" as one possible solution. However, one may follow Wentzel van Huyssteen, who pointed out that Davies' "mere choice for mystical ways of understanding is ultimately still not really satisfactory." (1998: 73) As a result of the foregoing thoughts it should be clear that it indeed could not be satisfying to leave aside any rationality at the very point where science stops (as this is implied by Davies). If we are seeking a comprehensive explanation of *all our* experience, reflecting also for instance on the very possibility of science itself, we ought to seek for rational ways to embrace also those aspects of life that might be of uttermost importance to us, despite the fact that they are not dealt with by science. If we are true psychosomatic unities, it is not reasonable to rely on rationality in the scientific realm, and turn totally away from any rational approach for the rest. Here is the place where the distinct qualities of theology become important. For "theology too is a distinct form of human knowledge, i.e., a distinct form of rational reflection on religious experience that not only could be markedly different from mysticism, but which could in fact, as a reasoning strategy, share important overlaps with the rationality of the natural sciences" (van Huyssteen 1998: 73).

Science seeks explanation by reducing different kinds of phenomena to the broader framework of a theory. The history of science appears as an ongoing process of reducing "accidental" events to laws, laws to theories, and so on until there might be only one TOE left. This reduces different kinds of contingent phenomena to ever fewer laws, and makes the outcome "necessary," provided the theory and the boundary conditions are given. Nevertheless, we could see that this scientific account could not solve fundamental contingencies. To say that that chain of explanation does not continue forever but stops within God transfers the contingency of the world into God's sovereignty. However, on pure, logical grounds it is not *per se* a better explanation of the reality science describes to assume God at that point where the "chain of turtles" stops. This demands the autonomy of science concerning its causal explanations.[31] However, if there are strong evidences for believing in a reality that goes beyond what is detected by science, if one believes in a God who by God's grace makes life in all its fullness possible, then it would be very reasonable to assume that the "chain of turtles" stops within God, who needs no other explanation, for God is believed in as the ultimate reality. Happy are those who have the good fortune to believe that this ultimate reality is not only the cool ground of being but has also a personal face, that this God has the face of Christ.

The bridge across the gulf that separates the scientific account of reality from the broader setting of personal life is partly built by scientists, for they come to points where the proper boundaries of science make them stop *as* scientists. The other side of the bridge can be built by all sorts of religious or philosophical interpretations and *Weltanschauungen*. Christian theologians are called to build the bridge on this other side in order to render an intelligible description of the whole reality as seen and experienced by the Christian community. As with any image, so does this have a shortcoming. Even if the bridge were built, there would still not be a secure and cogent path from science to theology. Reason does not replace revelation. Therefore not everybody will see the specific *theological* contribution to such an explanation of reality as necessary, but in some way or another everyone has to make metaphysical decisions. The god-of-the-gaps resulted in theology having an argument with science. Now, instead, theology is rather to be seen as having an argument with other religious and philosophical traditions, with other *weltanschauungen* on the interpretation of the scientific account. There is no "Christian science." Nevertheless, there is need for a Christian interpretation of scientific explanations. This interpretation is closely linked to the valuations one makes elsewhere in life. Concerning this interpretation of the scientific account of reality, and concerning the evaluation of life as experienced by oneself in community, Christians cannot but compete with other interpretations, be they agnostic, pantheistic, or otherwise.

NOTES

1. In the following I will mainly deal with questions arising from physics, because the subject matter is mainly related to this discipline.
2. This dichotomy, however, seems to result from the very fact that one does *not* meet the self-assessment of religious communities.
3. This refers only to the level of causal explanation and not, for instance, to the general presuppositions of science or its ethical implications.
4. In addition, I suppose the prevailing positivism in the twentieth century contributed to that separation by its emphasis on the uniqueness of the scientific method.
5. Cf. for instance Ian Barbour, who says that "most scientists are incurably realist" (1998: 118); likewise John C. Polkinghorne: "The decision made by the vast majority of working scientists, consciously or unconsciously, is to opt for critical realism . . ." (1998: 53).
6. This, of course, does not say anything about the *truth* of religious assertions. It only says that there can hardly be a dichotomy between the experiences of a scientist *as* a scientist and the experience of a scientist *as* a believer or *as* a non-believer.
7. Surely I am not superimposing any scientific rationality to theology. I just want to stress that *even* from a solely scientific-critical realist's viewpoint a bifurcation of reality into two separate realms is to be questioned. This is to make the dialogue with scientists easier and help them to see why a "bifurcation of nature" is not even consistent from *their* point of view.
8. Ian Barbour (1990: 17–20, 1998: 90–93) has made this proposal to start some kind of science and religion dialogue with boundary or limit questions.
9. The *causae formalis et finalis* were dismissed. One might say that partially the *causa materialis* was still accepted (by Hume, for instance), but in the long run it was also reduced to *causa efficiens,* cf. Holmes Rolston (1987: 35).
10. Cf. Thomas F. Torrance (1981: 74): "Throughout modern times it has generally been held proper for natural science to confine itself to intramundane connections and explanations, in methodological exclusion of all reference to extramundane relations. It would seem no less proper for natural science to recognize that this exclusion is only methodological and does not imply that there is no reality beyond what is open to investigation through its own methods and instruments or is accessible to understanding and formalization within the limits of its own conceptual framework—otherwise it would be guilty of the fallacy of identifying the real with what is conceivable to the natural scientific reason alone."
11. Cf. Torrance (1981: 74): "By focussing on the determination of observable regularities in nature and their formalization as logico-causal continuities, to the exclusion of all extra-causal and extra-logical factors, science has steadily cre-

ated an immensely powerful and successful conceptual machinery which has generated a momentum of its own, and functions as though it were a law to itself."

12. I deliberately avoid using the phrase "scientific world view," because strictly speaking it tends to diminish the distinction that is of great importance in this context, namely between the scientific *description* of reality, and that which can be called world view or *Weltanschauung.*

13. Quantum field theory, to be sure, allows for certain violations of this rule, but only within Heisenberg's uncertainty principle.

14. One might argue, for example, that biological evolution is anything but elegant because of its randomness. (F. Crick does so.) But this is not necessarily the case: If you "played the tape of evolution" not only once, but several times, you would get similar melodic elements appearing in each, as van Valen maintains. Hence one could indeed see "beauty" even in the evolutionary process (cf. Rolston 1999: 20).

15. As I see it, this argument is valid even if one, for good reasons, rejects the notion of a deistic designer. For it is not consistent to think of God's creation as both bringing order into chaotic situations—as God is understood, for example, in important traditions of the Old Testament—and at the same time overruling orderly structures. Again, this does not at all exclude God's active role in the process of the world; it only states that God's action does not compete with the natural causes.

16. Of course, this does *not* imply any reductionist assumption. It does not exclude distinct higher-level properties; it only states that the higher level at each time has to obey the lower-level rules.

17. Cf. also Wentzel van Huyssteen (1998: 71), who uses this—as we will do soon—as an argument for the limits of scientific rationality. However, I submit that van Huyssteen makes too much of a claim in saying that "*therefore* exist unprovable truths" (italics added). As Moore (1991: 173) says, we have "no reason to suppose" that "there is some true set-theoretical statement s such that, given any axiomatic base A for set theory, s cannot be proved using A." It *might be* that there exist such unprovable truths, but this could not be inferred from Gödel's theorem.

18. All this is not to say that the kind of TOE that physicists are striving for could not be found some day. On the contrary, I believe it is not unlikely that such a TOE can be found in the future, which might even include other branches of science. However, it must be clear that it will just not explain *everything.*

19. Cf. Torrance (1981: 74): "Undoubtedly modern science does accept the idea that the universe is contingent, for that is the regulative assumption behind its reliance upon experiment and its operation with the interrelation of experiment and theory."

20. See the above section entitled Is Total Independence Sufficient? Moreover, I submit this can also be defended because of the downfall of positivism, that is, the fact that a sheer dichotomy between scientific experience and other sorts of experience is not tenable.

21. But the most that might be said would be that one does not need any certain initial conditions in the literal sense of the meaning, such as certain values of energy or the like. Even supposing this could be achieved, the values of the

natural constants are still not determined. This, however, might be seen as a feature of the natural *laws*. So, in the end, it might be that the contingency of initial conditions could—at least in principle—be reduced to that of laws. This diminishing importance of the distinction between initial conditions and laws on a cosmological level is also emphasized by Davies (1992: 91).

22. Cf. Davies (1992: 170): "My conclusion, then, is that the physical universe is not compelled to exist as it is; it could have been otherwise."

23. The phrase "*deterministic* chaos" does certainly not *per se* say anything about the ontological status of chaos. It only says that our treatment of these phenomena is a deterministic one, that is, that we use classical (i.e., Newtonian) mechanics and not quantum mechanics for our calculations. This is a methodological restriction in order to be able to calculate.

24. "Perfectly random" can of course only be said for a long sequence of numbers, but let us assume that would be the case.

25. This, of course, need not imply a voluntarist concept of God. Even if one rejects a voluntarist concept of God and sees God's *potentia* as limited to do the good, God surely still has enough freedom to create the world in a way God wanted it—since there is not only one good world possible.

26. This argument is used by Ian Barbour (1998: 187–88) to repudiate Pollard's approach, within which God providentially controls the world through quantum mechanical events.

27. Even if quantum mechanics did not have any influence on the behavior of dynamical systems as they are, if we were to determine the *exact* initial conditions of *any* system, we finally come to a realm where quantum mechanics *will* be important. We simply cannot determine for instance the place of any object with infinite accuracy.

28. Cf. Polkinghorne (1998: 61–63; 1991: ch. 3). As mentioned before, Polkinghorne is critical about the influence of quantum mechanics on dynamical systems. I maintain, however, if one remains on the grounds of pure classical physics (without any quantum mechanics), the problem arises that phase space trajectories simply do not cross (which is of course due to causality). This means that even if adjacent states of a system lie infinitely close to each other, I see no chance that the system "jumps" from one phase space trajectory to another without any energy input. To violate this law would be similar to violating energy conservation. In pure classical mechanics even "active information" cannot change the system's state without violating one of these rules. Hence I do maintain (among others, see Kellert above) quantum mechanics as being important for the ontological indeterminacy of chaotic events.

29. Murphy (1997: 348) differs from Polkinghorne in the interpretation of the ontological status of chaotic events. Polkinghorne thinks chaotic processes reveal ontological openness, while Murphy stresses the epistemological openness: "The room God needs is not space to work within a causally determined order—ontological room—but rather room to work within our perceptions of natural order—epistemological room." I do not agree with her, because her position implies only a "pseudo"-freedom of humans. However, it might be that the question is unsolvable whether or not this is to be seen as an ontological or just an epistemological indeterminacy. For if you assume a Laplacean demon should calculate a totally deterministic system of the whole universe, it would

114   BERG

get incredibly complicated. One could probably say that even for a comparatively small macroscopic system any exact calculation with the fastest computers imagined would take much longer than the age of our universe. That
implies in a way that the universe simulates itself (cf. Davies/Gribbin 1992:
42). In other words: Is it reasonable to uphold the distinction between epistemological and ontological indeterminacy in this case, if any calculation takes
longer than the real system?
30. That is to say that the question of limitation of God's power is simply not
addressed here. It would, of course, be at issue if we were to discuss the question to what extent God influences quantum events, and whether or not God
influences all of them and the like.
31. Again, if it *were* a better explanation of the reality science describes, it would
compete with scientific explanations.

REFERENCES

Barbour, Ian G. 1974. *Myths, Models, and Paradigms. A Comparative Study in
Science and Religion.* New York, Evanston, San Francisco, London: Harper &
Row.
———. 1990. *Religion in an Age of Science. The Gifford Lectures 1989–1991,
Volume 1.* San Francisco: Harper & Row.
———. 1998. *Religion and Science. Historical and Contemporary Issues.* San
Francisco: Harper/London: SCM Press.
Brook, John Hedley. 1991. *Science and Religion. Some Historical Perspectives.*
Cambridge: Cambridge University Press.
Davies, Paul. 1992. *The Mind of God. The Scientific Basis for a Rational World.* New
York, London, Toronto, Sydney, Tokyo, Singapore: Simon & Schuster.
Davies, Paul and John Gribbin. 1992. *The Matter Myth. Dramatic Discoveries That
Challenge Our Understanding of Physical Reality.* New York, London, Toronto,
Sydney, Tokyo, Singapore: Simon & Schuster.
Gould, Stephen J. 1999. *Rocks of Ages. Science and Religion in the Fullness of Life.*
New York: The Ballantine Publishing Group.
Hawking, Stephen. 1988. *A Brief History of Time.* Toronto, New York, London.
Sydney, Auckland: Bantam Books.
Kellert, Stephen H. 1993. *In the Wake of Chaos. Unpredictable Order in Dynamical
Systems.* Chicago, London: The University of Chicago Press.
Moore, A.W. 1991. *The Infinite.* London, New York: Routledge.
Murphy, Nancey. 1997. "Divine Action in the Natural Order," in *Chaos and
Complexity. Scientific Perspectives on Divine Action,* ed. Robert J. Russell,
Nancey Murphy, Arthur Peacocke. 2nd ed. Vatican State: Vatican Observatory
Publications, 325–57.
Polkinghorne, John C. 1989. *The Quantum World.* Princeton: Princeton University
Press.
———. 1991. *Reason and Reality. The Relationship between Science and Theology.*
Valley Forge: Trinity Press International.

———. 1993. "Theological Notions of Creation and Divine Causality," in *Science and Theology. Questions at the Interface,* ed. Murray Rae, Hilary Regan, John Stenhouse. Grand Rapids, Michigan: Eerdmans, 225–37.

———. 1996. *Beyond Science. The Wider Human Context.* Cambridge: Cambridge University Press.

———. 1998. *Belief in God in an Age of Science.* New Haven, London: Yale University Press.

Rolston, Holmes III. 1987. *Science and Religion. A Critical Survey.* New York: Random House.

———. 1999. *Genes, Genesis, and God. Values and Their Origins in Natural and Human History. The Gifford Lectures 1997–1998.* Cambridge: Cambridge University Press.

Russell, Robert J. 1995. "Theistic Evolution: Does God Really Act in Nature?", in *Center for Theology and the Natural Sciences Bulletin* (winter 1995): 19–32.

Tipler, Frank J. 1994. *The Physics of Immortality. Modern Cosmology, God, and the Resurrection of the Dead.* New York, London, Toronto, Sydney, Auckland: Doubleday.

Torrance, Thomas F. 1981. *Divine and Contingent Order.* Oxford, New York, Toronto, Melbourne: Oxford University Press.

van Huyssteen, J. Wentzel. 1997. "Critical Realism and God. Can There Be Faith after Foundationalism?"in *Essays in Postfoundationalist Theology,* ed. by W. van Huyssteen. Grand Rapids/Cambridge (U.K.): Eerdmans, 40–52.

———. 1998. *Duet or Duel. Theology and Science in a Postmodern World.* Harrisburg: Trinity Press International.

This chapter was originally published in *Koinonia Journal* vol. 12, no. 2 (fall 2000).

CHAPTER 7

Cosmic Endgame: Theological Reflections on Recent Scientific Speculations on the Ultimate Fate of the Universe

JOHN JEFFERSON DAVIS

Dr. Davis earned a Ph.D. in systematic theology from Duke University in 1975. He is currently professor of systematic theology and Christian ethics at Gordon-Conwell Theological Seminary in South Hamilton, MA. He is the author of *Evangelical Ethics: Issues Facing the Church Today*, as well as of numerous books, articles, and scholarly reviews.

"I hope with these lectures," stated Freeman Dyson, a physicist at the Institute for Advanced Study in Princeton, New Jersey, "to hasten the arrival of the day when eschatology, the study of the end of the universe, will be a respectable scientific discipline and not merely a branch of theology."[1] In a seminal and far-ranging set of speculative lectures originally delivered at New York University in 1978, Dyson set out to challenge the prevailing pessimism of scientific opinion concerning the ultimate fate of the physical universe. Boldly extrapolating the known laws of physics into the most remote reaches of time, he challenged the dominant view that "we have only the choice of being fried in a closed universe or frozen in an open one."[2] Some form of intelligent "life"—perhaps only in the form of a computer-chip like structure—might be able to continue to exist in the outer darkness and extreme coldness of an unendingly expanding universe, long after *Homo sapiens* and other forms of carbon-based life had perished from the cosmos. Making no apologies for mixing "philosophical speculations with mathematical equations," Dyson boldly disregarded the traditional scientific reluctance to mix scientific analysis with questions of the ultimate purpose and meaning of life.

Dyson was, in effect, issuing an invitation to faith communities to engage in a conversation that related religious understandings of the end of the universe to the new scientific "eschatologies." This chapter will attempt to reflect theologically on recent scientific attempts like that of Dyson's to avoid the pessimistic conclusions about the fate of the universe that have dominated the scientific community since the development of modern thermodynamics and its notion of the "heat death" of the universe. This chapter will attempt to assess the intellectual challenges and the apologetic opportunities for the church's witness in the face of these scientific "eschatologies."

The Rise of Modern Scientific Eschatologies

The development of the discipline of thermodynamics in the nineteenth century gave rise to scientific speculations about the ultimate fate of the universe that have continued down to the present day. In a public lecture delivered in 1854 titled "On the Interaction of Natural Forces," Hermann Helmholtz, professor of physics at the University of Berlin, reflected on the implications of the second law of thermodynamics for the very long-term prospects of the human race. The second law, which came to be recognized as one of the fundamental principles of physics, states that in any closed physical system, the amount of energy available for useful work decreases over time. Or stated another way, the amount of *entropy* or disorder in a system tends to increase over time.[3] The useful energy in physical systems inevitably tends to dissipate or "run down," just as a clock, once wound up, will eventually run down. Helmholtz and other physicists recognized that the universe as a whole is "running down": eventually, over the vast reaches of cosmic time, the sun and all the stars will have exhausted their fuel, and the cosmos will face the unending darkness and coldness of the "heat death" of the universe.

According to Helmholtz, the "inexorable laws of mechanics" indicate that the store of available energy in the universe must finally be exhausted. The second law of thermodynamics permits the human race ". . . a long but not an endless existence; it threatens us with a day of judgment, the dawn of which is still happily obscured." Eventually, the inescapable working of the laws of physics will force the human race to perish and give way to ". . . new and more complete forms, as the lizards and the mammoth have given place to us."[4]

As the nineteenth century progressed, the pessimistic conclusions of the physicists began to influence leaders in the other scientific disciplines. Charles Darwin, for example, had, on the basis of his evolutionary views, come to expect greater perfection and progress for the human race over time. The implications of the second law, however, challenged this optimism in a fundamental way. For Darwin, it was an "intolerable thought" that the human race and all sentient beings were inevitably "doomed to complete annihilation" after long-continued ages of slow progress. In his autobiography, begun in 1876 but not first published until 1887, Darwin admitted that it seemed a scientific inevitability that "the sun with all the planets will in time grow too cold for life." To those who had a strong faith in the immortality of the human soul, such a prospect might not appear to be so dreadful, but he could not number himself among that company.[5]

In the earlier decades of the twentieth century the implications of thermodynamics were communicated to the general public by the British astronomers Arthur Eddington and James Jeans. In his Gifford Lectures of 1927, Eddington, professor of astronomy at Cambridge, spoke about the "Running Down of the Universe." "Whoever wishes for a universe which can continue indefinitely in activity," he stated, "must lead a crusade against the second law of thermodynamics." The final fate of the universe, according to Eddington, was a state of "chaotic changelessness." In his view such a fate, while certainly a gloomy prospect, was to be preferred to suggestions that the universe might undergo endless cycles of expansion and collapse. "I would feel more content that the universe . . . having achieved whatever may be achieved, lapse back into chaotic changelessness, than that its purpose be banalised by continual repetition." To Eddington it seemed ". . . rather stupid to be doing the same thing over and over again."[6] It is worth noting that Eddington's discussion of the second law led him to address questions of meaning and *purpose* that had generally been excluded from scientific discourse by the positivistic philosophies of science of the nineteenth century.

In a series of popular lectures later published under the title *The Universe Around Us*, Sir James Jeans discussed questions of "Beginnings and Endings" and the long-term implications of the second law. "Energy cannot run downhill forever," he noted, "And so the universe cannot go on forever . . . the active life of the universe must cease." In the very far distant future, the result will be ". . . a dead, although possibly warm universe—a 'heat death.' Such is the teaching of modern thermodynamics." In spite of this gloomy conclusion, Jeans was surprisingly optimistic about the prospects of the human race prior to the final end: ". . . a day of almost unthinkable length stretches before us with unimaginable opportunities for accomplishment."[7] For this British astronomer, the ultimately pessimistic implications of thermodynamics were evidently mitigated by a nearer-term optimism growing out of a faith in the powers of modern science and technology.

One of the best-known responses in the twentieth century to the gloomy message of thermodynamics was the often-quoted passage in Bertrand Russell's book, *Why I Am Not a Christian*. Russell summarized the implications of modern science as he understood it for the human future in this way:

> That man is the product of causes which had no prevision of the end they were achieving; that his origin, his growth, his hopes and fears, his loves and his beliefs, are but the outcome of accidental collocation of atoms; that no fire, no heroism, no intensity of thought and feeling, can preserve an individual life beyond the grave; that all the labors of the ages, all the devotion, all the inspiration, all the noonday brightness of human genius, are destined to extinction in the vast death of the solar system, and the whole temple of Man's achievement must inevitably be buried beneath the debris of a universe in ruins—all these things, if not quite beyond dispute, are yet so nearly certain that no philosophy which rejects them can hope to stand . . . only on the firm foundations of unyielding despair, can the soul's habitation henceforth be safely built.

Despite this eloquent expression of scientific and philosophic despair, Russell went on to say that in practice this gloomy scenario would have little impact on the average person's everyday life. No one really worries much about the fate of the universe millions of years into the future; such considerations merely lead one to "turn your attention to other things."[8] It seems for Russell that the only way that modern man can cope with the gloomy truth that human life must inevitably die out is to live in what psychologists would call a permanent state of avoidance and denial.

More recently in the twentieth century the tradition of what might be called "thermodynamic pessimism" has been expressed in the writing of the Nobel prize-winning American physicist Steven Weinberg. In his widely read book of 1977, *The First Three Minutes: A*

Modern View of the Origin of the Universe, Weinberg brought to the attention of the general public modern science's attempts to apply the methods of elementary particle physics to the understanding of the universe's development in the very first minutes after the "Big Bang." At the end of this book Weinberg offered his personal reflections on the human meaning of the current scientific picture of the origins of the universe and its ultimate fate. It is "almost irresistible," he noted, for human beings to believe that we have a special place in the universe, and that human life is not just some "farcical outcome of a chain of accidents reaching back to the first three minutes." It is not easy for human beings to come to grips with the scientific picture of an earth that is just a "tiny part of an overwhelmingly hostile universe," and the prospect that the present universe "faces a future extinction of endless cold or intolerable heat." The inevitably gloomy conclusion of this analysis, according to Weinberg, in a much-quoted statement, is that "The more the universe seems comprehensible, the more it also seems pointless."[9]

Weinberg's response to such a scenario differs from Bertrand Russell's strategy of avoidance and denial. There may be no comfort in the results of modern science, but perhaps man may find some solace in the process of research itself. For Weinberg, the very attempt to understand the universe lifts human life above the level of farce and meaninglessness, and "gives it some of the grace of tragedy."[10] Human life may have no enduring purpose or meaning, but perhaps it can have the stoical dignity of an honest and scientifically informed self-awareness.

Recent Expressions of Cosmic Optimism

During the last two decades there have been several notable attempts by physicists to challenge the dominant "thermodynamic pessimism" stemming from the nineteenth century.[11] The pioneering effort in this regard was the series of lectures delivered in 1978 at New York University by Freeman Dyson, already noted above. Dyson set himself the task of answering the question of whether intelligent life could continue to exist indefinitely in an "open" universe that continued to expand and cool forever. In order to proceed with his calculations Dyson had to make a number of assumptions. He predicated an "open" universe, that is, a universe in which the total mass of the cosmos was insufficient to halt through gravitational attraction the expansion begun at the "Big Bang." Dyson had already come to the conclusion that if the universe were "closed," that is, if the cosmic expansion would ultimately halt and the universe finally collapse upon itself in a "Big Crunch," then life could not exist forever. In such a case, he reluctantly conceded, "we have no escape from frying." No matter how far the human race might try to burrow itself into the earth to shield itself from the "ever increasing fury" of the background radiation, we could "only postpone by a few million years our miserable end."[12]

Dyson also assumed (l) that the laws of physics did not change over time, and (2) that the relevant laws of physics were already adequately known. With regard to the latter assumption, Dyson was, of course, incorporating the principles of quantum mechanics and discoveries in cosmology such as the evidence for the "Big Bang" that were not known by the nineteenth-century thermodynamicists. To make such assumptions seemed reasonable enough, and without them the calculations could hardly proceed. Dyson freely admitted the highly speculative nature of his investigation, but argued that it was nevertheless intellectually worthwhile to explore the consequences of known physical laws "as far as we can reach into the past or the future," because such extrapolations of known laws into new territory could lead to the asking of important new questions.[13]

Dyson began his investigation by studying the physical processes that would occur in an expanding universe over very long periods of time. He concluded that in about 10^{14} years all the stars would have exhausted their hydrogen fuel and burned out, finally reaching a cold, dark state as white dwarfs, neutron stars, or black holes. After 10^{64} years black holes would have "evaporated" by the emission of heat radiation by the Hawking process. After 10^{65} years, because of a quantum-mechanical effect known as "barrier penetration" (or "quantum tunneling"), the molecules in all remaining solid objects would have moved and rearranged themselves in somewhat random fashion, behaving like the molecules in a liquid, flowing into diffuse, spherical shapes under the influence of gravity. After the incredibly long period of 10^{1500} years, because of nuclear processes, all elements will have decayed or fused into iron. Finally, in the most remote imaginable future, depending on the minimum mass required to form a black hole, all matter will have disappeared into radiation, or else last forever in form of microscopic grains of iron dust.[14]

Having explored the nature of physical processes far into the most remote future, Dyson then turned to the question of the continuance of intelligent life under the extremely cold and dark conditions of an ever-expanding open universe. What forms of sentient life might be able to persist long after *Homo sapiens* and other forms of carbon-based life had become extinct? Answering such a question, of course, involved making certain assumptions about the nature and definition of "life." For the purposes of his calculations, Dyson assumed that the basis of consciousness was not a particular type of matter but rather a particular type of complex *structure,* and that a computer or computer-like structure (such as an organized dust cloud) could be sentient and so considered "alive." Dyson admitted that neither of these assumptions could be known to be true given our present state of knowledge. Proceeding under these assumptions, however, he envisioned a distant future when life would have evolved away from flesh and blood and become embodied in something like a cloud, ". . . a large assemblage of dust grains carrying positive and negative charges, organizing itself and communicating with itself by means of electromagnetic forces."[15]

Having made these assumptions, Dyson proceeded with calculations concerning the energy requirements of such a form of life. This life-form would need to maintain an internal temperature greater than that of the universal background radiation as the universe continued to expand, and would need to continue to radiate waste heat into space. He further postulated that the life-form would adopt a strategy of "hibernation" in order to conserve energy, with increasingly long periods of "sleep" alternating with shorter and shorter cycles of "wakefulness" as the universe continued to cool and expand into the outer darkness. Dyson then calculated that a life-form with a cognitive complexity equivalent to that of the present human species could maintain itself forever, needing only about as much energy as the sun radiates in eight hours.[16] By using the technology of analog rather than digital computers, this life-cloud could enjoy a memory and subjective experience of "endlessly growing capacity." Dyson cheerfully concluded that he had demonstrated the possibility of "a universe of life surviving forever . . . growing without limit in richness and complexity."[17]

Dyson's optimistic vision of the universe's distant future contrasts sharply with the pessimism of Weinberg and the nineteenth-century thermodynamicists. Just how plausible is such a scenario? Apart from strictly quantitative considerations of energy requirements, at the level of "quality of life" considerations the Dyson scenario would seem to leave much to be desired. He assumes that a computer or computer-like structure such as a dust cloud could be sentient; he does not discuss the question of whether such a being would also experience the emotional and affective states that we consider essential to a genuine human existence. The human brain—the most complex entity in the known universe—supports such affective states, but could a computer chip or dust cloud maintain the level of internal complexity needed for endless eons of time under the extreme conditions of cold that Dyson envisions? One might easily imagine a "man-in-the-street" reaction to this vision of a computer-chip existence in the outer darkness of a world forever approaching the coldness of absolute zero: "If that's the best that Dyson has to offer, then I don't want it. I would prefer a normal human life—and death—to the 'life everlasting' of the physicists." Indeed, Dyson's vision of the remote future seems to bear more resemblance to the endless cryo-preservation of a human body in a persistent vegetative state or to the "outer darkness" of the gospel tradition than to the "abundant life" and "life everlasting" of the Christian eschatological hope.

Such qualitative issues aside, however, Dyson's intellectually daring analysis is worthy of the most serious consideration on its own quantitative terms. Even at this level the proposal appears to be seriously if not fatally flawed. Dyson had admitted that his analysis proceeded with the assumptions that (1) the proton does not decay, and (2) black holes of arbitrarily small mass cannot exist.[18] If *either* of these assumptions turns out to be untrue, then matter is unstable, all material objects would disappear leaving only radiation, and the stable structures necessary for life would be impossible.[19]

Furthermore—and this appears to be a fatal flaw in the Dyson proposal—it seems that the Princeton physicist has failed to adequately take into account in his vision of the remotest future a degenerative process which he himself has recognized. As previously noted, on the time scale of $T = 10^{65}$ years, because of the quantum-mechanical effect of barrier penetration, every solid object behaves like a liquid, flowing into a spherical shape like a liquid, its molecules diffusing about like the molecules in a water droplet.[20] This means that any physical object—including Dyson's computer-like "life-form"—will have its internal structure disorganized, given enough time. To restore the internal order and structure necessary for sentient life would require the expenditure of additional amounts of energy that have not been factored into Dyson's calculations.[21] How could this additional energy be captured, stored, and processed in an environment that is approaching absolute zero in temperature?

Furthermore, the life-form continues to dissipate waste heat into space even when it "hibernates" in its "sleeping" state. The energy stored by the life-form is finite. Even though Dyson's model is based on a "subjective time" as experienced by the life-form that *seems*, due to a slowed metabolism, to go on forever, in *real time* the physical processes of the second law of thermodynamics and the degenerative effects of quantum-mechanical barrier penetration continue to operate. A finite store of internal energy that continues to be dissipated into space can not forever support metabolism in real time; nor can an increasingly dilute store of energy in an ever-expanding space be effectively captured to repair the degenerative forces that inevitably destroy the life-form's internal structure. The consequence of this analysis is that Dyson's proposal ultimately fails: the "hibernation" strategy is finally defeated by the inexorable, degenerative effects of the laws of thermodynamics and quantum mechanics. There is no longer sufficient energy available to support even the most minimal level of metabolic activity. Dyson's life-form, after the longest eons of a "virtual-reality" existence, finally expires in the heat death and outer darkness of an ever-expanding universe.

The other scientific "eschatology" to be discussed in this chapter is that presented in John D. Barrow and Frank J. Tipler's *The Anthropic Cosmological Principle* (1986),[22] a major contribution to recent discussions of the issues of design in the universe and extraterrestrial life. In chapter ten of their book these authors address the question of "The Future of the Universe." They recognize that the generally prevailing understanding of the implications of the modern scientific worldview is that mankind is an "insignificant accident lost in the immensity of the Cosmos," that the human species was an "extremely fortuitous accident" unlikely to have occurred elsewhere in the visible universe, and that over the very longest reaches of time, "*Homo sapiens* must eventually become extinct."[23]

Barrow and Tipler develop a scenario concerning the ultimate fate of life in a closed universe, one that will finally collapse in upon itself in a "Big Crunch."[24] *Homo sapiens* may be inevitably doomed, but these authors believe that from a behavioral point of view, intelligent *machines* can be regarded as persons, and that under certain conditions they might be able to survive "forever" under the extreme conditions near the "Final State." These intelligent machines [plasma-like computers?] would be our descendants, transmitting the values of the human race into an arbitrarily distant future.[25]

In a scenario where the boundary between science fact and science fiction becomes very blurred, Barrow and Tipler tell us that life, beginning its expansion from earth, then proceeds to colonize outer space, and ultimately encompasses the entire universe, even affecting the dynamical evolution of the cosmos itself. More and more information is processed at ever faster rates as the universe begins to collapse and to approach the final "Big Crunch" singularity. In terms of the *subjective* time experienced by the intelligent machines, it seems that time lasts forever. Before the final Götterdämmerung-like collapse is reached, these machines attain what Barrow and Tipler call the "Omega Point," where life has gained control of all matter, has expanded into all universes that are logically possible, and will have stored an infinite amount of information—including every bit of information that it is logically possible to know. Life having achieved these God-like attributes, Barrow and Tipler modestly conclude that "this is the end."[26]

This emphatically "Promethean" vision of an aggressively expanding life contrasts starkly with Dyson's "minimalist" vision of hibernating life hanging on by the slenderest of threads in an ever-expanding, cold, dark universe. How much scientific plausibility does the Barrow-Tipler scenario in fact have?

One reviewer of Barrow and Tipler's work, the astronomer and physicist William Press of Harvard's Center for Astrophysics, acknowledges the considerable amount of valuable scientific and historical exposition in the book, but also points to its serious weaknesses. There is a distressing amount of "mathematical flim-flam," according to Press, that is, "quotation of precise results in a manner designed to mislead less-mathematical readers," leading them to jump to the authors' non-mathematical conclusions.[27] Like an inverted pyramid, the conclusions of Barrow and Tipler all too often represent very broad and sweeping generalizations supported by a rather narrow base of empirical data.

Another reviewer, Fred W. Hallberg, has pointed out that the Barrow-Tipler scenario is based on a chain of *nine* assumptions, each of which is quite debatable on empirical grounds. Some of these assumptions are that life and consciousness are inherently expansive, and would want to colonize the universe; that computers that could be pre-programmed to replicate themselves could actually be built; that digital computers could actually be conscious beings; that there would be a continuous upward trend in the amount of disposable income for future intelligent beings to afford the project of intergalactic colonization; that future life could actually be embodied in the form of plasmas or energy fields rather than the molecular structures of the present; that these beings could actually maintain their metabolisms by using exotic sources of gravitational energy as the universe approached its final fiery collapse.[28] Not one of these assumptions is known to be true, and if even *one* of the assumptions were false, then the entire Barrow-Tipler scenario of life in the remotest future would collapse.

One of the critical assumptions made by Barrow and Tipler is that life could in fact maintain itself under the conditions of extreme heat that would characterize the universe as it approached the final state. One is led to agree with the simple conclusion of Jamal Islam, that there ". . . is very little hope for life of any kind surviving the big crunch in a closed universe."[29] This critical assumption has been subjected to a devastating critique by Ellis and Coule. There is simply no known physical theory that could support the idea that the complex, hierarchical structures necessary for life (or a computer) could be maintained under the intense conditions prevailing near the final state. Any such structures would be torn apart by the intense background radiation in a fraction of a second; any computer-like structure would be burned up, torn apart, and melted down into its component parts. The complex structures needed for life could not avoid being buffeted ". . . by photons, electrons, positrons, quarks, and heavier particles at MeV [millions of electron volts] energies and beyond."[30] The Barrow-Tipler scenario inevitably fails as "life" is vaporized in the unspeakable heat of a universe in its final collapse.

Some Concluding Theological Reflections

This analysis has shown, then, that at the end of the day, the attempts by Dyson, Barrow, and Tipler to overcome the "thermodynamic pessimism" of the nineteenth century do not succeed. The inexorable working of the laws of physics, when extrapolated into the most remote reaches of time, provide no reasonable hope that sentient life can exist forever. Steven Weinberg's 1977 conclusion seems substantially correct: the final destiny of intelligent life[31] is to be "fried" in a closed universe or frozen in an open one. Despite the revolutionary new scientific discoveries that have occurred since the nineteenth century—special and general relativity, quantum mechanics, the expanding universe of "Big Bang" cosmology—the fundamental scientific outlook is still the same; thermodynamic pessimism finally prevails.[32]

From a theological perspective the new scientific eschatologies are significant even though they are not convincing on purely scientific grounds. The work of Dyson, Barrow, and Tipler could be seen as expressions at a particular historical period dominated by the scientific imagination of the perennial human search for *transcendence*. From the perspective of Christian theology, it is to be expected that human beings made in the image of God will seek in any culture and historical epoch to transcend the determinisms of circumstance and the iron necessities of physical law. Centuries ago St. Augustine expressed this irrepressible desire for transcendence, an implication of man's creation as *imago Dei,* in the well-known words of his *Confessions:* "Thou hast made us for Thyself, and our heart is restless until it rests in Thee."[33] The search for a scientifically-based immortality is one form that the human quest for transcendence can take at the present stage of history.

Another observation that could be drawn from this analysis is that the unsuccessful attempts by Dyson, Tipler, and Barrow to establish secular versions of "eternal life" provide yet another illustration of the wisdom of seeing the relationship of science and Christian faith as being one of *complementarity* rather than one of competition or dominance. That is to say, science and Christian faith inhabit a common universe and claim to know realities beyond the self, but know their respective realities through different methods, languages, and for quite different purposes.[34] Notable examples from the history of science, such as the Galileo affair in the seventeenth century,[35] and the development of modern geology in the late eighteenth and early nineteenth centuries,[36] show that Christian theologians went beyond the bounds of their proper competence when they attempted to substitute biblical exegesis for empirical research or to impose traditional interpretations of biblical texts regarding natural matters on the natural scientists. If churchmen have been tempted to engage in "cognitive imperialism" in the centuries when the Christian faith has been more socially dominant, then perhaps the opposite danger is more real today. The natural sciences are now cognitively dominant in most areas of modern industrialized societies, and religion plays a more marginal role in shaping public life than in previous centuries.[37] Dyson, Barrow, and Tipler appear to be overstepping proper boundaries from the opposite direction when they attempt to use the methods of physics to argue for conclusions that are metaphysical and religious in nature. The history of the science-religion relationship indicates that both disciplines are best served when theologians do not attempt to derive empirical results from their religious texts, and when physicists do not presume to settle issues of value, meaning, and purpose by the scientific method.

Finally, it might be suggested that these secular eschatologies provide the church with a useful "point of contact" for the communication of the Christian message in a scientific age.[38] The grim conclusions of physics are complemented by the biblical witness that attests that "God *alone* has immortality"[39]—all created beings and all forms of life are perishable and doomed to extinction unless God freely wills, through grace, to bestow upon these creatures everlasting life. If, however, the human species is to find ultimate *hope*[40] of unending life in the face of the history of species extinction on planet Earth, that hope cannot be realistically supplied by the laws of physics. In the face of the pessimism and ultimate hopelessness implied by the inexorable laws of thermodynamics, Christian faith would point modern man to the reality of the resurrection of Jesus Christ, in which God has redemptively transcended the forces of disintegration and death, and "brought life and immortality to light *through the gospel.*"[41] For Christian faith, the grim prospects of a "heat death" of the universe are transcended by the omnipotent power of God attested in the resurrection and by the hope of a transformed cosmos,[42] which will finally be liberated from its bondage to decay.

NOTES

1. Freeman J. Dyson, "Time Without End: Physics and Biology in an Open Universe," *Reviews of Modern Physics* 51:3 (1979): 447–460 at 447. For a more recent attempt to project the long-term future of an open universe, see Fred C. Adams and Gregory Laughlin, "A Dying Universe: The Long-Term Fate and Evolution of Astrophysical Objects," *Reviews of Modern Physics* 69 (1997): 337–372. A popular version of this latter article may be found in *Sky and Telescope* 96:2 (August 1998): 32–39. Unlike Dyson, however, Adams and Laughlin remain agnostic on the question of whether or not life and sentience could survive in the far distant future of such an open universe.

2. Ibid., p. 448.

3. For general introductions to thermodynamics and the second law, see Hans C. Ohanian, *Physics* (New York: W. W. Norton, 1985), pp. 520–525; George B. Arfken, David F. Griffing, Donald C. Kelly, and Joseph Priest, *University Physics* (New York: Academic Press, 1984), pp. 444–458; and C. J. Adkins, *An Introduction to Thermal Physics* (Cambridge: Cambridge University Press, 1987). For a more advanced treatment, see Mark W. Zemansky, *Heat and Thermodynamics,* 5th ed. (New York: McGraw-Hill, 1968), ch. 9, "Entropy," pp. 214–250. A readable discussion of thermodynamics for a general audience, with helpful insights on historical and philosophical dimensions of the subject, is provided by Martin and Inge F. Goldstein, *The Refrigerator and the Universe: Understanding the Laws of Energy* (Cambridge: Harvard University Press, 1993).

4. Hermann Helmholtz, *Popular Lectures on Scientific Subjects,* tr. E. Atkinson (London: Longmans, Green, & Co., 1884), pp. 137–171 at 170, 171. It was not widely recognized in the nineteenth century, but the second law implied a

finite age for the universe: if the available energy was indeed running down, it could not have been running down *forever*. For the attempts of the British physicist William Thompson (Lord Kelvin) to use the principles of thermodynamics to calculate an absolute date for the age of the earth, see Joe D. Burchfield, *Lord Kelvin and the Age of the Earth* (Chicago: University of Chicago Press, 1975; 1990).

5. Nora Barlow, ed. *The Autobiography of Charles Darwin: 1809–1882* (London: Collins, 1958), p. 92.

6. A. S. Eddington, *The Nature of the Physical World* (Cambridge: Cambridge University Press, 1928), p. 86.

7. James Jeans, *The Universe Around Us* (Cambridge: Cambridge University Press, 1929), p. 320.

8. The passage from Russell is quoted in John D. Barrow and Frank J. Tipler, *The Anthropic Cosmological Principle* (Oxford: Clarendon Press, 1986), p. 167.

9. Steven Weinberg, *The First Three Minutes* (London: Andre Deutsch, 1977), p. 154.

10. Ibid., p. 155.

11. Dyson (1979), op. cit., and Barrow and Tipler (1986), op. cit. These technical treatments, together with related issues, are discussed in more popular form in Jamal N. Islam, *The Ultimate Fate of the Universe* (Cambridge: Cambridge University Press, 1983); Frank Close, *End: Cosmic Catastrophe and the Fate of the Universe* (London: Simon & Schuster, 1988); Paul Davies, *The Last Three Minutes: Conjectures about the Fate of the Universe* (London: Weidenfeld & Nicolson, 1994); and Frank J. Tipler, *The Physics of Immortality* (London: Weidenfeld & Nicolson, 1994).

12. Dyson, op. cit., p. 448. New evidence reported in 1998 appears to indicate that the expansion of the universe is accelerating rather than decelerating, and that the universe is indeed open, destined to expand forever: John Wilford, "Shocked Cosmologists Find Universe Expanding Faster," *New York Times* on the Web, March 3, 1998; Ann K. Finkbeiner, "Cosmic Yardsticks: Supernovae and the Fate of the Universe," *Sky and Telescope* 96:3 (September 1998): 38–45.

13. Ibid., pp. 449, 450.

14. These results, and others, together with Dyson's detailed calculations and assumptions, are found on pp. 450–453.

15. Ibid., p. 454. Dyson's discussion of biological processes, from which the following citations and calculations are cited, is found on pp. 453–457. It is significant that Dyson works with a rather minimalist model of sentient life, one based on computers and information processing. Of the two processes that biologists would consider essential to the definition of life—*metabolism* and *replication*—Dyson focuses only on the former and essentially ignores the latter. His calculations are concerned to show that some future life-form might be able to store and metabolize energy indefinitely, without the necessity of reproducing itself.

16. Dyson deals only with the amount of energy presumably needed to support the life-form, and does not deal with the "detailed architectural problems" of what physical structures and mechanisms might actually be able to capture this energy from the environment, store it, and then use it metabolically.

17. Ibid., p. 459. Dyson also offers calculations (pp. 457–459) that presumably show that such life-forms could continue to communicate with each other across the vast reaches of space in an ever-expanding universe, but these calculations will not be considered in the present discussion.
18. Ibid., pp. 450, 453.
19. At the time of this writing (1998), the empirical evidence concerning the stability or decay of the proton is inconclusive. Strictly speaking, if the proton does decay with an expected lifetime on the order of 10^{31} years, as predicted by Grand Unification Theories, not *all* matter would cease to exist: there would still be a plasma-like cosmos consisting of electrons, positrons, neutrinos, and photons. Nevertheless, it is difficult to imagine a world in which the stable structures necessary for sentient life could be maintained with such components. In such a case there is the additional difficulty of preventing the electrons and positrons from annihilating one another in bursts of radiation.
20. Dyson, op. cit., p. 452.
21. This criticism is also raised in the important article by Steven Frautschi, "Entropy in an Expanding Universe," *Science* 217: 4560 (13 August 1982): 593–599 at 599. At the time of writing Frautschi was a professor of physics at Caltech in Pasadena.
22. See note 8 above. This same general point of view regarding the ultimate fate of the universe is presented in a somewhat more popular form in Tipler's highly speculative book, *The Physics of Immortality: Modern Cosmology, God, and the Resurrection of the Dead* (New York: Doubleday, 1994).
23. Barrow and Tipler, op. cit., pp. 613, 615.
24. As of 1996 astronomers generally believed that the available evidence was insufficient to decide the question of whether the universe is closed or open. In one recent discussion of this issue, on the basis of their reading of evidence from the Hubble space telescope, Petersen and Brandt conclude that it is somewhat more likely that "we are constrained to live in [an open] universe that is expanding forever": Carolyn Collins Petersen and John C. Brandt, *Hubble Vision: Astronomy with the Hubble Space Telescope* (Cambridge: Cambridge University Press, 1995), p. 229. Cf. the new evidence reported in 1998, which also appears to favor an open universe, cited in note 12 above.
25. Barrow and Tipler, op. cit., p. 615.
26. Ibid., pp. 675–677: the end of their book, and the end [final state] of life in the universe.
27. William H. Press, "A Place for Teleology?" *Nature* 320 (27 March 1986): 315–316 at 315.
28. Fred W. Hallberg, "Barrow and Tipler's Anthropic Cosmological Principle," *Zygon* 23:2 (June 1988): 139–157 at 147–151. Hallberg points out that Barrow and Tipler seem to be inspired by the evolutionary speculations of the French Jesuit Teilhard de Chardin, *The Phenomenon of Man* (1959), in which de Chardin envisions life moving toward an "Omega Point" of higher cosmic consciousness. The Barrow-Tipler thesis is also severely criticized by W. R. Stoeger and G. F. R. Ellis, "A Response to Tipler's Omega-Point Theory" [Tipler, *The Physics of Immortality* (1994), a further extension of the Barrow-Tipler position of 1986], *Science and Christian Belief* 7:2 (1995): 163–172: in terms of its

major elements, the theory " . . . is not testable even in principle, either scientifically or theologically—certainly not relative to its key conclusions," p. 167.

29. Islam, op. cit. (n. 11 above), p. 114. Islam also raises (p. 134) the perceptive question, "Can intelligent beings survive indefinitely the social conflicts . . . that beset [modern] society?" The Barrow-Tipler thesis naively seems to expect that beings in the far distant future will not be afflicted with the wars, violence, crime, and other socially destructive behaviors that have plagued all known societies from the dawn of history.

30. G. F. R. Ellis and D. H. Coule, "Life at the End of the Universe?" *General Relativity and Gravitation* 26:7 (1994): 731–739 at 738.

31. Apart, of course, from the possibility of divine intervention—a possibility not entertained from Weinberg's naturalistic standpoint.

32. This is also the conclusion of Martin and Inge Goldstein, op. cit. (n. 3 above), p. 388: "So it appears that in spite of the new insights of quantum mechanics and relativity, the grim inference for the future drawn from the second law in the nineteenth century is not far wrong."

33. Saint Augustine, *Confessions,* tr. Vernon J. Bourke (Washington, D.C.: Catholic University of America Press, 1953), Bk. I, ch. 1.

34. For a helpful discussion of various ways of understanding the relationship between religion and the natural sciences, see Ian G. Barbour, *Religion in an Age of Science* (London: SCM Press, 1990), esp. pp. 3–92, "Ways of Relating Science and Religion."

35. Jerome J. Langford, *Galileo, Science, and the Church,* 3rd ed. (Ann Arbor: University of Michigan Press, 1966; 1992) provides a cogent analysis of the historical, scientific, and political dimensions of this pivotal controversy. The best analysis of the important role of presuppositions concerning biblical interpretation and theology is found in Richard J. Blackwell, *Galileo, Bellarmine, and the Bible* (Notre Dame, IN: University of Notre Dame Press, 1991).

36. The valuable articles by Davis A. Young, "Scripture in the Hands of the Geologists," *Westminster Theological Journal* 49 (1987): 1–34 and 257–304, document the misguided attempts by some Christian workers during the early years of geology to derive geological data directly from the texts of Scripture. It would seem that the "Creation Science" movement today is repeating the errors of the past by continuing to treat biblical texts as (potentially) primary sources for strictly scientific conclusions. The most comprehensive scholarly account of the history and development of the modern "Creation Science" movement is provided by Ronald L. Numbers, *The Creationists: The Evolution of Scientific Creationism* (Berkeley, CA: University of California Press, 1992).

37. The thesis of the "privatization" of religion in modern industrial societies has been developed in various ways by Peter Berger, *The Sacred Canopy: A Sociological Theory of Religion* (Garden City, NY: Doubleday, 1969), and David F. Wells, *God In the Wasteland: The Reality of Truth in a World of Fading Dreams* (Grand Rapids: Eerdmans, 1994).

38. The concept of a "point of contact" in the culture for the Christian message has been discussed, for example, by Helmut Thielicke, *The Evangelical Faith:* v. I: *Prolegomena: The Relation of Theology to Modern Thought Forms,* tr. Geoffrey W. Bromiley (Grand Rapids: Eerdmans, 1974), pp. 39, 139, 144ff. See also the discussion in a previous theological era by Paul Tillich of his "method of corre-

lation" ("The method of correlation explains the contents of the Christian faith through existential questions and theological answers in mutual interdependence") and "apologetic theology" ("Apologetic theology . . . answers the question implied in the 'situation' in the power of the eternal message, and with the means provided by the situation whose questions it answers") in Paul Tillich, *Systematic Theology: Three Volumes in One* (Chicago: University of Chicago Press, 1967), v. I, pp. 6, 60.

39. 1 Timothy 6:16, emphasis added. The fossil record shows that in the history of life on earth, extinction is the rule and not the exception: David M. Raup, *Extinction: Bad Genes or Bad Luck?* (New York: W. W. Norton, 1991). The average life span of a species in the fossil record is on the order of four million years.

40. In recent Protestant theology the theme of *hope* has been most systematically developed by Jürgen Moltmann, *Theology of Hope: On the Ground and the Implications of a Christian Eschatology,* tr. James W. Leitch (London: SCM Press, 1967). For Moltmann, hope is " . . . the foundation and the mainspring of theological thinking as such," and the resurrection of Christ is not only a " . . . consolation in a life . . . doomed to die, but it is God's contradiction of suffering and death" (pp. 19, 21). In a secular context, the importance of a future hope as a critical factor in the experience of many who survived the Nazi death camps is documented in the fascinating work of the Viennese psychiatrist Viktor E. Frankl, *Man's Search For Meaning: An Introduction to Logotherapy* (Boston: Beacon Press, 1962). The story of how the Christian church and its message provided a sense of hope to many pagans amidst the growing pessimism of late antiquity is documented in E. R. Dodds, *Pagan and Christian in an Age of Anxiety* (Cambridge: Cambridge University Press, 1965), focusing on the period from Marcus Aurelius to Constantine.

41. 2 Timothy 1:10, emphasis added.

42. Romans 8:21, 22; Revelation 21:1.

This chapter was originally published in *Science and Christian Belief* vol. 11, no. 1 (April 1999): 15–27.

CHAPTER 8

A Brief Note on the Problem of the Beginning: From the Modern Cosmology and "Transcendental Hikmah" Perspectives

PIROOZ FATOORCHI

Pirooz Fatoorchi is a researcher at the Institute for Humanities and Cultural Studies, Tehran, Iran, and editor of *Science and Religion Bulletin* (in Persian). His publications (all in Persian) include *The Problem of the Beginning from Modern Cosmology and Transcendent Hikmah* as well as several essays on theology and science.

Cosmology is derived from two Greek words, *Kosmos* (meaning "order," "harmony," and "the world") and *Logos* (signifying "word" or "discourse"). Cosmology in its broad sense is the study of Cosmos—the universe at large.

Until the early twentieth century, cosmology was not a scientific discipline, but following the classification of Christian Wolff it was considered to be a branch of metaphysics. In his classificatory scheme of philosophy, cosmology became the new denomination of the traditional "natural philosophy" and along with theology and psychology became a subdomain of "special metaphysics." After him, this classification was accepted as standard, so that Kant in his discussions about the domains of traditional metaphysics followed Wolff's scheme (Agazzi 1991: 44, 45).

Einstein's "Cosmological Considerations on the General Theory of Relativity" (1917) is regarded as the starting point of a new phase in cosmology. Using his theory of general relativity, he proposed the first detailed model for the large-scale structure of the universe. Subsequently, the developing of innovative experiments and theories, and the accessing of new sources of empirical data via the use of some modern technologies, resulted in cosmology's acceptance as a scientific discipline. Modern cosmology is that branch of science (chiefly astronomy and physics) concerned with the universe as a whole (Lightman and Brawer 1990: 1).

Did the cosmos begin or has it existed forever? Once this question was regarded exclusively in the philosophical or theological context, but nowadays, the "problem of the beginning" is also one of the central concerns of modern cosmologists. Although the scientific approach to this problem has its own characteristics that distinguish it from metaphysical and theological views, the nature of the problem is such that, almost from the beginning, presenting cosmological models and theories has been associated with a wide range of conclusions, implications, and responses in the realm of "philosophy" and "theology." Furthermore, it is striking that even some cosmologists who are among eminent scientists have evidently incorporated their philosophical inclinations into their choice or preference of different theories. Some instances will be mentioned later.

The current interdisciplinary inquiries of "science and theology" study the "problem of the beginning" widely from various cosmological and philosophical/theological points of view, hence involving a significant number of scientists, philosophers, and theologians in the related debates. Due to the metaphysical and theological dimensions of this study, deliberate and appropriate involvement of "Islamic philosophy" (Hikmah), particularly, "Transcendental Hikmah," could help enrich the field and enlighten some of the difficult issues. In the genuine sources of Islamic thought, there are norms and principles from which useful statements can be inferred concerning the "problem of the beginning." This, of course, is provided by sufficient analysis and cautious examination, following necessary conditions and avoiding confusion of philosophical debates with scientific concepts and theories.

Modern Cosmology and the Problem of the Beginning

Steady-State Theory and the Backgrounds of the Big Bang Cosmology

Among a few of astronomical beliefs that remained even after the Copernican revolution was the belief in a static universe. Based on this belief, celestial bodies, despite their complex and various motions, always remained the same; they did not expand and change. The astronomical observations were consonant with this idea and even after the invention of the telescope, no evidence was obtained to the contrary. It was this belief that led Einstein, initially, to alter his original equations via adding a "cosmological constant." He later called this mutilation "the biggest blunder of my life" (Parker 1988: 44; Pagels 1984: 50). Meanwhile, Friedmann, the Russian mathematician and meteorologist, began studying Einstein's original equations and their cosmological implications. In 1922, he suggested some solutions and models that allowed him to predict the expansion of the cosmos seven years before the Hubble discovery. So it was Friedmann not Einstein who founded the theoretical and mathematical basis of what came to be called the Big Bang cosmology (Lightman and Brawer 1990: 4). In 1929, using astronomical evidence, Edwin Hubble showed that the galaxies are speeding away from one another, and that the recessional speed is proportional to distance. This means that the universe is expanding—perhaps the most important discovery of modern cosmology. In this way, then, the static picture of the universe was to be refuted.

With the discovery of the general expansion of the universe, it seemed natural that if the universe is expanding, then as we move backward in time the universe should be more and more condensed until we arrive at an infinitely dense and small point from which the universe began—the same as the concept of the Big Bang theory. Although Hubble's discoveries implied this picture, they were not, on their own, sufficient to force scientists to accept the Big Bang theory. The steady-state theory, for instance, while accepting the expansion of the universe, attempted to suggest an interpretation that nevertheless avoided any "beginning" or "end" of the cosmos (Brush 1992: 37; Davies 1992: 51). Bondi, Gold, and Hoyle were the originators of this theory in 1948, and for about two decades it was considered the leading competitor to the Big Bang theory. According to the steady-state theory, if the universe is expanding forever, there is no need for the initial Big Bang. To justify this picture, it was postulated that the density of matter remains constant through continuous creation of "new matter" (Hawking 1989: 66). The universe would therefore look more or less the same at all times and one could say that it is not static but in a steady state.

Today, regarding evidence for the Big Bang theory especially from the COBE satellite, almost all cosmologists have no interest in the steady-state theory (Lightman and Brawer 1990: 20; Weinberg 1993: 180)—though, in 1990, Hoyle and a few of his colleagues tried to revive it in a new form (Brush 1992: 40).

The Big Bang Theory

The Big Bang theory provides a mathematical description for the evolution of the cosmos, according to which the universe started from an infinite density and very high temperature and then expanded, thinned out, and cooled.

The general theory of relativity is the basis of Big Bang cosmology. One of the essential features of general relativity is that it correlates the affairs of matter with the affairs of space and time. This correlation has significant implications for the beginning of the universe. Thus, as we move backward in time, the galaxies get closer and closer together until they merge. Then the galactic material gets squeezed more and more until a singular point of enormous density is reached. At this "singularity," the gravitational force and the density of matter are infinite. Since there is a mutual relationship between space and matter, the infinite compression of matter involves the infinite shrinkage of space. And the correlation of matter, space, and time further implies that "time" must disappear too. Thus, the material singularity is also a space-time singularity (Davies 1992: 48, 50). According to the Big Bang cosmology, the universe has a beginning: after an initial singularity, the entire cosmos came into existence abruptly in a sort of a gigantic explosion. This explosion did not occur at a point in space or time, but according to this model, space and time themselves came into being. Therefore, the question of the Big Bang's "when" and "where" is meaningless. As Paul Davies puts it:

> . . . the question "what happened before the Big Bang" is meaningless. There was no such epoch as "before the Big Bang," because time began with the Big Bang (Davies 1996: 32).

Because all our laws of physics are formulated in terms of space and time, these laws cannot apply beyond the point at which space and time cease to exist. Rather, these laws will break down at the "initial singularity" and they will not enable one to predict events after the Big Bang. Similarly, there is no way that one can determine what happened before the Big Bang from a knowledge of events after the Big Bang (Hawking 1989: 66). This "singularity" in the equations of many cosmological models is shown by "$t = 0$" (Stoeger 1988: 222). At the same time, $t = 0$ exhibits the limitations of the explanatory power of this model. In principle, every cosmological model attempts to interpret the universe within its conceptual framework and to push back the boundaries of intelligibility of the universe. Yet, every model has its own limitations and is unable to answer some questions. Milton Munitz, a philosopher, calls these limitations the "conceptual horizons" (Munitz 1986: 167). The concepts such as "singularity," "beginning of time," or "t = 0" exhibits the incapacity of the Big Bang theory in those conditions, because at "t = 0"—and even in the very early universe—the classical general theory of relativity cannot apply. Therefore, these concepts have their meaning only within the context of the Big Bang theory and according to its limitations, and do not necessarily refer to an actual ontological states of affairs (Stoeger 1988: 222; Munitz 1986: 175).

This, of course, does not means that there is anything wrong with the Big Bang theory, but merely exhibits the limitations of its explanatory power, and there is no doubt about the theory within its limits. Although there are some unresolved and difficult issues (such as how the galaxies were formed), all the evidence—especially recent discoveries—indicates that the Big Bang cosmology provides an accurate accounting of the evolution of the universe from 0. 01 seconds after the Bang [singularity] until today, some fifteen or so billion years later (Turner 1985, quoted in Drees 1990: 375).

In spite of the increasing success of the Big Bang theory after the 1930s, some cosmologists was not satisfied with the theory. This dissatisfaction was not always based on scientific grounds alone, but, as we shall see, in some cases it was due to nonscientific motivations. There are other cosmological models and theories that could be useful in our discussion:

- ⚜ Oscillating Universe Hypothesis
- ⚜ Inflationary Theory
- ⚜ Chaotic Inflation Model
- ⚜ Quantum Cosmology

Here, because of severe limits of space, we only deal with quantum cosmology, in brief.

Quantum Cosmology

In some respects, the quantum cosmological models affect the "problem of the beginning" more powerfully than the Big Bang cosmology. Is it possible to explain the very early universe using the methods of theoretical physics? For many years following the development of the Big Bang model, the answer to this question was thought to be "no." At *Planck time,* when the universe was a tiny fraction of a second old (about 10^{-43} sec., after the beginning of the universe in the Big Bang model), the universe had a density of 10^{93} grams per cubic centimeter, and space-time was shrunk to very small dimensions. Under such circumstances, the quantum theory has a very significant role. The study of this era is called "quantum cosmology" (Lightman and Brawer 1990: 38; Drees 1991: 374). Within the last twenty years much effort has been directed toward the goal of constructing a genuine quantum cosmological theory (Halliwell 1991: 82; Isham 1993: 51). One of the most important proposals was offered by John Hartle and Stephen Hawking in the early 1980s. The Hartle-Hawking proposal avoids the initial singularity or t = 0 as in the Big Bang theory, and this does not mean a past or future infinity. According to this proposal, space-time has no edge, though the cosmos will have a beginning and an end without any singularity (Drees 1991: 381; Russell 1994: 561). Closer to the singularity in the Big Bang model, time gradually loses its ordinary properties and begins to "turn into" space. In the Hartle-Hawking proposal, time emerges continuously and does not switch on abruptly. Thus, in Hartle and Hawking's theory there is no initial singularity where the theory breaks down. Only our interpretation, in terms of our usual notion of time, breaks down. Hawking in his writings suggests that the cosmos is finite but unbounded just as the surface of the earth is finite but unbounded (Hawking 1988: 135).

Although there are some serious difficulties in quantum cosmological models and they are far from any kind of direct empirical testing, eventually it seems that quantum cosmology must be dealt with to understand the very early universe (Lightman and Brawer 1990: 39).

Nowadays, the number of cosmological models is increasing and their speculation and abstract nature is increasing, as well. Hence, Steven Weinberg in the afterward added to the new edition of *The First Three Minutes* (1993), wrote, " . . . a gap has opened between what theorists are led to speculate and what astronomers are able to observe" (Weinberg 1993: 190).

"Transcendental Hikmah" and the Contingency of the Universe

As indicated before, in order to deduce the viewpoints of "Transcendental Hikmah" about the "beginning of the cosmos" and benefit from these perspectives in the relevant debates of "science and theology," one should focus on those topics that discuss the issue of the "contingency" (coming-into-being) of the universe. In this study, it is also desirable to highlight the distinctions of "Transcendental Hikmah" from other schools of philosophy and theology to illustrate its merit and eminence.

The issue of the contingency of the cosmos has always attracted great minds of religion and wisdom. Besides its deep trace in the long history of human thought, the significance of this issue is readily measured through a quick glance at various theological and philosophical methodologies among Islamic thinkers. The problem of the contingency of the universe has been one of the most controversial topics among followers of different schools of thought.

Both groups of Islamic philosophers and theologians accept the essence of the contingency of the cosmos and that it is preceded by "nonbeing." However, there is a clear diversity in how the "contingency" is perceived, and this diversion is particularly tractable between philosophers and theologians preceding Sadra (the founder of "Transcendental Hikmah"). Three major factors, independently or together, play a fundamental role in how Islamic scholars perceive the issue: (a) their view of the world of nature, (b) their approach toward knowledge of the Divine, and (c) their interpretation of religious understanding.

The Perspective of the Classical Islamic Theologians (Mutakallimun)

The classical Islamic theologians have presented a strictly temporal picture of the creation of the world *(huduth e 'alam)* and have taken the usages of Islamic texts and Law to imply this very same type of contingency (coming-into-being). Their outlook on nature as well as their method of theology is in line with this type of understanding of religious texts. The method of the theologians was that they would first prove the createdness of the world, and then from the temporal contingency of the world they would conclude the existence of God. Finally in explaining the attributes of God they would take the temporal contingency *(huduth e zamani)* of the world as a proof of His power and freedom.

The following diagram summarizes this method:

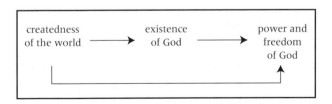

According to the most important proofs that are considered in many authoritative books on *Kalam* (classical Islamic theology), the natural world—that is, the "world of bodies"—is a finite collection, the parts of which, due to their movements and stillness, are all temporal contingents. So it is concluded that the world of bodies—or the natural world—is also a temporal contingent (Tusi 1986: 170).

The Opinions of the Peripatetic (Mashsha i) and Illuminationist (Ishraqi) Philosophers before Sadra

Contrary to the theologians, Peripatetic philosophers *(Mashsha iun)* did not base their proofs of the existence of God and His Divine attributes on the temporal contingency of the world. In a similar vein, they explicated the Divine attributes in such a way so as to make inappropriate and unnecessary the supposition that the acts of God are limited and intermittent. According to them, it is precisely because of the fact that the Divine essence is from all perspectives absolutely necessary that Its activity is most complete and Its effusion absolute. So if, like the theologians, we also hold the world to be a temporal contingency, then it would lead to the nullification of Divine generosity as well as the limitation of His attributes. Hence it is this type of theology on the part of the philosophers that has called them to hold the natural world to be an eternal and unceasing act of God. In the words of Tusi:

> Now it is because the First Principle is, according to them [classical theologians], eternal and perfect in activity that they have decreed the world, which is Its act, to be eternal; and this is to be found in their theological sciences (Tusi 1983: 82).

The opinions of the Illuminationists *(Ishraqiun)* on this issue coincide with those of the Peripatetic philosophers. Shaykh al-Ishraq (Suhrawardi) explains this view in the first and third chapters of the third section of *Hikmat al-Ishraq*. In the third chapter he does so in the following concise way:

> The Divine effusion is eternal; so as the Agent is neither changing nor diminishing, the world perpetuates with Its perpetuity (Suhrawardi 1952: 181).

On the other hand, still in line with the view that the Islamic philosophers have of the natural world and in consideration of certain philosophical proofs—as are to be found in the authoritative texts of the

Peripatetics and the Illuminationists—it is held that preceding any given temporal contingent there exists an infinite chain of temporal contingents that are prior to it. In other words, no matter how far back we go in time, and continue to trace the chain of events, we will never reach an end. This is the very same thing as what the philosophers term an "infinite regression of accidental supplementary causes." Sometimes they also say that "events have no beginning." They not only hold this "infinity" to be just possible but rather know it to be necessary—this case being different from the infinite regress of "complete essential causes," which is impossible (Ibn Sina 1984a: 265).

It was this particular trend of the philosophers before Mulla Sadra that led them to speak of the pre-eternity of the world during their expositions of the Divine attributes and natural order. In spite of this fact, as has already been covered, this group of philosophers accept, in principle, the creation of the world but believe in a type of contingency applying to it that is termed "essential contingency" *(al-huduth al-dhati)* and that requires an "essential nonexistence" to precede every "possible existent." They feel that just this belief by itself suffices to fulfill the criteria of the religious scriptures on the subject (Lahiji 1985: 150).

The Novel Approach of "Transcendental Hikmah"

The issue of creation in "Transcendental Hikmah" took to itself a completely new form—making it stand out and apart from the approaches of both the theologians and the ancient philosophers. Sadra (Sadr al-Din Shirazi, also called "Mulla Sadra," 1572–1640; one of the greatest Islamic philosophers and the founder of "Transcendental Hikmah") attempted to resolve the issue in a novel way by drawing upon Qur'anic verses, traditions, and the principles of "Transcendental Hikmah" as well as by referring to the inspirations of true Islamic mysticism. In this new approach, the positive points of the opinions of past theologians and philosophers are kept while the negative and problematic ones are avoided. Moreover, in this perspective an ontological view of nature has led to the formation of a new natural philosophy within the framework of Islamic philosophy.

The underlying reason for this development must be sought for amidst the main features and proofs of the theory of "trans-substantial motion" *(al-harakat al-jawhariyyah* or "motion in the category of substance"). To explain, the apparent motion within bodies falling under any one or more of the "accidental categories" has always been a readily accepted fact amongst intellectuals; but that the essence and substance of a thing can also undergo gradual change and "motion" has been thought by most to be tantamount to the negation of the subsistence of the subject of motion (Ibn Sina 1984b: 98). According to the precepts of "Transcendent Hikmah," however, motion is an aspect of existence itself—revealing the innate reality of the moving subject. It is not something extraneous that needs to be "added" to the subject. The disparity between "motion" and the "subject of motion" is a function of analysis in the mind. It is only a conceptual disparity and "otherness," for *in concreto* they are one and the same thing.

To explain more fully: the proofs for the theory of " trans-substantial motion" indicate that the roots and basis for the apparent and accidental movements of bodies lie in changes and transformations occurring within the substance and essences of those very same bodies. Hence attempting to explain accidental transformations without recourse to essential ones is an exercise in futility. In the words of Sabzawari (the great Islamic philosopher; 1797/98–1878), "Trans-substantial motion is to an accidental one as a spirit is to a body" (Sabzawari 1981: 97). It is in this manner that "flux" and change find their way into the very substance of natural existents and indeed encompass all aspects of their being. This perspective has lead to existence being fundamentally classified as either *fixed* or *in flux,* flux and change being seen as a modality of existence and an analytical attribute derived from an ontological analysis of natural essences and substances (Sadra 1981b: 131; Sadra 1981c: 282).

One of the corollaries of "trans-substantial motion" is that all the accidental categories, which are nothing but different levels and manifestations of substance, undergo change and transformation in lieu of the motion within that substance. Hence motion within the category of substance in no way negates the subsistence of the subject undergoing that motion. By this, the difficulty with accepting trans-substantial motion, which was alluded to earlier, is easily removed (Sadra 1981b: 85, 86).

Now because "time" is the quantity or amount of motion and change, it follows that trans-substantial motion defines trans-substantial time *(al-zaman al-jawhari)*—the latter only exemplifying the amount of motion or change in a substance. It is quintessential to note that according to "Transcendent Hikmah," "time" like "motion" is a modality of "gradual" existence *(al-wujud al-mutedarej*—being in its aspect of becoming). It cannot be counted as just an external container for the subject in motion. Similarly, even though motion and time are different and separate from an analytic and conceptual point of view, they are, ontologically speaking, one and the same reality. That is they are one existence in flux seen from two perspectives. Sadra says:

> It is certain that any differentiation between "motion" and "time" is feasible only in the domain of thought. Their existence in the real world is unified by one "being," as previously noted in this book (Sadra 1981b: 200).

When change comes to form the very being of any existent, that existent is at every moment renewed—every renewal being is an independent event and "becoming," taking place in time and on the level of the essence or substance of the thing. This is what is termed as a "temporal-substantial contingency" *(al-huduth al-zamani al-jawhari)*. All this implies that every natural existent, in all its aspects, is at every moment and in its very substance continuously being renewed and recreated—that is, it is temporally contingent. Now because the natural world is nothing but the sum total of natural existents it follows that the natural world is also being recreated every instant and is, in this meaning, temporally contingent. Sadra puts it in *Al-Mashair* (The book of metaphysical penetrations):

> The existence of the universe, with all it contains, is preceded by its nonbeing in a temporal sense. This means that the nonexistence of every entity precedes its existence in time, as its being precedes its disappearance when it annihilates. In general, all material substances, celestial or elemental, soul or body, possess evolutional characteristics, and their being is renewing and inconstant (Sadra 1983: 339–342).

Commonalities and Points of Divergence between "Transcendental Hikmah" and the Opinions of the Islamic Theologians and Philosophers

1. In "Transcendent Hikmah," under the section of metaphysics in its particular sense, the role played by what is called the "Proof of the Veracious," in proving the existence of God, is much more central and fundamental than those arguments that are based upon the creation of the world. (The former is based on analyzing the existence qua existence—the Ontological Argument par excellence.) Hence it can be concluded that the method of "Transcendental

Hikmah" is closer to the way of the Islamic philosophers preceding
Sadra than it is to that of the classical theologians.

2. Sadra is in agreement with the theologians in that the religious
   texts and holy scriptures do in fact allude to the world being temporally contingent or created in time—its being logically or essentially contingent is not enough (Sadra 1987: 186). But what becomes apparent after turning to the key places in his works where
   the matter of the creation of the world is discussed (especially the
   tenth station of the third journey of his book *Al-Hikmat al-muta
   aliyah* and his treatise *Risalah fi Huduth al-'Alam*) is his disagreement with the theologians on what is meant by "world" (universe) and exactly how it is "temporally contingent." In speaking
   of the natural world, theologians imply a "total whole" that includes the past, present, and future. This conglomeration they call
   the world. Accordingly, they attribute temporal contingency to this
   totality. Mulla Sadra on the other hand denies any such universal
   and totalistic existence of past events:

   > Past events cannot be identified as a "collected whole" to ne-
   > cessitate the argue of whether or not this whole is preceded
   > by its nonbeing; because what is past does not exist and
   > nonexistence by no means utilizes a whole, hence, cannot
   > carry any statement (Sadra 1981c: 311).

   In these same places, he holds that this "total" world is a mentally
   posited idea to which real existence cannot be attributed—the existent world not being independent of its constituent parts. Now
   because an existential attribute like "temporally contingency" or
   "eternity" *(al-qidam)* cannot be given to a mentally posited concept, it follows that the world in its meaning of a total whole is
   neither temporally contingent nor eternal. In Sadra's opinion, the
   natural world is nothing but the collection of its parts. It is the latter that are in reality subject to temporal contingency. Each and
   every part, at every moment and for perpetuity, is being created
   and hence is temporally contingent. The following text is an example of such an analysis:

   > So it has been established and made definite that bodies, all
   > of them, are in their essence "being in flux" and that their
   > form is a form of change and transmutation and every one of
   > them is a created, contingent being, with a prior temporal
   > nonbeing. They are generated and corrupted; there being no

continuity to their existential ipseity, their given natures, nor their universal concepts—for a "universal" has no *in concreto* existence. They have no collective *in concreto* existence either, for it to be attributed as temporally contingent or eternal. So just as a "universal" has no existence but through (its) particulars, in the same way the collectivity or total also has no existence but the existence of its parts. As the existent parts are many, so too are their temporal contingencies, multiple contingencies (Sadra 1981c: 297).

3. One of the results that comes to the fore while proving the theory of "trans-substantial motion" is that "time" is a part of the substantial ipseity of things and is not just an external "container" or place in which events happen. Nor must it be taken to be an accident occurring to subjects undergoing motion and change. Now it is because the classical theologians perceived time to be outside of and apart from natural existents and thought of the world as the total collection of natural existents that they imagined the temporal contingency of the world in terms of a unique historical event. In this way they felt that if we only go back far enough in time we will reach the temporal point of origin of the world. A study of the attempts of the theologians to prove the temporal contingency of the world clearly shows this to be true (Tusi 1980: 208).

   Opposing the classical theologians on this count, Sadra does not accept their interpretation of the temporal contingency of the world. He does not explain it as an historical event, but rather pictures it as an all-comprehensive and perpetual process. According to this view, temporal contingency is an ontological principle true of all natural existents, at every moment. It can even be said that temporal contingency is the very ipseity and existence of every natural existent and not an external accident occurring to it (Sadra 1981b: 251, 252).

4. As has been mentioned, the Islamic philosophers preceding Sadra, taking the perfection of the effusion of the Necessary Being and the eternity of His acts as a premise, would go on to deduce from it the eternity of the universe and all possible existents. Sadra also accepted this premise as necessary and in fact put emphasis on it, but he did not go on from there to conclude the pre-eternity of possibles or the eternity of the world; rather he took the premise to mean merely the nonintermittence of Divine effusions and their perpetuity.

It becomes clear from what we have stated that the generosity of the absolute Benefactor is perpetual, the creation of the true Creator is pre-eternal and His effusion upon all things is eternally uniform; but, as has been previously covered, the perpetuity of the Originator's generosity and His originating does not necessitate the eternity of "possible beings"—not all of them and not some of them, neither of their universal nor of their particulars. Now if the philosophers had sufficed themselves with just this much then their words would surely have been correct and true, but the late comers amongst them have added to this and have conjectured that these ideas necessitate the eternity of the world (Sadra 1981c: 305–307).

In a similar vein, in the third chapter of the tenth station of the book *Al-Hikmat al-Muta aliyah,* after first summarizing the opinions of the philosophers and their proofs regarding the eternity of the world, he evaluates their premises and conclusions in this fashion:

These premises are all correct and necessarily true but in spite of this the eternity of the world does not follow from them (Sadra 1981c: 300).

So even though Sadra accepts the opinion of the Islamic philosophers in holding that the chain of events has no end, he sees this infinity, however, as stemming from the perpetuity of Divine effusions which, as has been shown already, is quite compatible with temporal contingency and the instant by instant renewal of the world (Sadra 1981a: 138). It must also be said that according to "Transcendental Hikmah" an "eternal temporal entity" *(al-qadim al-zamani)* is a concept that has no external referent and extension *in concreto* [Fayd Kashani 1983:119].

Modern Cosmology, "Transcendent Hikmah," and the Problem of the Beginning

As pointed out earlier, in analyzing the "problem of the beginning" from "Transcendental Hikmah" and modern cosmology perspectives, we are, in reality, studying one of the basic themes of the "science and theology" debates. In the last few decades, the "science and theology" field in general and the theme of "modern cosmology and theology" in particular were burgeoning. A rich diversity of scholars has made significant contributions to the discussion of the relation of theology and modern cosmology from both sides of the issue. However, this theme has not yet been examined seriously from the Islamic philosophy (Hikmah) point of view.

Any one wishing to study the relationship between "Transcendental Hikmah" and modern cosmology needs to become familiar with "Transcendent Hikmah," as well as with the literature concerning the theme "modern cosmology and theology." Of course it must be noted that there are significant differences between modern cosmology and "Transcendent Hikmah." These differences are on a number of matters of considerable importance, such as the mode of dealing with the universe, resources and methods of inquiry, presuppositions, principles, and so on.

In what follows, I will try to present as much as possible, in the space available, the recent positions and to offer some critical approaches from the "Transcendental Hikmah" point of view.

Philosophical Trends in Modern Cosmology

Apart from various philosophical and theological responses, the philosophical trends among eminent cosmologists have been serious, as well; and in some cases, they have had a guiding influence. Here are only some instances:

- F. Hoyle, who is one of the main originators of the steady-state theory, has been opposed to the Big Bang theory for about the last fifty years. In his opposition to the Big Bang, the philosophical and especially atheistical grounds are important. He considers Big Bang cosmology as a form of religious fundamentalism and compares its new versions to medieval theology (quoted in Horgan 1995: 25). Hence, Barbour writes:

  Hoyle's writings make clear that he favored the steady-state theory not just on scientific grounds, but partly because he thought infinite time was more compatible with his own atheistic beliefs (Barbour 1990: 129).

- Steven Weinberg, the physicist and Nobel prize winner, is among the scientists who favor philosophical views in mode of preference to cosmological theories and models. He once remarked that for him the principal appeal of the steady-state theory was that it offered the least possible resemblance to the traditional religious picture of the creation of the universe as given in Genesis (quoted in Barrow 1988: 226).

❧ Stephen Hawking, an eminent cosmologist, in one of his articles, after explaining Big Bang singularity and before describing other cosmological models, wrote:

> Many people disliked the idea that time had a beginning or will have an end because it smacked of Divine intervention (Hawking 1989: 66).

❧ In contrast, there are scientists such as Wittaker, Milne, Weisskopf, and Jastrow, who claimed correspondence or resemblance between findings of modern cosmology and religious belief. Wittaker's statements about the accord between the Christian tradition and the picture of the expanding universe were inspiring for Pope Pius XII (quoted in Barrow 1988: 226).

Weisskopf also considers that the Judeo-Christian tradition describes the beginning of the universe in a way that is surprisingly similar to the scientific model (quoted in Rolston 1987: 72). Jastrow holds that "the astronomical evidence leads to a biblical view of the origin of the world" (quoted in Barbour 1990: 128).

Philosophical/Theological Responses and Implications

Direct Confirmation

Among the cosmological models and theories, the theory of the Big Bang and its related interpretations have evoked the most active responses and implications in philosophy and theology. Direct confirmation of *creato ex nihilo* by the Big Bang theory was one of the first responses to this theory and to "t = 0." In this context, the most important and well-known response came from Pope Pius XII in an address to the Pontifical Academy of Science (1951). He praised cosmologists for disclosing astrophysical evidence that was entirely compatible with theological convictions about Divine creation. His optimism was to the extent that he reckoned that the Big Bang theory was a valid argument for the existence of God (quoted in Russell 1989: 185). Some scientists such as Jastrow and Wittaker also strengthened this position by advocating the "direct confirmation" approach.

The approach of "direct confirmation" sees the content of the Big Bang cosmology concerning the beginning of the cosmos as an interpretation of *creato ex nihilo*. Ted Peters, a systematic theologian, believes that the content of "t = 0" in the Big Bang cosmology interprets the meaning of "creation" and "the dependence of the universe on God," so that, in his opinion, the concept of this dependence would not be well understood if one ignored the consequences of the Big Bang theory (Peters 1988: 288). The theistic philosopher William Craig also claims that if the Big Bang model is correct, "it does seem to constitute a powerful argument for the existence of a Creator of the universe" (Craig 1995: 276).

The adherents of this position, in general, have paid special attention to the boundedness of the universe. From this perspective, the universe has boundary in the past and has the "beginning" as well. This would necessitate that the universe be created by the Creator. Therefore, if the Big Bang theory indicates the boundedness and "temporal beginning" of the universe, it indeed would be a direct confirmation of the creation of the material beings and existence of God. Thus regarding what was mentioned about the Big Bang cosmology in the first section of this chapter, we can summarize the method of the "direct confirmation position" in the following diagram:

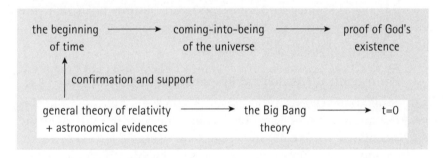

A part of the deductive method used in the above diagram is a throwback to the method used by Islamic theologians in proving the existence of God. By referring to the material covered in the second section of this chapter—that is, the explanation of the point of view of "Transcendental Hikmah" and its variance with that of the other schools of thought, especially that of the theologians—the place of "Transcendental Hikmah" and the positions it holds with respect to the "Direct Confirmation" approach come to the fore. In evaluating the "Direct Confirmation" approach the following points must be considered:

1. It was mentioned in the first section that in spite of the dazzling successes that the Big Bang theory has shown of itself to our day—mainly by explaining the various aspects of the structure, growth, and evolution of the cosmos—it has failed to explain the events preceding Planck time. Science has not been able to speak

of that period yet in any satisfactory way. Hence the initial "singularity" or "beginning of time" that Big Bang cosmology postulates speaks more to an "explanatory" or theoretical boundedness of the universe than it does to a real temporal boundedness. For this reason, it is not fitting to expect the Big Bang theory to prove anything of what clearly falls outside its purview.

2. To claim direct confirmation of the creation of the universe by way of the results of a scientific theory—assuming that they even agree with the correct scientific and theological understanding, in the first place—is to bring about a situation where any weaknesses or a possible nullification of the theory directly affects the initial belief and opens the doors to some sorts of misunderstandings and fallacies regarding it. It was alluded to earlier that some cosmological theories—such as quantum cosmology—attempt to escape from being bound to the ides of singularity and t = 0 as understood by Big Bang cosmology. It is obvious that if any of these theories comes to be proven, then the direct confirmation of the creation of the world will come under its influence and possibly lead to incorrect conclusions being drawn.

3. As has been mentioned, in "Transcendental Hikmah" temporal contingency and the "creation" of the world do not imply a temporal boundedness to the universe—nor is the "creation" an historical event—so that we need search for an edge to the world—assuming that such an "edge" or "shoreline" even exists. According to "Transcendental Hikmah" creation is eternal and is never interrupted; it does not end at any bound or limit. This is a fundamental difference between "Transcendental Hikmah" and the "Direct Confirmation" approach and bears heavily on how each sees "creation" and explains the temporal contingency of the world. It must be noted that proving the existence of God by referring to what is nowadays termed the "edge of time or of the universe" is in reality to make deductions from premises that science is either silent on or has very little to say about. Many scientists make the claim that, in principle, science will one day be able to explain this edge of the world—an edge that may more accurately be called the "periphery" of modern science. They see the quantum cosmological models to be the first step in this direction— even though, due to fundamental difficulties, they consider the actualization of such an event in the near future to be very unlikely. Now the fundamental approach of "Transcendental Hikmah" and Islamic philosophy in proving important theological

matters has been to stay away from unknown natural phenomena and the uncharted realms of knowledge.

4. In proving the existence of God, overemphasizing and paying excessive attention to the "beginning of the universe" inevitably leads one to construe that the creation of the Creator is either limited to the beginning of the world or at least is much more visible in that time frame. From this it is imagined that the need of the world for a Lord is more readily a function of the initial creation and origin—an event that once occurred in the far past—than of the subsistence and continuation of the world. But according to Islamic philosophy, the dependence of the world is not only due to its creation and contingency (coming-into-being), but, as a fact, the subsistence and continuance of the world also requires the creating of a Creator. The natural world is not just a structure that a builder has once made and then stepped aside from. In other words, the Creator is the cause of both the creation and contingency of the world as well as its subsistence. What's more, according to "Transcendent Hikmah," the temporal contingency of the world is not a one-time event, rather—as has previously been explained—it is a recurring reality that is repeated every instant and in this case both the "creation" and the "subsistence" or perpetuity of the natural world—due to the latter's gradual and influxive nature—are one and the same thing. In the words of Sadra as recorded in his book *Al-Shawahid al-rububiyyah:*

> Now because the material world in its individuation is gradual, in flux existence, and as the time of creation and the time of subsistence is the same in every gradual existence, it follows that the time of creation and subsistence of this world is one and the same (Sadra 1981d: 92).

All this given, it must be said that the causality of the Creator with regard to the temporal contingency and creation of the world is eternal and is not just a one-time affair residing on the edge of the universe.

Impartial Position

Although, nowadays, the majority of scholars in the realm of science and theology do not agree with the absolute segregation of these two fields, they do not agree with the "direct confirmation" approach, either. Despite their arguments in depicting the nature of the relationship between theology and modern cosmology, these scholars emphasize the ontological meaning of *creatio ex nihilo* and that it does not necessarily indicate temporal beginning of the universe, but merely its ontological dependence on God.

Naturally, this ontological dependence should be permanent with no preference to a particular period or instant of time. Thus, one cannot relate the meaning of "beginning" in the Big Bang theory to the concept of "creation." Langdon Gilkey, the neo-orthodox theologian, in his book *Maker of Heaven and Earth* (1959), made a proper distinction between historical and ontological origination. In his opinion, the latter is the essential meaning of "creation" in Christian tradition (quoted in Russell 1993: 294). In *Issues in Science and Religion* (1966), Barbour explicitly agreed with Gilkey on the meaning of creation (Barbour 1971: 414). More recently he has mentioned: "The message of creation ex nihilo applies to the whole of the cosmos at every moment . . . it is an ontological and not a historical assertion" (Barbour 1990: 45).

Arthur Peacocke and John Polkinghorne support the impartial position of theology concerning the Big Bang theory and the beginning of the cosmos. Polkinghorne says:

> There never was a theological stake in preferring Big Bang cosmology to steady-state cosmology . . . if physical cosmology were to abolish a datable beginning for the world, no great theological upheaval would follow (Polkinghorne 1995: 64).

William Stoeger, an astrophysicist and scholar in "science and theology," clearly mentions that *creato ex nihilo* states nothing about the cosmological concepts, and does not prefer any particular theory and would be consonant with current cosmological theories (Stoeger 1992: 62, 63).

Consonance Approach

Ernan McMullin, a philosopher and scholar in "science and theology," originally suggested what is called the "consonance" between theology and modern cosmology. He does not accept any kind of direct interrelation between theology and modern cosmology, and does not welcome a neutral position, either. He believes we should aim at a "coherence of world-view" in which theology and modern cosmology are consonant in their contributions. Applied to the "problem of the beginning," if the universe began in time through the act of a Creator, from our vantage point it would look something like the Big Bang that cosmologists are now talking about. But this does not mean "direct confirmation" or making a firm correlation (quoted in Russell 1989: 188).

Interaction Attitude

Robert John Russell is one of the scholars who tries to develop a framework for the consonance relationship. By using Imre Lakatos's methodology in philosophy of science and its applications to the methodology of theology, Russell attempts to build a framework as well as a method for what he denotes as interaction between theology and modern cosmology. Inspired with Lakatos's ideas and using his terms, Russell posits the following as the core of a "theological research program": *creato ex nihilo* means ontological dependence. Russell deploys a series of auxiliary hypotheses that use philosophical categories (especially the concept of "temporal finitude") to surround the core. This allows him to relate theology with modern cosmology. The auxiliary hypotheses constitute the main realm of relationship between theology and modern cosmology and are subject to confirmation and disconfirmation. By lying between the core and the data, the auxiliary hypotheses immunize the core from immediate falsification by anomalous data. Thus the interaction between a theological core and modern cosmology cannot be direct. The falsification of a particular cosmological theory leads to auxiliary hypotheses being changed and in turn provides the ground for a new relationship (Russell 1996: 201–224).

An Approach Based on "Transcendental Hikmah"

In order to establish a proper foundation that is consistent with the "Transcendent Hikmah," it is desirable to consider not only constructive consequences of the above approaches but also the conceptual and methodological consequences of the "Transcendent Hikmah." Paying attention to the remarks of those scholars who support impartiality of theology before modern cosmology would effectively help us realize the difficulties and limitations of relating modern cosmology to any theological system. These scholars typically emphasize two major issues: a) "Creation" has an ontological meaning and hence is equitable to whether or not the cosmos has a beginning; and b) The theories of cosmology are based on certain assumptions and convey certain limitations. Ignoring these limitations might lead theologians to incorrect and scientifically unjustified implications.

If one intends to benefit from the fruits of the "Transcendental Hikmah" in discussions of modern cosmology and theology, it is imperative that one avoid any illusion of simplicity and plainness; restrictions of the cosmological theories must be carefully regarded, and naive implications and interpretations must be skeptically scrutinized. In this regard, the "direct confirmation" position could not be welcomed.

Although considering "creation" as an ontological concept is consistent with the fundamentals of the "Transcendent Hikmah," taking a neutral position does not seem to be quite along the style of this school of philosophy. The "Transcendental Hikmah" not only sees creation as a truth of the matter, but also elaborates the details of creation through the Divine Names, specifically those effectual Names that indicate the absolute deity of the Almighty. In the theodicean discussions of the Divine names and attributes, a general and explicit principle states the eternity of the Divine generosity and continuity of His effusion, despite the renewing and changing of the creation (natural world) in every moment.

This principle has a significant role in describing the Divine action, so that Sadra has dedicated one whole chapter (station 10) of his remarkable book, *Al-Hikmat al-Muta aliyah*, to this topic, and clearly states the generality and strength of this principle in the title:

> Station Ten: On the perpetuity of the First-Principle generosity and permanence of His power, and in that His effusion has never been discontinued and will never be, and His act will never terminate, yet, the universe is renewing, becoming and perishing (Sadra 1981c: 282).

A necessary corollary of the generality of the above mentioned principle which directly refers to the natural realm—that is, all beings lower than the Divine and immaterial orders—is that despite the temporal and substantial contingency of the natural world, Divine effusion *(fayd)* has never been absent from this realm and moreover has always had an extension and referent in it. In explaining such general principles and laws, it has been the practice of the Hukama (Islamic philosophers), that if in lieu of the generality of a philosophical rule and principle and the event of cases where ambiguities and doubts are raised or could even possibly be imagined, to address these ambiguities and to remove any points of contention.

Deliberation upon the past discussions gives way to fields in which cosmological theories and models address the question of the origin of the universe, whether pro or con, and include in themselves various theological/philosophical leanings and conclusions. In such cases, applying what may be called a type of "mutual explanation" between

"Transcendental Hikmah" and modern cosmology will be effective and useful. Now because these cases—which we may term as the new or recent issues of "Transcendental Hikmah"—have mainly sprung from modern cosmology, naturally the expository part played by cosmological theories and models will be major and decisive. In the course of this "mutual explanation," it is fitting that "Transcendental Hikmah," by using the appropriate philosophical concepts and categories—which hail mainly from what is called "the secondary philosophical intelligibles" *(al-m'aqulat al-thaniyyah al-falsafiyyah)*—attempt to explain these cases within its own expository framework, and in doing so make clear the state of the possible referents and particulars of its general concepts and principles. Benefiting from and putting to use the theological/philosophical positions that sometimes even cosmologists themselves disclose can go a long way toward arriving at a "mutual explanation."

It appears that these types of "mutual explanation" can produce new corollaries of the general laws and principles of "Transcendental Hikmah" and in this way cause it to blossom all the more. Hence, regarding the problem of the beginning of the universe, it is not appropriate, as in "impartial position," to declare "Transcendental Hikmah" as indifferent toward modern cosmology and the theological/philosophical responses and implications of the issue.

As regards the "consonance approach," we must state that even though this opinion, due to its denial of the "direct confirmation" method and acknowledgment of the insufficiency of an impartial and unbiased position along with its acceptance of some possible reconciliations and consonance, is closer to the method of "mutual explanation." It seems that with a little deliberation upon the material already covered, it will become evident that the purport of the Big Bang theory— assuming it gives evidence to a temporal beginning of the universe— does not bear resemblance to the purport of the explanations of "Transcendent Hikmah," and it is for this reason that the instances that MacMullin puts forth as evidence of consonance cannot be accepted. Now of course if, ignoring scientific standards of acceptance, we take mere resemblance to be our only yardstick, then those models and theories that are in some fashion concordant with continuous creation begin to bear more resemblance to the outlook of "Transcendental Hikmah" on the beginning of the universe.

What has been said above should not be taken to mean that the Big Bang theory is substantially in opposition to the law of perpetual Divine effusion. As previously emphasized, in the moments preceding Planck time, the most apparent aspect of this theory is its silence and inability of interpretation. Hence, the Big Bang theory proves nothing about what has been termed the "moment of creation." Such expressions are nonscientific conclusions that have resulted from this theory, sometimes by way of a direct confirmation. What is clear is that the Big Bang theory does not say that there was nothing in existence before Planck time; rather it speaks of a presiding state of affairs that is outside of the ability of modern science to explain. In light of the fact that certain characteristics of this state, such as infinite mass and density and high temperatures among others, are often mentioned, we can say that in that period it is not correct, from the point of view of philosophy, to speak of "absolute nonexistence." This is because pure nothingness cannot have such attributes. Now if an existent has such real attributes and they do not fit those of an immaterial existent then without any doubt, from the point of view of Islamic philosophy, the existent is a natural existent. Of course, it can be said that in the period under question, "natural existence" comes with characteristics so abnormal that it is difficult to speak of it in usual terms and with popular concepts such as "nature," "matter," "motion," and "time." At the same time, philosophical concepts and categories such as nature, matter, motion, and time do have the necessary scope to include such unusual configurations and conglomerations of nature and in their applicability they need not have usual characteristics. Hence, from the point of view of philosophy, natural existence does indeed have a referent in the external world in the time preceding Planck time. With the above explanations, it becomes clear that the content of the Big Bang theory does not oppose the law of perpetuity of Divine effusion.

We will end this article by a cursory study of Russell's proposal. Russell's attention towards the part played by philosophical concepts and categories in creating a link between theology and modern cosmology is of importance, especially because he enters the field in a systematic and orderly fashion and explains the method of application of these categories.

Russell in his presentation of the concept of finitude only entertains the temporal finitude of the universe and in its most general sense takes it to include both the bounded temporal finitude and the unbounded temporal finitude. But it must be noted that temporal finitude or infinitude is but a consequence and corollary of the temporal perpetuity of the natural universe; according to the fundamentals of "Transcendental Hikmah" it is abundantly clear that the world, at every moment, is being renewed and that it does not even subsist for any two moments so how could it be, temporally speaking, considered to be either finite or infinite? Of course, "existential" finitude and limitation is another matter, considered both true and demonstrable by "Transcendent Hikmah."

REFERENCES

Arabic/Persian

al-Allamah al-Helli, Ibn al-Mutahhar. *Kashf al-Murad.* Qum, 1986.

Fayd Kashani, Mulla Muhsin. *Usul al-ma arif.* Qum, 1983.

Ibn Sina (Avicenna). *Kitab al-Shifa: al-Ilahi yyat (Metaphysics).* Qum, 1984a.

———. *Kitab al-Shifa: al-Tabi yyat (Physics).* vol. 1. Qum, 1984b.

Lahiji, 'Abd al-Razzaq. *Gawhar-i murad.* Edited by S. Muwahhid. Tehran, 1985.

Sabzawari, Mulla Hadi. *Commentary on Shirazi, Sadr al-Din's al-Hikmat al-Muta, aliyah fi'l-asfar al-aqliyyat al-arba ah.* vol. 3. Beirut, 1981.

Sadra (Shirazi, Sadr al-Din). *Al-Hikmat al-Muta aliyah fi'l-asfar al-aqliyyat al-arba ah.* vol. 2. Beirut, 1981a.

———. *Al-Hikmat al-Muta aliyah fi'l-asfar al-aqliyyat al-arba ah.* vol. 3. Beirut, 1981b.

———. *Al-Hikmat al-Muta aliyah fi'l-asfar al-aqliyyat al-arba ah.* vol. 7. Beirut, 1981c.

———. *Huduth al-alam.* Tehran, 1987.

———. *Al-Masha ir.* Qum, 1983.

———. *Al-Shawahid al-rububiyyah fi'l-manahij al-sulukiyyah.* Tehran, 1981d.

al-Sayuri al-Helli, Jamal al-Din Meqdad. *Irshad al-Talebin ila Nahj al-Mostarshedin.* Qum, 1984.

Suhrawardi, Shihab al-Din. *Hikmat al-Ishraq.* Tehran, 1952.

Tusi, Nasir al-Din. *Commentary on Avicenna's Kitab al-Isharat.* Tehran, 1983.

———. *Naqd al-muhassal.* Tehran, 1980.

———. *Tajrid al-i tiqad.* Qum, 1986.

English

Agazzi, Evandro. "The Universe as a Scientific and Philosophical Problem," in *Philosophy and the Origin and Evolution of the Universe,* edited by E. Agazzi and A. Cordero. Dordrecht, Netherlands: Kluwer Academic Publishers, 1991.

Barbour, Ian. *Issues in Science and Religion.* 2nd ed. New York: First Torch Book, 1971.

———. *Religion in an Age of Science.* San Francisco: Harper, 1990.

Barrow, John D. *The World Within the World.* Oxford: Oxford University Press, 1988.

Brush, Stephen G. "How Cosmology Became a Science?" in *Scientific American* (August 1992), pp. 34–40.

Craig, William Lane. "A Criticism of the Cosmological Argument for God's Non-existence," in *Theism, Atheism, and Big Bang Cosmology*, by W. L. Craig and Q. Smith. Oxford: Oxford University Press, 1995.

Davies, Paul. "The Day Time Began," in *New Scientist* (27 April 1996), pp. 30–35.

————. *The Mind of God*. New York: Touchstone, 1992.

Drees, Willem B. "Quantum Cosmologies and the Beginning," in *Zygon: Journal of Religion and Science*, vol. 26, no. 3. (1991), pp. 373–395.

————. "Theology and Cosmology Beyond the Big Bang Theory," in *Science and Religion: One World—Changing Perspectives on Reality*, edited by J. Fennema and I. Paul. Dordrecht, Netherlands: Kluwer Academic Publishers, 1990.

Gilkey, Langdon. *Maker of Heaven and Earth*. Lanham, Maryland: University Press of America, 1959.

Halliwell, Jonathan J. "Quantum Cosmology and the Creation of the Universe," in *Scientific American* (December 1991), pp. 76–85.

Hawking, Stephen. *A Brief History of Time: From the Big Bang to Black Holes*. London: Bantam Press, 1988.

————. "The Edge of Spacetime," in *The New Physics*, edited by Paul Davies. Cambridge: Cambridge University Press, 1989.

Horgan, John. "The Return of the Maverick," in *Scientific American* (March 1995).

Isham, Chris J. "Quantum Theories of the Creation of the Universe," in *Quantum Cosmology and the Laws of Nature*, edited by R. J Russell, N. Murphy, and C. J. Isham. Berkeley, California: Vatican Observatory and CTNS, 1993.

Lightman, Alan, and Roberto Brawer, eds. *Origins: The Lives and Works of Modern Cosmologists*. Cambridge, Massachusetts: Harvard University Press, 1990.

Munitz, Milton K. *Cosmic Understanding: Philosophy and Science of the Universe*. Princeton, New Jersey: Princeton University Press, 1986.

————. "Cosmology," in *The Encyclopedia of Philosophy*, vol. 2, edited by Paul Edwards. New York: Macmillan, 1967.

Pagels, Heinz R. *The Cosmic Code*. London: Pelican Books, 1984.

Parker, Barry. *Creation: The Story of the Origin and Evolution of the Universe*. New York: Plenum, 1988.

Peters, Ted. "On Creating the Cosmos," in *Physics, Philosophy, and Theology: A Common Quest for Understanding*, edited by R. J. Russell, W. R. Stoeger, and G. Coyne. Vatican City State: Vatican Observatory, 1988.

Polkinghorne, John. *Serious Talk: Science and Religion in Dialogue*. London: SCM Press, 1995.

Rolston III, Holmes. *Science and Religion: A Critical Survey*. Philadelphia: Temple University Press, 1987.

Russell, Robert John. "Cosmology from Alpha to Omega," in *Zygon: Journal of Religion and Science*, vol. 29, no. 4 (1994), pp. 557–577.

————. "Cosmology, Creation, and Contingency," in *Cosmos as Creation*, edited by Ted Peters. Nashville: Abingdon Press, 1989.

————. "Finite Creation Without a Beginning," in *Quantum Cosmology and the Laws of Nature*, edited by R. J. Russell, N. Murphy, and C. J. Isham. Berkeley, California: Vatican Observatory and CTNS, 1993.

————. "T = 0: Is Theologically Significant?" in *Religion and Science: History, Method, Dialogue*, edited by W. Mark Richardson and W. J. Wildman. London: Routledge, 1996.

Stoeger, William R. "Contemporary Cosmology and Its Implications for the Science-Religion Dialogue," in *Physics, Philosophy, and Theology: A Common Quest for Understanding*, edited by R. J. Russell, W. R. Stoeger, and G. Coyne. Vatican City State: Vatican Observatory, 1988.

————. "The Origin of the Universe in Science and Religion," in *Cosmos, Bios, Theos*, edited by H. Margenau and R. A. Varghese. La Salle: Open Court, 1992.

Weinberg, Steven. *The First Three Minutes*. New York: Basic Books [updated edition], 1993.

This chapter was originally published in Persian in *Science and Religion Bulletin*, Institute for Humanities and Cultural Studies, Tehran (spring/summer 1999).

CHAPTER 9

Three Views of Creation and Evolution

RICHARD H. BUBE

Richard Bube is professor emeritus of materials science and electrical engineering at Stanford University, Stanford, CA.

Introduction

One definition that attempts to be true to authentic science is this: "Authentic science is *a* way of knowing based upon *testable descriptions* of the world obtained through the *human interpretation* in *natural categories* of publicly observable and reproducible *sense data*, obtained by interaction with the natural world."

This definition emphasizes that science does not provide the only way of knowing, gives descriptions of what the world *is like* and not exclusive explanations of what the world *is*, is the result of human activity, is limited by choice to natural categories to define the area of applicability and not because of an atheistic worldview, and involves the testing of human hypotheses by comparison with phenomena in the natural world. Although it is recognized that no human activity can be a truly objective activity free of all inputs from personal faith systems or philosophical guidelines, it is the goal to carry out science in as objective a way as possible, seeking to understand how the physical world functions "as it presents itself to us." Authentic science cannot be carried out for the purpose of attempting to show the validity of previously assumed philosophical, metaphysical, or religious conclusions. The essential emphasis is that mechanisms chosen for scientific descriptions must be susceptible to such scientific tests.

If, in the course of scientific research, we arrive at the point where we cannot find a scientifically acceptable description of an observable phenomenon in the world, (1) we can conclude that no such description is possible, and that we have encountered a genuine case of God's direct action, or (2) we can conclude that the subject must remain open, since the possibility always exists that further investigation may lead us to a scientific description of God's activity after all. Acceptance of the first point is not more consistent with a Christian worldview and commitment than acceptance of the second.

It is unfortunate that a false definition of science as the "explanation of everything" has been embraced so widely in the creation/evolution debate. The person committed to an atheistic worldview argues that since God is not included in scientific explanations, the successes of science show that there is no God. Meanwhile, the person committed to a literal, biblical worldview argues that the absence of specific divine activity from current scientific explanations is the cause for this lack of evidence for the existence of God, and that therefore the existence of God must be acknowledged by changing the scientific process itself into a "theistic science" so that God's activity can be admitted into it as a scientific explanation.

In order to come to a reliable description of all of the features of reality, the inputs from authentic science and the inputs from authentic theology must be seen as interacting, complementary descriptions, each bringing valid and vital partial insights from their own domains. They must be allowed to guide overall perspectives as the result of an attempt to integrate them in a way that preserves the qualities of authentic description relevant to each.

If one wishes to resolve the apparent conflict between science and theology, the way to proceed is by challenging the claim that non-biblical philosophical conclusions have the authority of authentic science, and not by attempting to reconstruct the scientific method by insisting that God's activity must be inserted into that procedure as a scientific hypothesis or mechanism.

The Importance of Definitions

Misunderstanding, disagreement, and apparent conflict between different views of creation and evolution can often be traced to basic differences in the definitions that are assumed for essential terms and concepts.

Limited Terms Versus Worldviews

One of the most fundamental distinctions lies in the recognition of the difference between certain limited words (science, natural, deterministic, chance, creation, evolution) and the general philosophical worldviews extrapolated from them on faith by absolutizing them (Scientism, Naturalism, Determinism, Chance, Creation, Creationism, Evolutionism).

Science is a limited human activity as defined above. Scientism is a worldview chosen on faith that matter is all that exists, and that science provides the only knowledge of truth possible—it presupposes an atheistic worldview. Christians embrace science and reject Scientism.

"Natural" is an adjective describing the types of material and phenomena observable in the physical world and describable, at least in principle, by science—it can be seen as a description of God's regular activity in the physical world. Naturalism is a worldview chosen on faith that there is no reality beyond the material physical world investigated by science—it presupposes an atheistic worldview. Christians embrace the natural as God's activity and reject Naturalism. No more damaging confusion is caused than that which arises from assuming that to call something "natural" means that God is not involved, and that the involvement of God can be assured only by the treatment of specific phenomena as exclusively "supernatural."

A deterministic scientific description is one in which future properties of a system can be accurately predicted from a knowledge of present properties. A worldview of Determinism asserts that all events taking place in the world are determined to occur, as in the concept of "fate," and that such concepts as "individual choice" or "personal responsibility" are only illusions.

A chance scientific description is one in which only probabilities concerning future properties of a system can be accurately predicted from a knowledge of present properties. A worldview of Chance asserts that all events taking place in the world happen spontaneously so that such concepts as meaningfulness or God's Providence are irrelevant. Since evolution is often described as a "chance" process, this represents an objection for those who hold that a scientific chance description automatically supports a meaningless Chance worldview. It is important to recognize the limited utility of deterministic and chance scientific descriptions, and to see such descriptions as applicable to God's activity in the world, while rejecting the absolute worldview positions of Determinism and Chance.

"To create" is a verb describing the origin of novelty in the world through the continuing activity of God. In principle it could occur either as a continuous process susceptible to scientific description, or as an instantaneous act of God not describable scientifically. Creation with a capital C refers to a foundational biblical worldview based on faith in

God, the Maker of Heaven and Earth, as described more fully in the summary section at the end of this chapter. Creationism is a worldview in which the specific mechanism of this activity must be identified with instantaneous, non-scientifically describable acts of God. Christians generally embrace the biblical worldview of Creation and creation by God through a variety of possible mechanisms; Christians committed to a literal biblical interpretation embrace Creationism.

Evolution is a description of a possible mechanism that we can use to describe the process of coming into being of something new, which did not exist in that form before, through certain scientifically describable processes—it is in the form of a theory whose suitability for the description of the actual events occurring in the physical world is impressive, but incomplete, open to question, and constantly subjected to test. Evolutionism is a worldview in which it is assumed on faith that all that was, is, or ever will be is the product of meaningless chance events that result in transforming changes—it is in the form of a faith commitment that assesses all observations and data in terms of an atheistic perspective. Whereas many Christians accept the possibility and utility of evolution as a description of God's activity in creation, they reject Evolutionism.

Methodological Naturalism

"Methodological naturalism" has become a battle cry in many science versus faith debates. This use of words implies that the methodology adopted in science by choice, that is, the limitation of scientific descriptions to natural categories, results from or leads to the acceptance of Naturalism, an atheistic worldview.

To the practicing Christian scientist the limitation of scientific descriptions to natural categories is not at all the necessary result of an atheistic worldview, but simply a choice to make it possible for science to be a well-defined and reliable, albeit limited, activity. The adoption of such a methodology insists that for a particular approach to be considered *science*, it must be subject to experimental test and shown to be an accurate indication, within limits, of what reality *is like*, consistent with the definition of science given above.

The Christian involved in doing science may agree that science is based on methodological naturalism, meaning that science is a discipline involving the human interpretation of phenomena in natural categories only. This is a choice made to define the capabilities and limitations of science. In this context "methodological naturalism" has no philosophical or theological significance, since the Christian scientist believes in general that all authentic scientific descriptions correspond to descriptions of what God's activity in the world appears to be. It specifically does not involve embracing the worldview of Naturalism.

The possibility remains open that some phenomena in the world may not be describable in natural categories. But the Christian scientist seeks to maintain a situation where the term "scientific" carries some specific meaning and assurance of validity, and hence insists that non-scientifically describable phenomena should not be called "science."

Intelligent Design

A major theme in the history of Christian apologetics has been the so-called Argument from Purpose and Design, also known as the Teleological Argument. When one looks at the unique properties of matter and the earth that allow the existence of human life, one is struck by the amount of evidence that can be interpreted as indicating that all of this has been designed by a Great Designer.

All such evidence for the existence of a Great Designer from phenomena in the natural world are powerfully consistent for the person who has a personal relationship with God the Creator and Sustainer. Whether they are accepted as evidence for the activity of the God of the Bible, however, depends primarily on the faith commitment of the person who is considering them. It is logically possible to dismiss them simply as a grand "shake of the dice," which happened in a one-in-a-trillion toss to lead to a universe that will sustain human life; if it had not happened, we would not be here to think about it. Or they may be considered as mysterious evidence for the existence of some kind of Life Force with little or no relationship to the God of the Bible.

There is no objection to using the concept of "intelligent design" as a guide in suggesting how to construct suitable models of physical reality, provided that these models are capable of being subjected to test and description in natural categories before they are accepted as scientific. *Intelligent design for the Christian is a general concept underlying all descriptions, scientific and non-scientific, affirming the creative and sustaining activity of God.* But if the concept of "intelligent design" is advanced as a substitute for natural categories of description, limiting the specific instances being concerned to acts of God's "intervention" in the "gaps" in our understanding, and considering "intelligent design" itself as a valid scientific description, critical harm is done to our concepts of the relationship between scientific descriptions and God's continuing activity in creating and sustaining.

There is also the whole area of interaction between such concepts as "natural law" and "God's intervention" in the world. Many writers speak of "natural law" as though "laws" were self-existing elements that God called into existence to rule the physical world. *Within the area of science, "natural laws" are human descriptions of God's regular creative and sustaining activity. Laws do not cause anything to happen; they are descriptive, not prescriptive.* For God to act in a way different from this regular creative and sustaining activity—as for example, in the doing of a "miracle"—He does not have to "break His laws," "set aside His laws," or "intervene in His laws" to accomplish His purpose. Just as we can understand the ordinary "laws" of nature as our descriptions of God's regular activity, so we can understand a "miracle" as our description of God's special activity.

Summary

The worldview summarized in the biblical doctrine of Creation reveals to us that the God who loves us is also the God who created us and all things, and establishes the identity between the God of religious faith and the God of physical reality. Our belief in Creation underlies our trust in the reality of a physical and moral structure to the universe; enables us to see that the universe and everything in it depends moment-by-moment upon the sustaining power and activity of God; and provides the foundation for our faith that we are not the end-products of meaningless processes in an impersonal universe, but men and women made in the image of a personal God.

Our belief in "creation out of nothing" affirms that God created the universe freely and separately, and rejects the alternatives of dualism and pantheism. To worship God as Creator is to emphasize both His transcendence over the natural order and His imminence in the natural order. Appreciation of God as Creator provides the rationale for scientific investigation, the assurance of ultimate personal meaning in life, and the nature of evil as an aberration on a good creation.

The biblical doctrine of Creation plays such a foundational role in all of the biblical revelation that it is unfortunate when the word "creation" is used narrowly and restrictively to refer—not to the fact of Creation—but to a possible mechanism in the creative activity. *When it is implied that Creation and evolution are necessarily mutually exclusive, or when the word Creation is used as if it were primarily a scientific mechanism for origins, a profound confusion of categories is involved. The key to much of the evolution controversy lies in the recognition of the necessity and propriety of descriptions of the same phenomena on different levels of reality.*

Even a complete biological description does not do away with the need for a theological description, any more than a complete theological description does away with the possibility of a biological description. Biological evolution *can* be considered without denying creation; creation *can* be accepted without excluding biological evolution. If it is true that the evolutionist must realize that he has little scientific support for extrapolating biological evolution into a general principle of life, the Christian anti-evolutionist must realize that he has little religious justification upon which to attack a scientific theory dealing with biological mechanisms.

This chapter is a revised condensation of "Final Reflections on the Dialogue, Reflection 1" from: *Maker of Heaven and Earth: Three Views on the Creation-Evolution Controversy.* Edited by J. P. Moreland and J. M. Reynolds. Grand Rapids, Michigan: Zondervan, 1998.

CHAPTER 10

The Scientist as Believer

RICHARD RICE

Richard Rice is a professor of religion at Loma Linda University, Loma Linda, CA. He received his Ph.D. in systematic theology from the University of Chicago. His latest book, written with Clark Pinnock and others, is *The Openness of God*.

The expression "science and religion" is abstract. It refers loftily to bodies of knowledge or approaches to truth. My primary concern in this chapter is the people who do science, specifically people with religious convictions who engage in scientific inquiry, and more particularly those who do so within the setting of a church-related college or university. In other words, I am interested in the questioner, not just the question.

For, as "postmodern" thinkers insist, beliefs do not float around in some ethereal stratosphere of meaning, disembodied and unattached. They belong to flesh and blood human beings—to people, whose perspectives are always affected by particularizing features such as body, gender, class, race, and nationality. So we can talk about beliefs all we want to, but we won't get to the heart of the matter unless we talk about those who hold these beliefs, why they hold them, and what impact holding them has on their lives.

A scientist who is a believer will encounter tension on three different levels, or three different areas, of experience. One is the tension between faith and reason, which is experienced to some degree by all believers who are intellectually responsible. A second is the tension between two intellectual activities, namely science and theology. Theology applies reason to the contents of faith. Science applies rational inquiry to the natural world, the world accessible to empirical investigation. A third area of tension concerns the two communities to which the Adventist scientist belongs, viz., the community of faith and

the community of scientific inquiry. These communities are characterized by different qualities, they serve different purposes, they contain
quite different memberships. Can a person fulfill the obligations involved in both communities at the same time?

Let us begin by sounding a note of optimism and confidence. Too
many Christians approach this issue of science and religion as a tremendous problem. They accept the perception that science and religion are
locked in combat, with religion a decided underdog. Given its compelling effectiveness in explaining our world and transforming our environment, science clearly has the upper hand, they believe. The most
religion can hope for is to keep the fight going and avoid getting
knocked out.

The attitude is understandable, but it is not unavoidable, and we
should not succumb to it. Our heritage as Christians, and as Adventists,
gives us a wonderful perspective on reality. The mandate for it lies in
biblical affirmations such as these: "In the beginning God created the
heavens and the earth."[1] "The heavens are telling the glory of God; and
the firmament proclaims his handiwork."[2] "Ever since the creation of
the world his eternal power and divine nature . . . have been understood and seen through the things he has made."[3] "Fear God and give
him glory for the hour of judgment has come; and worship him who
made heaven and earth, the sea and the springs of water."[4]

Our understanding of God's creative power and love provides a basis for affirming the universe as something wonderful—as valuable, intelligible, and filled with beauty and mystery. We see the world as the manifestation of a God of infinite wisdom and love, who reaches out to us and
speaks to us through the glories of the world around us and the depths of
the world within us. This confidence should never degenerate into a presumption that offers easy answers to difficult questions or a self-congrat-
ulatory smugness that dismisses all opinions but our own. But a view of
God that is faithful to the Bible and sensitive to the accumulated insights
of the Christian community provides us a basis for exploring the universe, the planet, and ourselves with wonder and gratitude.

Faith and Reason

As thinkers and believers, Adventist scientists must relate their trust in
God to the activity of careful reflection and the quest for evidence to
support all truth claims. There is a fundamental contrast between faith
and reason. Faith is the most important category in personal religion,

and it refers to several things. As described by the apostle Paul, it means trust in God to save us apart from any of our own accomplishments. The word is also used to refer to the Christian life in general, as a synonym for "Christian experience." And people also apply it to the beliefs characteristic of Christianity or to the Christian tradition as a whole. In a general, nonreligious sense, faith means trust, particularly in the absence of evidence or proof. To take someone's word for something rather than finding it out for yourself is to "take it on faith."

"Reason" has a similarly broad range of meaning. It can refer to our mental faculties, generally to discursive reasoning, and to the results of rational investigation. Reason is the process of finding reasons for things and drawing conclusions from evidence. In contrast to faith, reason involves having a demonstrable basis for what you believe, one you can show to other people.

Over the centuries, most Christians have taken the position that faith and reason are both gifts from God, and that both lead us ultimately to him. Our relation to God is based on faith, but we can also find evidence to support our confidence, so it makes sense for us to believe. Believing in God never makes perfect sense, however, so we never outgrow a need for trust. The relation of faith and reason is not a simple one, and many people have a tendency to emphasize one at the expense of the other.

My greatest challenges as a religion teacher typically come from two different sorts of students. Some students feel that their religious convictions are obviously true and need no examination. Others insist that religion is so obviously false that it does not deserve serious consideration. We should simply dismiss it and move on.

I had a couple of students long ago who epitomized these opposing attitudes. Dan was a tall, dark ministerial student, who hated every class he took from me, and the program unfortunately required him to take several. He disliked thinking seriously about religion, and his disdain for the process was obvious. He sat in the middle of the classroom with a look of studied boredom on his face. He never took notes, never asked a question, never spoke up except to complain. He felt that theological ideas were nothing but mind games played by misguided people. He wanted nothing more than to get out of school and get on with the real work of the church.

Dave was equally disenchanted with his courses from me, but for entirely different reasons. He was convinced that religion had nothing to recommend it to thinking people such as himself, so he openly ridiculed anyone who believed the stuff. And he accused those who defended it, like me, of rationalizing a hopeless position because they were either unwilling to think or else afraid to let people know what they really believed.

In response to both the Dans and Daves in my classes I always present religion as something that both needs and deserves careful investigation. So, I urge believers to think, and I encourage thinkers to believe.

For most of Christian history people assumed the importance of faith and questioned the value of reason. But about two hundred years ago a momentous change in Western thought took place, and the burden of proof shifted to the other side. As Tom Stoppard puts it, "There is presumably a calendar date—a *moment*—when the onus of proof passed from the atheist to the believer; when, quite suddenly secretly, the noes had it."[5] That is true of most educated people today. They take reason for granted, and view faith as problematic. In response, some believers regard serious thinking as a threat to faith, and they look for ways to avoid it. But this is not an option for scientists, who are thinkers by inclination and training, so we need to look for another approach.

The truth is that reason is not inherently a threat to faith, and can be a tremendous help to it. Careful thinking can strengthen religious commitment, once faith is already present. And it can open the way for faith, helping to prepare people for religious commitment. Let's examine these contributions.

According to the Bible, careful thinking and growth in knowledge are important elements in the Christian life. The letter of 2 Peter, for example, exhorts its readers to "make every effort to supplement your faith with virtue, and virtue with knowledge, and knowledge with self-control. . . . "[6] Acts of the Apostles praises the Jews of Berea, "for they received the word with all eagerness, examining the scriptures daily. . . ."[7]

The Bible also criticizes Christians for a lack of intellectual growth. The letter of Hebrews bemoans its readers' failure to advance beyond a rudimentary grasp of God's word, and urges them to go on to maturity.[8] Similarly Paul calls Christians in Corinth "babes in Christ," because they are still of the flesh and unready for solid food.[9]

The New Testament also tells us what role understanding should play in the Christian life. It leads to a life of fruitful activity. It contributes to the general upbuilding of the Christian community. And most important, it strengthens faith. Careful thinking increases comprehension, and increased comprehension deepens religious commitment. Colossians 2:2 links together the ideas of knowledge, understanding, and conviction, with the hope that Christians will "come to the full wealth of conviction which understanding brings" (NEB).

Besides helping us understand what we believe, careful thinking can also help us respond to questions or doubts. The typical path of personal faith is not a smooth, uninterrupted growth in confidence. Sooner or later, we all meet with obstacles that test our trust in God. When this happens, reason can help us. Finding answers to difficult questions can greatly strengthen our confidence. In fact, many people believe that dispelling doubt is the most important contribution reason can make to religious experience. This seems to have been true of Ellen White. Her well-known statement on faith and evidence appears in a chapter in *Steps to Christ* entitled "What to Do With Doubt."

In addition to increasing commitment and overcoming doubt, reason also affects the way we look at our beliefs. When we examine our beliefs, their relative importance can increase or decrease. Beliefs may become more or less important to us than we previously thought. Rational scrutiny can also affect our confidence in certain beliefs. People sometimes realize that some long-held ideas are not as well founded as they had thought. And sometimes they find new evidence to support their beliefs.

This shows there is always an element of risk involved when we start to think seriously about faith. We can never guarantee the outcome. Careful thinking can increase our understanding and deepen our commitment. But it may also expose inadequate arguments, raise questions, and introduce doubt.

Refusing to examine our beliefs, however, contradicts the very nature of faith. Faith means having the confidence to stake your life on what you believe. People who refuse to ask or answer questions give the impression that they are not sure of what they believe.

Although reason can make an important contribution to faith, it would be a serious mistake to overestimate it. Logic alone can never take someone all the way from unbelief to trust in God. People virtually never come to believe through a straightforward process of rational investigation, and it is doubtful that arguments have ever converted anybody. Instead, the factors that lead to faith are largely nonrational in character.

Jesus compares the new birth to the wind. "The wind blows where it wills, and you hear the sound of it, but you do not know whence it comes or whither it goes; so it is with every one who is born of the Spirit."[10] We can chart the general course of faith development but its origin is always a mystery.

The very nature of faith also limits the role of reason. Faith is a free decision. Like love, it can't be forced. If trust in God were the only conclusion reason allowed, it would eliminate freedom from faith. And if reason could produce faith, then faith would be a human achievement, a form of intellectual works righteousness, and not a response to God's grace. Furthermore, faith involves more confidence than reason can provide. Faith means trusting God without reservation. But rational inquiry can only achieve a high degree of probability, so it cannot produce the trusting certainty of faith. This is why faith always "goes beyond" the available evidence. It affirms and trusts in more than reason can demonstrate.

Since faith is not a rational product, there will always be room for doubt. We are never so close to God that we could never drift away. The Bible's most outstanding examples of faith faced their greatest trials as mature believers. Job and Abraham had their faith tested after years of walking with God. As their experience shows, faith is never a permanent achievement, something we acquire once and for all. We must affirm it again and again as life goes on.

All this prevents us from expecting either too little or too much from rational inquiry. Scientist-believers should view the search for truth as something fully compatible with their religious convictions. The desire to know and the capacity to discover are gifts from God. He intends us to use them. Scientist-believers also need to appreciate the role that reason plays in faith. By showing that faith is intellectually responsible, reason can prepare the way for faith. And once faith is present, reason can make it stronger. So, it is a grave mistake to disregard what reason says to religion. It is equally mistaken, however, to overemphasize what reason can do. Believers have a responsibility to think. But thinking alone will never be all there is to faith.

Science and Theology

Bill, Bob, and Sam all teach in the biology department of a fictitious Adventist university. They were close friends in college but over the years their thinking has led them in different directions. Lifelong Seventh-day Adventists, all three grew up listening to Bible stories and learning about nature from family camping trips, Pathfinder club and summer camps, and science teachers who used animal stories to illustrate religious lessons. It all turned them on to the world of living things. In fact, one reason each of them went into biology was the conviction that God speaks to us through nature.

They still share that conviction, but graduate study and their own research activities raise questions about the things they were taught as children. The earth seems a lot older than six thousand years. The geological column points to a long succession of life forms. And the notion of evolution gives a plausible explanation for the way different species have adapted to their environments. In addition, predation is endemic in the scheme of things from the cellular level on up, so it is difficult to attribute the origin of death to a single historical event. So, they have all faced questions about the relation between prevailing scientific views and what they read in the Bible.

Our three fictional friends respond to this challenge in different ways. For Bill, everything depends on the concept that the Bible is God's word. Behind the various biblical writings, he believes, there is one divine author, who guided their composition and compilation to insure that the Bible contains just what he wants to say the way he wants to say it. Since God does not inspire error, the Bible is fully reliable in all its contents, and accurate in everything it touches on—from our relation to God, to the origins of life on earth, to the history of the ancient Near East. And since the Bible is the basis of all true knowledge, it guides us when we look at the natural world. If what we see supports what we find in the Bible, we know the evidence is reliable. If it doesn't, then we know something is wrong with our interpretation. So, we rely on the Bible to help us interpret nature, not the other way around. Our task is not to subject God's word to human reason, but to submit human reason to the authority of God's word.

Bob finds it difficult to reconcile some of the Bible's claims with the results of scientific investigation. Like Bill, he believes that God inspired the Bible, but he's not sure that makes the Bible an infallible authority on every area of human inquiry. The Bible was obviously written before the development of modern science and many passages seem to reflect a prescientific view of the world. Furthermore, Bob doesn't know what it means for a scientist to "yield" to biblical authority or to any authority for that matter. As a scientist, Bob looks for explanations that best account for the data he collects. The phenomena under investigation determine the conclusions of his research. To set up an external standard that his results must meet, in other words, to have an outside source dictate what a scientific investigation is supposed to find, Bob feels, would interfere with the process. It wouldn't be science. When his study of the natural world leads to one conclusion and his study of the Bible leads to another, he takes both of them seriously. He continues to look for ways to harmonize the two, but he believes that we'll have to live with some unanswered questions until the Lord comes.

Sam takes a different tack. He sees no conflict between science and the Bible because the two belong to wholly different realms of experience. The Bible deals with spiritual matters. It concerns our relation to God. Its purpose is to make us wise unto salvation, not to inform us about the natural world. It is obvious that the Bible is not a textbook in mathematics or physics. It would be equally mistaken, he believes, to view it as a textbook in biology or in astronomy or geology, for that matter. Sam reads the Bible faithfully for spiritual guidance. He participates enthusiastically in the life of the church. But he keeps the scientific and religious parts of his life separate. The great nineteenth-century physicist Michael Faraday was a committed Christian believer. People said that when he went into his laboratory he forgot his religion and when he came out again he forgot his science.[11] Sam doesn't like to think that he ignores either science or religion. He believes that the world is God's creation. So, his religious convictions support the scientific task in a general way. But he doesn't believe that the idea of creation makes certain scientific theories more credible than others.

How then should Adventist scientists relate their scientific conclusions to their religious convictions? If their religious community teaches one thing and their scientific study teaches something else, what happens? What if God's two books seem to tell different stories? What do they do then?

I suppose the first thing to do is ask, so what? If we are strong believers, why should we care if prevailing scientific theories diverge from our religious doctrines? The reason this discrepancy creates an internal conflict for many of us is the tremendous influence that science exerts in our thinking. And the reason science is so influential is the fact that it is so effective. As Ian Barbour states at the beginning of his Gifford Lectures, "The first major challenge to religion in an age of science is the success of the methods of science."[12]

Let's face it: science is the most reliable means we have of acquiring knowledge. It provides us with enormous amounts of information. Moreover, the process of scientific inquiry is self-correcting and cumulative. Science perfectly exemplifies Bernard Lonergan's definition of a method. It is "a normative pattern of recurrent and related operations yielding cumulative and progressive results."[13] In other words, science keeps getting better. It not only keeps discovering more and more, it keeps finding better ways to do it. Consequently, science is the one area of human experience that exhibits its demonstrable progress. There is no evidence that human beings are improving in moral judgment or aesthetic sensitivity. But there is no doubt that we know a lot more than we did before.

It is no wonder that the development of science, as John Herman Randall notes, was more important than any other factor in shaping the modern mind.[14] Like it or not, our view of the world is largely framed by science. So, behind the apparent conflict between scientific conclusions and religious convictions lies our immense confidence in the strategy of science and the view of reality it seems to support.

According to the conventional view science is an autonomous rational enterprise that follows its own internal logic in testing hypotheses against reliable observations. The scientist accumulates data, formulates a theory to account for it, and then tests the theory against further data. So, there is an inductive move from data to theory and a hypothetical-deductive move from theory to data. The data either confirm or disprove the theory. And the scientist moves on to make further observations, formulate and test additional theories. Over time a reliable body of truths accumulates.[15]

It is customary for people to look at religion with this general view of science in mind. And religion naturally suffers by comparison. "In this popular stereotype," to quote Ian Barbour, "the scientist is seen as open-minded, the theologian as closed-minded. The scientist's theories are tentative hypotheses that are continually criticized and revised, while religious beliefs are unchanging dogmas that the faithful accept without question." Accordingly, "science alone is objective, open-minded, universal, cumulative, and progressive." In contrast, religion is "subjective, closed-minded, parochial, uncritical, and resistant to change."[16] So the very nature of religious conviction seems to separate it from science. If scientific inquiry is the paragon of intellectual achievement, then religion is intellectually irresponsible. If you are truly religious, then you can't think scientifically.

People respond to this challenge in several different ways. Some grant that religion is purely subjective and proceed to make a virtue of it. According to nonrealists, there is no conflict between science and religion, and there never could be, because they pertain to completely different things. Science tells us about reality, religion expresses our reaction to reality. For Don Cupitt of Cambridge University religious beliefs can be entirely a matter of personal choice. We select them not because they are true, but because they are helpful. We follow a religious tradition not because it describes reality, but because it helps us cope with reality.[17] I once heard him say that he prays every day even though he does not believe that there is a God. Cupitt's position is extreme, to say the least, but there are others who follow a similar strategy. A much less radical example is George Lindbeck of Yale Divinity School. He interprets Christian doctrines as rules of discourse, which guide individual and communal life. They express a self-contained cultural system and do not describe the objective universe.[18]

To formulate the issue precisely we should speak of science and theology, rather than science and religion. Theology is to religion what science is to sensory experience. It carefully examines the beliefs of a religious community. It identifies these beliefs, explores their meaning, assesses their truth, and sometimes responds to criticisms about them. Like science, theology examines data, formulates theories, and tests its theories against further data. Like scientific theories, theological ideas, or doctrines, must meet the basic criteria of adequacy to the data, coherence, comprehensiveness, and fertility. In spite of their general structural similarity, theology differs from science in significant ways, too. The most obvious is the sort of data with which it deals. Christian theology by definition takes the Bible as its basic source. It draws its theories or doctrines from the Bible and tests them by further examining the Bible.[19] The notion of divine revelation distinguishes the Bible from any of the data to which science appeals. Scientific data are in principle accessible to any inquirer and further discovery may significantly alter the data on which we rely. But the contents of the Bible are perceptible only to those who have faith, and Christians believe that nothing will ever supersede the Bible. So the Bible enjoys a position of authority for theology unlike anything in the realm of scientific inquiry.[20]

This helps to explain why scientific change is less traumatic than theological change. We rather expect scientists to change their minds over time, but we are not at all sure that theologians should do so. As Iain Pears asks in his recent novel, *An Instance of the Fingerpost*, "How is that when a man of God shifts his opinion it proves the weakness of his views, and when a man of science does so it demonstrates the value of his method?"[21]

Religious experience also makes an important contribution to theology, and this, too, distinguishes it from science. Scientific data are in principle public, that is, accessible to any observer with sufficient patience and skill. But religious experiences are notoriously private. Sometimes they involve dramatic, sensational events, such as the fire that descended on Mount Carmel. But for the most part they are internal, known only to the person who has them.

So, what are we to do when scientific evidence points in one direction and our religious convictions run in another? Is there any way to resolve this tension? I don't have a simple answer to this question, but there are several things that hint at a resolution, without promising that we can actually reach one.

On the side of religion there are doctrinal considerations that may be helpful. Our perspective on humanity prevents us from being either overly optimistic or overly pessimistic about our ability to understand. On the one hand, the world is the creation of an intelligent Being, who placed his image on humans and gave us sovereignty over what he had made. Consequently, we should have confidence in both the possibility and the value of exploring the universe. Intellectual inquiry is good, and it leads to truth. On the other hand, the results of the fall are significant and pervasive. Sin affects both our powers of inquiry and the world we investigate. And this requires us to qualify our claims to knowledge.

The doctrine of creation provides a strong foundation for serious scientific endeavor. And the doctrine of the fall prevents us from taking the results too seriously. I believe this gives us a basis for the sort of qualified optimism that seems to characterize scientific endeavor at its best wherever it takes place. We follow the evidence where it leads, we develop the conclusions it calls for, but we recognize the limitations of all human inquiry so we keep the issues on the table for further discussion.

If all this discourages people from trying to integrate or coordinate their science and their theology, they should take heart from the fact that recent developments point to a more positive relation between the two. The disciplines are not as dissimilar as many people think, and there are indications that each has something to contribute to the other.

First of all, science is not as "scientific" as people used to think. From the work of Thomas Kuhn and others, it is clear that the course science actually follows does not fit the conventional view of science we described earlier. The picture of dispassionate investigators accumulating data, generalizing, and objectively testing their theories is a caricature. It doesn't fit the facts. The truth is that all data are theory laden. Without some sort of theory we wouldn't know what to count as data and investigation could never start. Then, too, theories are not mere generalizations from the data.

They require imaginative insights, which data alone could never produce. Furthermore, scientists operate within the framework of large-scale, widely shared assumptions, or "paradigms." In other words, they take a lot of important ideas for granted. And when scientists exchange one paradigm for another, their reasons for doing so are never entirely "reasonable." Data alone don't require it. Finally the whole enterprise of science rests on the fundamental conviction that the natural world is orderly and trustworthy. "Without faith that nature is subject to law" wrote Norbert Wiener, the founder of cybernetics, "there can be no science. No amount of demonstration can ever prove that nature is subject to law."[22]

The fact that science rests on unprovable assumptions, that it relies on paradigms and requires an imaginative interaction between theory and data, gives it a strong similarity to theology.

Theologians have also said some things during the past few years that may help us to coordinate, if not integrate, religious and scientific beliefs more effectively. The statements I have in mind reject the idea that we can construct a system of thought that ties our beliefs together in a tight logical package and situate them firmly on a foundation of self-evident truths. This sort of rational system is unattainable anywhere, these theologians argue. It doesn't even work for science—as William Placher notes, the case for science's distinctive rationality has disappeared[23]—and it won't work for theology either. This doesn't mean we have to give up the quest for rationality but we have to find a different way of construing it. And when we do, it will apply to both religious and scientific beliefs.

This is the general position of Nancey Murphy of Fuller Theological Seminary. In her book *Theology in the Age of Scientific Reasoning,* Murphy argues that theology can meet the standards of scientific inquiry when they are properly formulated.[24] For Imre Lakatos, science is a "research program" comprising a set of theories and a body of data. Central to the program is a "hard core" theory. Surrounding it are auxiliary hypotheses that connect it to the data and change as the data require. Murphy maintains that this is a good way to think of theology. Our religious beliefs form a cluster, with some beliefs more central than others, and we modify them as new evidence requires. On this view there is an openness, a flexibility to theology that allows for both continuity and change in our beliefs over time, and opens us to relevant information wherever it comes from. According to Murphy, this approach not only gives theology a scientific form, it envisions a way for theology and science to communicate with and contribute to each other.

One of the most encouraging developments in this general area is the new openness of scientific theories to the presence of God in the universe. In its cover story of July 10, 1998, *Newsweek* notes the growing visibility of religious conviction among scientists today and reviews some of the reasons they give for believing in God. They include the remarkable ability of the human mind to understand the workings of the universe—"The world follows rules that human minds can figure out"—and various signs that the cosmos is "custom-made for life and consciousness." There are also scientists who believe that big-bang cosmology evolution, chaos theory, and quantum mechanics allow for divine participation in the natural world. The article concludes with this observation: "Once, science and religion were viewed as two fundamentally different, even antagonistic, ways of pursuing the quest to understand the world, and science stood accused of smothering faith and killing God. Now, it may strengthen belief. And although it cannot prove God's existence science might whisper to believers where to seek the divine."[25]

In a related development, Darwin's theory of evolution has come under increasing suspicion over the years. And many people now question its adequacy as a scientific explanation of life's history on this planet. Tom Bethell, Phil Johnson, and Michael Behe have made important contributions to this discussion. So, there seems to be less rigidity to some prevalent scientific theories than there used to be, and greater openness on the part of scientists to religion.

While we welcome these developments as ways to ease the tension between science and theology or to ease the tension within believers who are scientists, an important caveat is in order. It is essential for us to recognize just what this openness of science to theology and theology to science does and does not do. Science can contribute to natural theology the search for public evidence to support the reality of God. It can also contribute to a theology of nature, an interpretation of the natural world as the object of God's creating and sustaining love. Religion can inform the overall perspective of the scientist and suggest questions for scientific investigation. But this mutual openness does not provide a basis for something like "religious science," that is to say religiously authorized scientific statements, or scientific theories that have only religious authority to support them. If religion tells science what to say— more accurately if religious authorities tell scientists what to say—both science and religion are the poorer. For all the value of interrelating science and theology, we need to respect their integrity as discrete disciplines and not allow one to dictate the contents of the other. Scientific theories require the support of empirical data. Theological statements require the support of religious data. Coordinating them is helpful; conflating them is not.

There is another significant difference between theology and science, which anyone who does theology has discovered. This is the role that religious beliefs play in the life of the believer and the community of faith. Influential ideas always die hard. People are reluctant to part with concepts and perspectives that have served them well. This is true in science, but it is doubly true in religion. A religious doctrine is analogous to a scientific theory only to a point. It purports to make sense of evidence and remain open to revision and reformulation. But, in fact, it does much more. Theological doctrines deal with the deepest convictions and highest values that people hold. Their tentacles involve the strongest feelings we have. Moreover, religious beliefs are a unifying factor in people's lives. Common convictions are the binding force that holds religious communities together. For this reason, religious communities are enormously resistant to doctrinal changes. And anyone dealing with issues of this nature must be sensitive to this fact.[26]

The Community of Scientists and the Community of Faith

Tom and Ted were classmates thirty years ago at another imaginary Adventist college. Tom went to graduate school and returned to their alma mater to teach chemistry. He's tried hard to do all the things expected of small-college teachers. He has received several modest research grants, and he is known as an effective classroom communicator. His students generally do well on the Medical College Admission Test, and several of them have gone to graduate work and careers in chemistry. He makes it a point to keep in touch.

Ted went into the ministry and worked his way up the administrative ladder to become president of a constituent conference. Ted's first love is soul winning. He longs to see the message go to all the world and the work finished. So he is deeply committed to evangelism. He urges all his pastors to hold evangelistic series, and he wants to do more outreach with radio and television. As a member of the college board, Ted knows how much money it takes to run a college and, quite frankly, he wonders if the payoff is worth it. He asks himself how many people would join the church if they put the college subsidy into evangelism. Ted also wonders if our colleges are doing their job. He is disturbed by reports that students sometimes have their faith shaken by things their teachers say. He wants assurances that faculty members support the church's fundamental beliefs.

What should someone like Tom say to someone like Ted? How do we justify our involvement in education? And what is the role of the scientist in an Adventist institution?

It is obvious that Adventists have made a tremendous investment in education. In fact, it is one of the distinctive things about our denomination. We have the largest unified private-school system in the world, in spite of our modest size. In North America alone, where Adventists number less than a million, we support a dozen colleges and universities. With higher education growing more expensive every year, it is no wonder that people have begun to question the value of our investment. If the central work of the church is mission, it is natural to ask how scholarship fits into the picture. To some, education distracts us from the church's work. So, what is the role of education in Adventism?

There are certain religious communities that subsume their schools under their evangelistic endeavors. My wife and I conducted a workshop at a Bible college in Oakland, California, a couple of years ago. The campus surrounded a large church and was part of an extensive school program that went from kindergarten all the way up. The whole program was supported by a large congregation that grew up several decades back as the result of an evangelistic effort in that city. The evangelist is the church pastor; her two daughters serve as president and dean of the college. At a place like this, evangelism is primary; education is secondary.

For Adventists, however, the situation is quite different. For important reasons, education stands, not at the edge, but at the center of our mission and our identity. One is our holistic concept of salvation. According to Ellen White, the work of education and the work of redemption are one.[27] Because a human being is a multi-dimensional unity, a physical, mental, and spiritual reality, religion is not just a spiritual matter. It affects the entire person. It enhances all the powers of human life. It not only heals the soul, it elevates the mind. Our commitment to education reflects the conviction that salvation affects the whole person.

It also reflects our understanding that salvation is a lifelong experience. For Adventists, justification and sanctification are complementary aspects of God's saving work in human life. He not only forgives our sins and restores us to our place in his family, he imparts his Spirit to us in order to transform our lives and make us partakers of the divine nature. With other Christians, we emphasize the importance of helping others come to Christ and join the church, but we are also concerned with everything that happens afterward. We see salvation as a lifelong experience. For Adventists, church growth is more than just increasing membership, it is spiritual development as long as time lasts. Nurture is essential to the meaning of salvation.

Another factor that elevates education is our doctrine of creation. If this is our Father's world, then it is worth exploring and understanding. It deserves all the attention we can give it. And if we are creatures whose origin and destiny are linked to this planet, then we need to view ourselves within the framework of this larger reality.

For a number of reasons, then, education is central to Adventism. The academy is not irrelevant to the church. It is not incidental to the church. It is part and parcel of what the church is all about. Adventist theology thus provides an important mandate for the work of the scientist-believer.

It is not enough, however, to applaud the work of academics as important to the general mission of the church. We need to say something about their role within the Christian community. What are the church's responsibilities to its scientists? What are their responsibilities to the church?

On a general level, the church owes its scientists what it owes all its members—an inclusive, supportive community. And this requires a commitment to the full scope of the community's life. Beliefs are important to the life of any religious community. But belonging to a community involves more than doctrinal assent. It involves participating in the life of the community. The church is not just a believing community but a caring and worshiping community as well, so open communication is vital to its life. Consequently, all of us in the church must strive to develop an atmosphere of trust where people can ask serious questions and explore difficult issues without fear that they will generate suspicion or lead to repercussions.

On a more specific level, the church also needs to affirm and respect the value of the scientific enterprise. Since the integrity of scientific inquiry requires a degree of autonomy, the church must allow its scientists the freedom they need to pursue their work.

While we're thinking about what the church owes its scientists, we should also consider what our scientists owe each other. Scientists should offer each the same trust that they want from the church as a whole. Scientist-believers need to cultivate a culture of conversation. They need to communicate with each other frankly, honestly, charitably. This can only happen where there is trust on all sides. If we are afraid that sharing our concerns and our questions will arouse suspicion and limit our influence, then real conversation will never take place.

The church not only owes its scientists something, scientists owe the church a great deal, too. In particular; they have a responsibility to help prepare our young people for life in the larger world. This involves training students for the rigorous work required of them in graduate school and professional programs. It means preparing them for the questions and challenges that believing Christians will face in the larger academic world. And, most important of all, it includes mentoring—personally demonstrating what it means to be both scientist and believer.

Scientist-believers can also help the church fulfill its mission to extend the gospel into all areas of human endeavor and explore the implications of the gospel for all of life. In recent years a number of conservative Christian thinkers have been examining the relationship between Christianity and scholarship. They issue ringing appeals to Christians in the academy to say more about the impact of their faith on their scholarship. In *The Scandal of the Evangelical Mind,* Mark Noll bemoans how little evangelical Christians have contributed to serious scholarship. Evangelicalism is a large and influential movement on the religious scene, but what great ideas has it communicated to the larger world? What scholarly impact has it had in the natural sciences, in the social sciences, in the humanities, in the fine arts? Not enough, he asserts, not nearly enough in comparison to its potential.[28]

George Marsden issues a similar challenge. In *The Outrageous Idea of Christian Scholarship* he argues that a creationist, incarnational view of reality should reverberate throughout the academy. Naturally it will affect different disciplines in different ways, but as he says, "there would be huge implications when [believing] scientists relate their subjects to the larger issues of life." In particular, they will oppose the view that materialism "provides the best account of reality."[29]

No one offers a more urgent appeal along these lines than Alvin Plantinga, a distinguished philosopher of religion. In a recent address, he argues that scholarship and science are anything but neutral. To the contrary, he sees a tremendous struggle between Christianity and two rival perspectives—perennial naturalism, the view that human beings are simply parts of nature, and creative antirealism, the view that all ideas are nothing more than mental constructs and projections. To counter the pervasive influence of these movements, Plantinga calls on Christian scholars to extend their religious convictions into the scholarly arena. Since Christians have the means to make sense of the whole range of human experience, including things such as love, knowledge, aggression, beauty, humor, and sensitivity, we must not abandon the field to purely naturalistic, reductionistic perspectives. "As Christians we need and want answers to the sorts of questions that arise in the theoretical and interpretative disciplines," he states. And "what we know as Christians is crucially relevant to . . . a proper understanding; therefore . . . [we] should pursue these disciplines from a specifically Christian perspective."[30]

Let us conclude on the same confident note with which we began. The church, the academy, and the world need the contributions of Christian scientists.

NOTES

1. Gen. 1:1 (REB).
2. Ps. 19:1 (NRSV).
3. Rom. 1:20 (NRSV).
4. Rev. 14:7 (NRSV).
5. Tom Stoppard, *Jumpers* (New York: Grove Press, 1972), p. 25.
6. 2 Pet. 1:5–7 (RSV).
7. Acts 17:11 (RSV).
8. Heb. 5:11–13; 6:1.
9. 1 Cor. 3:1–3 (RSV).
10. John 3:8 (KJV).
11. John Polkinghorne, *One World: The Interaction of Science and Theology* (Princeton, NJ: Princeton University Press, 1986), p. 97.
12. Ian Barbour, *Religion in an Age of Science: The Gifford Lectures,* 2 vols. (San Francisco: Harper, 1990, 1993).
13. Bernard Lonergan, *Method in Theology* (New York: Herder & Herder, 1972), p. 4.
14. John Herman Randall, Jr., *The Making of the Modern Mind: A Survey of the Intellectual Background of the Present Age* (New York: Columbia University Press, 1977), p. 164.
15. Barbour, *Religion,* pp. 31–32. We could expand every element of this account. For example, scientists evaluate their theories in light of four criteria. The most important, of course, is agreement with the data. The others are coherence with other theories, explanatory comprehensiveness—the best theories explain a lot of material—and fertility in providing a framework for further investigation.
16. Barbour, *Religion,* p. 5.
17. Don Cupitt, *The Sea of Faith* (New York: Cambridge University Press, 1988).
18. Cited in Barbour, *Religion,* p. 14
19. Other factors, too, inevitably play a role in this theological reflection—notably tradition, experience, and reason—but theologians differ as to whether we should construe them as sources alongside the Bible, or aids to help us understand the Bible.

20. Another feature of the Bible that distinguishes it from scientific data—at least a good deal of scientific data—is its historical character. The events of which the Bible speaks, like all historical events, are unrepeatable. We cannot reproduce the data under different conditions. This is not unlike the data that some sciences deal with, such as cosmology and paleontology, but it distinguishes theology from a good deal of scientific endeavor. Theologians must develop their theories on the basis of data that accumulated a long time ago.

21. Iain Pears, *An Instance at the Fingerpost* (New York: Riverhead Books, 1988), p. 551.

22. Quoted in David N. Livingstone, "Farewell to Arms: Reflections on the Encounter between Science and Faith," in *Christian Faith and Practice in the Modern World: Theology from an Evangelical Point of View*, ed. Mark A. Noll and David F. Wells (Grand Rapids, MI: Eerdmans, 1988), p. 260.

23. William C. Placher, *Unapologetic Theology: A Christian Voice in a Pluralistic Conversation* (Louisville, KY: Westminster John Knox, 1989).

24. Nancey Murphy, *Theology in the Age of Scientific Reasoning* (Ithaca: Cornell University Press, 1990).

25. *Newsweek*, 10 July 1998, p. 61. One of those featured in the article is John Polkinghorne, a physicist who entered the Anglican clergy. As one of his book titles indicates, *One World* (see no. 11 above), Polkinghorne affirms the fundamental harmony of science and theology. He believes that they have the same ultimate objective—seeking to understand reality—and are capable of mutual and fruitful interaction.

26. Galileo wasn't sensitive, according to a careful reading of his confrontation with church authorities, and instead of changing minds quickly and radically as he intended, he hardened them against his views. There are lessons to be learned from all sides of that experience. See Jerome J. Langford, *Galileo, Science, and the Church* (South Bend, IN: Saint Augustine's Press, 1998).

27. E. G. White, *Education* (Mountain View, CA: Pacific Press, 1905), p. 50.

28. Mark A. Noll, *The Scandal of the Evangelical Mind* (Grand Rapids, MI: Eerdmans, 1996).

29. George M. Marsden, *The Outrageous Idea of Christian Scholarship* (New York: Oxford University Press, 1997), p. 92.

30. Plantinga's views on scholarship are spelled out in several articles at the following Web site: www.hisdefense.org/articles.htm. Or visit www.ucsb.edu/fscf/library/plantinga/OCS.html.

This chapter was originally published in *Spectrum* (spring 1999), pp. 21–31.

CHAPTER 11

A New Immortality?

BRIAN G. EDGAR

Rev. Dr. Brian Edgar is convenor of the Australian Evangelical Alliance Theological Commission and academic dean of the Bible College of Victoria, Melbourne, Australia, where he teaches theology and ethics, including courses on the relationship of science and theology. He has a particular interest in the implications of bio-science and technology for a theology of the human person.

One of the theological challenges of the twentieth century has been to respond to those issues relating to the *creation* of human life. Whether theology has adequately met the challenge or not, birth control and enhancement techniques must rank as one of the major social developments of the century. The contraceptive pill and abortion have had an enormous impact on social structures, family relations, female and male roles, sexual attitudes, work patterns, and global economics. Birth-enhancement techniques, including the various reproductive technologies, in vitro fertilization, genetic engineering, cloning, genetic screening, and gene therapy, are set to have a similar impact. All of these developments require a theological understanding of the nature of the person and of the way in which humanity reflects the image of God both individually and socially, and it is likely that the twenty-first century will not see any easing of the imperative to describe the nature of the human person in theological terms. In fact, it is more likely that an even more intense scrutiny of theoanthropology[1] (the theology of the human person) will be needed due to developments concerning the *extension* and then the *ending* of human life. This will come about because of the probability that we are soon to be presented with the prospect of medical technology, known as telomere therapy, which will enable human life to be extended by hundreds of years and perhaps indefinitely. This chapter will focus on the theological implications for the

understanding of immortality in the context of this possible development in the third millennium.

Telomere Therapy[2]

It is a serious possibility that telomere therapy will be available for extending life span between 2005 and 2015.[3] The technology involved goes beyond attempting to establish optimum standards of good health in order
to achieve greater longevity, and well beyond attempts to eliminate individual diseases. Telomere therapy is aimed at investigating and manipulating the most fundamental aging mechanisms of the human body so
that there can be an almost unlimited extension of human life. One of the
simplest ways for anyone to gauge the social significance of such a discovery is to ask happily married people what they think it would be like to be
married "till death us do part" if both partners were going to live four
hundred years. There are enough significant implications for career and
work patterns, global population, marriage and family structures, and social relationships to guarantee a large-scale social transformation.

The various component organs of the body have different cells,
which function in a variety of ways according to the needs of the particular organ and which reproduce themselves at different rates. The life
of the whole organism is longer than that of any of the individual cells
of the body but the life span of the organism as a whole is restricted if
the various organs are not able to reproduce cells. Until the early 1960s
it was generally assumed that cells could, theoretically, reproduce
themselves perpetually and that the failure of cells to do so was simply
the result of an accumulation of degenerating conditions. In 1961,
Leonard Hayflick and Paul Moorhead demonstrated the falsity of this
and showed that even under optimal conditions cells would only reproduce a finite number of times.[4] Each cell type has its own reproductive
limit, now known as the Hayflick limit. Some cells, however, do not
seem to have this limitation. The very problem with cancer cells is that
they reproduce indefinitely, to the point where the sheer number of
cells overwhelms the normal functioning of the host. If the processes
that control this can be discovered and manipulated, might it not be
possible to find a way to cause cancer cells to reach a reproductive limit
and also to persuade normal bodily cells to reproduce indefinitely and
thus extend the life span of the organism as a whole?

Telomeres are structures found at the ends of eukaryotic linear
chromosomes and consist of thousands of tandem repeats of the DNA

sequence TTAGGG. These terminal repeats are highly conserved among all vertebrates. Every time a cell divides, the chromosome is duplicated and its telomeres get shorter. In 1986, Howard Cooke of the Medical Research Council in Edinburgh[8] noticed that telomeres in reproductive cells were longer than those in shorter-lived somatic cells such as those found in skin and muscle. Most normal somatic cells have Hayflick limits that are comparable but some cells, including the reproductive cells, need to divide more than would normally be the case. Cooke speculated that the somatic cells might not be able to make an enzyme to repair their telomeres and that this would account for them reaching their Hayflick limit after less replications than reproductive cells. And it seems that he is right—it is likely that the telomeres are the molecular clock that triggers replicative senescence. Once a threshold number of TTAGGG repeats is reached, cells become unable to divide. Some cells, however, produce an enzyme called telomerase, which rebuilds and maintains the telomeres and thus extends their replicative life. Telomerase has now been found in a number of classes of normal cells (including stem cells, gonadal germ cells, and skin fibroblast cells) and all of them are cells with a high turnover rate or which are in a continuously replicating pool of differentiating cells. It seems that an extended replicative life is made possible by the presence of telomerase. It is also significant that the level of telomerase in these cells is still significantly less than that found in cancer cells, which are virtually "immortal."[5]

In 1998, several studies were conducted in which human cells were cloned. Some were telomerase negative and they exhibited telomere shortening and normal cell senescence. In one study those cells that were telomerase positive exhibited both elongated telomeres and delayed senescence, exceeding their normal life span by at least twenty doublings, thus indicating that perhaps telomere loss is the intrinsic timing mechanism in human cells. To be able to treat human cells with telomerase in this way is thus a significant step forward not only in the search for significantly extended life span but also, more immediately, in the treatment of certain aging problems including atrophy of the skin, muscular degeneration, and atherosclerosis.[6] People with Down's syndrome or failed bone-marrow transplants could also benefit from telomerase treatment[7] and it may be an answer for those with Hutchinson Gilford syndrome,[8] who have an average life span of 12.7 years (and, significantly, skin fibroblasts with telomere lengths characteristic of cells from far older patients[9]).

The role of the telomeres in this is only one part of a broader theory. Human aging is controlled by gene expression and operates through free radical damage to the cell. Senescent cells have altered function (through gene-expression changes such as altered patterns of collagen production) and increased damage (as a result of poorer control of free-radical metabolism). Such senescent cells introduce dysfunction at the cell and organ levels of operation. Altogether, the process is a complex picture of senescent gene expression regulated by telomeres and the telomeres are only part of the picture. They are, though, the part of the process that has had the focus. Fossel says that "shortly after the year 2000 telomere therapy will be available for treating cancer and telomere therapy will be available for extending your life span between 2005 and 2015."[10]

This is not to say that even the greatest success with telomere therapy would eliminate death. Even if this scenario turns out to be right, people will still be able to wear out and die and no one will be immune from other diseases and accidents. Perhaps talking in terms of an indefinite life span is more accurate as it leaves open the question of the ultimate human life expectancy.

Even though in relatively recent times there have been significant changes to mortality rates, it seems that over the past forty thousand years at least there has not been any significant change in potential life span. The fact that no Neanderthal skeletal remains have been discovered that give any indication of a life span of more than thirty or forty years simply indicates that this was the maximum possible given the very significant environmental dangers that were faced. Even two to three thousand years ago, environmental conditions meant that the average life expectancy was low, but evidence from ancient Egyptian, Hebrew, Greek, and other cultures point to a reasonably consistent picture in which the maximum human life span in optimum conditions is seventy to one hundred years.[11]

Nor is the general constancy of the maximum human life span negated by great changes to mortality rates in the twentieth century. In this century in western society there has been an increase in average life span of around 25 years. For example, in Australia in the 1990s the average life expectancy was around 80.5 years for females and around 74.5 years for males instead of about 48 and 51 years respectively at the turn of the century. But this average increase is obviously achieved by keeping people alive longer, especially by reducing infant mortality, rather than by extending the maximum possible life span, which has not significantly changed. To illustrate this one may ask how much longer a person can expect to live, assuming a person avoids disease and accident and survives to 65. In the United States in 1900 it was a further 11.5 years (male) or 12.2 years (female). Today it is only three to five years more than that. In short, medical science has had significant success in increasing the average life expectancy but so far has only managed a modest improvement in the normal maximum life span.

Competing Theories of Aging

It this likely to change? Or is telomere therapy one more scientific theory that has suffered from overoptimism? Steve Austad[12] makes the case against telomere as the overall solution to human aging. While telomere research is extremely important, Austad thinks that the study of the growth of cells since Hayflick has been mistaken to the extent that it assumes that it is a study of aging as such. Austad argues that cell research is very relevant to aging but is not aging itself. He distinguishes between *mechanisms* and *causes* and argues that senescent gene expression, even if controlled by the telomeres, is a mechanistic theory of how a certain part of the aging process takes place rather than a causal theory of why humans age. Austad reviews the three present causal theories of aging: the "good of the species" theory; the "rate of living" theory; and the "evolutionary aging" theory. Each will attribute to telomere therapy a different role and status in the aging process.

The "good-of-the-species" understanding of cellular behavior argues that evolutionary theory requires that any process as ubiquitous as aging must benefit the population as a whole apart from any benefit to the individual entity or its immediate offspring. Therefore cellular senescence should not be equated with human aging per se but rather should be seen as a normal part of bodily development by which the body avoids its own destruction through unlimited cell reproduction. Without a limitation on cell reproduction it would not be possible for the body to survive. The Hayflick limit is therefore a part of the normal growth and development of the body, a necessary protective device against cancer, and an important mechanism in the cell processes of the body. It is neither a pathological disorder nor an overall causal explanation of aging. If this interpretation is correct, then the search goes on for a broader causal understanding of the aging process.

Austad rejects this theory however, arguing that it emerges from a misunderstanding of evolutionary theory when it requires a benefit to the population as a whole. Most traits or processes that are beneficial to an individual or his or her immediate offspring will also be beneficial to the species as a whole, but not all. For example, a propensity to reproduce more offspring can certainly be beneficial to the individual entity and immediate offspring but it may not be beneficial to the species as a whole if, say, food supplies are limited. Where there is a conflict will the interests of the individual or that of the species prevail? There is an analogy with the reproduction of cancer cells where there is a conflict between reproduction of the cancer cells—reproduction is certainly advantageous for the cells and their "offspring" but it is not advantageous for the host organism or the overall population of cells that constitute the organ. Just as the individual cancer cell wins out at the expense of the whole, so too must we say the same about aging. That is to say, we should not assume, along with the "good of the species" theory, that aging is a process that is necessarily beneficial to the species as a whole. The implications of this for understanding the aging process and the telomere theory of replicative control are that these processes need not be presumed to be best understood as a theory or cause of aging of the organism as a whole but need only be seen as having their purpose in the basic requirements for the proper development of the individual entity alone.

Austad discusses two other possible causal explanations of aging—the "rate of living" or metabolism theory in which the rate of energy use is seen as causing aging via the collateral damage of biomechanical processes through the production of toxic by-products or by oxygen-free radicals (oxidants). However, he declares it to be a theory that is now "as dead as the proverbial doornail."[13] Like cell senescence these processes may play a part in the aging mechanism but the scientific evidence for elongated life span based upon, for example, antioxidant vitamins is not convincing, despite popular support. In the search for a causal theory one would be better to revert to the investigation of telomerase or to move to a broader "evolutionary aging" theory. Austad prefers the latter.

He notes that a reduced vulnerability to environmental accidents leads to slower aging. This is seen experimentally in research with certain insect and animal populations and is consistent with the general trend for larger animals to live longer—because they are less susceptible to external threats. In the context of reduced danger the imperative to move through the life cycle rapidly is diminished. The theory is a general one and the processes by which it is implemented can include a variety of mechanisms, including cellular behavior. The point Austad makes is that discovering a mechanism is not the same as discovering an overall theory and telomerase therapy is, in principle, not going to provide the answers that some people expect.

"Top Down" Versus "Bottom Up"

How does the theologian or other lay-scientist assess the value of these competing views? In terms developed by Arthur Peacocke the conflict is between "top down" and "bottom up" approaches to explaining causes.[14] Generally, scientific explanations are tightly locked into the concept of causality and any detection of a causal sequence of the kind that event "x" causes event "y" is frequently taken to be a sufficient explanation of the process and sometimes also a predictor of event "z." The final value of such inductive reasoning has been the subject of philosophical debate (concerning the extent to which a sequence of events can be logically predictive) and it ultimately requires some intelligible explanation in terms of underlying relationships. Yet despite the problems that exist with the fundamental uncertainty of complex systems, the overall effectiveness of simple induction cannot be denied. Methodologically, scientific reductionism, whereby complex situations are broken down into simple units for analysis, has been responsible for scientific progress to the point where "bottom up" causality has frequently been perceived as the *only* form of causation. Telomere theory as an explanation of aging is a form of "bottom up" causation.

"Top down" causation in contrast refers to the influence of the state of the system as a whole on the behavior of its components so that changes occur to the components of a system because of their incorporation in the system.[15] Recognition of "top down" causation is important, not least because science is typically reductionist and never fails to look for "bottom up" causation whereas recognition of "top down" is less frequent. Properly understood, the processes of causation have a dual character—an "up and down" interaction. Peacocke identifies four levels that are able to interact in terms of causation.[16] The first level is that of the *physical world* of matter and energy existing in space-time. The physical sciences typically focus on this level. The second level is that of *living organisms* of cells and bodies and so forth, which is the interest of the biological sciences. The third level concerns the *behavior of living organisms* and is attended to by the behavioral sciences including psychology. Finally, the fourth level is the domain of *human culture* including art, economics, literature, and science. These levels interact and it is quite appropriate, for example, for the level 1 physical sciences to indicate to level 2 researchers those systems of causation that influence events in the realm of level 2. But it is also right to reflect on the influence of the system as a whole and to seek downward influences as well.

Indeed Peacocke argues that "'top down' causation has increasing significance in those kind of complex systems that are living."[17]

The recognition of the role of such "top down" causation in no way
detracts from that of "bottom up" theories. The two are able to exist har-
moniously. In the present case cellular theory is intrinsically a "bottom
up" mechanistic explanation, which need not be in competition with
"top down" causal theories. If a conflict does occur, then one or the
other or both theories must be modified. But it is not impossible for such
conflicts to be more apparent than real. Conflict is expressed in the present case when Fossel sees the limitation on the reproduction of cells according to the Hayflick limit as problematic and the fundamental reason
for aging. Cellular senescence is pathological and degenerative. He interprets this as a problem to be overcome in the search for longevity.

From a different point of view Austad sees the Hayflick limit and
the behavior of cells with limited life as being necessary and normal
parts of life that enable normal bodily development. He sees Fossel's
pathological interpretation of this cellular behavior as misleading and
argues that cellular behavior is mechanistic rather than causal in that it
might explain *how* aging takes place but not *why*. He prefers an explanation at a higher level. This is not to say that he repudiates the value or
even the findings of telomere research but he does have a different assessment of the primary purpose of the Hayflick limit (which is not so
much to do with aging as it is to do with a necessary defense against
cancer); he also has a different view of the overall cause of aging.

Our assessment of this situation and its various interpretations
needs to include the following observations. Both sides are agreed that
serious progress can be made in the next twenty to fifty years (at the
most) concerning the aging processes and the possibility of significantly
extending the human life span. There is agreement that the examination of cellular behavior is very relevant and will play a part in understanding the process. The reductionist, "bottom up" approaches tend to
be more optimistic, but ultimately those who require a "top down" approach will have to be satisfied—a holistic explanation will be needed
in order to fully comprehend the situation. With regard to the debate
concerning the role of telomeres in cell behavior, there is no fundamental reason why the process of cellular senescence cannot be *both* normal
and developmental as well as ultimately pathological and degenerative.

Finally, we note that reductionist "bottom up" approaches have
been enormously successful and it would be unwise to rule out some of
the possibilities envisaged by some of its advocates. Nor is it simply
wishful thinking to put a timescale on the likely developments. It is true

that many revolutionary scientific discoveries have been quite unpredictable not only as to the timing of their discovery but also as to the very idea. For instance, no one said, "I think that today I'll invent a machine that will allow us to look through a person's skin and muscle so that we can see their bones and other internal organs." Such an idea would rightly have been considered extremely improbable but it came about, quite unpredictably, as the by-product of research of a different nature. At other times though the progress of scientific discovery is much more predictable—though never certain—as science moves along generally predictable lines once fundamental principles have been established. Telomere therapy may be one such development and even if it is not the final answer it will still constitute a major step forward in understanding the mechanisms of the aging process, and the focus of research will simply move on to another area with the advantage of a greater understanding of cellular aging processes.

Immortality: Conflict, Integration, and Dialogue

If a twenty-first-century theology of the person is likely to focus on the *ending or non-ending nature* of human life, then the theology of death and immortality will need to be re-examined. Given the propensity of human nature to repeat itself, it is likely that the exploration of these new issues will follow a pattern similar to that of earlier science-faith interactions, which have frequently been characterized in terms of "conflict," "dialogue," and "integration."[18] It would be tempting to hope that there will be no such conflict when the general discussion about increased life spans comes to the fore and, no doubt, many will easily assume that the two "immortalities"—extended temporal life and the eschatological "life everlasting" of the Apostles' Creed—need not be played off against each other in any way. Nonetheless a conflict is likely not only because there have been similar confrontations but also because a debate over immortality would in fact simply be a repetition of a conflict extending back to the earliest days of modern medicine.

Hans Küng observes that it was no coincidence that it was after a surge of materialism that Antoine de Concordat, in a mood of medical optimism, described in his *Outline of an Historical Presentation of the Progress of the Human Mind* (1794) the ultimate goal of modern medicine as being the abolition, or at least the considerable postponement, of death. This was an expression of the agenda that medical science has pursued vigorously ever since. In the context of a reductionist scientific world-view, everything can be explained by physical and chemical processes; when it comes to the threat of death, medical science provides an alternate form of salvation and as a consequence "atheism went hand in hand with the Utopia of an earthly immortality."[19] However, de Concordat's vision has not been fully realized because, despite the incredible success of modern medicine, in the absence of any final solution to the problems of sickness and death, it is difficult for a scientifically reductionist point of view to persuade everyone that religious faith in the resurrection is superfluous. But the closer science comes to understanding human aging, the more tempting—though not necessarily the more valid—that proposition becomes and the greater is the possibility of confusion concerning the meaning of "immortality." It is used in a number of different ways and some clarification is needed.

The first immortality might best be called *genetic immortality* and it is found in writings such as those of Richard Dawkins, who proposed that the aspect of human behavior normally referred to as altruism was, in fact, the outcome of a genetic selfishness aimed at maximizing the chance of an entity's own genetic material surviving into the future. The aim is genetic immortality. Despite the metaphorically personal terminology frequently used of the genes, in which deliberate intention is attributed to them, this form of immortality does not include personal survival of any kind. It is simply the continuous replication of the genetic code.

The second form of immortality is *cellular immortality*, which is the process whereby a population of cells is able to keep reproducing indefinitely. In no situation can individual cells be immortal. It is only certain cell populations as a whole that can be "immortal," that is, exist indefinitely by replication. It is therefore properly a "corporate" or "cell population" immortality.[20]

At the third level there is *organismal immortality*, which refers to the possibility of certain more complex organs having an indefinite life. This is predicated on the possibility of cellular or cell population immortality and is distinguished from it only by the fact that it refers to a more complex, functioning, interactive bodily organ or set of organs such as an animal or human person that is able to survive indefinitely because of the continual replication of various types of cells. The indefinitely replicating organism (or person) is still subject to illness, disease, and accident, and is a form of life that still has a guarantee of death.

In all cases the "immortality" is temporal, relative, indefinite, and corporate in nature. It is *temporal* in that any continued existence takes place in time. It is *relative* in the sense that immortality is not intrinsic to the entity in question and is dependent on suitable conditions including the absence of fatal accidents and so forth. The potential life span is therefore *indefinite* rather than infinite. Finally it is *corporate* in the sense that while the whole may be immortal, the constituent parts are not, although they may be indefinitely replicated.

Of course, it is also necessary to include a fourth definition, which is more theological than scientific in nature. It is that immortality which is primarily defined in terms of a qualitative relationship with God in Jesus Christ (John 17:3). It is not an intrinsic quality of human life but a gracious gift of God, a sharing in the divine nature (2 Peter 1:4). Now a definition expressed in biblical and theological terms such as these suggests that there is no necessary connection with any of the previous definitions of immortality. Therefore there can be no conflict if they are referring to different kinds of events. Indeed, treating theological immortality as something of a completely different order might be as useful as the recognition of the different orders of causation can be in eliminating the forced choice in the creation debate: Darwin *or* God. But it is not that simple; the problem that emerges is that any genuine dialogue can be expected not only to point to differences but also to look for similarities, especially methodological parallels in what are otherwise different areas. There is no doubt that the interpretation of the fourth level of "theological immortality" is influenced by the way that the first three levels of "scientific immortality" are understood as temporal, relative, indefinite, and corporate. The temporal and corporate dimensions are of particular importance.

Parallels in Scientific and Theological Immortalities

Temporality

All three of the definitions noted above assume an understanding of immortality that is temporal. In contrast, classic theology understands immortality as atemporal. But there have been philosophical problems with the concept of atemporality. Karl Barth objects to "the Babylonian captivity of an abstract opposite to the concept of time."[21] Clark Pinnock objects to its apparent determinism.[22] J. W. Cooper rejects the notion of timeless eternity; as part of his defense of anthropological dualism and the concept of the intermediate state, he argues that on death the person does not move out of spatio-temporal conditions.[23] J. R. Lucas claims that the temporality of God is essential because "to deny that God is temporal is to deny that he is personal in any sense in which we can understand personality."[24] The consequence of this is that, while an identification of the theological concept of immortality with the temporal "immortality" of scientific endeavor is not automatic, at least one of the one of the previously essential differences has been minimized.

Personality

It was also noted that scientific versions of immortality are fundamentally corporate in nature. It is cell populations, genetic codes, and whole entities rather than constituent parts that are described as being "immortal." The focus is upon the continuation of the species or the population as a whole rather than any individual constituent. This stands in contrast to the classic picture of immortality, which is essentially personal in nature. However, objections have been raised concerning the personal nature of immortality. It is argued that the general emphasis in eschatology has been too individualistic and anthropocentric and thus too subjective and selfish.[25] This common, anthropocentric approach, it is said, has distorted the construction of what ought to be a more directly theological framework built on the foundation of God. Thus, there is in process theology a stress on "objective" forms of immortality. By this, it is meant that the symbols of "resurrection" and "immortality" are ways of saying that all experiences and all relationships that have been known and realized have been received by God into the divine life. The manner in which this history is conserved and guaranteed is not so important as the fact that their preservation illustrates the tremendous significance given to them.

Whitehead held to a neutral stance so that subjective immortality was neither definitely affirmed nor denied, even though it is obvious that Whitehead's own tendency was to deny the possibility of it. Others are quite clear that there is definitely no subjective immortality at all. It is, as Hartshorne says, an idea that is an invention[26] and as Ogden says, "The only immortality or resurrection that is essential to Christian hope is not our own subjective survival of death, but our objective immortality or resurrection in God, our being finally accepted and judged by his love, and thus imperishably united with all creation into his own unending life."[27]

From these two examples we can see that as science begins to consider seriously the possibility of indefinite life span, the tendency is to describe this "immortality" in temporal and corporate terms. It is no coincidence that at broadly the same time some theological definitions of immortality have shifted away from classic atemporal and personal notions of immortality to a view that is more likely to lead to a fundamental agreement. There is likely to be a significant minimization of difference between scientific and theological understandings where there is a commitment to the view that "God is subject to the same principles which govern all reality," as in process theology.[28]

Defining Immortality Theologically

In this situation how are we to be more precise in the definition of the fourth, more theological, level of immortality? There are at least three possible interpretations, each of which relates the theological to the scientific to a different degree. The first possibility is to understand immortality as *personal and qualitative immortality* and therefore defined in terms of the survival of transformed, resurrected persons in an atemporal context. This "classic" understanding of immortality is unlikely to be equated or even loosely related to the "immortality" of medical science.

The second possibility is that of immortality as *personal and quantitative*. This involves persons in an infinitely extended temporal life span. It is the quantitative extension of the physical, emotional, intellectual, and spiritual life of a person. This view is held by those such as Cooper who says, "eschatological time is historical time."[29] This form of immortality, which comes about as a result of the eschatological action of God through the resurrection of Christ, does not have to be identified with the indefinitely extended life span sought by medical science, but an identification or partial identification is less problematic than for the first definition and can occur.

The final option is *corporate and quantitative immortality* in which immortality is not a quality attributable to persons. People constitute a temporal event in the life of an organic whole and only exist beyond death as part of the history of the infinitely but temporally existing whole known as God. Once again, this immortality, found in various forms of process theology, is not necessarily to be identified with the immortality sought by medical science, but some form of connection is probably inevitable given the search for a thoroughgoing integration of the religious and scientific levels of immortality.

In evaluating the merits of these three broad interpretations of immortality the critical questions revolve around the extent to which *temporality* and *personality* are essential constituents of immortality. So it is to these two issues that we now turn.

Temporality and Immortality

The "classic" Christian conviction is that immortality is a presence with Christ that is more than extended duration and so it can only be described as timelessness. This belief is protected by being tied very closely to the principal attributes of God. The notion of timelessness emerges from a belief in the immutability of God and, in turn, it provides a defense of divine omnipotence.

Timelessness emerges from the immutability of God because, as Aquinas says, "the idea of eternity follows immutability, as the idea of time follows movement . . . as God is supremely immutable, it supremely belongs to him to be eternal." Divine eternity arises out of divine immutability because "in a thing bereft of movement, which is always the same, there is no before and after." In this, classic western Christian theism has followed Boethius's definition of eternity as the "simultaneous possession of endless life." This divine "timelessness" enables God to avoid being subject to the changing events of the world and by his simultaneous knowledge of all things, and by not being subject to time, God's omnipotence in his relationships with the world is preserved.

This understanding of time and eternity has been popular but it has not won universal theological approval because the linking of immutability with eternity in the classic tradition meant that God became a static entity. Hence the reservations of those such as Pinnock, Cooper, Lucas, Barth, Whitehead, Ogden, and Hartshorne. In particular, A. N. Whitehead and process theology in general have specifically aimed to eliminate that "vicious separation of the flux from the permanence" of classic theology, which produced a changing world but an entirely static God with whom it seemed impossible to have any real relationship.

Scientifically, it has also been found wanting. In the modern era the classic Boethian-Anselmian-Thomistic tradition of eternity has been interpreted by reference to the Newtonian method of science. Newton identified space and time with the omnipresence and eternity of God which, together, constitute the infinite container of all creaturely existence. Space and time are thus considered absolutely, in themselves without relation to anything external. As attributes of an immutable God they are absolute and unchanging and they embrace all things within the universe and as such they are the ultimate reference system. However, it has been necessary to move forward beyond the classic notions of time and eternity. The theories of Newton have been superseded by those of Einstein, Bohr, Heisenberg, and others. The *receptacle* concept of time and space was replaced by the *relational* theory of time and space so that instead of understanding time as a line or boundary it was understood as a succession of states of personal activity. Time is never given independently of a given situation. The theory of relativity has reminded us of this: that there is no absolute time. Just as there is no space without an object, so too there is no moment without an action and no person without a relation. Time is the form and shape of our actions. We now have to talk of time *for whom*. Once it was believed that there was a spatial center to the universe and that all directions could be defined by reference to it. Now it is understood that position is defined in relation to the observer. In fact, there is no fixed position, only relations between bodies. Similarly, time is dependent on the observer.

Any contemporary view of immortality has to work with these changes to the understanding of time. The fundamental conviction of the classic view that immortality is more than extended duration need not be altered, but the description of this in terms of timelessness is soon shown to be less than helpful. What is required is an immortality that is defined neither in terms of time nor in terms of the opposition to time, but as an immortality that is trans-temporality—beyond temporality and yet embracing it. Such a relationship of temporality and eternity can be clarified by analogy with the relationship that exists in classic theism between the omnipresence (immensity) and the spirituality (a-spatiality) of God.

The notion of omnipresence asserts that there is no place in the universe where God is not. This attribute is actually *defended* (rather than negated) by the assertion that God is a "spiritual" being, which is to say that there is a real sense in which God is, in fact, spaceless or in *no* space. If God were to be in space in the same way as other forms of reality, then there is no "space" for anything else. In other words, the assertion that God is in space and in every space *requires* as a corollary the statement that there is a sense in which God is in "no space." In a similar way, the assertion that God is in *every* time requires the assertion that God is, in a sense, in *no* time *in the same way that other things are*. This is an eternity of God that is not threatening to the "timefullness" of God any more than the "spirituality" of God threatens his omnipresence. In this way it is possible to come to the idea of eternity as *timelessness* by stressing the *temporality* of God.

This stands in opposition to the classic method of deducing the timelessness of God, which is by working from his immutability. What has happened in classic theism is that God's eternity has been primarily described in terms of the negative quality of timelessness *without sufficient recognition of his temporality*. But the method of reaching eternity via time does not run into the problem of relating time and eternity, as the classic method does, because it is clear from the start that *time and eternity are, asymmetrically, each the ground of the other*. We come to an understanding of eternity as supra-temporality (rather than atemporality) not by denying involvement in time, but by stressing it. Eternity is understood positively, with its primary meaning being more than simply the absence of time. It is the positive description of God's time that is not external to God but included in his duration.

Given this, it is possible to see a direction forward. Earlier in our discussion, immortality was understood as *either* essentially temporal or as essentially atemporal. Now we can see that, as far as God is concerned, the possession of temporality is not limiting provided that time is not understood in an absolute, singular, or non-relational manner. The temporality of the world is derived from the eternity of God, which is, partially at least, understood as a relational multi-temporality. This understanding of eternity may exhibit a form of "simultaneity" in that God is related to all times, but this does not imply "temporal" simultaneity because time is not absolute, time is not the medium of association. Different events cannot be said to be "simultaneous" *to each other* even though each one of them is present to God and all events are simultaneous *in him*: "He is before all things, and in him all things hold together." In this way it is possible to affirm an immortality that goes beyond those purely quantitative notions of immortality put forward as alternatives to what has been described as the classic view. However, the classic view must recognize the role that temporality plays in divine eternity in that the point of connection between eternity and time, between God and humanity, is found in the mystery of the incarnation. Here is one who is temporal and eternal, and time and eternity are united in each person as the person is united in Christ, as the image of God in the person is fulfilled.

Personality and Immortality

The question of (a)temporality is closely connected to that of personality. J. R. Lucas claims that the temporality of God is essential because "to deny that God is temporal is to deny that he is personal in any sense in which we can understand personality."[30] In a contrary move process theology uses a temporal understanding of immortality to *deny*[31] the possibility of personal immortality.[32] According to Hartshorne "my everlastingness is neither more nor less than my entire earthly career as a contribution to the divine life."[33] Eternity is not continued personal existence—it is purely God's enjoyment of our past life. This, says Hartshorne, does not mean that there is no immortality or that at death people become unreal. "Once an individual is there to refer to, he continues to be there even after death, as object of reference, as a life which really has been lived."[34]

There are obvious parallels with the relative, temporal, indefinite, and corporate immortality of scientific speculation. In cellular immortality individual cells are not immortal but do participate in the ongoing life of the whole cell population and in organismal immortality, complex organisms survive indefinitely because of the continual replication of various types of cells. In a similar manner, process immortality is corporate in that the individual humanly person does not survive but does contribute to the continuing immortality of the whole God/cosmos. The person is no longer present as the subject of a life but only as "an object of reference" in the experiences of many people.[35] God's continuing experience or memory of me is *my* immortality. But it is so only in the sense that it is an experience for God that is based on an experience involving me, although not in the sense that I am the subject of the experience.

For some people this is immediately problematic and the view is immediately repudiated as it constitutes the end of personal existence. Unfortunately, however disconcerting this thought may be, it is a possibility that cannot be ruled out simply because it is an unpleasant thought. It is possible, however, to claim that it is a view presented using somewhat misleading terminology. If my personal immortality ("my everlastingness" according to Hartshorne,[36] or "our objective immortality" according to Ogden[37]) consists in God's remembrance of me in a manner analogous to any person's remembrance of me[38] then I may protest that another person's memory is not normally seen as part of *my* reality and the same must apply with respect to God's remembrance of me. It is therefore misleading to suggest that God's remembrance of me can be spoken of as my immortality.

However, a linguistic correction such as this does not indicate that the proposition is essentially wrong. Consistency with biblical data is more of a problem though. The process view of immortality involves the conviction that there is no personal activity in immortal life. There

will be no addition to the experiences of the person; death is understood as the affixing of the quantum of the reality of a life;[39] resurrection is simply the synthesizing of one's life in God. While Hartshorne
claims that this view is superior to the traditional alternatives,[40] he certainly has difficulties establishing this by comparison with the biblical
data concerning death and resurrection life.

Death

In process thought death takes the individual person into a *total
losing* of self, a losing of personal identity and the absorption of the total
history of the person into the life of God for God's gain and benefit. The
scriptural material indicates, though, that the *ultimate* resolution of the
transitoriness of life is not death *per se*, it is the final *gaining* of self in
the next life through resurrection and transformation as the consummation of a life that is "lost" in the present in the service of God in
Christ. "For those who want to save their life will lose it, and those who
lose their life for my sake will find it" (Matthew 16:25). This is a finding
of life, a gain which is to the benefit of the person as well as to God.

Resurrection

Ironically, the process notion of eternal life is more like the biblical
notion of death, involving, as it does, a completely static, depersonalized,
and unchanging "existence." In contrast, the biblical picture, symbolic
though it may be, is of a continued, dynamic, developed life lived in relationship with God (Titus 1:2; 1 Peter 5:10; Revelation 3:20–5:14; 21–22).

Beyond linguistic clarity and biblical consistency a third approach
is to question the rationality of the fundamental rationale behind the
process approach to immortality. David Pailin, in discussing the claim
that the Whiteheadian position is wrong because it does not involve the
survival of the self, puts very simply the process belief that most modern expressions of immortality are hopelessly individualistic. "The
strength of this objection to objective immortality depends upon the
credibility of holding that our individual lives are so important that
their continuation is a requirement of rationality and meaningfulness of
reality."[41] Pailin therefore dismisses the objection on the basis that
while it may be hurtful to our pride, there is in fact no absolute necessity for us to survive at all and that to assume so is to exaggerate our
own importance. "Our aim in life must be to enhance our contribution
as much as we are able and our satisfaction lies in knowing that nothing
we achieve will ever be lost. All will become part of the concrete reality

of God."[42] However unpalatable this may seem, the possibility must be faced. Ogden expresses the issue theologically by saying that the expectation of personal survival is nothing other than an idolatrous hope. He argues that historically such an individualistic view of immortality is the superimposition of a Gnostic hope onto a Jewish apocalypticism, and what is produced is "nothing specifically Christian."[43] In a similar vein Hartshorne says, "my contention that wanting to be immortal in the specified sense is a form of wanting to be God."[44] Such a claim could not be more serious. Is a belief in a personal afterlife a form of idolatry? Is it appropriate to set oneself up as an "object" or "end"?

There is no doubt that biblical teaching is consistently opposed to self-centeredness and it is opposed to those who seek to arrange their lives in a way that is focused on themselves. Positively, it stresses the need to direct life toward God's glory. What Hartshorne has overlooked is that, while any self-centered thought or action is idolatrous, a belief in immortality is not necessarily self-centered. It is not idolatrous if it arises from a belief that personal survival is a gracious act of God (a gift rather than a necessary action) arising out of his love (not the result of inexorable logic or self-love) and revealed as a possibility in which the person of faith can hope (not as a demonstrable fact).

If God says that the individual will be part of, and participant in, the eschatological future, then it is not a "setting up of oneself" but the reception of the gracious promise of God and the evidence for this lies in the incarnation, ministry, teaching, death, and resurrection of Jesus and the ensuing tradition of the church. The fact, manner, and effect of the incarnation are understood to teach not only the existence of God but, above all else, his extraordinary love for the world. This demonstrates the value he attributes to the world and the particular esteem in which he holds people. This love is not the natural or inevitable result of some inherent value or of inexorable logic; it is purely a matter of grace. A belief in personal survival need not be idolatrous. Stressing, as process theology does, that the symbols of future life have a primary reference to the glory of God, does not require the elimination of continuing personal involvement in that life.

Conclusion: God and Immortality

The indefinite and relative immortality that can be achieved by continuous replication of cells and that has no final solution for death is not the infinite immortality that is a final presence with Christ and not simply a continued presence in this world. This participation in the divine nature (2 Peter 1:4) is an immortality that is not in conflict with the temporal, relative, impersonal, indefinite immortality of scientific expectation. But nor is it completely unrelated. It is an immortality that cannot be defined in temporal terms as it extends beyond temporality but nor is it a radical atemporality as it does not exclude all elements of temporality. Rather it is the fulfillment of temporality. It is a transformation of this life rather than a rejection of it, a taking up of temporality into eternity. As such it is a genuinely personal immortality rather than the continuation of any genetic code or population. It is personal life emerging out of God's graciousness rather than from any fundamental anthropocentricity or genetic or personal selfishness.

There is nothing in a genuine theology of immortality that conflicts with the relative "immortality" that is a radically extended life span. Nor is there anything in this theology of life in Christ that makes a scientific search for this relative "immortality" wrong. For God a thousand years is as a day (Psalms 90:4) and a life lived for two thousand years is one that can be lived in honor of God as much as one lived for three-score-and-ten years or a life lived only for twenty minutes. A life lived for seventy years is a life lived twenty-five thousand times longer than a life lived only for a day. Yet both can have their own completeness in God. If people were to be able to live a mere fifty times longer than at present and survive for five thousand years, would that detract from the immortality of grace, which is an eternity with Christ? I think not. Given the huge amount of time involved in God's work of creation prior to the presence of any human being, it is hard to imagine him being concerned about a few thousand years! There is nothing in this scientific hope of extended life that causes concern with regard to a genuinely theological understanding of immortality. The two "immortalities" can live in dialogue rather than in conflict. This is not to say, however, that there are no problems at all with the search for an end to aging, simply that if there are problems, they will emerge elsewhere. Extended life span is not a threat to God's immortality but it may well be a threat to significant aspects of human life and social relationships, but these will have to be dealt with elsewhere.

NOTES

1. Theoanthropology is simply a conflation of "theological anthropology." It is a convenient way of referring to the theological understanding of humanity that avoids the non-inclusiveness of "doctrine of man" and the absence of conve-

nient nouns and adjectives relating to the "doctrine of humanity." It is, of course, possible to use "anthropology" and "anthropological," but these refer to the study of humanity in the widest possible sense and when used without qualification are usually taken to refer to what is more properly called "cultural anthropology."

2. Acknowledgment is made of the assistance of Edmund Sim of the University of Queensland, who read this chapter and made valuable suggestions regarding some of the scientific details.

3. M. Fossel, *Reversing Human Aging* (New York: William Morrow and Co., 1996), p. 222.

4. L. Hayflick and P. S. Moorhead, *Experimental Cell Research*, 25 (1961), pp. 585–621.

5. W. Wright, M. Piatszek, M. Rainey, W. Byrd, and J. Shay, *Developmental Genetics* 18, pp. 173–179.

6. A. Bodnar et al., "Extension of Life-Span by Introduction of Telomerase into Normal Human Cells," *Science*, (January 16, 1998), pp. 349ff.

7. L. DeFrancesco, "Looking into Longevity with Telomere Detection Kits," *The Scientist*, vol. 12:7 (March 30, 1998).

8. Juvenile progeria—an aging disorder.

9. M. Fossel, *Senescent Gene Expression, Telomeres, and Aging*, http://faculty.ucr. edu/~browley/ telomere.htm.

10. Fossel, *Reversing Human Aging*, p. 222.

11. In Ancient Egypt it was not considered completely inappropriate to aspire to live 110 years and the reign of 67 years of Ramses II points to a death at around 90 years of age. Plato and Sophocles were considered old when they died at about 80 and 90 and of course there is the biblical "three score years and ten" (D. B. Bromley, *The Psychology of Human Aging* (Baltimore: Penguin Books, 1966), p. 37; S. Austad, *Why We Age: What Science Is Discovering about the Body's Journey through Life* (New York: John Wiley, 1997, p. 37). Nor does the evidence of Genesis 5 run counter to this general picture. Prior to the eighteenth century the long lives attributed to Adam, Seth, Methuselah, and others were generally accepted as real descriptions of life span. However, the combined effect of biblical criticism and biological evolution led to them being more generally reckoned to be artificially exaggerated life spans. It is important to note that large figures such as these are not only a Hebraic phenomenon but are consistent with certain Sumerian king lists of about 2000 B.C. R. K. Harrison sees the apparent life spans of Genesis as the result of some combination of an enhanced reckoning by the family and a mathematical manipulation by an archivist with the intention of honoring significant people—in accord with a broader ancient Near Eastern tradition, which also influenced the form of the Sumerian king list material (R. K. Harrison, "From Adam to Noah: A Reconsideration of the Antediluvian Patriarchs' Ages," in *Journal of the Evangelical Theological Society* 37: 2 [June 1994], pp. 161–168). Other interpreters find somewhat different versions of this answer but whatever the nature of the precise solution it would seem that these figures are best taken as cultural phenomenon rather than as biological data.

12. S. Austad, *Why We Age: What Science Is Discovering about the Body's Journey through Life* (New York: John Wiley, 1997, p. 37).

13. Ibid., p. 93.
14. A. Peacocke, *Theology for a Scientific Age* (Minneapolis: Fortress, 1993), especially pp. 44–45.
15. Ibid., pp. 53–54.
16. Ibid., pp. 213–244.
17. Ibid., p. 55.
18. For example, as in I. Barbour, *Religion in an Age of Science* (London: SCM, 1990), pp. 3–31.
19. H. Küng, *Eternal Life?* (London: Collins, 1984), pp. 7–8.
20. As discussed earlier, it was Hayflick who first showed that "cell populations could be classified into two distinct categories characterized chiefly by whether they were mortal or immortal." L. Hayflick, "Mortality and Immortality at the Cellular Level: A Review" in *Biochemistry,* vol. 62, no. 11 (1997).
21. Karl Barth, *Church Dogmatics* II/I, ed. G. W. Bromily and T. F. Torrance (Edinburgh: T and T Clark, 1957), p. 611.
22. For example, as Clark Pinnock has said, "We are not impressed when classical theism tells us that God takes in the whole of history in a single glance, because what that means to us is that history is meaningless. If the day after tomorrow is as fixed in God's timeless present as the day before yesterday, then there is no meaning to our freedom and power to shape what will be in the future." "Between Classical and Process Theism" in R. Nash, ed., *On Process Theology* (Grand Rapids: Baker, 1987) pp. 309–328.
23. J. W. Cooper, *Body, Soul, and Life Everlasting* (Grand Rapids: Eerdmans, 1989), p. 210.
24. J. R. Lucas, "The Temporality of God" in R. J. Russell, N. Murphy, C. J. Isham, eds., *Quantum Cosmology and the Laws of Nature: Scientific Perspectives on Divine Action* (Vatican City State: Vatican Observatory and Center for Theology and the Natural Sciences, 1993), p. 235.
25. "Another factor which has tended to make talk about the 'after-life' less than appealing may be found in the feeling that too much of that talk about it is highly self-centered—a matter of "glory for me" . . . men and women nowadays are uncomfortable with any position which would be so *totally* individualistic . . . the presentation of the Christian gospel as purely individual 'salvation' appears to be outrageous." Norman Pittenger, *After Death: Life in God* (London: SCM, 1980), p. 13.
26. See Charles Hartshorne, "Time, Death, and Everlasting Life" in John Hick, ed., *Classical and Contemporary Readings in the Philosophy of Religion* (Englewood Cliffs: Prentice Hall, 1970), pp. 357–369; *Omnipotence and Other Theological Mistakes* (Albany: State University of New York Press), pp. 36–37; "Response to Debate" in T. L. Miethe, ed., *Did Jesus Rise From the Dead?* (San Francisco: Harper and Row, 1984), pp. 137–142.
27. Schubert M. Ogden, "The Meaning of Christian Hope," in H. J. Cargas and B. Lee, eds., *Religious Experience and Process Theology* (New York: Paulist, 1976), pp. 206.
28. Hartshorne, "Time, Death, and Everlasting Life," pp. 362.
29. J. W. Cooper, *Body, Soul,* p. 210.
30. J. R. Lucas, "The Temporality of God," pp. 235.
31. Or, at best, leave open the question of subjective immortality.

32. It is important to recognize that some process theologians do affirm subjective immortality, such as John Cobb and David Griffin. However, subjective immortality is not a necessary development of process principles and has to be based on other material, as Whitehead recognized.

33. Hartshorne, "Response," p. 137.

34. Hartshorne, "Time, Death, and Everlasting Life," p. 359.

35. The "retained actuality" of a person is that which was part of his or her "thoughts, feelings, decisions, perceptions" (Hartshorne, "Time, Death, and Everlasting Life," 361). In this context it is impossible to forget Woody Allen's comment, "I don't want to live forever by having my art remembered, I want to live forever by not dying."

36. Hartshorne, "Response," p. 139.

37. Ogden, "Christian Hope," p. 206.

38. For Hartshorne the only difference between a human remembrance of me and the divine remembrance is that no human person can perfectly remember me. "In short, our adequate immortality can only be God's omniscience of us" (Hartshorne, "Time, Death, and Everlasting Life," p. 362). God alone really knows us and can recall us and only in him can we have what might be called immortality.

39. Hartshorne, "Time, Death, and Everlasting Life," p. 364.

40. He argues that this view is preferable because it transcends the present form of self-identity as human beings, which is "at best, an extremely partial preservation of the actual quality of life" (Hartshorne, "Beyond Enlightened Self-Interest," p. 309).

41. David A. Pailin, *Groundwork of Philosophy of Religion* (London: Epworth, 1986), p. 196.

42. Ibid., p. 197.

43. Ogden, "Christian Hope," pp. 203–209.

44. Hartshorne, "Response," p. 138.

This chapter was originally published in *Evangelical Review of Theology* vol. 23, no. 4 (October 1999), pp. 363–382.

CHAPTER 12

God Among Immortal Humans!

KURUVILLA PANDIKATTU, S.J.

Kuruvilla Pandikattu is a professor of physics, philosophy, and theology at Jnana-Deepa Vidyapeeth, Pontifical Institute of Philosophy and Religion, Pune, India. He has three master's degrees and two doctorates and concentrates on the dialogical dimension of life. His two major books are *Idols to Die, Symbols to Live* and *Dialogue as Way of Life.*

"Living for ever on this earth! It is impossible! God will not allow it. I do not want it." These are the spontaneous and instinctive comments of many committed believers when they hear of the possibility of humans living forever! Religion has taken for granted that humans have to die one day and that at least then they will be confronted face to face with God! In this chapter an attempt is made to show that personal mortality is not necessarily an imperative for religious belief. We shall first try to show the theoretical plausibility of human immortality and then see briefly the theological responses to it. Our aim in this chapter is to broaden our vision of human life and divine agency, so that the spiritual quest in humans need not be made possible only because of the contingency—in this case physical death—of humans!

Introduction

We first begin with an ancient mythical story from Mahabharata, which deals directly with the human search for immortality and how narrowly humans miss it!

The *devas* ("the godly") assemble on Mount Meru and want to drink *amrta,* the nectar that bestows immortality to them. *Amrta* can be acquired only by churning the ocean. God Visnu helps them to bring Mount Mandara to the ocean so that they can use the mountain as a churning stick. The giant snake Vasuki offers its help to be used as the churning rope. The *asuras* ("the evil ones") hold the head of Vasuki and *devas* the tail of the snake. As the churning proceeds, the sea is disturbed, many creatures die, the Mandara mount is turned upside down. Both the *asuras* and *devas* get tired and want to stop churning. But God Visnu encourages them to carry on. Finally after many hindrances the *amrta* surfaces. The *asuras* rush to grab it. But God Visnu takes the form of a seductive woman and she becomes the arbitrator between the *asuras* and the *devas* for *amrta*. The woman distributes the *amrta* to the *devas* only. But one *asura*, Rahu, disguises himself as a *deva* and succeeds in sipping it. Informed by the Sun and the Moon, Visnu severs the head of the *asura* before the immortality-bestowing *amrta* can reach his stomach. In the fierce battle that ensues the *asuras* are defeated and they do not achieve immortality.[1]

This story illustrates the futility of the human search for immortality. Many believers are convinced that since God is the author of life he reserves the destiny of humans (death) to Himself. What we want to show in this chapter is not the possibility but the theoretical plausibility for immortal human life and a theological response to it.

Plausibility of Human Life Forever

It is theoretically possible to conceive of the cosmos and life—not necessarily human life—as existing forever.[2] But our concern here is more about the immortality of human life. Although no scientist today talks seriously of the possibility of human immortality, there are very clear indications that it could become a possibility at least in the far future. In this section we deal with four main areas of research that enable us to make such a claim: the cryonics movement, stem cells research, Human Genome Mapping, and exploration into artificial intelligence. All of these fields are advancing so rapidly that we cannot figure out the possibilities. Some of the theories may even be contradicting each other. Still there are some clear indications that immortality may be viewed as a theoretical plausibility.

Cryonics Movement

Following R. C. W. Ettinger's *The Prospect of Immortality*, published in 1965, the cryonics movement has been claiming to provide immortality even to those who have already died. Followers of this movement claim that in the very near future immortality may become a real possibility. Indeed, in theory it is possible now, for if one is to be deep-frozen and stored away it is inevitable that in fifty, or a hundred, or a thousand years surgery will have progressed to the point where damage to cells that is at present irreparable will be able to be repaired. The difficulty at the moment is that the present methods of freezing and unfreezing are so crude that a great deal more damage is done in the process. They further claim that the possibility of immortality is a "sober, scientific, and logical argument founded on undeniable fact: that a body deep-frozen stands a better chance of being revived than one rotting in the ground."[3] So they have actually organized themselves, called for people to donate money so that their bodies could be kept frozen either immediately before or after death. There are a few dozen bodies kept in specially prepared laboratories waiting to be made immortal in the near future.

Stem Cells Research

Stem cells have the ability to divide for indefinite periods in culture and to give rise to specialized cells. They may be pluripotent or totipotent. Pluripotent cells are capable of giving rise to most tissues of an organism, but not to the embryos. Totipotent cells have unlimited capability to multiply. They have the capacity to differentiate into extraembryonic membranes and tissues, the embryo, and all postembryonic tissues and organs. Research into such stem cells has lead to tremendous possibilities, especially when coupled with telomerase research.[4]

Telomerase is an enzyme that extends the replicative life span of cells indefinitely. It is an RNA-dependent DNA polymerase that adds nucleotide repeats to the ends (or telomeres) of each chromosome. This enzymatic process maintains the integrity of the telomeres during cell replication and enables the cell to continue replicating indefinitely. In normal somatic cells telomeric length is reduced with each round of cell division. When a critically short telomeric length is reached, somatic cells typically reach a state of "replicative senescence" and can no longer divide and multiply. Scientists have shown that restoring telomerase activity by gene transfer into normal cells will allow those cells to continue to divide indefinitely without conferring any abnormal or cancerous characteristics to the cells.

Telomerase reactivation in the differentiated cells derived from human pluripotent stem cells (hPSCs) makes large-scale production of transplantable cells feasible. Without telomerase reactivation by gene transfer, differentiated descendants of hPSCs would eventually cease replicating. By reactivating telomerase, the differentiated cells are expected to retain their ability to divide so that limitless quantities of cells can be generated for the repair of degenerating organs. Therefore "it should be possible to permanently repair the damaged portions of these patients' nervous systems by means of the transplantation of *immortalised* differentiated neurons produced from hPSCs."[5] If immortalised cells could be produced today, its extension to the whole body could be seen as at least a viable quest.

Human Genome Mapping

It is well established that human nature and even longevity are controlled by genes and the DNA that constitutes them. Conventional scientific wisdom affirms that having the complete genetic blueprint for humans will transform medicine—with new drugs, new treatment, and prevention of possible disease. Doctors even promise to diagnose sicknesses before they occur and to prescribe custom-made medications to fit the sick individual's genetic makeup, once every one of our one million genes have been studied and mapped.

The Genome Project, a public agency, divided the full complement of human DNA into 22,000 segments, each 150,000 letters long. The positions of these segments were carefully mapped and then each was cloned several times. The agency hopes that before 2003 they will be able to give the mapping of the whole human genome.

As against this method Craig Venter of Celera Genomics uses a faster and a more risky method of "whole genome shotgunning." He clones a genome several times, blasting the clones into 60 million bits, each between 2,000 and 10,000 letters long. The bits are being decoded by a robot. He has already announced that he has filed provisional patents on hundreds of newly discovered genes. He hopes that by 2001 his project of mapping the whole human genes will be over.[6]

It is conceivable that with the genes totally mapped, the medicines for all the possible diseases found, the next logical step would be not just to alter the genes that cause aging, but to stop aging altogether. With the powerful and comparatively simple tool of genetic engineering available to scientists, it will not be an all-too-impossible task!

Progress in Artificial Intelligence

The tremendous advances made in artificial intelligence and computer programming also enable us to visualize immortality for us.[7]

Obviously, it is not assumed that humans will lead an immortal life in their own physical bodies. The assumption is that humans will be able to modify their own physical bodies and their brains to suit the new situations and adapt themselves to live forever. Computer chips and memory will enable humans to replace their own bodies with computer robots.

According to Ian Pearson, a British futurologist, within about 150 years people will find the body a liability and will go in for "voluntary extinction" of themselves as biological entities and yet continue to live. One can take a backup of one's mind on the network before one dies (in the biological sense) and offload it onto an android. This is facilitated by the nano technologies that will be all-pervasive. Nano technology aims at extreme dwarfing of objects by manipulating individual atoms and molecules. He affirms: "My guess is that we'll do [migration to other planets] using nano technology, where we encapture the mind on a tiny chip and send it to colonise other planets and stars."[8]

It has not been our resolve to show that human immortality is possible or even desirable.[9] The arguments in this chapter only focus the issue on the possibility of immortality—at least theoretically. I am aware that no mainstream scientists of today will make serious claims on human immortality. Therefore, our concern in this chapter is not to show that such an immortal future for human beings is possible, but to affirm that it has become a theoretical plausibility and catches the imagination of the people. It will get into the mythic subconscious of the people and will have tremendous influence on the way people live and react—even if objectively immortality may still elude us. The four cases mentioned above add to the plausibility of immortality and influence the collective human psyche.

If immortality has become even a theoretical plausibility, it has profound theological implications. In the next section I try to indicate that religions do not need to be defensive in the face of the plausibility (or even possibility) of human immortality.

Theological Considerations

God as God of the Living

It would be beneficial to keep the terminological difference between contingency (perishability and dependence) and immortality (non-perishability). Only the temporal contingency is ruled out by immortality. Again it is useful to recall that God is God of life and is life enhancing. Further, both science and religion as human enterprises foster and promote life.

The monotheistic religions affirm in no uncertain ways that God is the sole creator and sustainer of the world and specifically of human life. Theologically, this means that we are eternally dependent on Him, not that human life necessarily needs to be finite. The crucial point to be noted is that even a temporally immortal life is totally and completely dependent ontologically on God.[10] The angels, for instance, are examples of beings who are immortal and at the same time eternally dependent on God. So God as creator of human beings does not necessarily imply that humans need to be or to remain mortal.[11]

We should very well ask if the immortality that science promises brings along with it betterment of other human contingencies. Does human immortality necessarily eliminate suffering and pain? It may be remembered that immortal life is not identical to the eternal life that Jesus promises to give. It may be assumed that we cannot have eternal life without immortality, not vice versa. Eternal life implies the fullness—eschatological—of life. Eschatological concerns are valid even in an immortal human existence. The eschatological fullness deals with human "salvation" or final, ultimate "yes" to human life and it involves axiological, ontological fulfillment, besides the temporal fulfillment: only the last is assured by immortality. Immortality does not rule out total ontological dependency.

Thus ethical concerns are still valid in an immortal human society. These ethical concerns have to inform human behavior and life even if the life lived is immortal. Only that can lead to human fullness. Besides ethical concerns, the ontological dependency of humans on God also needs to be asserted even in an immortal (temporal fullness) human life.

With these cautions, we can say that since God is life affirming, the human task—both from religious and scientific perspectives—will be to seek immortality, if such a task is ever feasible. So the search for immortality can very well be conceived of as a "sacred duty" or "holy task" provided we do realise that such a task does not imply replacing God or "playing God."[12]

We worship God not because we will die, but because we are alive. God is the God of the living, not of the dead or the would-be-dead. Therefore theologically, belief in God is not necessarily for the concerns of future only; the concerns of the present are enough to postulate or affirm God.[13]

If the "glory of God is man fully alive," then obviously a human being who is "immortal" gives "more" glory to God. Such humans are more to the image of God. Creation of such humans make us "created co-creators"[14] in its most appropriate sense. This implies that the God we believe in is not the "God of the gaps," the God who satisfies one only at the limit-situation of one's death. We do not need crisis moments to lead us to God. It is the conviction of a genuine believer that God can be found in the depths of the daily lives and not necessarily at the end of daily lives. God is present both in the limit-situations and in the everyday life of the people as well in the glorious human achievements.

Theology as a Critique

The state of immortality, if at all attained, will not even lead us to the "paradise" of Adam and Eve or to the "Kingdom of God," which Jesus came to proclaim. Still it is our task as religious believers and scientists to search for immortality provided other ethical concerns are respected. The issue of human significance and meaning is not at all exhausted by immortality.

It must be remembered that the venture of seeking immortality is beset with many dangers and fallacies. We simply cannot be blind to the totality of life and be one-sidedly enamoured by the promise of scientific immortality. It is here that religious spirit and ethics have to encounter technology to justify, correct, critique, and strengthen the search for immortality. Religion can collaborate and interact with such a venture.[15]

We must be cautious that it is not human hubris that is at work here. It has been the traditional teaching of all religions that hubris leads inevitably to destruction. If our search for immortality stems from hubris—replacing God by ourselves, idolizing—then such a search cannot be religiously justified. But it is our contention that we can genuinely seek immortality with humility, with respect, and with awe before the infinite power of the Divine.

But we also need to be aware of the wider dimensions of justice and love. Some vital questions need to be faced: Does immortality for humans imply immortality for a select few (the elite) and mortality for other humans and non-human beings? Do immortal humans become machines—similar to the "soulless computer"?

Our search for immortality calls for humility, openness, respect both to the whole cosmos and to the Divine. It urges us to widen our vision, to deepen our insight, and to purify our faith: widening our vision of humanity, deepening our insights on God, and purifying our faith in God and in human beings. It leads us to focus our faith on the "depth dimension" of existence. It encourages us to search for further answers scientifically, technologically, religiously, and ethically.

This calls for serious dialogue between scientific and religious quests. It calls for mutual collaboration between the two. It also requires that each perform an informed critique of the other. One needs to be aware of the ulterior motives and unspoken assumptions and unconscious considerations.

Conclusion

So we must admit that human beings as we know them will perish one day. It is possible that new forms of life, including immortal human beings, may emerge. The crucial questions are: Will the immortal human still be capable of hoping and loving? Without the three traditional human virtues of faith, hope, and love, it is very difficult to conceive of these immortal forms of life as human or super-being, as proposed by Karl Rahner. Will we become immortal and reduce ourselves to intelligent, but soulless machines? Will artificial intelligence have anything to say to the "soul" of the human person? Will we reduce ourselves to immortal human beings who can not enjoy life, who cannot feel the simple pleasures of existence, who cannot love and hope? Or will we demonstrate that immortal humans who can love and laugh, who have something to hope for, someone to trust in, approach more closely and humbly the mystery of the Divine? If so, drinking *amrta* will make *asuras* have a humbler and wider vision of humanity and of the cosmos.

NOTES

1. Subhash Anand, *Story as Theology: An Interpretative Study of Five Episodes from the Mahabharata* (New Delhi: Intercultural Pub, 1996), pp. 2–3.
2. See Kuruvilla Pandikattu, "Eschatology: Arena for Creative Encounter between Science and Religion," *Jeevadhara* (April 1999), pp. 45ff.
3. See their Web site cryonics.org. Also Kuruvilla Pandikattu, *Meaning Through Science and Religion* (Pune: JDV, 1999), p. 124. See also Anupama Bhattacharya, "Crucible of Immortality," *Life Positive* 3/12 (March 1999), pp. 40–50.
4. Cf. Workshop Reader, Berkeley Introductory Workshop, January 13–18, 2000. See Geron Corporation, Q & A, May 1999.

5. See http://www.geron.com/News/QandA.html. Italics added.
6. Dick Thompson, "The Gene Machine," *Time* (January 24, 2000), p. 40. The sequence was announced in 2001.
7. The philosophical assumption that the human being is a "ghost in the machine" and the Cartesian duality must be seriously taken into account here.
8. *Times of India,* Pune (February 5, 2000), p. 1.
9. There are many philosophical and ethical issues involved here needing further elaboration.
10. This may call to mind the finite regress that is discussed in connection with the "proofs for God's existence."
11. This raises the issue if God wanted humans to be immortal when he created humans. The answer to this question can only be guessed. Scripturally there does not seem to be any conclusive evidence for one way or another.
12. Ted Peters, *Playing God: Genetic Determinism and Human Freedom* (London: Routledge, 1997).
13. P. Tillich and E. Gilson are two theologians who are significant in this area.
14. Ted Peters, "Genes, Theology, and Social Ethics: Are We Playing God?" in Ted Peters, ed., *Genetics: Issues of Social Justice* (Cleveland: The Pilgrim Press, 1998), p. 33.
15. It may be noted that the religious critique goes further than the ethical critique. Religious critique goes further than the ethical norms: It asks the most basic questions of what is a human being and what is immortality? Philosophical considerations play a significant role here.

This chapter was originally published in *The Month* (London, July 2000).

CHAPTER 13

Divine and Artificial Life:
A Theological Exploration

PETER G. HELTZEL

Peter Heltzel is a doctoral student in theology at Boston University. He received his M.Div. degree from Gordon-Conwell Theological Seminary in 1998. An ordained minister in the Christian Church (Disciples of Christ), he serves Park Street Church in Boston as a minister to college students.

Can you imagine having a witty conversation with your own personal robot, similar in construction to C3PO from *Star Wars,* while he takes care of your laundry, dishes, and waste disposal? By constructing "smart" machines and robots like C3PO, the artificial intelligence community hopes to improve the quality of human life. For example, the construction of a humanoid robot named Cog is currently underway at the Artificial Intelligence Laboratory at MIT. When the possibility of "artificial humanity" is considered, it seems that "natural humanity" has reached a new height of creative power.[1] What is the source of the human creativity that makes the construction of a robot possible? Is it simply evolutionary development or does human creativity have its source in something that transcends human life? What kind of deity, if any, is implied in the creation of artificial intelligence?

Artificial intelligence (AI) sheds significant light on contemporary Christian theology.[2] This programmatic chapter asserts three primary hypotheses. First, the attribute of human creativity is clearly illustrated in AI's attempt to construct a humanoid robot. Second, the creativity expressed in AI points to a creative transcendent being. The creative actions of the God of Christianity will be employed as a case study to put forward one explanation for the existence of human creativity. Third, AI, like all human creations, is an example of humans being "created co-creators" with God; as such, it can be used for good or evil.

Artificial intelligence is a scientific discipline that studies all facets of the human mind culminating in the construction of useful artifacts based on human intelligence. Launched at the 1956 Dartmouth conference as a systematic research program, AI is directed toward getting computers and robots to be "smart" and do "smart" things to assist humans in daily and vocational tasks. AI also employs computers and robots to simulate activities of human beings, so that we can deepen our understanding of how humans work.[3] AI is becoming increasingly a reflexive science, constantly benefiting from a dialectic between computers and the human mind.[4] This symbiosis allows for immense creativity through the development of many different engineering applications, including robotics, vision systems, language systems, and circuit design technology.

Cog, a Humanoid Robot

A major advance in the creative human spirit is occurring at the MIT AI lab in its current attempt to construct an artificial human, like the fictitious Lt. Commander Data on *Star Trek: The Next Generation*. The construction of such a robot named Cog testifies to the remarkable creativity of AI. Isaac Asimov's dream in his short story "I, Robot" of a positronic android brain with human-like consciousness is slowly becoming a reality. Margaret Boden argues that developments such as the construction of Cog have increased the sense of wonder among scientists today, wonder over the possibility of representation, meaning, and mind.[5] One reason for the "wonder" factor within AI is due to the fact that the human mind and body is a mysterious and complex frontier. In visual art, drawing and painting the human figure is the most difficult creative challenge; likewise, in AI building a humanoid robot is a formidable task. Although only the upper torso is complete on this fabricated man, Cog will be fully operational soon.

The justification for Cog comes out of a new trend in AI toward embodied intelligence (*contra* Dreyfus),[6] challenging the traditional symbolic approach, which asserts that intelligence is ultimately abstract formal symbol manipulation that is independent of the medium in which the symbols are embodied.[7] Rodney Brooks, in contrast, sees human-like embodiments as critical to the development of human-like intelligence. Embodied intelligence is a point of contact in the dialogue between AI and Christian theology, which affirms the psychosomatic unity of the human person.[8] The central premise behind embodied intelligence is that human consciousness is human because it is formed in a human, physical body. Although humanoid robots are not human, since they are not complex biological systems with a brain and central nervous system, James Sennett hypothesizes that they can still be thought of as persons (though not *human* persons) when they exhibit "self-consciousness" (e.g., the ability to assess their own states).[9]

During the past decade AI has run into several roadblocks in constructing a humanoid robot. For example, in terms of the development of mind, emotions remain an enigma. In contrast to Cartesian rationalism, recent neurological evidence suggests that emotions are not a luxury, but rather that they are essential for rational decision making.[10] Many studies are currently underway in cognitive robotics that attempt to model human emotion, further expressing creativity in the lab.[11] Every step of the way, teams of AI engineers must be creative as they integrate new systems and abilities into Cog. The creative problem solving and sense of wonder in AI research is present in other research fields, but embodied in AI's goal of building a human-like robot, from the inside out, is a unique challenge. Where does this creativity point?

Analogy and the Image of God

Jewish and Christian theologians are especially interested in AI's attempt to build a humanoid robot because of their belief that humanity is created in the image of God *(imago Dei)*.[12] The concept of *imago Dei* claims analogically that in some sense humanity "images" God. Analogies show similarity *in* difference. There is a fundamental difference between humans (and humanoid robots) and God—namely the difference between created and uncreated, material and immaterial, reality. Medieval theologian Thomas Aquinas wrote, "No term can be used of God in quite the same sense *(univoce)* as it is of other things."[13] Although analogies are limited, they can deepen our understanding of God.

Analogy is also a central form of reasoning within science, including AI. The central thesis of AI—that human mental activities are similar to the activities of a computer—is based on analogy. Instead of seeing humans as made in the image of God, humans are viewed as machines. Such reasoning is creatively employed by AI engineers daily as they try to build a robot analogous to humans. The ultimate success of AI's analogical approach depends on the adequacy of a mechanistic and functionalistic explanation of humanity.[14] Daniel Dennet has become one of the chief proponents of the functionalist view of human life. In *Consciousness Explained* Dennet argues that human consciousness can be explained comprehensively and decisively in purely material terms.

Roger Penrose counters that human consciousness is beyond the algorithms of computational science. When we say that human beings are self-conscious, we mean that there is such a thing as being *human:* human beings have subjectivity. The subjectivity of the human person is a starting point for many modern theologians, including Wolfhart Pannenberg.[15] This theological approach is typically called "theological anthropology"; it attempts to discover the theological significance of human self-consciousness as described by the natural and human sciences, which today includes AI. Creativity is one aspect of human consciousness and intelligence.

The creativity of God is a sufficient explanation of the creativity of the human mind, but not a necessary one. There are alternative and competing theories that are equally viable, but these do not have to exclude a theist option. If Penrose is right, that a computational explanation of consciousness is inadequate, maybe another approach will succeed in explaining and constructing human-like consciousness. For example, the embodied approach employed in the Cog project may eventually succeed in producing autonomous, self-conscious intelligence. If this end is accomplished, many naturalists will claim that this human attainment proves God's nonexistence. However, this would only be the second time that autonomous intelligence was created, the first being the creation of human intelligence.

When one considers all of the intellectual capital—both in theory and infrastructure—that has gone into developing science and technology throughout human history to place AI on the platform to possibly create autonomous robots, it is an unlikely conclusion that this is an accident of cultural evolution; a great deal of time, planning, and cumulative, collective human intelligence would have gone into the successful creation of an autonomous humanoid robot. Why are we not to conclude that this deliberate, laborious process points to an even greater preexistent intelligence? Thus, this chapter will proceed by correlating the human creation of robots with the divine creation of the world.

THE ANALOGICAL ARGUMENT

Source Analogy (Creator)	Target Analogy (Created)
God	Humanity *(imago Dei)*
Humanity (imago Dei)	Humanoid Robot *(imago humanitatis)*

The source of human creativity is coherently explained by the paradigmatic biblical creation accounts. The creativity demonstrated in AI reflects the creativity of God;[16] creativity, which is a central part of human personhood, finds its source within God, the Creator of the universe who continues creative activity throughout human history. The similarity in the analogy is that humans building robots mirrors God's creation of mankind. One difference is that humans were originally created perfect *(imago Dei)*, whereas cognitive robots will never be perfect because of human fallenness *(imago humanitatis)*. Therefore, robots made in our image inherit both our beauty and our ugliness. Because human existence is divided between good and evil, AI (and all human endeavors) have the potential for good and evil.

The second hypothesis of this chapter, that the creativity expressed in AI points to a creative transcendent being, is questioned by some scientists. For example, Karl Popper contends that theories should be, in principle, falsifiable.[17] Since the concept of the creativity of God implies the existence of a deity, which is an unfalsifiable belief, Popper would claim the second hypothesis of this chapter inadequate. However, Popper's positivist epistemology has now been questioned by many post-foundationalist philosophers including Kuhn and Lakatos. It is the methodological work of Imre Lakatos (*via* Nancey Murphy) that is especially helpful in getting around this roadblock to religious discourse.[18]

In contrast to Popper's concern with the falsifiability of theories, Lakatos emphasizes commitment to a certain "research program." He urges that our attention be directed not to individual hypotheses and theoretical networks at any one point in time, but to developing research programs over a span of time, such as the Newtonian program to treat the universe as a mechanical system. Lakatos holds that the "hard core" of a program (like Newton's laws) is exempt from falsification so that positive possibilities can be explored. Therefore, this chapter will proceed with the Triune God of Christianity as the "hard core" while exploring the possibility of the Christian God being the source of human creativity exhibited in AI. This "gamble on transcendence," as George Steiner describes it, suggests that all human creative efforts imply the existence of a God. It is the *imago Dei* that serves as the essential link between humanity and God in the biblical narratives.

In the Old Testament, the image of God is only mentioned directly in three passages (Gen. 1:26–27; 5:1–3; 9:5–6). This chapter emphasizes creativity as one way humans reflect God.[19] The idea of humanity's creativity being a reflection of God's own creative power has a long poetic heritage. For example, British Romantic poet Samuel Taylor Coleridge asserts in his *Biographia Literaria* that it is in the act of human creation that we truly express the *imago Dei.*[20] Coleridge defined imagination as "the primary Power and prime Agent of all human Perception, and as a repetition in the finite mind of the eternal act of creation in the infinite I AM."[21] Coleridge asserts, intuitively, that human creativity points to a creative transcendent being.

Is this transcendent creativity an abstract principle or a personal God? Rejecting speculative metaphysics and focusing on human creativity, humanist theologian H. N. Wieman claimed that God is "Creativity."[22] The notion of person implicit in the Christian doctrine of the Trinity (one essence and three persons: Father, Son, and Holy Spirit) does not allow for a deity who is simply an abstract principle of creativity. The Christian understanding of the triune God brings together human creativity and divine creativity in the doctrine of *Creatio continua:* since the initial creation of the world, God continually and creatively sustains it. There is a significant sense in which the act of humans building humanoid robots mirrors God's creation of and continued interaction with humanity. Furthermore, humans as creative agents have freedom to "co-create" with God through making artifacts out of natural materials.

The Creative God

Theologian Robert Neville argues that creation is the root doctrine of Christian theology and a paradigm for human creativity.[23] Creation means the work of God in bringing into being, without the use of any preexisting materials, everything that is. The biblical story affirms that God brought the whole world into existence *ex nihilo*—out of nothing.[24] Although the initial creation was immediate, there has also been a mediate or derivative creation, God's subsequent work of developing and fashioning what was originally brought into existence. In Book 12 of his *Confessions,* Augustine describes the subsequent origination of new entities fashioned from the previously created material that the Bible calls "formless and void" (Gen.1:2).[25] From this invisible myriad of atoms, God continues to fashion the universe progressively by bringing forth matter throughout the first chapter of Genesis. God says, "Let the waters bring forth . . ." (v. 20), and "Let the earth bring forth . . ." (v. 24). Furthermore, the description of the forming of Adam suggests the use of some type of material—"dust from the ground" (2:7). According to Augustine's exegesis it may well be that what God did originally was merely to create from nothing, and then in subsequent creative activity, God fashioned everything from the atoms initially created. Therefore, the various species created at the later time would be just as much God's doing as was the origin of matter.

If God does at least part of the creative work through immanent means, the origination of the various later species through the law of genetics—even recent hybrid varieties of roses, corn, cattle, and horses—is God's creative work. In these cases humans are often partners with God in producing what comes to be, "imaging forth" artifacts as God did in creation. Thus, from this perspective, God is involved in AI as engineers construct robotics out of various metals, circuits, and chips. God's initial creation becomes a paradigm for the ongoing creative process in the world.

After sparse mention in the early twentieth century, the doctrine of creation has enjoyed a recent renaissance in Christian theology, related to contemporary environmental concerns. Earlier understandings of creation emphasized the initial act, and particularly the uniqueness of God's power to create *ex nihilo*, while human beings are always dependent on preexisting materials for our creative acts. More recent considerations of the doctrine of creation, however, have emphasized the continuing creativity of God, highlighting the similarity between divine and human creativity through the recognition that God, like us, also creates by rearranging preexisting materials.

This renaissance in the doctrine of creation has been enriched by the contributions of theologians from a variety of perspectives.[26] The concept of *Creatio continua* makes three primary affirmations: (1) Creation is an ongoing process in which God is continuously active; (2) God is everywhere present, affecting the creation at every moment and at every level of complexity; (3) the future of creation is open-ended.[27] These affirmations show that God may be seen as one who accompanies the evolution of the cosmos, sustaining and influencing its development.[28] If God is continuing to create new forms and new possibilities, what is humanity's role in this continuing creation?

Co-Creating in Artificial Intelligence: A Concluding Proposal

Human work, especially technological innovation, may be seen as partnership with God in the continuing work of creation. Some have suggested the term "co-creation" to describe this role for humans. Karl Barth was leery of this term because it implied an unsubstantiated equality with God, which has been articulated by some AI researchers.[29] Philip Hefner's more nuanced version, *created co-creators,* is more appropriate: "The human being is God's created co-creator, whose purpose is the modifying and enabling of existing systems of nature so that they can participate in God's purposes."[30]

Through science, we gain a greater comprehension of the natural processes through which God creates. For example, cognitive robotics is gradually helping us understand the complex interaction of all the human systems that make for human consciousness. With a deeper understanding of these processes, human beings can participate in the ongoing creativity of God.[31] From this perspective, science and technology serve God's ongoing creative work.

When seen in this light, cognitive robotics is a new modality for divine agency, as are other forms of technology. This is not to take away from the high level of human creative intelligence demonstrated in projects such as the construction of Cog. Rather, this Christian concept of God goes beyond both deism and naturalism. *Creatio continua* opens up the possibility that God continues to act creatively in sustaining the world.

The concept of created co-creators implies that we actively take part in God's ongoing creativity. Thus, we also have responsibility for our creations. Frightening images of Frankenstein and Golem loom large in the cultural imagination of the West. AI can be applied for good or evil ends. Therefore, it is in the technological assessment of AI that a dialogue between science and religion can be helpful. AI challenges traditional Christian theologians to resist their neo-Luddite impulse and critically embrace our changing world. At the same time, Christian theology challenges AI researchers to think profoundly about the nature, responsibility, and purpose of humanity. Together, scientists and theologians can begin to discuss the plethora of pressing questions raised by this creative advance.[32]

Instead of subverting human creativity, the Christian concept of an active, personal, Creator God provides a compelling explanation for humanity's creative prowess. This dynamic view of the creative God as a spiritual explanation for the evolution of human creativity provides an alternative to Dennet's naturalistic explanation. Seen in this light, AI is a shadow-box show of the continuing creativity of God.

NOTES

1. The term "artificial humanity" is used by Rodney Brooks and others within the field of cognitive robotics (a subdiscipline within AI) to indicate the goal of constructing an autonomous humanoid robot.
2. A general and flexible use of Artificial Intelligence (AI) will be employed throughout this chapter to describe both the scientific discipline, as well as the community of scientists and engineers who carry out research in this field.
3. Brooks and Stein.
4. Cf. Wiener, p. 11ff.; Cf. Stein, pp. 393–407.
5. Boden.
6. Brooks and Steels; Foerst "Cog, A Humanoid Robot, and the Question of the Image of God," pp. 99–102. Cf. Dreyfus.
7. For an explanation of the symbolic approach see Haugeland's discussion of "Good Old Fashioned AI (GOFAI)" in *Artificial Intelligence: The Very Idea.*
8. The classical Christian affirmation of embodied humanity (*contra* gnosticism) is reinforced by the doctrines of the incarnation of Jesus Christ and the resurrection of the dead. Cf. a modern treatment of embodiment, T. Tracy.
9. Sennett, p. 197. cf. Lillegard; Richardson and Wildman.
10. Damasio; LeDoux; Picard.
11. Velasquez; Pfeifer.
12. See Foerst, "Cog, A Humanoid Robot, and the Question of the Image of God."
13. Aquinas, 1.32, p. 143.
14. Foerst, "Artificial Intelligence: Walking the Boundary," p. 685.
15. Pannenberg.
16. On the warrants of analogy in theological construction, see T. Tracy, pp. 405–445.
17. Popper.
18. Murphy.
19. Scholem, pp. 63, 64; Sayers.
20. Coleridge, part 13, 14.
21. Coleridge, part 1, p. 199.
22. Wieman.
23. Neville.
24. Gen. 1:1; cf. John 1:1–3; Rev. 4:11; Rom. 4:17; May.
25. Augustine, 2.12.1–17, pp. 289–328.
26. For example, Whiteheadian process theologians (John Cobb and David Griffin), scientist-theologians (Arthur Peacocke and John Polkinghorne), and trinitarian theologians (Jürgen Moltmann and Thomas Torrance).
27. The openness of the future, the third point, is the most theologically debatable of the three affirmations of *Creatio continua.* The future is open in terms of the creative potential of human beings; however, the future of the cosmos is certain from an eschatological standpoint. Limiting God's knowledge of the future is problematic for the traditional understanding of the omniscience of God. For a defense of God's omniscience, focusing on the issue of quantum indeterminacy, see Davis.
28. Peacocke; Polkinghorne.

29. Theologian Karl Barth argues that the primary continuing creative work of God is building the new creation, the church. See Barth III/1.
30. Hefner, p. 212.
31. The idea that humans can co-create does not mean that all human creative activities are divinely inspired.
32. Pressing ethical and philosophical questions raised by AI remain for further discussion: for example, How will these robots be used—for the benefit or destruction of humanity? Do robots have souls? What moral and ethical properties do robots have? How will the existence of thinking machines that are smarter than humans affect our self-understanding? May the conversation continue!

BIBLIOGRAPHY

Aquinas, Thomas. *Against the Gentiles.* vol. 1, trans. Anton C. Pegis. Notre Dame: University, 1955.
Augustine. *Confessions,* trans. William Watts. Cambridge, MA: Harvard, 1912.
Barth, Karl. *Church Dogmatics* III/1, eds. Bromiley, G. W. and T. F. Torrance. Edinburgh: T and T Clark, 1958.
Boden, Margaret A. "Wonder and Understanding." *Zygon* 20:4 (1985), pp. 391–400.
Brooks, R. A., and L. A. Steels, eds. *The Artificial Life Route to Artificial Intelligence: Building Embodied, Situated Agents.* Hillsdale, NJ: Lawrence Erlbaum Associates, 1995.
Brooks, R. A., and Lynn Stein. "Building Brains for Bodies." *Autonomous Robots* 1 (1994), pp. 7–25.
Cobb, John B., Jr., and David Ray Griffin. *Process Theology: An Introductory Exposition.* Philadelphia: Westminster Press, 1976.
Coleridge, Samuel Taylor. *The Collected Works of Samuel Taylor Coleridge,* vol. 7, *Biographia Literaria,* ed. James Engell and W. Jackson Bate. Princeton: University, 1983.
Damasio, A. *Descartes's Error: Emotion, Reason, and the Human Brain.* New York: Grosset/Putnam, 1994.
Davis, John J. "Quantum Indeterminacy and the Omniscience of God." *Science and Christian Belief* 9: 2 (1997), pp. 129–144.
Dennet, Daniel. *Consciousness Explained.* Boston: Little, Brown and Co., 1991.
Dreyfus, Hubert L. *What Computers Still Can't Do: A Critique of Artificial Intelligence.* Cambridge, MA: MIT, 1992.
Foerst, Anne. "Artificial Intelligence: Walking the Boundary." *Zygon* 31:4 (December 1996), pp. 681–693.
———. "Cog, A Humanoid Robot, and the Question of the Image of God." *Zygon* 33:1 (March 1998), pp. 99–111.
Haugeland, John. *Artificial Intelligence: The Very Idea.* Cambridge, MA: MIT Press, 1985.
Hefner, Philip. "The Evolution of the Created Co-creator," in *The Cosmos as Creation: Theology and Science in Consonance,* ed. T. Peters. Nashville: Abingdon Press, 1989.
Kuhn, Thomas S. *The Structure of Scientific Revolutions.* Chicago: University, 1962.
Lakatos, Imre. "Falsification and the Methodology of Scientific Research Programmes," in I. Lakatos and A. Musgrave, *Criticism and the Growth of Knowledge.* Cambridge: University, 1970.

LeDoux, J. *The Emotional Brain.* New York: Simon and Schuster, 1996.

Lillegard, Norman. "No Good News for Data." *Cross Currents* 44: 1 (Spring 1994), pp. 28–42.

May, Gerhard. *Creatio Ex Nihilo: The Doctrine of Creation out of Nothing in Early Christian Thought,* trans. A. S. Worral. Edinburgh: T and T Clark, 1995.

Moltmann, Jürgen. *God in Creation: A New Theology of Creation and the Spirit of God.* The Gifford Lectures 1984–1985. trans. M. Kohl. San Francisco: Harper and Row.

Moravec, Robert. *Mind Children.* Cambridge, MA: Harvard University Press, 1988.

Murphy, Nancey. *Theology in the Age of Scientific Reasoning.* Ithaca: Cornell University Press, 1990.

Neville, Robert Cummings. *Creativity and God.* New York: The Seabury Press, 1980.

Pannenberg, Wolfhart. *What is Man?* trans. Duane A. Priebe. Philadelphia: Fortress, 1970.

Peacocke, Arthur. *Creation and the World of Science.* Oxford and New York: Oxford University Press, 1979.

Penrose, Roger. *Shadows of the Mind: A Search for the Missing Science of Consciousness.* Oxford and New York: Oxford University Press, 1994.

Pfeifer, R. "Artificial Intelligence Models of Emotion." *Cognitive Perspectives on Emotion and Motivation,* ed. G. Hamilton, G. Bower, and N. Frijda. Netherlands: Kluwet, 1988, pp. 287–320.

Picard, Rosalind. *Affective Computing.* Cambridge, MA: MIT, 1997.

Polkinghorne, John. *Science and Providence.* Cambridge: University of Cambridge, 1989.

Popper, Karl. *Conjectures and Refutations.* London: Routledge, 1963.

Richardson, W. Mark, and Wesley Wildman. *Religion and Science: History, Method, Dialogue.* New York and London: Routledge, 1996.

Sayers, Dorothy. *The Mind of the Maker.* London: Religious Book Club, 1942.

Scholem, Gershom. "The Golem of Prague and the Golem of Rehovot." *Commentary* 1 (1966), pp. 62–65.

Sennett, James. "Requiem for an Android?" *Cross Currents* 46:2 (summer 1996), pp. 195–214.

Stein, L. A. "Imagination as Situated Cognition." *Journal of Experimental and Theoretical Intelligence* 6 (1994), pp. 393–407.

Torrance, T. F. *The Christian Doctrine of God: One Being, Three Persons.* Edinburgh: T and T Clark, 1996.

Tracy, Thomas. *God, Action, and Embodiment.* Grand Rapids: Eerdmans, 1993.

Velasquez, J. "Modeling Emotions and Other Motivations in Synthetic Agents." *Proceedings of the Fourteenth National Conference on Artificial Intelligence.* Providence, RI: AAAI Press/MIT, 1997.

Wieman, Henry Nelson. *Religious Experience and Scientific Method.* New York: Macmillan, 1926.

Wiener, Norbet. *God and Golem, Inc.* Cambridge, MA: MIT, 1964.

This chapter was originally published in *The Journal of Faith and Science Exchange* vol. 2 (June 1999), pp. 21–30

PART II

NEW VISIONS OF
Theology

Toward a Kenotic Pneumatology: Quantum Field Theory and the Theology of the Cross

ERNEST L. SIMMONS

Dr. Simmons is professor in the Department of Religion at Concordia College, Moorhead, Minnesota, and director of the Dovre Center for Faith and Learning. He is also the co-chair of the National Working Group on Religion and Science of the American Academy of Religion.

"Science without religion is lame and religion without science is blind."
ALBERT EINSTEIN

"The material principle of the Doctrine of the Trinity is the cross. The formal principle of the Theology of the Cross is the Doctrine of the Trinity."
JÜRGEN MOLTMANN

Introduction

I first became interested in the relationship of field theory to the understanding of the Spirit through the writing of Wolfhart Pannenberg. Many theologians are interested in unity and the priority of the whole over the part in understanding God's relationship to the creation. Drawing upon the earlier work of Thomas Torrance, Pannenberg observes:

> Field theories from Faraday to Einstein claim a priority for the whole over the parts. This is of theological significance, because God has to be conceived as the unifying ground of the whole universe if he is to be conceived as the creator and redeemer of the world. The field concept could be used in theology to make the effective presence of God in every single phenomenon intelligible.[1]

He concludes, "The concept of a field of force could be used to make effective our understanding of the spiritual presence of God in natural phenomena."[2] Pannenberg here has in mind classical field theory (such as the electromagnetic field) and hopes to derive from it divine ubiquity (omnipresence), "the effective presence of God in every single phenomenon."

However, there are problems with using classical field theory as an analogy for understanding divine presence in the world, as John Polkinghorne has pointed out.[3] First of all, according to classical field theory, effects are local. What one does "here" does not necessarily affect what happens "there." In other words, occurrences in a classical field are collections of parts, not a whole. Secondly, there is no possibility of entanglement or connection between the parts. And finally, superposition—the presence of more than one state at a time—is not possible. Classical fields are "determinate entities" and "local entities."[4] Dr. Polkinghorne suggests that if theologians want to find a picture for the "priority of the whole over the parts," derived from contemporary science, they should look at quantum theory and in particular, quantum field theory.[5] He observes, "All established modern accounts of the structure of matter are quantum field theories. A field is an extended system, taking values at all points of space and instants of time." Quantum field theory does suggest nonlocality, superposition, and entanglement.[6] The quantum world displays a universe in which local phenomena are built upon a nonlocal reality.[7] This would seem to be exactly what Pannenberg ordered if one is to speak of the "spiritual presence of God in natural phenomenon." Quantum theory, however, also involves indeterminacy and that too must be taken into account in any theological reflection.

To respond to the issue of quantum indeterminacy, I would like to employ the idea of divine kenosis[8] (self-emptying or self-limitation) to create "room" theologically for indeterminacy within the created world. As a theological analogy, I would thus propose a kenotic understanding of the activity of the Holy Spirit, to characterize divine love in relation to a creation filled with indeterminacy. In regard to the theology/physics dialogue the question can then be asked, "Does quantum field theory's (QFT) understanding of a nonlocal, relational holism involving particle entanglement, indeterminacy, and superposition provide an exploratory analogy for understanding the activity of the kenotic Spirit?"

My thesis is that kenosis is a form of divine entanglement with the world, which entails nonlocal, relational holism through which the Holy Spirit is actively present as sanctifying agapaic love. This would then lead to a "kenotic pneumatology" (understanding of the Holy Spirit), which would be consistent with a kenotic understanding of the cross and creation, indeed a kenotic Trinity. It is this same Spirit that was also active in the self-limiting emptying of God into the creation itself and that continues to sustain the creation by emptying unto sanctification.

Such a proposal has implications both for theological reflection and for the relation of theology and science. There are thus two types of theoretical issues at stake: One is the direct theological concern of a kenotic understanding of the Spirit. The other is the consideration of the activity of the Spirit in the theology and science dialogue. In this chapter my primary emphasis will be upon the latter, but some theological discussion of kenotic theory and the theology of the cross must precede our discussion of quantum field theory. This discussion will focus only upon the divine presence of the Spirit in creation and will not address other activities of the Spirit: the Spirit's "gifts," the activity of sustaining the church, or Eucharistic presence.

Please do not misunderstand my intentions. I am not calling for a "Pentecostal physics" or for "charismatic quarks," even though some of them may indeed be "charmed." What I am calling for is a serious consideration of the presence of the Holy Spirit in creation as the expression of divine love characterized by self-emptying upon the cross. What would such a kenotic Spirit then mean in relation to contemporary physics as the most sophisticated understanding of the physical world? In this constructive exercise the goal will be to see if current understanding in quantum field theory can serve as an *analogical aid* for the understanding of the activity of the Holy Spirit in the world, *not* as an explanation for such activity.

I would like to begin with a brief overview of the theology of the cross, which involves the self-emptying of God such that God's action becomes hidden in the world. This hiddenness is at the heart of kenosis. The discussion of the theology of the cross will lead to an overview of the understanding of kenosis in creation and a kenosis of the Holy Spirit in creation. After clarifying the nature and value of a kenotic understanding of the Spirit, we may then turn to a consideration of quantum field theory and the possibilities it offers as an analogy for understanding the activity of the emptying Spirit in the world. This chapter is an exercise in constructive theology, which always has about it a tentative and exploratory character, and is subject to further revision. I am not a physicist, so in the paragraphs that follow I would like to sketch out briefly the argument as I see it developing and ask for your assistance in

its refinement. Let us begin with a brief reflection on theological
method.

Theological Method

"Theology is the proposing of relations between the testimony of a
community of faith and the life of that community in nature and history."[9] As such it involves a method of correlation between the testimony of the faith tradition (scriptures, creeds, and confessions) and life
experience, including not only what humans do to one another (history) but also the wider ecosystem of which they are a part (nature). As
such, theology is dynamic and dialectical (relational) and an exercise in
the use of the analogical imagination. In this sense theology is a form of
theory construction similar to other human forms of knowing. Theology,
however, will never be complete, for divine reality always transcends
human knowing and will remain hidden from its grasp. That is why
theology is an exercise in faith reflection *(fides quarens intellectum)* undertaken within, and in service to, a community of faith.

Theology of the Cross (Kenotic Christology)

The principle of the incarnation is that the spiritual is manifest in the
material, that the "Word became flesh" (John 1:14). Out of the incarnation flows God's justifying grace and forgiveness of sins. By becoming
creature the Creator has sanctified human earthly existence, reconciling
us not only to God but also to one another and the earth. The earliest
scriptural analogy for understanding this divine action is found in
Philippians 2:6–8. Most biblical scholars believe it was an extant, liturgical hymn that Paul or another author employed to express his understanding of *how* God could be present in human history.[10] It is also believed that he added his own touch to this hymn with the phrase "even
death on a cross," to characterize the depth of divine emptying. In the
Christian tradition the cross is the lens through which God is viewed,
albeit "darkly."[11] The cross is a paradoxical and complex disclosure of
the divine.[12]

There is a paradoxical, two-fold hiddenness involved in God's disclosure on the cross. First, there is the "form of the opposite" where
power comes in weakness, victory in defeat, and life in death. Second,
there is the totality of divine reality, God in God's self, the *mysterium
tremendum et fascinans,* which is beyond the disclosure of God in Christ.

God is more than God's self-disclosure in Christ. This gives us both a critical and a material principle for theological reflection. Critically, it tells us that the work of God on Calvary must be related to all Christian thought. The cross alone is our theology *(crux sola nostra theologia)* and functions as a *critical principle* for the assessment of theological formulation. The material principle is the character of divine love as agape or self-giving love, which I believe can be understood as the expression of divine kenosis. Divine love, to enter the world, must self-limit itself in order not to destroy the creation it loves and which is a product of that love.[13] Kenosis is a means for the expression of divine love. Divine self-limitation makes possible divine self-giving. A kenotic Christology leads directly to a kenotic understanding of creation.

Kenotic Creation

In this theological model, kenosis is understood as the way God relates to the world. Creation is a work of love and that love is made possible by God's self-limitation both in creating "space" for a free creation to occur within divine power and in the self-giving love which makes creation possible at all.[14] John Polkinghorne argues that such divine self-limitation may be three-fold not only in omnipotence and omniscience but also in agency. He observes, "I am suggesting further that divine self-emptying extends to a kenosis of the status of agency, so that special providence is exercised as a cause among causes, active within the cloudy unpredictabilities of created process."[15] God would be seen to interact with creaturely history but not overrule the acts of creatures.[16]

The "emptying" of God into creation however is not a full disclosure of who God is. Just as in the cross, God remains hidden behind the masks of materiality. The creation too becomes *larva dei*, the "mask of God." In faith one may appeal to God as Creator, but one cannot prove such a creation by observation of the natural world. Scientific analysis can neither prove nor disprove the presence of God in creation. Divine kenosis involves the emptying of divinity in order for the creation to occur. The creation is not divine although it is related to the divine. The kenosis of God in creating allows for true relationship and community, by creating the "other" to which God can be related. In this sense, the incarnation is an intensification of the kenotic process of creation. George Murphy observes, "The most profound aspect of the cross is that *God himself* shares in the suffering of the world. In the incarnation, God becomes a participant in the evolutionary process, sharing in the evolutionary history which links humanity with the rest of the bios-phere."[17] Through the incarnation the Creator further self-limits and empties in order to enter the suffering "other" of the creation itself. This then leads to what I am calling a "kenotic logic" of the Trinity and therefore of the Spirit.[18]

Kenotic Pneumatology

In the Christian tradition, the fullest disclosure of God is confessed to be in Christ. This Christological disclosure reveals the kenotic character of divine love, which gives us insight into the nature of divine creation. By the internal consistency of the divine nature the spirit too must be kenotic. The logic is as follows: a kenotic Christology yields a kenotic understanding of divine activity, which yields the self-emptying of God to allow for the creation, a kenotic creation. This two-fold relational ac-tivity of God can lead to a kenotic understanding of the divine nature of love which, in turn, brings about a kenotic understanding of the activity of the Holy Spirit, in effect, a kenotic Trinity.

Alternatively, since the Holy Spirit in the West is understood to proceed from both "the Father and the Son" and since the activity of both divine persons *(hypostases)* can be understood through the idea of kenosis, then so too can the third person, the Holy Spirit. Love entails kenosis and, since God is love (1 John 4:16), God also entails kenosis in order to express this self-limiting love. Jürgen Moltmann puts it this way, " The Spirit is the Spirit of surrender of the Father and the Son. He [sic] is creative love proceeding out of the Father's pain and the Son's self-surrender and comes to forsaken human beings in order to open them to a future for life."[19] The Spirit is the self-emptying, self-limiting agapaic love of God sanctifying the creation toward life and fulfillment. Is it possible to find any resources in science that would help further understand this kenotic activity of the Spirit? I believe QFT can provide useful analogies, though certainly not explanations.

Quantum Field Theory and Kenosis

QFT involves, through the EPR Effect and Bell's theorem, a demonstra-tion of two things very helpful for this discussion.[20] First of all, through the entanglement of the potentialities of paired photons, nonlocal rela-tionality has apparently been demonstrated. Nonlocal relationality car-ries with it some form of "action at a distance" or connectedness between particles. Secondly, holism is understood in such a way that the part seems to derive from the whole and superposition is possible. Particles come in and out of existence as excitations within the field of the quantum vacuum, like ripples on a pond of energy. A photon is a quantum of the electromagnetic field and an electron a quantum of the electron field. These characteristics emerge when the wave/particle duality is brought to bear on the field excitation. One could say, in a sense, that the universe is not "filled" with the vacuum but is "written" on it.[21] What analogical implications would this have for understanding spiritual presence in physical existence? Let us begin with the understanding of entanglement and nonlocality.

For nonlocal relations to be possible, particles, such as photons in Alain Aspect's experiment, must be phase entangled from the beginning. This is an entanglement of potentiality that proceeds out of the quantum holism within the wave function potential of the quantum field. The entanglement proceeds out of a holistic phase potential, which is not destroyed when the particles are emitted. Nick Herbert puts it this way, "Since there is nothing that is not ultimately a quantum system, if the quantum phase connection is 'real,' then it links *all systems that have once interacted at some time in the past*—not just twin-state photons—into a single waveform whose remotest parts are joined in a manner unmediated, unmitigated, and immediate."[22] This is, of course, an indeterminate potential until such time as measurement is done. Then the entanglement of potentials becomes definite; for example, polarization is measured in Aspect's experiment.

Now what does this have to do with theology? The concept of nonlocality in quantum field theory provides an excellent analogy for understanding God's entanglement with the creation. First, we begin by employing a method of *analogia relationis* (analogy of relationship) rather than an *analogia entis* (analogy of being). We can thus understand that God's kenotic self-limitation, in order to generate possibility for the creation, proceeds out of a divine potentiality. The divine potentiality grounds an entanglement with the potentiality of the creation. There is a divine holism operative prior to the creation. This could be seen as analogous to quantum holism in such a way that God is forever related to the world by virtue of the entanglement of divine potentiality. In effect it could be said that God influences the creation, but the entanglement is reciprocal such that the creation also influences God. Divine entanglement could be one way of developing the understanding of panentheism, which defines God as being in the world but more than the world.[23] The divine potentiality is not exhausted by the creation but is self-limited by it. The kenotic turn to incarnation would entail an intensification of entanglement with the creation, whereby future possibilities are conjoined. The continuing entanglement of God with the creation is one way in which God sustains the creation, keeping it from chaos.[24]

Second, this entanglement of divine future-oriented field potential with the creation's field of potential could be understood as the sanctifying activity of the Holy Spirit. In effect this is analogous to a superposition of wave functions within the field, which eventuates in providential presence in the midst of indeterminacy. The Spirit is the ongoing kenotic entanglement of the Father and the Son with the creation, the sanctifying embodiment of the agapaic love of God. Since the kenotic nature of divine activity also involves hiddenness, it is no surprise that the activity of the Spirit would be hidden; we see only its influence. The Hebrew *ruach* (breath or wind) as well as the Greek *pneuma* (air)—from which words like pneumatic are derived—carry with them this understanding of an unseen force whose effects can be experienced. It would not be possible, therefore, to disentangle the spiritual presence in the "gossamer" of creation from all other causes and potentials in the field.

There is a difficulty here, however, and it is that the field potentials in quantum theory are always indeterminate until measurement takes place.[25] All one can know is that the results will be correlated after measurement, not what the results will be beforehand. This is where entangled quantum potentials run head-on into quantum indeterminacy. Does this present an insurmountable obstacle to using quantum field theory as an analogy? I do not think so, if we realize that the creation is indeed free and at the same time that God is related to all the possible potentials of that creation. True novelty is possible but it is not unrelated to God. Indeed love is as interested in process as in outcome. Therefore God need not push for efficacy over growth, and divine self-limitation allows openness of outcome for the authentic reciprocity of love on the part of the creation.

Also, what would result if we consider that divine relation is analogous to measurement? Positing divine becoming in relation to creation, could God's self-understanding constitute a measurement of the divine potential in relation to the creation, in such a way that a correlate definiteness emerges in the creation? In other words, does God's own becoming in relation to the creation function as an operator field assisting the creation in actualizing its own field-state potential? If this understanding works, then the activity of the Holy Spirit could be seen as analogous to a field operator that makes various field states possible but nevertheless remains hidden within the field. This could bring to mind Whitehead's particular providence for particular occasions. Divine phase potential could then be seen as a superposition upon the creation's own phase potential. Could this be a relational effect of divine kenotic entanglement and one possible role of the Spirit in creation? I believe so.

Finally, because the Spirit and the creation are entangled from the beginning, we do not have the need for a "causal joint" here because they are part of the same holistic quantum potential. Rather, we might speak of a "causal potentiality" in which the entanglement brings forth respective quantifications from the quantum field. There is distinction as well as relatedness between God and the creation. Quantum field theory might indeed help give a useful analogy for understanding such a panentheistic relationship.[26]

Conclusion

The human question of why always hangs suspended between the finite and the infinite. Between logos and ethos we exercise our pathos, as we seek meaning before our own beginnings and after our demise. We encounter God through "masks," the masks of kenotic self-limitation, for that is the only way that the infinite can enter into the finite without destroying it. Perhaps QFT in collaboration with kenotic theology can provide a way for us to understand a bit more of that divine mask and a way to perceive the self-emptying love of God behind it. Quantum field theory may offer the following:

- Through quantum field holism it may provide a physical analogy for the whole within the parts in such a way as to illuminate the idea of God being both in the world and beyond it at the same time, affirming divine ubiquity and panentheism.
- Through phase entanglement and nonlocal effects it may provide analogy for the activity of the Holy Spirit in sustaining and sanctifying the creation from within, in a hidden fashion.
- Through quantum indeterminacy it may affirm the freedom and openness of the creation in relation to divine self-limitation.
- Through such physical analogies it may show that a kenotic pneumatology can be a meaningful understanding of spirituality for contemporary Christianity and assist reflection on the role of the Spirit in the theology and science dialogue.

The task before us, as I see it, is to make this discussion more explicit, and to ask what additional insights reflection on the Holy Spirit might contribute to the theology and science dialogue.

NOTES

1. Wolfhart Pannenberg, "The Doctrine of Creation and Modern Science," in *Cosmos as Creation*, ed. Ted Peters (Nashville: Abingdon Press, 1989), 164. Also quoted in John Polkinghorne, *Reason and Reality* (Philadelphia: Trinity Press, 1991), 93.
2. Pannenberg, "The Doctrine of Creation and Modern Science," 175.
3. See John Polkinghorne, "Pannenberg's Engagement with the Natural Sciences," *Zygon* 34 (March 1999): 151–158.
4. Ibid., 6. See also Polkinghorne, *Reason and Reality*, 93.
5. Polkinghorne, *Reason and Reality*, 92–93.
6. On quantum theory see John Polkinghorne, *Serious Talk: Science and Religion in Dialogue* (Philadelphia: Trinity Press, 1995); idem, *The Particle Play* (Oxford; San Francisco: W. H. Freeman, 1979); idem, *The Quantum World* (Princeton, NJ: Princeton University Press, 1984); idem, *One World* (Princeton, NJ: Princeton University Press, 1986). In addition, see Bernard d'Espagnat, *Reality and the Physicist: Knowledge, Duration, and the Quantum World* (Cambridge: Cambridge University Press, 1989); Ian Barbour, *Religion and Science: Historical and Contemporary Issues* (San Francisco: Harper SanFrancisco, 1997).
7. Nick Herbert, *Quantum Reality* (Garden City, NY: Anchor Press/Doubleday, 1985), 230. In my opinion, this text is one of the best introductions to quantum theory for the nonspecialist that is currently available. An excellent anthology on the relation of physics to philosophy and theology is *Physics, Philosophy, and Theology: A Common Quest for Understanding*, ed. Robert Russell, William Stoeger, and George Coyne (Vatican City State: CTNS and The Vatican Observatory, 1988). Within the philosophy of science see *Philosophical Foundations of Quantum Field Theory*, ed. H. R. Brown and R. Harré (Oxford: Clarendon Press, 1990).
8. See "Kenosis," *Theological Dictionary of the New Testament* (Grand Rapids, MI: Eerdmans, 1965), 3: 661–662. For a more complete recent treatment of kenosis see Lucien Richard, *Christ, The Self-Emptying of God* (New York: Paulist Press, 1997).
9. Joseph Sittler, *Essays on Nature and Grace* (Philadelphia: Fortress Press, 1972).
10. See Richard, *Christ, The Self-Emptying of God*, chapter 4, "In the Form of a Servant: The Kenotic Hymn."
11. See Jürgen Moltmann, *The Crucified God*, trans. R.A. Wilson and John Bowden (New York: Harper and Row, 1974).
12. See George Murphy's articles, "The Theology of the Cross and God's Work in the World," *Zygon* 33 (June 1998): 221–231; "The Third Article in the Science-Theology Dialogue," *Perspectives on Science and Christian Faith* 45 (September 1993): 162–168.

13. The idea that divine power would be destructive or coercive unless limited is commonly asserted, but it has also been challenged by theologians such as Anna Case-Winters in *God's Power: Traditional Understandings and Contemporary Challenges* (Louisville, KY: Westminster/John Knox Press, 1990).

14. See Jürgen Moltmann, *God in Creation: A New Theology of Creation and the Spirit of God: The Gifford Lectures, 1984–1985* (San Francisco: Harper and Row, 1985); John Polkinghorne, "God in Relation to Nature: Kenotic Creation and Divine Action" (Queen's College, Cambridge, July 1998, photocopy); Richard, *Christ, The Self-Emptying of God,* chapter 8, "Kenotic Creation."

15. Polkinghorne, "God in Relation to Nature: Kenotic Creation and Divine Action," 16. See also John Polkinghorne, *The Faith of a Physicist: Reflections of a Bottom-up Thinker: The Gifford Lectures, 1993–1994* (Minneapolis, MN: Fortress Press, 1996); idem, *Science and Providence: God's Interaction with the World* (London: SPCK, 1989).

16. For an interesting comparison of several leading "scientist theologians" on this topic, among others, see John Polkinghorne's *Scientists as Theologians: A Comparison of the Writings of Ian Barbour, Arthur Peacocke, and John Polkinghorne* (London: SPCK, 1996).

17. George Murphy, "'Chiasmic Cosmology' and the 'Same Old Story': Two Lutheran Approaches to Natural Theology," in *Facets of Faith and Science,* vol. 4, *Interpreting God's Action in the World,* ed. Jitse van der Meer (Ancasater, Ontario: The Pascal Centre and Lanham/New York/London: University Press of America, 1996), 137.

18. See also Richard, *Christ, The Self-Emptying of God,* chapter 7, "Kenosis and the Holy Trinity."

19. Jürgen Moltmann, "The Crucified God: A Trinitarian Theology of the Cross," *Interpretation* (1972): 294–295.

20. See Herbert, *Quantum Reality*; Polkinghorne, *Reason and Reality,* chapter 7; Polkinghorne, *Serious Talk,* chapter 2.

21. Ian Marshall and Danah Zohar, *Who's Afraid of Schrödinger's Cat? All the New Science Ideas You Need to Keep up with the New Thinking* (New York: William Morrow, 1997), 304.

22. Herbert, *Quantum Reality,* 223.

23. "Panentheism," in *The Oxford Dictionary of the Christian Church,* ed. Cross and Livingstone (Oxford: Oxford University Press, 1974), 1027.

24. The subject of divine action is currently a major focus in the science and theology dialogue and so the literature is growing quickly. J. Polkinghorne, A. Peacocke, R. Russell, P. Clayton, N. Murphy, T. Tracy, and I. Barbour among others are writing on the subject. For a good overview of the issues and perspectives see *Chaos and Complexity: Scientific Perspectives on Divine Action,* ed. Robert Russell, Nancey Murphy, and Arthur Peacocke (Vatican City State: CTNS and The Vatican Observatory, 1995); and Philip Clayton, *God and Contemporary Science* (Grand Rapids, MI: Eerdmans, 1997). Also see John Polkinghorne, "Creatio Continua and Divine Action," *Science and Christian Belief* 7 (1995): 101–115; Lyndon Harris, "Divine Action: An Interview with John Polkinghorne," *Cross Currents* (Spring 1998): 3–14; Robert John Russell, "Does 'The God Who Acts' Really Act? New Approaches to Divine Action in Light of Science," *Theology Today* 54 (April 1997): 43–65. Russell prefers to approach this issue

of divine action from the "bottom up" employing quantum theory, while Polkinghorne prefers to approach it "top down" employing chaos theory.

25. This is one of Polkinghorne's reasons for preferring chaos theory over quantum theory to explain divine action. See John Polkinghorne, "The Metaphysics of Divine Action," in *Chaos and Complexity,* as well as idem, *Serious Talk,* chapters 2 and 7.

26. See Robert John Russell, "Cosmology from Alpha to Omega," *Zygon* 29 (December 1994): 572

This chapter was originally published in *Center for Theology and the Natural Sciences Bulletin* vol. 19, no. 2 (Spring 2000). Research for this article was made possible by a grant from the Pew Charitable Trusts in their funding of the Calvin College Faculty Summer Seminars.

CHAPTER 15

A Pantheist Vision of God:
The Divine Universe

PAUL HARRISON

Dr. Paul Harrison is an environmentalist and author living in London. He is the founder and president of the World Pantheist Movement (www.pantheism.net), and author of *The Elements of Pantheism* (Element Books). He has worked as a consultant for many UN agencies such as the United Nations Population Fund, Food and Agriculture Organization, and the World Bank, and written many books and reports on environment, population, and development, including *Inside the Third World* and *The Third Revolution* (both Penguin). In 1988 he received a United Nations Environment Programme Global 500 Award for services to the environment through his writing. Dr. Harrison has master's degrees from Cambridge in European languages and literature, and in sociology from the London School of Economics, and a doctorate in earth sciences from Cambridge.

Two core beliefs lie at the heart of pantheism. All pantheists believe that the Universe is divine, or that there is no distinction or separation between the Universe and God. And they believe that the Universe is in the deepest sense a unified whole of which all individual things are interdependent parts.

For pantheists there is no part of God or the divinity held in reserve, somewhere beyond the edge of time and space. God did not precede the Universe. God does not extend outside the Universe. God is not greater than the Universe. Some scientists speculate that there may be other universes beyond the one we can see with our telescopes—but if so, these would still be part of the bigger Universe or Omniverse, the totality of everything that exists.

Why Pantheists Believe the Universe Is Divine

Some pantheists have tried to prove that God and the Universe are identical through logical argument. Spinoza used complicated scholastic definitions to try to prove that nothing except God could possibly exist. But Spinoza believed that God possessed infinite attributes beyond mind and space and time, and so strictly he did not believe that God and the Universe were identical.

There are simpler proofs of the central pantheist belief. According to theists, before the Creation nothing existed except God. Therefore the only thing out of which he could make creation was his own substance. By this argument the Universe would be, or would at least be part of, God's substance.

Another proof starts with the theological definition, provided by St. Anselm of Canterbury, that God is "that being than whom no greater can be conceived." Now if we define the Universe as the totality of everything that exists, then it is impossible to conceive of anything greater than the Universe. So the Universe itself must be Anselm's greatest being, and therefore the Universe is God or the true "supreme being."

Another approach to grounding the central pantheist belief in the divinity of the Universe is by comparing its real powers with the powers that people think God possesses.

Throughout the ages, sceptics have suggested that the supposed powers of the gods were myths, based on the real powers of nature. So Zeus or Thor embodied the power of storms. Apollo symbolized the power of the sun, Neptune that of the sea, and so on.

Pantheists take this argument further and suggest that the main characteristics of the God of Judaism, Christianity, and Islam are based on nature and the Universe.

God is said to be the creator: overwhelmingly powerful, all-knowing, omnipresent, infinite, and eternal. Pantheists would argue that the Universe itself possesses most of these qualities usually attributed to God. It is indeed the only thing we know to possess these qualities, and our only source of experience of these qualities.

The Universe is *our creator*. We are made of star stuff: our hydrogen and helium emerged in the first few minutes after the big bang; the rest of our elements were forged by fusion inside stars and strewn across space in novae and supernovae. Finally they were regathered in the solar system, allowing life to evolve.

The Universe can also destroy us. In past mass extinctions, it has wiped out most life on earth through large meteor collisions or nearby supernovae, and it could do so again in the future. The power of nature can destroy us through earthquakes, volcanic eruptions, storms and floods, epidemics.

So in a very real sense the Universe and nature are, as far as we are concerned, *overwhelmingly powerful.*

The Universe is *omnipresent* because it is filled with energy spreading from every part to every other part. Radiation of various types, mostly in the form of photons, reaches us from every corner of the Universe and from the deepest reaches of time past—we are constantly bathed in microwave radiation from the earliest moments of the Universe's existence.

In the human sense, the Universe is not *all-knowing.* Yet every part of it is, in a sense, "aware" of every other through the exchange of photons conveying messages about the state of even the most distant regions.

The universe our telescopes can detect does not appear to be *infinite.* What we can see today covers a diameter of no more than 20 to 30 billion light years. Nor is the universe as far as we know *eternal*—cosmologists estimate it to be between 10 and 15 billion years old. But from our tiny human perspective, these times and distances are virtually eternal and infinite.

The most prevalent modern hypothesis of cosmic origins, the inflation theory of Allan Guth and Andrei Linde, predicts that our local universe is just one of a foam of universes bubbling into existence from a dense energy field. The totality of all these universes, the greater Universe, or Multiverse, or Omniverse, would in fact be truly infinite and eternal.

The Universe as Eternal, or as Its Own Creator

Humans are naturally impelled to seek the causes of everything. That urge explains a large part of our success as a species, and has driven us to investigate links and to develop new technologies.

This same urge has led people to seek the *cause* of the whole Universe. Theists like Thomas Aquinas have argued that we see from experience that nothing exists without a cause. Since it is unacceptable for a chain of causes to be infinite, the Universe itself must have a first cause. This has been one of the main arguments for the existence of a creator God.

Sceptics have always challenged this argument. Since we have no problems imagining an infinite future, it is hard to see any good reason why the chain of causes in the past should not be infinite.

The argument for a separate creator God has a serious logical flaw. It assumes that everything requires a cause, and yet theists accept that one thing does exist without a cause: God Himself. As sceptics have pointed out, this tends to undermine the basic premise of the argument. If one thing can be self-existing, why can this one thing not be the Universe itself?

When we say something has a cause, we mean that something preceded it which brought it about—cause precedes effect. But by definition the Universe includes all time and space, and no time could have preceded it. It seems unreasonable to ask for the cause of a totality that includes all space and all time.

Moreover, the idea of a creator God does not really answer the question of cause, but simply pushes it back one level. The question of the cause of God's own existence remains unanswered, yet theists draw a boundary here to our urge to question causes.

As the Scottish philosopher David Hume remarked:

> If I am still to remain in utter ignorance of causes . . . I shall never esteem it any advantage to shove off for a moment a difficulty which . . . must immediately, in its full force, recur upon me. . . . It were better, therefore, never to look beyond the present material world. By supposing it to contain the principle of its order within itself, we really assert it to be God; and the sooner we arrive at that divinity, the better.

But if the Universe had no external creator, then where did it come from?

One possibility is that the Universe "created" itself, or rather emerged spontaneously out of virtually nothing. Several modern theories of cosmology assume that the Universe began as a fluctuation in a quantum vacuum, or arose from an energy field empty of matter.

Another possibility is that it existed eternally and had no beginning. This does not appear to be true of our own local universe, but it could be true of the Multiverse, the bubbling foam of universes that several theories of cosmology believe to exist.

British cosmologist Stephen Hawking has suggested that space-time might be curved back on itself like the surface of a sphere, and like a sphere it may have no beginning or end. "The universe would be completely self-contained and not affected by anything outside it," he writes in *A Brief History of Time*. "It would just BE. . . . What place, then, for a creator?"

Evolution as the Great Designer

One of the most powerful arguments for the existence of God has been the argument from *design:* if nature has the appearance of careful design, then there must have been a designer. But pantheists do not accept the idea of a designer separate from the Universe. They believe that the Universe designed itself through evolution.

The design argument was classically put by English clergyman William Paley in 1802. Suppose, said Paley, that we found a watch lying on the ground, in perfect working order, with all its parts moulded and assembled to tell the time of day. We would immediately assume that the watch had a designer. Since nature shows evidence of very complex and beautiful design, it follows, Paley argued, that the Universe must have a maker and designer.

This mechanism being observed, the inference . . . is inevitable that the watch must have had a maker; that there must have existed, at some time, and at some place or other, an artificer or artificers who formed it for the purpose which we find it actually to answer; who comprehended its construction, and designed its use.

The Scottish sceptic philosopher David Hume had already provided a telling answer to the design argument in his *Dialogues on Natural Religion,* published in 1776. Hume showed how apparent design could arise purely by chance in a universe of countless particles in motion. Given an infinite length of time, the particles would eventually hit on every possible combination. And some of those combinations would be forms of order which, once hit upon, would perpetuate themselves for a very long time.

Two centuries later we have more knowledge and better theories to flesh out what Hume claimed. We know how gravity gathers matter together into galaxies and then into stars that begin burning. We know how solar systems can form from rotating clouds of dust. We do not know exactly how life originated, but we do have a number of plausible theories. We know that organic molecules exist even in space. We know the physics and chemistry of how DNA reproduces itself and makes the vast diversity of organisms on this planet.

The science of *self-organization* is showing how inanimate matter can form quite spontaneously into regular patterns. No one imagines that a quartz crystal requires a designer: it is the inevitable result of the way in which the atoms that make it up behave. Sand piles arrange themselves into mounds with very specific angles of slope, not because there is an invisible sandpile designer at work, but simply because of gravity and the shape and weight of the grains.

Above all, in the theory of *evolution,* we have a brilliantly success-ful scientific explanation of how design emerges in the most complex things: living creatures.

Evolution is a wonderful mechanism for perfecting design, and like any good designer, it has both creativity and rigorous discipline. Its main sources of creativity for new variations are random mutations and sexual recombinations of genes. Its disciplined weeding out of poor de-sign is done by the environment. Organisms that are best adapted to the environment thrive better and produce more offspring. Those that are less well adapted die out.

For pantheists evolution is a universal force that works even on non-living things. From the very first instant of our universe, every in-dividual thing has existed in the midst of other things, and has had to adapt to them. Evolution is at work even in the realms of mind and of society. Ideas, scientific theories, technologies, and products are tested against each other and the most effective survive.

Was the Whole Universe Designed so That We Should Evolve?

The modern form of the design argument is much more sophisticated and challenging than Paley's. It is based on the idea that, if we are here to observe it, the whole universe must be structured in such a way that conscious intelligent beings would evolve. This argument is known as the Anthropic Cosmological Principle.

In its weak form the argument simply states the obvious: if the universe were not structured in that way, then there would be no one around to observe it. But in its strong form the Anthropic Cosmological Principle suggests a lot more. It claims that the universe shows sign of having been deliberately designed with the goal of creating conscious observers like us.

The principle has some arresting evidence to back it. For example, if the universe had been a fraction of one per cent more or less "flat" than it is, the universe would have recollapsed or expanded before stars, planets, and life had time to evolve. There are many other constants that seem to be incredibly finely tuned to make life possible.

But even the strong form of the Anthropic Cosmological Principle can't prove that conscious beings are the *purpose* for which the universe was designed. If this is so, it's not clear why humans have been planned to evolve on a planet that is periodically hit by meteorites or mass lava flows big enough to wipe out a large proportion of all species on earth.

And if the universe is tuned so that consciousness can emerge and evolve, this implies that intelligent life has probably emerged on countless billions of other planets—so humans would have no special status in the design.

Those who believe the universe designed itself have several possible answers to the strong Anthropic Cosmological Principle. One is that the basic physical constants had to turn out one way or another, and our particular arrangement is no less likely than any of the others. It only seems miraculous from our human-centred viewpoint, just as a lucky spin on the roulette table might seem to the winner like the hand of destiny.

The chaotic inflation theory of Andrei Linde proposes that our universe is just one of an infinite number of universes—each one of which may have slightly different initial conditions and laws of physics. Given so many, all permutations are possible, and our own universe is just one of them. There would be many others where life was not possible.

Cosmologist Lee Smolin suggests that black holes spew matter into new dimensions, creating new universes with laws slightly different from ours. Over time a kind of evolution would operate and favour the kind of universe that produces black holes. This just happens to be the same kind of universe that allows stars to exist for long periods of time. In other words, our kind of universe is likely to be the most common.

The Universe Has the Emotional Impact of a God or Divinity

Another approach to showing how the Universe can be considered divine is to look at the emotions it awakes in us, and compare these with the feelings that believers have toward a personal God.

In 1917, the German theologian Rudolf Otto wrote his classic work *The Idea of the Holy*. Based on comparative study of religions East and West, Otto tried to establish exactly what qualities people felt were possessed by things seen as divine—whether these were the personal creator Gods of Western religions, or impersonal things like the Tao, Brahman, or nirvana in the East.

Otto decided that above all divinity was a *mysterium tremendum et fascinans*—an awesome yet fascinating mystery. The three key elements were mystery, awesome power, and capacity to fascinate. Pantheists believe that the Universe itself is the only entity we know of that possesses these qualities, and therefore has the highest claim to be considered as divine.

Mystery is the feeling that the divinity is something wholly other, something extraordinary and incomprehensible, producing blank wonder and astonishment in us. The Universe has the capacity to do this like nothing else in our experience. Earlier generations, as they gazed at the starry heavens on a clear night, could have had some sense of this, though the universe was thought of as actually very small, not much bigger than the solar system.

But the twentieth century is the first to have the privilege of knowing the vast scope of the universe, from the smallest sub-atomic particles to the farthest quasars and clusters of infant galaxies. Today we have the priceless asset of the Hubble Space Telescope, which reveals exploding stars, colliding galaxies, and luminous gas clouds birthing solar systems like our own.

Although science is continually discovering more about the inner workings of all this, what it can never do is take away our astonishment that all this stupendous immensity exists. It is all so very distant from our everyday experience that it will never cease to leave people breathless with wonder and excitement. The mystery of the ultimate origins of our universe, before the big bang, before the first tiny fraction of a nanosecond, may well remain forever unsolved. And the most basic mystery of all: why does anything exist? is inherently unanswerable.

Newton thought that matter was made up of hard little particles moving around predictably as they bumped into each other. Modern science has discovered that matter is far stranger and more mysterious. Its picture of reality is one that common sense cannot grasp at all, however hard it tries.

The theory of relativity teaches that as we approach the speed of light, time lengthens, length shortens, and mass increases. Quantum mechanics tells us that the ultimate particles of light, photons, are not distinct particles in one place but are fuzzy waves of probability smeared out in space. And yet whenever we put up apparatus to detect them, they only ever show up as particles, pin-point dots on a detector screen. They can behave both as waves and as particles, yet humans cannot imagine anything that could be both.

All this goes so much against everyday experience and everyday human ways of understanding things that quantum mechanics is a profound mystery even to physicists working in the field. As Nobel prize winner Richard Feynman remarked to his students: "Do not keep saying to yourself 'But how can it be like that?' because you will get into a blind alley from which nobody has yet escaped. Nobody knows how it can be like that."

Otto's second aspect of divinity is the *dread* it inspires: the sense of an overwhelming and uncontrollable power that can transfix anyone who comes near it, a power that instills a sense of its absolute superiority, and makes us feel our personal submission to it and submergence in it.

No one has ever seen the power of the God of Judaism, Christianity, and Islam, and whenever this power is written or spoken about it is described in terms of the power of nature: when God smites people, he does so with thunderbolts, earthquakes, plagues, and other natural means.

In fact pantheists believe that claims about God's awesome power are simply symbolic expressions of the real power of nature and the Universe. No one who has witnessed or seen films of lightning, volcanic eruptions, or arching solar flares can be other than awestruck at the terrifying levels of power involved. The sun alone is so powerful that we cannot gaze at it directly even for more than a few seconds without being blinded.

Jews, Christians, and Muslims see all these things as expressions of the power of God. Pantheists see them as expressions of the power of nature herself, and recognizing that power, acknowledge that nature should be regarded as divine.

The final quality of divinity that Otto identified is its *beauty* and power to fascinate and inspire love. "The believer," Otto wrote, "feels a something which captivates and transports him with a strange ravishment, rising often to the pitch of dizzying intoxication."

Here too pantheists would claim—and most non-pantheists would acknowledge—that these same feelings can be inspired by the beauty of nature. A forest or a pounding ocean, scudding clouds, still pools, or leaves falling on an autumn day can inspire the deepest feelings of love, peace, and belonging.

Wordsworth expresses these feelings intensely in his 1799 *Prelude:*

> among the hills I sate,
> Alone upon some jutting eminence
> At the first hour of morning, when the vale
> Lay quiet in utter solitude . . .
> Oft in those moments such a holy calm
> Did overspread my soul that I forgot
> The agency of sight.

Again, images from the Hubble Space Telescope have shown us the indescribable beauty of the universe, from the radiance of whirlpool galaxies, to the diaphanous veils of glowing dust clouds, to the exotic blossoms of planetary nebulae.

What Kind of a God Is the Pantheist God?

The pantheist God is quite different from the God of Judaism, Christianity, or Islam. Indeed many pantheists prefer to avoid using the word God at all, because it brings up in most listeners' minds ideas of the particular God they have read about in the Bible or Koran or were taught about as children. Other pantheists, however, see the word God as simply a name for the highest object of reverence, and believe they have as much right to use it as others.

The pantheist divinity is the existing Universe. *It is not a personal God.* It is not a loving father, conscious of and caring for each one of us. It is simply the Reality of Being, just as it is. It is beyond personality, in any human sense. It cannot really love us, but it cannot hate us either. As Spinoza wrote in his *Ethics,*

> God is without passions, neither is he affected by any emotion of pleasure or pain. . . . Strictly speaking, God does not love anyone. . . . He who loves God cannot endeavour that God should love him in return.

To some people this may seem like a cold, unwelcoming sort of God, a hard God to love. The best way to answer this is to think of some part of nature that you love—a particular forest, say. Do you expect the forest to love you back? Does it worry you that the forest cannot love you back? Does it make you love the forest any the less?

People who do like to think in terms of love can think about love assessed by deeds rather than by possession of emotions, and reflect that the Universe has provided us all with an indescribably beautiful home and a consciousness with which to appreciate it. True, it could wipe us out tomorrow in a hurricane or a meteor strike—but then so could the "loving" God of theist religion. Natural disasters are easier to accept if you do not imagine there is a personal God sending them to destroy the innocent and the guilty alike, or creating a world in which such things can happen.

The pantheist divinity is not a good God. It is neither good nor evil. The human categories of good and evil do not apply. It simply *is*. Again, this conception is easier to square with reality than the idea of an omnipotent and perfectly good God, who allows or even causes events that in human terms would be seen as evil, such as devastating hurricanes, floods, and epidemics claiming millions of lives.

The question why God would allow pain and evil to exist is one of the most difficult of all for theists to answer. Pantheists do not have to answer it: the Universe is what it is.

The pantheist divinity is not a judging God. It will not assess each one of us at the end of our lives, and assign each of us to everlasting bliss or agony. It is not listening to our every breath and thought, marking them down in our account to be held for or against us after our death. For many pantheists, even conscientious pantheists who strive to do good in their lives, the freedom from a judging God inside one's brain is a liberating experience. There is no need to be self-conscious all the time, aware of how your every thought might be assessed by a vigilant listener who has the power to punish you for all eternity.

The divinity of pantheism is not, in the normal human sense of the word, conscious. Some pantheists, such as the Stoics or Hegel and many modern pagans, have believed that the Universe does have some kind of collective mind or soul and sense of purpose.

Naturalistic or scientific pantheism, however, does not believe there is anything resembling a soul or spirit to the Universe. There are no galactic neurones, no stellar databanks thinking collective thoughts. But we humans are part of the Universe. We are conscious and aware of the Universe. So in this sense the Universe has consciousness within it.

The pantheist divinity has a number of character traits that are quite different from the God of Judaism, Christianity, and Islam. It is in a state of permanent change and motion, at every level from the restless flitting of electrons and the lightspeed motion of photons, to the slow rotation of galaxies over aeons.

Everything is in a state of flux, a flux that can at times be creative, and at times destructive. The destruction is an essential part of the creation. The elements for life were made available only by stars blowing off part of their substance as supernovae. The rise of the mammals was made possible only by the extinction of the dinosaurs.

The Divine Unity

So far I have been referring to the pantheist divinity as an "It." But in fact all individual things are part of it. We are not set over against it in distinction from it. We have a share in the divinity. This is what modern pagans mean when they say: "Thou art God." Not that each one of us is a separate little god in our own right, with supernatural powers and demanding to be worshipped, but that we are all part of the same universal divinity.

Each one of us is just as much part of the divinity as a venerable old tree or a bright star. The pantheist God is the community of all beings. It is not a He, or a She, or an It. It is a "We."

The major Western religions are all monotheistic. They all insist on the unity of God (though in the Christian case this unity has also to accommodate the Trinity).

Pantheists too are in a sense monotheistic. Their one divinity is the Universe, and they have a profound belief in the unity of all things in nature and the Universe. Indeed the pantheist belief in unity is in a sense stronger than the theistic one. Theists believe that God and the Universe are separate things. For pantheists there is only one all-embracing Reality: the Universe.

Some pantheists have simply asserted this unity. Others such as Spinoza have tried to prove it logically. But the unity of the Universe and nature is not just a feeling or an abstract belief: it has a solid basis in science.

Everything in our universe shares a common origin. The standard big bang cosmology holds that the whole universe originated as a microscopic bubble no more than one hundredth of a millimetre across. Thus everything that makes up the universe of today was once in the most intimate contact. As Italian novelist Italo Calvino wrote in his comic short story *All at One Point:* "Every point of each of us coincided with every point of each of the others."

But unity is not just based on a shared history. It continues throughout the present. Every single particle, every star, every being in the universe is linked by the force of gravity. A quasar on the edge of the observable universe has some effect, however small, on each of our bodies.

The whole universe is a tightly woven mesh of electromagnetic radiation. Everything emits photons of energy which race in all directions. Everything is made of the same sub-atomic constituents, held together by the same forces. And everything transmutes into everything else. The day before yesterday we were atoms in the heart of a burning star, yesterday we were dust in a collapsing proto-star, today we are living humans, tomorrow we may be soil, beetles, grass, trees, birds.

Some idealist pantheists, like Parmenides from Elea in Southern Italy, or the authors of the Upanishads, have taken the idea of unity to extremes, and suggest that nothing really exists except the divine unity. All the everyday things we see around us, they suggest, are really just illusions.

But most modern pantheists are realists. They accept the reality that individual things exist independently of our minds: tables, cats, moons, and so on. Although nothing is exactly the same even from one moment to the next, individual things do have a temporary existence, which can be very long in human terms.

Such is the creativity of matter that every single thing is different from every other. No two people are alike, no two clouds are alike, no two pebbles on the beach are identical. Without individuality, the divine unity would be utterly drab and could have no more beauty than an empty room.

Yet all these individual things are part of the same universe, just as, on the ocean, every wave is different and partly separate, yet every wave remains part of the same ocean.

The Place of Humans in the Divine Unity

People who object to pantheism are often concerned that it seems to give humans an insignificant role in the cosmos.

Pantheists freely accept that we are physically tiny in the scale of the cosmos, as indeed everyone must accept. Far gone are the days when we believed the earth to be the centre of the universe. Our sun is just one of over 100 billion stars in the Milky Way galaxy, which in turn is just one of perhaps 30 billion galaxies in the visible universe.

However, this does not mean that we are insignificant. In size terms we are no more and no less insignificant than anything else in the universe. Every individual thing from a mouse to a mammoth or even a star is dwarfed by the immensity of the whole—but the whole is made up of its parts.

We humans are not made insignificant by the size of the universe, any more than each of us is made insignificant by the size of the earth or the size of the world population.

We are, with our brains and our societies and technologies, the most complex beings we know of so far. We are conscious observers of the Universe. Even if the Universe as a whole possesses no consciousness, we do. In this sense we can be said to be a part of the consciousness of the Universe, or of its self-consciousness.

And though our lives have no external purpose, we can give them the noble purpose of observing and understanding and loving the Universe and nature, and of preserving nature on our planet, and of creating societies where all humans can have dignity and the opportunity for fulfilment.

Most pantheists see such a self-chosen purpose as far preferable to the purpose humans have in the major Western religions. Even though, in Judaism and Christianity, humans are seen as central to the entire universe, the human role is not a distinguished one. Since God is seen as perfect and self-sufficient, it is not at all clear why God needed to create humans, or what purpose they serve to Him. Our role on earth seems to be to prove to God that we obey his commands and that we believe in him and worship him. If we fail in one short lifetime we will be punished for all of eternity. And the role of the earth, indeed of the whole vast cosmos, is simply to serve as the backdrop for this brief and tiny drama.

Unity Means That Union Is Possible

If all things are, in a fundamental sense, one, then we humans are not distinct from other things in the universe. We are not superior or set apart. We share a common origin, a common history, a common substance with everything else in nature and the universe. Our very atoms are recycled continually with our surroundings. Every single breath we take unites us with everything else on earth.

Of course we often imagine that we are separate. We can feel isolated, alone, threatened, or anxious in the face of nature and the Universe.

But with only a small effort of thought, we can realize that our isolation is only partial. Our deepest selves can never be separated from the divine unity. We are never alone; every one of us shares in the unity. We are all part of the unity at all times. It is with us and we with it, inseparably, forever.

BIBLIOGRAPHY

Bak, Per, *How Nature Works*, Oxford University Press, Oxford, 1997.

Barrow, John, & Frank Tipler, *The Anthropic Cosmological Principle*, Oxford University Press, New York, 1988.

Dawkins, Richard, *The Blind Watchmaker*, Penguin Books, London, 1988

Dennet, Daniel, *Darwin's Dangerous Idea*, Penguin Books, London, 1995.

Guth, Allan, *The Inflationary Universe*, Helix Books, Cambridge, MA, 1998.

Hawking, Stephen, *A Brief History of Time*, Bantam Doubleday Dell, New York, 1998.

Hume, David, *Dialogues Concerning Natural Religion*, Oxford University Press, New York, 1994.

Otto, Rudolf, *The Idea of the Holy*, trans. John Harvey, Oxford University Press, New York, 1968.

Sagan, Carl, *Pale Blue Dot*, Brilliance Corporation, Grand Haven, MI, 1994.

Smolin, Lee, *The Life of the Cosmos*, Oxford University Press, New York, 1998.

This chapter was originally published as Chapter 5 (pp. 56–67) of *The Elements of Pantheism*, by Paul Harrison, published by Element Books in May 1999 in their mainstream series "Elements of. . . ."

CHAPTER 16

God, Science, and Jnani: *A New Framework*

MICHAEL R. KING

Dr. King holds four degrees from British universities in the fields of art, science, and spirituality. His work as reader in computer art and animation at London Guildhall University enables him to work at the intersection of these three disciplines on the basis that each can represent a systematic and open inquiry into the deep structure of human experience.

The premise for this chapter is that a better framework for the science/religion debate arises when we take the mystical core of religion and contrast its goals and methods with the goals and methods of science. This requires the establishment of a few simple concepts. First of all, a natural division of spiritual and religious phenomena can be summed up in three terms: the "social," the "occult," and the "transcendent." The social in this context is the phenomenon of popular religion, including articles of faith, religious practice, priesthoods, and integration into the political life of a culture. These all evolve over centuries, usually from the teachings of a single religious founder (for example, Christ or the Buddha), and may bear only a nominal relationship to that individual's life or teachings.

By the "occult" I wish to denote a range of beliefs and practices that relate to a world of disembodied or spirit beings, the existence of which is neither posited nor denied by the use of the term. Teachers of occultism have existed throughout history and across the continents with considerable consistency in their statements, despite complete separation through time or location. One of the greatest such teachers in recent Western history has been Rudolf Steiner, while an account that is completely independent, but agreeing in many areas, originates at approximately the same time in the autobiography of Paramahansa Yogananda, an Indian yogi. Occult accounts vary in detail, but generally include descriptions of spirit beings, life after death, and the "occult powers" or *siddhis* of Indian and Buddhist tradition. Occultism usually also has a strong moral dimension, though in its perversion it may be described as "black" magic.

The term "transcendent" is used here to describe the core mystical experience, and is independent of the social and occult dimensions of religion, as defined here. It does, however, act as a vortex in history, around which religions grow, as crystals around seed matter, and is often mistaken for an occult phenomenon. As religions grow from the transcendent experiences of the geniuses of a particular religion, a popularization is inevitable. Occult accretions take place at the same time, often leading to a mainstream religion being shadowed by "esoteric" traditions that are often persecuted, or taught in secrecy. While popular religion has little in it that can constructively engage in science, the occult has, in the sense that it also represents an inquiry into the hidden nature of reality. However, one needs to examine the geniuses of this practice, such as Boehme, Blake, Swedenborg, Yogananda, and Steiner, rather than popularized versions, in order to establish a debate with science.

But how can we describe the transcendent? The answer given here is radical: *in two completely different ways.* The two forms of transcendence, or better, the two paths to the transcendent, can be simply delineated as devotional and non-devotional. We can immediately spot a problem here: the term "devotional" is easily understood, if not necessarily empathized with, but how can the term "non-devotional" be used to describe an exalted state or path to such a state? Our problem is of course a Western one: our language and culture have developed in the Christian context, which is devotional. We need to turn to the East to find a world religion that is non-devotional: Buddhism, and, we need to turn to Hinduism to give us a language that encompasses both paths or orientations—the terminology of *bhakti* and *jnani*. (The "jn" in *jnani* is pronounced as the "n" in the Italian "signor" or "signora.")

The term *bhakti* means devotional, and although its expression varies widely across the world, it is generally recognizable from a Christian perspective. Key concepts of a *bhakti* tradition will be love (of God, or a god, or maybe the divine element in a spiritual teacher or mythologized person), devotion, and surrender. The will of the individual is only important in as far as it is aligned to the divine will, and spiritual progress and understanding are acts of grace visited on the supplicant. In contrast, the term *jnani* describes a spirituality that is in the first instance more cerebral, more inclined to inquiry than surrender, more inclined to meditation than prayer, to see the goal in terms of wisdom rather than love, and to emphasize the will as a means to the goal. A *jnani* tradition may have no concept of God at all, certainly not a personal God, but is not atheistic. However, its teachings will generally use non-theistic concepts in contrast to the heavily theistic emphasis in a *bhakti* tradition.

To recap: religious phenomena can be understood in three categories: the social, the occult, and the transcendent. While science can only have a limited debate with the social or popular dimension of religion, it has more in common with the occult dimension because the occult can be seen as an attempt to penetrate behind appearances, but it has the most in common with the transcendent because it represents the purest inquiry into the deep structure of human experience. The transcendent itself can be understood in terms of two orientations: the devotional and the non-devotional, termed here *bhakti* and *jnani*. These terms, unfamiliar to the West, are vital to this thesis, and are presented as a Rosetta Stone in understanding the relationship between science and religion. It is the concept of *jnani* that is the most important and will be developed here as the central contribution to the debate.

It is proposed that the two spiritual orientations are spread about fifty-fifty in the individuals of any population. The dominant religion in any culture will, however, tend to emphasize one or the other orientation, usually depending on that of its founder, and hence roughly half of the population will find a mismatch between the religion of their birth and their religious instincts. This condition is mitigated to some degree by the way that religions develop, in that key players in this process (other than the religion's founder) may instinctively bend the religion toward their own, contrary, orientation. In Christianity, which is *bhakti* in origin, some of the greatest shapers of its tradition have had a *jnani* orientation, while in Buddhism, a *jnani* religion, some of its development has been clearly shaped by *bhakti* influences. Although there are interesting parallels in the developments of the two religions, there have been important historical differences, which make a mirror symmetry less than perfect. However, it is a fruitful comparison to make, because the key creative tensions in both religions can be understood in terms of the differences between *bhakti* and *jnani*. The major differences between East and West can also be seen in terms of this dichotomy, leading to an understanding of science as the outcome of a suppressed *jnani* instinct in the West, and the failure of the development of science in the East due to the relative fulfillment of the *jnani* instinct.

Some development of the *jnani* concept is needed before we go further into this. Christ and the Buddha are problematic in that we have no documents written by them, but even so we can, by going to the Gospels in one case and the Pali canon in the other, find useful contrasts. When Jesus was asked what one must do to inherit eternal life, he asked the questioner how he understood it, and assented to the answer: "Love the Lord with all your heart, and with all your soul, and with all your strength, and with all your mind" (Luke 10:27). This is the core of *bhakti*, and from it arises the central practice: prayer or worship, a heart-oriented practice. The Buddha in contrast opens the Dhammapada (a central Buddhist text) with the statement: "Our life is shaped by our mind: we become what we think."[1] He then offers eternal life *(nirvana)* as the fruit of meditation, a mind-oriented practice involving stilling of the mind. It is significant that the pope quite recently exhorted his followers to the practice of prayer, and to consider meditation as foreign to their religion: a clear indication that Christianity is *bhakti*, not *jnani*. Given that a picture of the *jnani* path and orientation needs to be built up or triangulated from many sources (preferably authenticated as genuine by scholarly research), and that these sources need to come from both East and West, it is hard to recommend a single work or even a small "canon." However, two texts might be put forward: the *Enneads* of Plotinus,[2] and Longchempa's *Kindly Bent to Ease Us (Part Three)*.[3] Both texts are tightly linked to a spiritual tradition, the first to Neoplatonism, and the second to Tibetan Buddhism, but both authors are also genuine *jnanis* in their own right, and of the first order. Both give directions for the stilling of the mind and, an indication of the central *jnani* experience, a transcendence of conditioned existence through a direct apprehension of the ground of being.

In pointing up Plotinus and Longchempa as Western and Eastern representatives of the *jnani* orientation and achievement, we are brought to the idea of the lost buddhas of the West. The term "buddha" is a title given to a perfected *jnani*, though few Buddhists use the term for any other than the historical Buddha, born as Siddhartha Gautama of the Sakya clan. (Instead, the *Bhodisattva* ideal was developed in one of the major Buddhist branches, as a term covering other perfected beings.) If we run through the spiritual history of the West, we can identify developed *jnani* individuals, both before and after Christ, including Pythagoras, Heraclitus, Socrates, Plotinus, Meister Eckhart, and Spinoza. In the modern period we could include Walt Whitman, Ramana Maharshi, Jiddu Krishnamurti, Douglas Harding, and Andrew Cohen. However, if it is contentious to posit other historical buddhas, it is even more so to claim this status for the living, so it is just left to mention that, if one has no doctrinal objection to it, instruction from a living *jnani* is worth a thousand instructions from the texts of dead ones.

We are now close to the point where we can examine the relationship between science and religion through the concept of *jnani*. Just one more distinction is required however—borrowing terms from Christianity this time, and using them in a slightly altered fashion: the terms *via positiva* and *via negativa* to indicate two possible relationships with the outside or so-called material world. In traditional Christian thinking these terms describe ways of thinking about God: the first describes Him through positive attributes, and the second describes Him via negating all attributes (also found in Hinduism as *neti-neti*—not this, not that). We have already noted, however, that the *jnani* traditions are generally non-theistic, and hence the terms *via positiva* and *via negativa* will have a slightly different meaning here. If the goal of the *jnani* is the disidentification with the ego, then there are logically two routes: to deny successively the identifications with body, home, family, and desires, leading to the renunciative lifestyle typical of early Buddhism and many other religions; or to identify successively with *everything*. The history of religion is generally the history of *via negativa*, in the sense defined. We do find elements of *via positiva* in all religious traditions, however, particularly in the Upanishads, though perhaps its best expression comes through the festivals and rituals of popular religion. The greatest single exponent of *via positiva*, and completely misunderstood by all but a few Hindu scholars, is Walt Whitman, of interest to the West usually as a poet, or possibly because of alleged homosexuality. In fact, he came close to founding a *jnani* religion and had disciples who saw him as one of the world's greatest gurus, though his bible, *Leaves of Grass*, was written by his own admission in such a way as to hide his teachings completely.

So, to science and *jnani*. Firstly, we can return to the proposition made earlier that science arose in the West because the *jnani* instincts of some of its greatest thinkers had no legitimate expression within Christianity. We are used to understanding the Middle Ages as a period where the early Christian church discouraged inquiry into the nature of the universe, and encouraged faith in the power of love and in the practice of prayer and service. This is a particular irony as Saint Augustine, one of the chief architects of this medieval world-view, renounced his Manichaean faith of ten years because one of its chief bishops gave him an answer to an astronomical question that did not fit the science of the time. After renouncing Manichaeism Augustine contemplated the views of the Neoplatonists (a European *jnani* tradition owing largely to Plotinus), but rejected them in favor of Christianity: Augustine was *bhakti* by orientation. The intellectuals of the Christian world tended to seek a *jnani* teaching to supplement their Christian heritage, and were thus instinctively drawn to the Greeks, resulting in a struggle within the church between the followers of Aristotle and the followers of Plato (the Neoplatonists). In Aquinas the victory goes to Aristotle, which allowed for the church to prune back the threat of Neoplatonism in favor of the more spiritually neutral terrain of Aristotle. In the Renaissance the struggle re-erupted with Neoplatonism appearing in the Academy of Ficino, but it had not the intellectual vigor to attract the disenfranchised Christians of the *jnani* orientation, and so we find a genius like Leonardo putting his faith in *observation* of the natural world. Galileo's discoveries then mark the beginning of the schism between church and science.

It is important to point out that the *jnani* of the Neoplatonists was *via negativa*, from Plato's emphasis on the *forms* and his rejection of the empirical, to Plotinus's quasi-Buddhism. Hence the Renaissance vigor of thought could not find in it an engagement with a physical world (newly discovered as more human-friendly than in the introspective period of the Dark Ages), and is roundly dismissed by Leonardo as a worshipping of the ancients. Christianity rejected it because Christianity remained a *bhakti* religion (despite the best efforts of its more intellectual clergy), and the new intellectual classes dismissed it because it was *via negativa*. In this climate the growth of science and its domination of Western culture became inevitable.

Christianity and Buddhism have a coincidence of propagation: both were taken up and made the state religion of an empire, by Constantine in Europe, and by Ashoka in India, and both were doctrinally formulated through religious councils under the chairmanship of the emperor. The Emperor Ashoka, after the conquest of a small kingdom called Kalinga in the third century B.C.E., experienced remorse for the resultant slaughter, converted to Buddhism (or at least took it up more seriously), and established a generally pacifist rule through the empire. Ashoka's Buddhism was tolerant of other faiths, principally those of the Brahmins, Jains, and Ajivikas, found in the empire, and this tolerance was encouraged by edicts in rock inscriptions found across the region. Constantine, in contrast, experienced a military victory after his original inspiration, which confirmed his conversion to Christianity, and made it the religion of the Roman Empire. The evolution of Christian thought for several centuries was centralized by the apparatus of the empire, in contrast to the evolution of Buddhism which, even in Ashoka's time, was allowed to absorb local influences. The central apparatus of Christian governance was one of the reasons for the unfortunate appearance of the Inquisition.

Thus the birth of science was painful, as it came in the middle of this long period of religious persecutions. There can be no doubt that the collective religious psyche of the West was traumatized by these events, and scientists also seem to be collectively aware that many of their kind were reviled, tortured, or even killed in pursuit of their science. The devout atheism of some of today's scientists and writers, such as Richard Dawkins and Gore Vidal, has a spleen that can only be explained by the residual effect of this historical trauma. The paradoxical result of the Christian history of the West is therefore both the rise of science as an outlet for the suppressed *jnani* instinct of its brightest intellectuals, and also the contempt held for religion by some of today's best scientists. However the goals and methods of the *jnani*, particularly when of a *via positiva* orientation, have much in common with the goals and methods of scientists. When John Polkinghorne states that "both science and religion are an inquiry into what is,"[4] he is right as far as the *jnani* religionist is concerned, but less so for the *bhakti*.

Einstein's personal writings show *jnani, via positiva* characteristics found in the writings of many great scientists, often expressed as a wonder or awe at the natural world, and at the order behind it, as revealed through the physical laws of science. He also tells us of a sympathy for Spinoza (whose extraordinary convoluted proofs of the existence of God can be read as the struggle of a highly gifted *jnani* to coexist with the *bhakti* traditions of Judaism and Christianity), and a general lack of engagement with the theistic doctrines of popular Western religion. Could his genius, the genius of doubt and inquiry, and the extraordinary ability to think the unthinkable, could this genius, in a *jnani* heritage, also express itself in a religious way? Is the real dialogue between science and religion yet to come, as the West absorbs Eastern ideas, comes to a more fluid conception of God, and considers, as the Buddha did, our interiority a worthy subject for systematic inquiry? Can the West contribute to this the concept of *via positiva,* resulting in an inquiry that embraces the inner as much as the outer, a spirituality that embraces the outer as much as the inner? I suggest that the answer is yes, and that from the concept of *jnani* we will be able to develop the true complement to our conventional, third-person science of the outer: a first-person science of the inner.

274 KING

NOTES

1. *Dhammapada* (trans. Eknath Easwaran; London: Arkana, 1986).
2. Plotinus, *Enneads* (trans. Stephen Mackenna; New York: Penguin, 1991).
3. Longchempa, *Kindly Bent to Ease Us, Part One: Mind* (Berkeley, CA: Dharma Publishing, 1975).
4. Polkinghorne, John, *Reason and Reality* (London: SPCK, 1991).

This chapter was originally published in *Network: The Scientific and Medical Network Review* (December 1999), pp. 15–17. (It is a summary of a forthcoming book, *Jnani: An Alternative Intellectual History of the West.*)

CHAPTER 17

A Theology for the Millennium:
Exploratory, Creative, Humble

ISAAC PADINJAREKUTTU

Dr. Padinjarekuttu is a Roman Catholic priest from India. He studied theology in Pune, India, and Frankfurt am Main, Germany, where he obtained his Ph.D. in theology. He is presently professor of theology in Jnana-Deepa Vidyapeeth, Institute of Philosophy and Religion, Pune, India, where he also heads the Department of Historical Theology. He is the author of *The Missionary Movement of the 19th and 20th Centuries and Its Encounter with India*.

What on earth are we doing? There is no figuring that out without both science and religion; there is no doing it right without integration of the two.[1]

Recently, the board of education of the state of Kansas, in the United States, decided to remove the topic of evolution from the science curriculum in schools. The eminent priest-scientist Arthur Peacocke rightly points out that such churlishness must be rectified "if the Christian faith is to be believable and have intellectual integrity enough to command attention, let alone the assent of thoughtful people at the beginning of the millennium."[2] What he said could be applied to all religions. Religions cannot afford to ignore the scientific discoveries of our age and still claim to mediate meaning to people in the twenty-first century. They must change constructively in the light of scientific advances so that their "speech about God"—theology—becomes broader, more humble, and "worthy of God." In this chapter, I will attempt to elucidate both these premises, not as a scientist, but as a historian and theologian who is keenly interested in the science-religion dialogue.

A New Way of Being Religious

It has now been recognized that one of the important contributions of the Enlightenment and its aftermath has been the concept of one humanity with a shared world and a shared history. At no point in time has humanity been more aware of its common heritage and destiny than at the present time. But at no point in time, too, has humanity been more aware of its differences than at the present time. One important question that engages humanity today, as always, is the perennial question of the meaning of life. Is life meaningful, purposeful, and intelligible? Is it directed to some end beyond itself? What is the inner meaning of the massive transformations that are taking place in the world? In other words, the question of religion has come to the forefront once again because our religious instinct is a thirst for meaning. The twentieth century made the great promise of secularization—the final demise of religion, but it has turned out to be a myth. Religion has not been vanquished; on the contrary, it is thriving, and it may be the beginning of a fundamental reordering of our worldviews, because "religion is an accurate barometer of a culture."[3] But the present interest in religion has a qualitatively different accent. At least in the West, it represents a new religious sensibility. According to Harvey Cox, the new religious movements, with new forms of expression and sources of inspiration, challenge traditional religions and their values: hierarchy, submission, abstraction, single meanings, and fixedness are rejected, and equality, participation, experience, multiple meanings, and plasticity are encouraged.[4] Not all religions seem to accept these values readily, and there are backlashes such as fundamentalism and religious terrorism. But it is reasonable to assume that in the one world, all will be influenced by them sooner or later.

The Scientific Challenge

This new way of being religious was brought about by a radical challenge to religion by science in the wake of the Enlightenment. There are different interpretations of the relationship between science and religion during the Enlightenment,[5] but the fact remains that it was a serious challenge, especially in the case of Christianity.[6] This challenge is still felt, especially from some areas of science more than others.[7] It would be arrogant and foolhardy on my part even to attempt to present these challenges in these pages. I can merely point to some of them.[8]

No one today doubts that without the scientific revolution in the West, the birth of the modern mind with its profoundly new vision of the universe and the human being would have been impossible. With its twin epistemological foundations, empiricism and rationalism, it claimed to free the human mind from the encompassing influence of the medieval church, indeed from religion itself. Under the spotlight of the demand for public, empirical corroboration of all statements of belief, the substance of religion seemed to wither away. In the twentieth century, the enormity of the challenges to religion from science became clearer. Led by Planck's isolation of quantum phenomena, Einstein's special and general theories of relativity, and the formulation of quantum mechanics by Bohr, Heisenberg, and others, astounding information about the universe and the human began to pour in from physics, astronomy, cosmology, biology, psychology, and the technological revolution,[9] much of which seemed to challenge the spiritual dimension of reality altogether. At the same time, the destructive potential of science also became apparent.[10] The same science that had dramatically lessened the hazards and burdens of human beings now presented to human survival its gravest menace. The environmental degradation, new diseases, and the moral dilemma arising from genetic engineering, cloning, nuclear weapons, and so on made the goals of science questionable. Chastened by this, science became self-critical and aware of its limitations in understanding the complexity, subtlety, and multivalence of reality. Karl Popper, Thomas Kuhn, and others, through their critical studies of the history and philosophy of science, contributed to the relativization of scientific knowledge. It was even proposed that science could be in perfect harmony with the human being's spiritual and religious beliefs.[11] But scientific explorations into the nature of the human person and the universe have continued unabated, and they continue to pose serious challenges to religion, especially Christianity: the relationship between cosmic and biological evolution and creation, chaos theory and divine action, quantum complementarity and Christology, information theory and revelation, molecular biology and human freedom, genetics and ethics, and so on, are just a few of them.[12] Can these momentous scientific discoveries help religion/theology to reorient itself toward a new self-understanding?

Toward a Theological Response

There is a saying attributed to Justice Oliver Wendell Holmes, Jr.: "I don't give a fig for the simplicity on this side of complexity, but I would die for the simplicity on the other side."[13] One of the tasks of religions has been to try to understand the complexity on the "other side" in a meaningful way, which alone will explain the complexity on "this side," namely, the multifaceted character of human existence in an increasingly mysterious universe. Science, too, tries to approach this problem in its own way. What can theology learn from the scientific endeavor? The theologian David Tracy perceptively says: "Amidst all the shoutings of the present, the reality of God has returned to the centre of theology. This is not the time to rush out new propositions on the reality of God. This is rather the time to allow wonder again at the overwhelming mystery of God—as some physicists and cosmologists seem so much more skilled at doing than many theologians are."[14] Scientists are in awe of the creative and provident God, while theologians are blasé and casual.

And therefore, the first task of a theology that is informed by science is the inculcation of the sense of wonder. The splendid panorama of scientific discoveries should be a stimulus to wonder, worship, and awe. A God who lets us prove everything about Him/Her is an idol. Mystics and great theologians of all religions have expressed the indescribably mysterious nature of the Ultimate. The only language proper to God is the language of paradox: a God who is at the same time *intimior intimo meo*—closer to me than I am to myself (Augustine) and who is *absconditus*—the hidden God (Isaiah 45). This Mystery is to be enjoyed, celebrated, and also explored humbly. The reason why to many people religion seems complicated and sophisticated is that God has been conceptualized and rationalized. The challenge to religions today is to communicate the mystery of God through their theologies, rituals, and morals, respectful of their great heritages, but in the light of the new visions and possibilities that come to us through science. To the extent they fail to do this, warns the physicist William Stoeger, "they will fail to articulate authentically and truthfully who we really are, what the world and the universe really is, and who God really is or is not."[15] This is a serious warning.

A second challenge to theology from science comes from the widely held scientific opinion that objectivism is a mirage. Religions, generally, claim the monopoly of objective, timeless truth. But today we know that reality is a process rather than a structure. Accordingly, revelation, too, is not a timeless truth but a historical manifestation of the divine. Theology cannot, therefore, speak in absolute statements about God (dogma), but can only wonder at God who is Mystery. All religious concepts and theories are approximations of truth, not truth itself. If religions see their creeds, rituals, and symbols as culturally and historically conditioned approximations, there would be less intolerance and authoritarianism, and more compassion and freedom. Ambiguity in religious language is not a deficiency but a climate of faith.[16] As Thomas Merton puts it: "The very obscurity of faith is an argument of its perfection."[17] A religion that does not allow for ambiguity and tension leads to artificial living, unworthy of the creator of our magnificent universe of immense creativity and painful uncertainty.

A third challenge to theology from science comes from the nature of the universe: its grandeur, size, and dynamism; its marvelous diversity and complexity; its uniqueness and individuality; but at the same time, its interconnectedness and interdependence. Concepts from modern science such as instant correlation and nonlocality are more than empty abstractions. We see this "systemic thought"[18] operative in everything, including cultures and religions. On the one hand, every religion is individual and autonomous, but on the other, it is part of a larger whole. This should relativize religions in a healthy way. As Abraham Heschel says: "The religions of the world are no more self-sufficient, no more independent, no more isolated than individuals or nations. . . . Horizons are wider, dangers are greater. No religion is an island. We are all involved with one another."[19] The total truth does not reside in only one religion or in one interpretation of one religion. Where does all this put us with our petty biases and rigid mind-sets? Openness to the universe alone will help religions to be tolerant to each other, and move them to do the things that only they are capable of doing: to be the informers of conscience, the providers of meaningful ethics, and the source of wisdom that comes, not from computers, but from God and thus be the soul of a culture.

The fourth challenge to theology from science, too, comes from the fundamental interconnectedness and interdependence in the universe, and also from a number of other scientific discoveries such as the increasing evidence that the universe is older and grander than we thought and that it is expanding; that the human species is a "latecomer" and a small player in it; that all the species in the universe exist with a purpose, and so on. In consequence, we need to rethink both the role of human beings in the universe, and the sustainability of the concept of progress that is considered as normal—in other words, the question of ecology. Progress through ecological degradation has been the result of a purely mechanistic view of science. But now science has become open to a more integrated view of reality,[20] and religions, too, should draw consequences from it. There are religions that advocate complete control of nature; others that reject the world; and yet others with a cosmic paradigm, with an ambiguous role for the human. Perhaps religions should learn from each other. For example, Christianity with its specific doctrine of creation and of the human person has developed a sense of responsibility to human society and to the earth, but lacks the cosmic sensitivity of Buddhism and Hinduism. But Hinduism and Buddhism have missed out on the social consequences of their spiritual doctrines. Is there not an opportunity to learn from one another and from science, and to develop a theology that will save the earth from destruction, because in this case, both religion and science prove to be an ambivalent savior.

A fifth challenge to theology from science comes from the fact that the human person is a microcosm of the universe. Psychology, sociobiology, and evolutionary sciences have shown us that the human person is as great a mystery as the universe. The human person is not a finished product but a dynamic process. This should challenge religions in at least two important ways. Firstly, it calls for a reevaluation of their ethical systems. It would be unfair to furnish ethical guidelines valid for all times without taking into account the scientific discoveries about human beings. A scientific approach should also reject moral selectivity—for example, in Christian ethics the one-sided emphasis on sexuality. If ethical teachings of religions do not respond adequately to contemporary knowledge, society will, sooner or later, ignore the objections of religions, and that will be perilous for a society that with amazing speed tries to transgress all limits. Secondly, the understanding of the human person as the microcosm of the universe calls for fundamental respect for the human. The creed of every religion should include an article on human dignity. In a new theological synthesis that is informed by the scientific findings on the human person, there is no place for discrimination against women, discrimination on the basis of race, color, or creed, and for the denial of fundamental human freedom.

A sixth challenge to theology from science comes as an invitation to end the deception of our senses by theological rationality, and to give due place to imagination, beauty, passion, humor, art, and so on, in religion. As Paul Ricoeur says: "Too often and too easily, we speak of the need for conversion, when it's not a conversion of the will that is needed but an expansion of the imagination."[21] Human multidimensionality cannot be explained by reason alone. There is place for imagination, passion, beauty, humor, art, aesthetics, and more in religion. How deprived our lives would be without these sources of joy. A typical religious attitude to these is expressed, in my view, by the blind Jorge, in Umberto Eco's classic novel, *The Name of the Rose,* when he says: "Laughter is weakness, corruption, the foolishness of our flesh. It is the peasant's entertainment, the drunkard's license. . . . Laughter frees the villain from fear of the devil."[22] Replace laughter with "passion," "beauty," "art," "aesthetics," "imagination," and the picture would be complete. Imagination calls us to creativity. Listening to and looking at the universe with its order and chaos calls upon theology to be creative, to go beyond the sterile and the predictable. It is this openness to transcend the predictable that enables scientists to make new discoveries. It is the same openness that theology is called upon to show today.

Conclusion

There are many more areas in which the enrichment of theology by science can take place, but it is not possible for me to elaborate them here. In conclusion, I would like to say that while it is clear that the new ways of looking at the world and human beings suggested by scientific advances have implications for theology, the precise nature of these implications is far from clear. I have not come across any major theological breakthrough that integrates all the issues raised by science. In fact, I do not believe that every scientific discovery should lead to immediate changes in religious doctrines, because they are two different disciplines. The real contribution of science to theology would be to increase the scope of human awareness, by making possible a broader, more flexible, and more imaginative human mind.[23] This would be possible if theology were to pay attention to science with greater care than it does today, in fact, with the same care it gives to scripture, tradition, and other sources. This is only beginning to take place. One can only hope that it will continue. "We shall not cease from exploration," although we know that "the end of all our exploring will be to arrive where we started, and know the place for the first time."[24]

NOTES

1. Holmes Rolston III, "Science, Religion, and the Future," in W. Mark Richardson and Wesley J. Wildman, eds., *Religion and Science: History, Method, Dialogue* (New York & London: Routledge, 1996), p. 80.
2. Arthur Peacocke, "Darwin: Friend Not Foe," *The Tablet* 21 (August 1999), p. 1126.

3. Harvey Cox, "The Myth of the Twentieth Century," *Harvard Divinity Bulletin* 28: 2/3 (1999), pp. 6–8.

4. Ibid., p. 8.

5. Two articles are particularly helpful from the historical point of view: John Hedley Brooke, "Science and Theology in the Enlightenment"; Claude Welch, "Dispelling Some Myths about the Split between Theology and Science in the Nineteenth Century," both in Richardson and Wildman, pp. 7–40.

6. See Richard Tarnas, *The Passion of the Western Mind* (New York: Ballantine Books, 1993), p. 305, for a description of the dilemma experienced by Christianity because of the unprecedented challenges from science.

7. Following Ian Barbour's four ways of relating science and religion, conflict, independence, dialogue, and integration, Holmes Rolston argues that at present there is more dialogue and integration in the physics-religion relationship and ample conflict and independence in the biology-religion relationship. See Holmes Rolston III, "Science, Religion, and the Future," in Richardson and Wildman, p. 62.

8. Most of the ideas in the following pages are not mine. I have been greatly helped by Richardson and Wildman (see note 1 above). I have not come across a better presentation of this theme anywhere else; Richard Tarnas (see note 6 above), chapter v, "The Modern World View," pp. 223–414; Lancelot Pereira, *The Enchanted Darkness* (Anand: Gujarat Sahithya Prakash, 1995); Kuruvilla Pandikattu, *Meaning through Science and Religion* (Pune: Jnana Deepa Vidyapeeth, 1999).

9. See Holmes Rolston III, "Science, Religion, and the Future," pp. 61–74.

10. Wesley J. Wildman, "The Quest for Harmony: An Interpretation of Contemporary Theology and Science," in Richardson and Wildman, pp. 43–47.

11. Fritjof Capra, *The Tao of Physics* (London: Fontana, 1976), p. 24.

12. See the case studies by William R. Stoeger, Robert John Russel, Karl Young, John Polkinghorne, Edward Mackinnon, James E. Loder and W. Jim Neidhardt, Christopher B. Kaiser, John C. Puddefoot, Arthur Peacocke, R. David Cole, W. Mark Richardson, William Irons, and Philip Hefner in Richardson and Wildman, pp. 183–224. Tarnas lists other important persons and their contributions: for example, Bateson's "ecology of mind," Bohm's theory of the implicate order, Sheldrake's theory of formative causation, McClintock's theory of genetic transposition, Prigogine's theory of dissipative structures and order by fluctuation, Lorenz and Feigenbaum's chaos theory, and Bell's theorem of nonlocality. Evelyn Fox Keller's recommendation that there be empathic identification with the object one is trying to understand is very important. See Tarnas, p. 405.

13. Quoted by M. Scott Peck, *The Road Less Travelled and Beyond* (New York: Touchstone, 1997), p. 13.

14. David Tracy, "The Return of God in Contemporary Theology," *Concilium* 6 (1994), p. 46.

15. William R. Stoeger, "Key Developments in Physics Challenging Philosophy and Theology," in Richardson and Wildman, 194.

16. See Richard M. Cote, "God Sings in the Night: Ambiguity as an Invitation to Believe," *Concilium* (1992/94), pp. 95–105.

17. Thomas Merton, *New Seeds of Contemplation* (London: Burns & Oates, 1962), p. 104.

18. See Fritjof Capra and David Steindl-Rast, *Belonging to the Universe* (San Francisco: Harper, 1995), pp. 72–74.
19. From "No Religion Is an Island," in Paul Griffiths, ed., *Christianity through Non-Christian Eyes* (Maryknoll: Orbis, 1990), pp. 28–29.
20. For example, Victor Weisskopf says: "The origin of the universe can be talked about not only in scientific terms, but also in poetic and spiritual language, an approach that is complementary to the scientific one." Ernst Mayr says about biology: "Virtually all biologists are religious, in the deeper sense of this word. . . . The unknown and maybe unknowable instills in us a sense of humility." Quoted by Holmes Rolston III, "Science, Religion, and the Future," pp. 63, 72.
21. Quoted by Kathleen Bryant, "Spirituality for the Future," *Human Development* 22 (Summer 1999), p. 18.
22. Umberto Eco, *The Name of the Rose* (trans. into English by William Weaver; New York: Harcourt Brace Jovanovich, 1983), p. 474.
23. Mary Gerhart and Allan Melvin Russel, "Mathematics, Empirical Science, and Religion," in Richardson and Wildman, p. 128.
24. T. S. Eliot, quoted by Lancelot Pereira (see note 8 above), p. 9.

This chapter was originally published in *Vidyajyoti: Journal of Theological Reflection* vol. 64, no. 1 (January 2000), pp. 18–25.

CHAPTER 18

Science and Religion:
A Marriage Made in Heaven?

RAMI M. SHAPIRO

Rabbi Shapiro is a graduate of the Hebrew Union College-Jewish
Institute of Religion and Union Graduate School. He is the senior rabbi of
Temple Beth Or in Miami, and directs the Simply Jewish Foundation, the
What Would a Mentsch Do Project, and the Sh'ma Center for Jewish
Meditation.

Santa Fe, 2007. A spokeswoman for the Physics and
Theology Institute said today that recent breakthroughs in
superstring theory have resulted in a startling discovery.
"Not only are we reading the mind of God," said Dr. Alice
Weinstock, "We have found the essence of the Creator. . . .
Scientists and theologians attending a recent PTI symposium
on "The New Science of God" announced a new era of cooperation between science and religion. "In the past religion
and science were often in conflict," said Rev. Frank
Macintosh, co-chair of the symposium, "but we are entering
a new age; an age of cooperation; an age where science and
religion both reveal the God of Creation."

Farfetched? Or just a matter of time? A growing number of scientists and theologians believe that the marriage of science and religion is
inevitable, and that science is revealing the very nature of God. But
what kind of God does science reveal? If science is reading the mind of
God, just what kind of thoughts is God thinking?

Almost four hundred years ago Galileo Galilei invited the church
fathers to look through his telescope and see for themselves that the
earth orbits the sun. They refused, insisting instead that Galileo stop
looking through the infernal device as well. Today the church has its

own telescope, and theologians turn to science for the latest revelations of God.

This shift is both revealing and misleading. Revealing in the sense that science is discovering that the fundamental unity spoken of by religious mystics throughout history permeates every strata of creation; misleading in that it lends itself to a reductionist view that shrinks God to the amoral building blocks of nature.

Religion and science are different lenses through which we can catch glimpses of God, but to lay one atop the other is to distort them both. Religion will never discover superstrings. Science will never imagine loving one's neighbor as oneself. And yet we persist in blurring the boundaries between religion and science in hopes of having the latter prove the claims of the former so that faith can be bolstered by fact.

The blurring occurs because, at present, we lack a map of reality that allows us to accept the truths of both science and religion without reducing either to a subset of the other. Such a map would allow us to unify (but not reduce) our sciences, both material and spiritual, and present an idea of God that incorporates and transcends them both. Such a map is not hard to find, and has appeared in every culture throughout recorded history. It is called the Great Chain of Being.

Transpersonal philosopher and theorist Ken Wilber has done the most to bring the Great Chain into the twenty-first century, and I am indebted to him for much of my understanding of it. Wilber's map is far more complex than the one I will use here, and speaks to issues far beyond the narrow scope of this chapter. My intention is to use the Great Chain of Being to present a unified but not homogenized vision of science and religion within the greater unity of God. In doing so I will present my own interpretation of the kabbalistic map of the Five Worlds.

In the same way that a Russian nesting doll conceals progressively smaller dolls within it, the Jewish mystics see all reality manifest as five distinct and nested dimensions, or worlds. Just as the smaller doll is included in and transcended by the next larger doll, so the less inclusive worlds are included in and transcended by the next more inclusive world, and the whole nested reality is included in and transcended by God, the unconditioned and unconditional source and substance of all that was, is, and will be.

The first and least inclusive of the Five Worlds is called Assiyah. This is the realm of quantum mechanics, superstring theory, chaos, and complexity. The world of Assiyah is primarily the domain of physics. It is a world of constant wonder, and, if Heisenberg is right, impenetrable

mystery. It also appears to be a world to which both physicist and theologian turn to read the mind of God. Listen to Sheldon Glashow speak
of superstring studies in Timothy Ferris's *Coming of Age in the Milky Way*
(New York: Doubleday, 1989, pp. 333–334):

> [Exploring superstrings may be an enterprise] as remote
> from conventional particle physics as particle physics is from
> chemistry, to be conducted in schools of divinity by future
> equivalents of medieval theologians. . . . For the first time
> since the Dark Ages, we can see how our noble search may
> end, with faith replacing science once again.

Do we really want science to be replaced by faith? What advantage is gained by reducing the dialogue between science and religion to
a monologue? And what kind of faith will this be? Glashow's vision is
not the wonderful marriage of science and religion that some imagine.
Spirit is replaced by superstrings, scientists by theologians, and faith in a
moral universe calling us to justice, compassion, and humility (Micah
6:8) is reduced to faith in amoral multidimensional superstrings that
speak to the origins of life, but not to its meaning or purpose.

The energies and forces studied by physicists in the Assiyah dimension of reality are called Nefesh, which kabbalists take to be
the most rudimentary manifestation of soul or consciousness. Without
Assiyah and Nefesh no other worlds can exist, but to imagine that
Assiyah reveals the final word (rather than the first) is to reduce the
five dimensions to one, and the least inclusive one at that.

The second world or dimension of reality is called Yetzirah. In
Yetzirah the quantum world of Assiyah reaches a new level of complexity, that dimension of life explored by biologists. Biology incorporates
physics and also transcends it. Biology reveals a level of complexity that
the world of quantum mechanics need not and cannot posit. Just as biology incorporates and yet goes beyond physics in its field of study, so
the world of Yetzirah incorporates and goes beyond the world of
Assiyah. The consciousness or soul manifest in Yetzirah is called Ruach.
Ruach, like Nefesh, is not self-aware. It is the level of instinct and law,
not yet reason and will.

Biology no less than physics has much to offer regarding the
majesty of creation, and the universe it reveals is of such intricacy and
wonder as to be a source of mystic amazement in and of itself. And
herein lies the danger. To lose oneself in the wonder of Yetzirah is to
fail to move beyond it.

Ursula Goodenough, professor of biology at Washington University, is a good representative of this:

> Our story [of nature] tells us of the sacredness of life, of the astonishing complexity of cells and organisms. . . . Reverence is the religious emotion elicited when we perceive the sacred. . . . And so, I profess my Faith: For me, the existence of all this complexity and awareness and intent and beauty, and my ability to apprehend it, serves as the ultimate meaning and the ultimate value (*The Sacred Depths of Nature*, New York: Oxford University Press, 1999, pp. 170–171).

I cannot understand how the wondrous complexity of cells is the ultimate meaning and value of life. True, without cells the world I truly revere could not exist, but to reduce that world to its cellular structure, or to point to cells as the carriers of meaning and value, seems extraordinarily reductionist.

A more reasoned approach comes from biologist Kenneth Miller of Brown University:

> God uses physics, chemistry, biology to fashion and run the physical universe. . . . (*Finding Darwin's God*, New York: HarperCollins, 1999, p. 281). To a religious person, science can be a pathway towards God, not away from Him . . . (ibid., p. 292).

Science can move us closer to God manifest as the physical world. It just cannot reach those dimensions of God that transcend it. Or, when science does try to explain the spiritual yearnings of humankind with the bio-logic of Yetzirah, the results are inevitably similar to E. O. Wilson's sociobiology, which reduces the grandest capacities of human life and culture to the amoral transmission of genetic code. It is not that the science of biology is wrong, it is only that the world of Yetzirah is too small.

Beriah, the third dimension of the kabbalistic map, is the world of self-conscious beings; beings, human and otherwise, who are aware of Creation, if not yet their place in it. It is in this world that life achieves the level of consciousness called Neshamah, ego, the self that imagines itself to be separate from other selves. The dominant science of Beriah is psychology.

Where the sciences of physics and biology reveal an all-inclusive unity underlying their respective dimensions, the unity revealed by psychology is an egoistic one, striving for an integration of forces present in the self to create a more harmonious self. Neshamah consciousness knows all about "I" but has yet to discover "Thou."

Just as a study of the physics of Assiyah does not require the biological complexity of Yetzirah, and the biological complexity of Yetzirah does not require the conscious ego of Beriah, so the psychology of Beriah does not mandate a more inclusive dimension of reality that incorporates and transcends it. On the contrary, speculation into an egoless spiritual unity and inclusivity is seen as an infantile wish to return to the supposed safety and security of the womb. Early forms of religion that do appear in this dimension are centered on the ego, its tribe, and its survival after death.

Higher, more inclusive expressions of religious consciousness, for example that which gives us Ethical Monotheism, the belief that One God necessitates one world, one humanity, and one moral code— justice and compassion for all—requires a transpersonal perspective that cannot be found in the self-preoccupied dimension of Beriah.

For this perspective we have to move to the fourth world, called Atzilut. It is at this level of reality that Neshamah consciousness evolves into Chayya consciousness, an appreciation of the transpersonal dimension of being. It is here that we find the creative energies of art, music, mathematics, religion, theology, literature, and the quality of mind capable of using them. The language of Chayya is nuanced: dream, myth, and metaphor. The science of Atzilut is transpersonal religion.

It is here that the sacred traditions of the world begin to recognize that the egoistic formulations of faith common to Beriah are too narrow, focusing as they do on division, chosenness, the saved and the damned. They begin to look beyond these differences to discover a common ground from which to build a more compassionate and peaceful world. The "scientists" of Atzilut tend to be the prophets and visionaries who peer over traditional boundaries to embrace the whole of life—cultural, psychological, biological, and physical—as a network of mutually supportive and interactive systems all within the domain of God.

As integrative as Atzilut is, however, it is still not the final level of inclusiveness and transcendence. For this we turn to the fifth world, Adam Kadmon, Primordial Being. It is here that all selves dissolve into a selfless unity characterized best by the Hindu phrase *sat chit ananda:* being, consciousness, bliss. Not surprisingly the level of consciousness that experiences this dimension of reality is called Yechida, or unity consciousness. This consciousness belongs to no one in particular, for it does not see any separate beings at all, but only the One from Whom all diversity flows.

The science of Adam Kadmon is mysticism, and her scientists are those rare beings—Abraham, Moses, Jesus, Mohammed, Lao Tzu, Buddha, Krishna, Eckhart, Hildegard of Bingen, to name but a few—who master rigorous spiritual disciplines and momentarily drop body, mind, ego, and soul to experience God as the greater unity that is the singular source and substance of all worlds and levels of consciousness.

There is often difficulty in distinguishing between the fourth and fifth dimensions as they seem to be saying similar, if not the same, things. The difference is the presence and absence of self. In the fourth dimension of Atzilut, Chayya consciousness is still a form of self-consciousness. The person manifesting Chayya consciousness is aware of both herself and her fundamental interdependence with all other selves. She is not without self, but sees that all selves are part of each other and a greater whole. It is this greater whole that is the realm of Adam Kadmon, the fifth world of the kabbalistic map. The Yechida consciousness that manifests in this fifth dimension is aware of a seamless unity that leaves no room for variation or selves of any kind. Yechida consciousness is not aware of itself, it is awareness itself; consciousness without content.

Does Yechida reveal the true nature of God? No more so than any of the other worlds. God is not limited to any one dimension. God is the parchment on which the map is drawn. God is present in every space, in every place. God permeates each and every dimension, for God is both the source and the substance of all reality. God is the superstring and the dark infinity of space. God is the cow in the stable and the neighbor next door. God is the immanent and the transcendent. There is nothing that is not God.

When we apply our Five Worlds map to our understanding of science and religion, we honor each discipline and its discoveries for what they are: various facets of an infinitely faceted God.

When the physicist exploring Assiyah uncovers the primary forces of existence and thus the mind of God, she reveals the truth, just not the whole truth. It is not that the eye of the physicist sees poorly. It is that the lens of physics sees only what it can.

When the biologist exploring Yetzirah discovers the vast interconnectedness of all life and thus the unity of God, he reveals the truth, just not the whole truth. It is not that the eye of the biologist sees poorly. It is that the lens of biology sees only what it can.

When the psychologist exploring Beriah lays bare the secrets of self and then suggests that God is only a projection of this self, she reveals the truth, just not the whole truth. It is not that the eye of the psychologist sees poorly. It is that the lens of psychology sees only what it can.

When the ardent religious disciple exploring Atzilut shows us the transpersonal ground from which all religions arise, he reveals the truth, just not the whole truth. It is not that the eye of the disciple sees poorly. It is that the lens of religion sees only what it can.

When the mystic exploring Adam Kadmon points toward the Source from which all form and being arise and to which they return, and if she suggests that this realm is the only true realm, and that all other dimensions are illusory, she reveals the truth, just not the whole truth. It is not that the eye of the mystic sees poorly. It is that the lens of mysticism sees only what it can.

Whatever lens we use to view reality, we are reducing reality to what that lens reveals. All attempts to align God exclusively with any one aspect of reality are flawed. Physics is not theology, and while good theology must incorporate the truths of science and not deny or violate them, it must do so in the process of offering a more inclusive view of reality than science can reveal. There is no conflict between good science and good religion; there should just not be an equation of the two.

The quantum paradoxes of Assiyah, the biological wonder of Yetzirah, the psychological genius of Beriah are all vital to the whole story of reality, but they do not contain the whole story. Physics may well be "nearing God" as Stephen Hawkins said in the *Observer* (11/23/97), and physicists may well desire with Albert Einstein "to know the thoughts of God," but they will only know the thoughts of God when God is thinking about the laws of physics.

What the kabbalistic map of the Five Worlds offers, indeed what all the expressions of the Great Chain of Being offer, is a means for integrating science and religion in a greater whole. It allows us to honor and pursue the sciences appropriate to each dimension without forcing any one science to work in all dimensions. It provides us with a schematic of reality that honors both science and religion, and reveals to us the truth that we are never apart from and always a part of that infinite Reality we call God.

This chapter was originally published in *Tikkun* (March/April 2000).

CHAPTER 19

Light of Science in Our Eyes: Envisioning a New Spiritual Epic

EDWARD SEARL

The Reverend Searl has been affiliated with the Unitarian Church of Hinsdale in Hinsdale, IL, for the last eighteen years. He received this theological degree from McGill University in Montreal in 1973. He is the author of two books, *In Memoriam: A Guide to Modern Funeral and Memorial Services* and *A Place of Your Own.*

The reconciliation of science and religion, especially from the vantage of religion, is an area of considerable concern as we enter the year 2001. The psychological threshold of a new millennium is rendered even more dramatic by a flood tide of science and technology.

What was unimaginable twenty years ago has become our almost unremarkable reality. Consider examples of what has become commonplace in recent years, months, weeks, and even days: a computer network that creates a world wide web; cloned mammals that have themselves sexually reproduced; a telescope traveling through space sending back clear and defined images of faraway planets and distant galaxies; DNA tracking that takes us back to a common mother in Africa; and particles—quark-gluon matter—created in a so-called Little Bang in a Geneva physics laboratory that replicated matter that existed in the first moments after the Big Bang, some 15 billion years ago.

For centuries, modern science has been undermining the supernaturalism and myth that supports traditional religions. As a result, religion is in crisis.

The Harvard biologist Edward O. Wilson, who helped popularize sociobiology, described this crisis succinctly and predicted an outcome in a millennium-heralding interview published in the January 1, 2000, edition of the *Wall Street Journal.* Dr. Wilson declared, "Make no mistake about it: the expansion of human knowledge with science and technology, especially neuroscience, genetics and evolution, renders traditional religious belief less and less tenable, more and more difficult to justify and argue logically. The more we understand from science about the way the world really works, all the way from subatomic particles up to the mind and on to the cosmos, the more difficult it is to base spirituality on our ancient mythologies."

Dr. Wilson has a healthy respect for the religious impulse in human beings. In his influential book of the 1970s, *On Human Nature,* he wrote: "the predisposition to religious belief is the most complex and powerful force in the human mind." In his New Year remarks, he argued that traditional religions would continue to decline. Those that refuse to accommodate the insights of science will simply become irrelevant. Those that do will become more secular as they accommodate the worldview of science. Yet the religious impulse will not diminish. (Human nature hasn't changed for at least one hundred thousand years, he reasoned, so it's not going to change in the foreseeable future.)

Taking such things into consideration, Dr. Wilson speculated, "The search for spirituality is going to be one of the major historical episodes of the 21st century. We realize that we are going to have to be proactive in seeking it and defining it instead of reactive in the traditional manner of taking the sacred texts and beliefs handed down to us and trying to adapt them to an evolving culture. That's just not working anymore." He concluded, "We need to create a new epic based on the origins of humanity."

Envisioning a New Spiritual Epic

I agree with Dr. Wilson on all counts. I'm particularly excited by the challenge and opportunity of creating a new epic—a spiritual epic concordant with science to take us into the twenty-first century, and indeed, into a third millennium of the Common Era.

It's thrilling to visualize the outline of such a New Spiritual Epic. Though realistic, it will still be rich in the particular meanings our humanity brings to it, including traditional religious emotions and sensibilities. Imagine with me three significant aspects of a New Spiritual Epic.

Let's begin at the beginning, *the story of Cosmic Creation:* the Big Bang. Every few weeks a new announcement from cosmologists or particle physicists brings us closer to that long ago event that sent matter exploding into the space-time continuum. Soon, we might expect, we will be peering into what is now imponderable—what "was" (though there "was" no *was,* since time didn't exist) before the speck of matter exploded to begin Creation. As I read the accounts, written for the consumption of laypersons like myself, of the initial and early intricate actions of particles and subatomic particles, of the emergence of time and the later appearance of light, of the subsequent formation of stars massing into galaxies, and of speculation about the future of the universe, I am in awe. Cosmic Creation swallows my being in its enormity of process, size, and time, and I am full of fear and trembling. Yet its design—intricacy of cause and effect on micro- and macrocosmic levels—strikes me with its beauty. Though majestic, it seems to accommodate me. I realize that wherever I might be in its vastness, I am at the center, or so it appears. Whatever I do affects it in some way, so it and I are engaged in an incredibly complex dance of existence. It may be dispassionate, but it is not indifferent, at least as I relate to It and It to me. I am embedded in a cosmic process. Such sensibilities and emotions have analogs in historical God language.

In compiling a New Spiritual Epic, we next look at *our own home, the earth,* curious because it contains just the right combination of factors to result in advanced life. It's not too close to or too far from our sun, allowing for water and not vapor or ice. The radiation levels aren't too high, the right chemical elements are abundant, sufficient gravity keeps an atmosphere ringing it and oceans covering it, the atmosphere helps keep meteor showers from bombarding the surface, and a large moon stabilizes the earth's tilt, allowing for mild seasons. As a closed system, a great biosphere hurtling through space at considerable speed, it begat varied and abundant life. That life began in the simplest biological forms, adapted and evolved into complex forms that eventually produced our species amid an incredible biodiversity that itself is a tenacious but fragile balance. All we need to do is look around at our earth home to realize that within creation there is an urge to come alive, to attain consciousness, and ultimately self-consciousness. Though the universe may appear to be dispassionate, we seem to prove by our existence that there is a passion that has followed successful strategies to gain a kind of immortality through the cycle of generations. There is a chain of life that has emerged from the inanimate stuff that was the speck of matter at the moment of the Big Bang when space-time began. We are, indeed, enchanted stardust, as nineteenth-century transcendentalists liked to poeticize. This realization makes me exceedingly grateful. With such a vision I must reverence all life forms and vow to do my ethical best not to harm any life when at all possible and to maintain the interdependent web of existence for the sake of all lives.

Scientists in recent years have argued that given the vastness of the universe, with hundreds of millions of galaxies and untold stars, there are probably millions of planets sustaining advanced life forms. One estimate posits 10 trillion habitable planets. We have come to accept this truly humbling probability—humbling our timeless pretensions of being the goal or end of creation. Yet, certain reputable scientists have challenged the hypothesis of a universe rich in advanced life forms. They use the earth as their guide. Its combination of so many fortuitous factors, they argue, must be applied to other planets. They speculate that there may be only a few and perhaps no other planet in the whole universe that can sustain the advanced life that earth is graced by. They concede that microbes might exist elsewhere, but the conditions for microbes to evolve into advanced life may not. Yet if this should prove so, this is humbling, too. Good fortune, like a great love, tends to evoke gratitude and with understanding edges into the humility that acknowledges how lucky we are to enjoy it.

Which brings me to a third aspect of a New Spiritual Epic, the place of *our human species*. We look around and see an abundance of sentient life in our time. In these abundant and diverse life forms, we recognize that some have a consciousness grounded in instinct, perhaps shaded by dim and inarticulate memories, certainly evidencing what we would call emotion, and in some instances able to reason. We have all that and more. Self-consciousness describes our extra, human level of awareness. It includes advanced cognition—intuition and reason plus imagination. We are aware of self and experience our individuality. We have a sense of time, including a future. We can think in abstractions, see relationships, draw metaphors. Our incredible mind allows us to communicate with one another, here and now, and to a degree in the past and to the future. I believe that our incredible mind is an expression of an urge in the universe to reflect on Itself and to reach beyond Itself toward the Transcendent. In our mind, as time and generations testify, but which we know first hand, there is the religious impulse, which may be simplified as the quest for meaning and purpose. Of creation, and representative of an urge within creation, our religious impulse also belongs to creation. And here enters the eternal question of Overarching Meaning.

We say "Wow!" and "Thank you!" but this does not preclude "Why?" Silence always edges toward a new horizon. Beyond the horizon is a compelling mystery that pulls inquiry forward.

Science, like religion, accepts mystery. Science will never reach a place where it has all the answers. In the January 1 article, Dr. Wilson remarked that "[T]he eternal frontier satisfies one of the deepest needs of the human mind and the human heart. Always moving out into a strange and surprising world—understanding more, fulfilling our potential more. Each quest brings us to a point where we see a new horizon stretching beyond. That is what science gives us."

Which brings me to my own speculation, make that intuitive musing, relative to a New Spiritual Epic. Creation itself, as will humankind first, in some distant time will come to an end. Our individual existence, we know all to well, that is existentially, is shaped by the mystery of being and non-being—of living and dying. Religion is driven to answer this mystery. If we are representative of an urge within Creation to become self-conscious, to understand Itself, my spiritual imagination wonders if Creation Itself isn't concerned with Its own space-time existence. Might It seek to know what brought It into existence and where It is destined? Might It, from Its own need, have evolved and continue to evolve conscious life to find an answer?

I've been imagining a spiritual epic that draws upon the understandings of three realms of science: 1) cosmology, astrophysics, and particle physics regarding a Creation Story; 2) earth sciences including biology to describe the uniqueness of earth and its interdependent web of existence; and 3) the scientific study of the human condition through neuroscience, psychology, social biology, and anthropology. I've even speculated that Creation brought us into being out of Itself to ask and seek answers to Its own meaning and purpose.

A "New" Natural Religion

It will take a bold and free religion to strive toward such a scientifically and humanly meaningful spiritual epic where dispassionate truth, understood empirically, meets passionate meaning experienced through the mind, heart, and soul. Such a church, sensitive to the universal human urge to spirituality, will develop a Natural Religion grounded in reason and science, always open to progressive thought. Today we sang a familiar hymn, words written 120 years ago by John Addington Symnonds,

> These Things Shall Be: a loftier race
> Than e'er the world hath known shall rise,
> With flame of freedom in their souls,
> And light of science in their eyes.

Throughout my twenty years as a minister, I've taken those words to heart and especially appreciated the last line: "And light of science in their eyes." Our free tradition has long embraced the advancements brought by science. We've already passed through what Edward O. Wilson predicted for the traditional religions in the twenty-first century: they will tip toward the empiricists, becoming more secular, while striving to preserve an inner core of spirituality through their psychologically powerful rituals and rites. This is something of a backward-looking way of reconciling science and religion. I envision a more forward-looking response. Our liberal tradition is poised to take the step Dr. Wilson recommends, the creation of a New Spiritual Epic drawing upon science and blended with human meaning. That epic is summarized by what our tradition has been developing for a century-and-a-half as Natural Religion.

The window that science provides lets us look out on an epic story of Creation and Evolution that leads to the most profound spiritual experiences, understandings, and sensibilities possible. That New Spiritual Epic will include all the timeless responses, emotions, and sensibilities associated with traditional religion, including a sense of adventure and mystery. It will create its own ethics and make moral demands.

As a matter of fact, this New Spiritual Epic has already been created, at least in its significant parts. The task of contemporary religion—our age's task—is to bring the parts together in a popular, meaningful mytho-poetic telling. A significant part of this endeavor will be assuring the religious traditionalists that this is a continuing revelation of all they hold sacred.

Revelation is not sealed. It never was and never will be. In our time revelation comes through science. It is religion's responsibility to transform ever-progressing scientific truths into a new spirituality—an epic for the twenty-first century, certainly, but also with an eye to the expanding horizons of a new millennium.

This chapter was originally a sermon given by the author and is published here with his permission.

PART III

HISTORICAL AND
PHILOSOPHICAL PERSPECTIVES ON THE
Science-Religion Dialogue

CHAPTER 20

The Mystery of the Self and the Enigma of Nature

ROGER L. SHINN

Roger L. Shinn is Reinhold Niebuhr Professor of Social Ethics, Emeritus, at Union Theological Seminary in New York. His distinguished career in the academy has been in three fields: religion, ethics, and economics. He has conducted extensive research on the relations of science and technology to ethics in various social systems in disparate areas of the world. He has chaired the National Council of Churches' Department of Church and Economic Life and its Task Force on Human Life and New Genetics. He is past president of the American Theological Society and the Society of Christian Ethics. His most recent books are the third edition of *Forced Options: Social Decisions for the 21st Century* and *The New Genetics: Challenges for Faith, Science, and Politics.*

As Christians enter the third millennium, we find ourselves re-thinking our relation to the realm of nature around us and within us. Like it or not, we have to do this, for two compelling reasons. First, the discoveries of modern science demolish many traditional understandings of nature and confer on humanity new powers, benevolent or threatening. The church has sometimes welcomed, sometimes resisted, the discoveries of Copernicus, Galileo, Newton, Darwin, Einstein, and Heisenberg. Now, new genetic science describes our inmost selves in ways that both exhilarate and jolt us. Second, ecological perils, some local and some planetary, warn us that our present ways of dealing with nature, while destroying much of what we call the environment, are also self-destructive, potentially on a grand scale.

The controversies that rage about these issues often focus on specific political and economic issues. They also reach deeply into our culture, engaging the values and sensitivities that form our thoughts and actions, often unconsciously. In this chapter, I resist two broad tendencies of our time: (1) those that neglect nature, depreciate it, or regard it as a warehouse of materials for human exploitation, and (2) those that cultivate pleasant illusions about nature or idealize it as a norm for human living. And I seek some "theological pointers" as guides to responsible living.

As a convenient starting point, think of a phrase heard frequently in contemporary arguments: "human intervention in natural processes." "Intervention" is here a curious word. When a hawk swoops upon a sparrow, we do not call that intervention in nature. It is one natural process clashing with another, as is common in nature. We human beings can talk of intervention only if, in some elusive way, we are more than or other than those processes. Philosophers from Plato to Descartes and after have tried to separate the self from nature, constructing dualisms of mind or soul and body. But that effort, always strained, gets less and less persuasive. The discoveries of science confirm what ancient people, including the Hebrews, knew intuitively. We are bodily beings, in and of nature, of earth, akin to plants and animals, and nature is in us. The processes of physics and chemistry and electronics have more to do with our physical and intellectual activity, our purposes and our spirituality, than we may like to think. We share the universal genetic code—that marvelous four-letter alphabet of A, G, C, and T—with chimpanzees, mice, and bacteria.

Systematic, dogmatic naturalists, of the "nothing but" school, may try to reduce all our activities to natural processes, to those complicated interactions of "chance and necessity"[1] that science investigates with startling results. But when they write books to persuade us of their theories, they engage in acts of imagination, rationality, and will. When they claim truth for their arguments, they rise above the unknowing and unintentional electrochemical processes that they describe. They illustrate a kind of transcendence—controversial word—of the self over nature, the transcendence that impressed Plato and Descartes, even though it misled them to incredible—I'd add harmful—conclusions.

So if we are part of nature, we are a unique part. We can conceive nature as an object, investigate it, talk about it, purposely act upon it, "intervene" in it. We can fleetingly and locally put our "Kilroy was here" upon nature. We may even prate foolishly about "conquering" space, or "managing" the environment, or "controlling" the genetic code. If we are sane enough to avoid such gloating, we, unlike other processes of nature, can write solemn essays about our relation to nature.

Yet, in any such acts, we confront the enigma of nature around us and within us. Out of its evolutionary processes has come human life. It sustains us, inspires us, threatens us, will kill every last one of us, and will outlast our entire species.

Macronature

Nature, when we dare to think of all of it, is an overwhelming reality. According to the currently dominant theory, our universe began with a Big Bang some thirteen or fourteen billion years ago, give or take a few hundred million years. Then a mass, somewhere between the size of a pea and a grapefruit, initiated the explosion that is still going on, shaping and unshaping galaxies. There are dissenters to this theory, and it may be modified in the next century—or month. But alternative theories pose comparable issues, so I use this one, simply as an example.

The Big Bang, it seems, made possible all that followed, including human life: our loves and fears, our artistic imagination, our sciences and intellectual attainments, our wars, our economies, our communities and political organizations, our visions and aspirations, our moral judgments. Yes, the Enlightenment of the Buddha and the Cross of Christ. I do not say that the Big Bang made all these inevitable; that kind of metaphysical determinism, familiar in the seventeenth and eighteenth centuries, gets more incredible year by year. But in the Big Bang were—somehow and in some sense—all these possibilities and many more, yet to be realized or never to be realized. If we love life, we'd better be grateful for the Big Bang.

In this universe, our sun, perhaps five billion years old, is one of billions of stars in this galaxy, which is one of billions of galaxies in this universe. These galaxies appear to be rushing outward at tremendous speed. Yet, now and then two of them collide with unimaginable explosions. Our galaxy appears to be moving toward a collision with the Andromeda galaxy, maybe five billion years in the future. With luck, we may only sideswipe it, although nobody on a burnt-out earth will drink a toast to that luck.

Some signs point toward the existence of many universes, rising out of many Big Bangs, "continually being created and destroyed like bubbles on the ocean."[2] But nobody—at least just now—can confirm or refute the theory for certain. In the vast array of nature, our planet and our sun are minute. Our brief temporality is equally tiny. Hinduism and

Pythagoreanism have projected earlier existence of persons, perhaps eternal. Wordsworth put it eloquently:

> . . . trailing clouds of glory do we come
> From God, who is our home.[3]

But such visions go far beyond any nature known to science.

A rash of observations, many made possible by the Hubble telescope floating in space, has been inspiring new observations monthly or weekly. As fresh knowledge seems to settle some old arguments, it engenders new ones. This is a bad time for dogmatists, a good time for inquirers.

Some scientists affirm the anthropic principle. In its most modest form, it is a truism: This is the kind of nature in which human life is possible. In the vastness of nature, through eons of time, conscious purposeful beings have emerged on one small plant and in one sliver of time—perhaps elsewhere, also, in times and places of which we have no certain knowledge.

In its stronger, controversial form, the anthropic principle holds that nature points toward the emergence of life. Processes of cosmology are precisely calibrated to make life possible. An extremely slight variation (one part in many millions) in the force of gravity or electromagnetism would have made this universe impossible, as would the most minute variation in the formation of such elements as hydrogen, helium, oxygen, and carbon. The Yale physicist Henry Margenau wrote, to the consternation of many colleagues, "the laws of nature are created by an omnipotent and omniscient God." The eminent astrophysicist Freeman Dyson is a little more reserved: "I do not feel like an alien in this universe. The more I examine the universe and the details of its architecture, the more evidence I find that the universe in some sense must have known that we were coming."[4]

Other scientists just as readily find nature utterly indifferent to human life and purposes. If natural processes temporarily support human life, they likewise support the forces that mutilate and destroy life. This is a universe of cosmic catastrophes, of annihilating events, of "black holes"—collapsed stars so dense that from them nothing, not even light, can escape.

On our planet, more congenial to human life than any other locale that we know about, nature is as perilous as it is supporting. If we formulate an anthropic principle, why not a viral principle? Nature supports viruses that combat human life and health, forces that by all signs have a far greater staying power than we. A microbe, wrote Dean Inge, "had the honor of killing Alexander the Great at the age of thirty-two and so changing the whole course of history."[5] Medical science inflicts many momentary defeats on microbes, but they keep coming back.

Biologists identify five great catastrophes—eruptions of volcanoes or strikes of meteorites—that have brought massive extinctions of earthly species. The most recent if not the greatest, it appears, destroyed the dinosaurs and many other forms of life about sixty-five million years ago. Recovery of biodiversity took twenty million years after that. E. O. Wilson reckons that such a catastrophe is likely every ten to one hundred million years.[6] Such an estimate tells us that science is not always a matter of precision. But it explodes any confident and comforting version of the anthropic principle.

"Science," writes Freeman Dyson, "is a mosaic of partial and conflicting visions."[7] When it has done its best, nature is an enigma. The seventeenth-century genius Blaise Pascal, the one person of great eminence in the history of both science and theology, saw the enigma well. Again and again he pointed to the grandeur and the weakness of the self, so frail in the midst of a perilous nature, yet so wonderful. "The eternal silence of these infinite spaces frightens me." "By space the universe encompasses and swallows me up like an atom; by thought I comprehend the world." Yet even our best thought is fragile. "How ludicrous is reason, blown with a breath in every direction!"[8] The enigma of nature meets the mystery of the self.

Micronature

To turn from macronature to micronature is to find more enigmas. From ancient times, the atom was thought to be a tiny, indivisible particle. By the time I got to high school, it was a miniature solar system of protons and electrons. Now, high school students enter that strange world of neutrons, leptons, photons, mesons, quarks and antiquarks, superstrings, and quantum foam, and more year by year. (That term "quark" was lifted out of James Joyce's *Finnegan's Wake*—an unusual fertilization of science by the humanities.) Quantum theory tells us that electrons have no simple location, that "wavicles" are best regarded as both waves and particles, that in microphysics statistical probability is the closest we can come to certainty. Einstein resisted quantum theory with his saying, "God does not play dice,"[9] but apparently Heisenberg has won the argument, at least for now, with his "uncertainty principle." If these esoteric theories remain unknown to most people, the technologies related to these theories affect all the world. Few people can explain Einstein's famous equation, $e = mc^2$, and fewer by far know how to derive it; but its effects touch all human life. When uranium was transformed into energy in the spontaneous nuclear reactor that ran for a hundred thousand years in Africa (in what is now Gabon) two billion years ago, no human beings existed to worry about it. Today, humanly constructed nuclear reactors—don't forget bombs—influence the world's economies and political structures, to the benefit or detriment of people everywhere.

With these discoveries and activities, the human power to direct and modify natural processes increases monstrously. At the same time, the divide between living and inanimate nature becomes less absolute.

As epoch-making as the nineteenth century's discoveries of the nucleus of the atom are the discoveries of the nuclei of biological cells. Here, we enter that micronature of the three billion bits of information carried by the DNA in the hundred thousand or so genes of the human cells. A fertilized egg, described as a millionth of the size of a pinhead, begins the divisions that lead to the hundred trillion cells of an adult human body. Investigators are learning to manipulate that DNA with the aim of overcoming disastrous disease, perhaps cloning human individuals, maybe reconstituting human nature in the directions, benign or malignant, of the wielders of new powers. In this realm of science, even more than in quantum theory, the enigma of nature joins the mystery of the human self.

Human Perspectives

Within nature, I have been saying, humanity has a unique place, both privileged and limited. We are not gods. We understand human nature from a human perspective. In the mid-twentieth century, the philosopher Ralph Barton Perry invented the term "the egocentric predicament." By that he meant that human beings—each of us individually and all of us collectively—can know the world only as it is accessible to our senses (or their extension in humanly devised instruments) and our thought. We lack the keen noses of dogs, the sharp eyes of eagles, and the irrepressible skill of bacteria in mutating and multiplying.

Most of us don't want to trade places with these other forms of life; we have our advantages. But we perceive the world only as the human species can perceive it, and we organize our knowledge around human interests. There is nothing shameful in these limitations. They become shameful and silly only if we pretend they are not there, acting as though our limited understandings are somehow final and absolute.

To do that is a frequent human failing, known to the Greeks as hubris, to the Hebrews as sin. The appropriate answer to it is a humility before the mysteries of self, nature, and God.

The egocentric predicament affects all our acts and thoughts. Think of the way we talk of environment. Among human beings, environmentalists are sensitive to the beauty of nature, the welfare of many species of life, and the needs of future generations. But the very word "environment" is egocentric; it distinguishes us from the nature outside ourselves. To the innumerable other species of life, *we* are environment, even though they do not know how to say so. We, the human species, are, temporarily, the most voracious and lethal of all beasts of prey. In terms of tenure on earth, cockroaches almost surely surpass us. Although we can sometimes best them in hand-to-hand or chemical combat, we must expect them to outlast us on earth. Maybe viruses outrank us *and* cockroaches. They are the real specialists in the arts of survival. Medical biologists warn us that we never know when they may invade us in forms that defy our best weapons of defense and counterattack.

Still, we do not envy these other beings in nature. They do not— we are virtually certain—build civilizations, write epic dramas, repent before God and their co-creatures, and envision more glorious futures.

We need not despair over the egocentric predicament. We had better beware of its limitations and deceptions. In this chapter, I have already unintentionally stumbled into it. Describing macronature, I have referred to thirteen or fourteen billion years. In my attempt to stretch our awareness beyond the boundaries of human life, I used a parochially human language. Why should anybody reckon cosmic time in *years*? A year is a humanly chosen unit of time, based on one elliptical movement of the earth around the sun. It is transcultural, a measurement shared by all of us on earth, but insignificant for other planets, other suns, other galaxies. Yet, we impose it on a universe in which our planet is an infinitesimal participant. I can propose no better measurement *for us*. I only point out that, to a cosmic angel, it might be a mild joke that people reckon the age of the universe in so absurdly provincial a unit as years.

Nature and Human History

In a recent fragment of terrestrial time, human life has emerged to question nature, celebrate and lament it, and act purposefully to change it. *Homo erectus* appeared in Africa some 1.8 million years ago, then spread to much of Europe and Asia. "Modern *Homo sapiens*" appeared 125,000 to 200,000 years ago and began to change irrevocably the history of nature on earth. Maybe something comparable has happened often in the multiverse. We shall never know, and perhaps our descendants will never know. But when persons interact with natural processes, we face ethical issues unknown to Big Bangs and to outward rushing or colliding galaxies. Are we somehow improving on natural processes, or are we creating a wreckage that desecrates the splendor of nature and portends our own ruin? How does the mystery of the self meet the enigma of nature?

One traditional answer is that nature is infused with purpose, either the gift of a divine Creator or an invincible immanent process. "Nature does nothing without purpose or uselessly," wrote Aristotle. In a very different context, Newton asked, "Whence is it that Nature doth nothing in vain; and whence arises all the Order and Beauty which we see in the world?" His answer was "a Being incorporeal, living, intelligent, omnipresent."[10]

But then came Charles Darwin. He was not the first to propose a hypothesis of organic evolution. However, he did it with both a comprehensiveness and a scientific attention to detail that were new. Christians sometimes rejected Darwinism with a literal reading of Genesis, which was an unnecessary and useless controversy. Still, the Darwinian explanation of the driving force of evolution as random variation followed by natural selection was more deeply disturbing, even to Darwin.

In the concluding paragraph of *On the Origin of Species,* Darwin tried hard to give an upbeat interpretation of his own work:

> Thus, from the war of nature, from famine and death, the most exalted object which we are capable of conceiving, namely the production of the higher animals, directly follows. There is grandeur in this view of life, with its several powers, having been originally breathed into a few forms or into one; and that, whilst this planet has gone cycling on according to the fixed law of gravity, from so simple a beginning endless forms most beautiful and most wonderful have been, and are being evolved.[11]

Privately, Darwin made a more disturbing exclamation: "What a book a Devil's chaplain might write on the clumsy, wasteful, blundering low & horridly cruel works of nature!"[12]

A century later, Richard Dawkins, picking up the metaphor of the eighteenth-century deist William Paley and turning it against him, wrote in *The Blind Watchmaker:*

> Natural selection . . . has no purpose in mind. It has no mind and no mind's eye. It does not plan for the future. It has no vision, no foresight, no sight at all. If it can be said to play the role of watchmaker in nature, it is the blind watchmaker.[13]

The last two centuries have aroused a host of swirling and conflicting thoughts about nature. Consider the questions of ethics. From ancient times, doctrines of natural law have affirmed ethical principles built into nature and knowable to humankind apart from any historical religious revelation. The belief, though pre-Christian in origin, was absorbed into centuries of Christian teaching and practice. But it had many definitions, many interpretations. The "nature" of natural law was rarely knowable by empirical observation of the processes of nature. More often, it was some cosmic principle of order or rationality, understood to apply to human conduct as well as to universal nature.

John Donne challenged the idea in an essay entitled "Nature Our Worst Guide" in 1633.[14] But the Romantic movement found a deep human rapport with nature. Wordsworth in 1798 found

> In nature and the language of the sense
> The anchor of my purest thoughts, the nurse,
> The guide, the guardian of my heart, and soul
> Of all my moral being.[15]

But Tennyson in 1850, just a few years before Darwin's *Origin of Species* (1859), grieved at "Nature, red in tooth and claw."[16]

A little later, Thomas Huxley, the doughty defender of Darwinism, called himself "Darwin's bulldog." But in his famous Romanes Lecture of 1893 he argued:

> . . . the practice of that which is ethically best—what we call goodness or virtue—involves a course of conduct which, in all respects, is opposed to that which leads to success in the cosmic struggle for existence. . . . It repudiates the gladiatorial theory of existence. . . . [T]he ethical progress of society depends, not on imitating the cosmic process, still less in running away from it, but in combating it.[17]

That is not the last work on evolution and ethics. Cooperation as well as competition is part of evolutionary survival. Both belong to the enigma of nature. Biologist Robert S. Morison has framed the issue:

> Perhaps the crucial Darwinian question for our time of crisis is whether or not man can broaden his culture, his concept of human brotherhood and his tolerance of variation so that it becomes coextensive with his gene pool.[18]

Morison affirms this without denying the cruelty and waste in the evolution of life.

Beneath the controversies about ethics were perplexing questions about the place of humankind in nature. While some Christians resisted evolution, for its apparent rejection of all natural teleology, others welcomed it. Henry Drummond in *The Descent of Man* (1894) declared that Christianity and evolution were identical. Lyman Abbott in *The Theology of an Evolutionist* (1898) rejoiced in "Redemption by Evolution." A poem by William Herbert Carruth, popular in my youth, included the lines:

> Some call it evolution,
> And others call it God.[19]

The secular culture had similar perplexities. The poet Swinburne exulted in his place at the apex of nature:

> Glory to man in the highest! For Man is the master of things.[20]

W. S. Gilbert (of Gilbert and Sullivan fame) could have been spoofing Swinburne when a few years later he wrote:

> Darwinian Man, though well-behaved,
> At best is only a monkey shaved

and,

> Man is Nature's sole mistake![21]

Probably neither Swinburne nor Gilbert knew the pre-Darwinian hymn of Reginal Heber, who could sing of at least some locales:

> Though every prospect pleases,
> And only man is vile . . .[22]

The continuing argument is not likely to be settled soon.

The Industrial Revolution had more direct impact on human habits and consciousness than Darwin's science. It gave rise to the conception of nature as a hoard of materials—smugly called "raw materials"—for human use and consumption. Of course, human beings had long exploited nature as voraciously as possible with their limited abilities. But industry brought new possibilities and ambitions. People who had never heard of Francis Bacon discovered for themselves that "knowledge is power." They did not always share Bacon's belief: "God almighty first planted a garden; and, indeed, it is the purest of human pleasures." Nor did they always treasure his insight: "Nature cannot be ordered about, except by obeying her."[23]

In this chaos of data and opinions, can we make any generalization about the mystery of the self and the enigma of nature? How do we relate to the nature that is our womb and our tomb? I see no unanimous judgments, no emerging consensus. Sometimes I turn to an exclamation of George Santayana that has reverberated in my memory for five decades:

> Great is this organism of mud and fire, terrible this vast, painful, glorious experiment. Why should we not look on the universe with piety? Is it not our substance? Are we made of other clay? All our possibilities lie from eternity hidden in its bosom. It is the dispenser of all our joys. We may address it without superstitious terrors; it is not wicked. It follows its own habits abstractly; it can be trusted to be true to its own word. Society is not impossible between it and us, and since it is the source of all our energies, the home of all our happiness, shall we not cling to it and praise it, seeing that it vegetates so grandly and so sadly, and that it is not for us to blame it for what, doubtless, it never knew that it did?[24]

That is not the last word. Noting the reference to the universe as an organism, I would like to nudge Santayana in the direction of Whitehead. But I find his natural piety one element in any adequate ethic of human interaction with nature. For a more robust ethic, I must turn (as Santayana did but not in the way he did) to a more specific religious heritage.

Theological Pointers

Why do I come to theology so late in this inquiry? Because it is a late arrival in the long story of human efforts to live with and cope with nature. The faith that theology seeks to understand never arises *ex nihilo*.

Its origins are not *sola scriptura*. It builds upon, invades, and transforms the varieties of human experience.

Theology does not replace the enigma of nature with a single, coherent vision. The Christian Scriptures are not a list of major premises from which believers can deduce moral rules for today's world. Nor is the Bible a grab bag of proof texts, although people use it as though it were. It expresses pervading motifs that guide thought and behavior but rarely with rigorous, consistent, prescriptive authority. In the diversity of biblical insights, Christians find guides to belief and activity. Our responses are rarely unanimous, as anybody can plainly see. From theology I expect *pensées* (Pascal) and fragments (Kierkegaard), rather than a systematic concept of the world and social policy. I encourage those who strive to weave the insights into a comprehensive understanding, but I am skeptical of their results. So I refer here to "theological pointers." The pointers are decisively important as guides in life and death. They confer on us the responsibility for discovering their significance for the mystery of the self and the enigma of nature.

We think immediately of the biblical belief in creation. Its rejection of pantheism and polytheism means that nature is not God and is not inhabited by gods. Nature is created by God. It is real—not *maya*, not a projection of shadows on the wall of Plato's cave. In the audacious refrain of Genesis 1, it is "good," yes, "very good." But good is not perfect. Lurking in the garden is the "crafty" serpent. Though God's creation, it is a tempter, a provocateur.

Although the Bible does not declare creation *ex nihilo*, Isaiah comes close:

> I form light and create darkness,
> I make peace and create evil.[25]

Christians today (and Jews, though others can speak more competently than I to that) rarely attribute directly to God all the acts ascribed to God in some parts of Scripture. Amos asks: "Does disaster befall a city, unless the Lord has done it?" Today, even we who love Amos believe that some disasters (e.g., the devastation of cities by bombs and floods that follow deforestation) are caused by people in defiance of God. Others (e.g., eruptions of volcanoes and the tornadoes that are frequent in history) are acts of an unknowing nature that is neither malicious nor benign. Nature, created by God and basically "good," has an order and disorder that stand between us and God. *Phusis*, the Greek word for nature with its inherent order, creeps into the New Testament, chiefly in the letters of Paul; the word does not appear in the Gospels. At the end of the beginning of the third millennium, science has explored the natural order, only partially, but sufficiently to influence any theology of nature.

Yet, biblical insights are as impressive as ever. *Homo sapiens* is one creature among others, created of the dust of the earth but bearing the divine image. Humanity, privileged above all other creatures, is granted the gift and responsibility of a limited dominion. That dominion does not extend to "the Pleiades and Orion" (Amos 5:8; cf. Job 9:9, 38:31) or even to such earthly creatures as Behemoth (Job 40:15) and Leviathan (Isa. 27:1; Pss. 74:14, 104:26; Job 41:1). Extravagant straining for power leads to destructive confusion, as at Babel.

As important as the doctrine of Creation, and more uniquely Christian, is the doctrine of Incarnation. In the famous words of William Temple,

> Christianity is the most avowedly materialistic of all the great religions. . . . Its own most central saying is: "The Word became flesh," where the last term was, no doubt, chosen because of its specifically materialistic association.[26]

Those who believe are bound to esteem human flesh, animal flesh, and the material world.

The biblical creation is not static. God acts in it. People act in it. Lions, wild goats, forest animals, birds, and sea creatures act in it. So do winds, clouds, fire, and springs (Ps. 104). God is capable of doing "a new thing" (Isa. 43:19). Modern theologians have sometimes implied that the biblical God acts in history, not nature. But that will not do. The exodus from Egypt is a conspicuous, certainly not the only, example of the merging of nature and history in divine activity.

The biblical ethic, in its calls for justice, constantly demands a sharing of God's gifts. The sharing extends to the family, the neighbor, the sojourner, the enemy. It extends also to future generations. If much of the New Testament portends an early day of final judgment, the Old Testament sees providence extending to "the thousandth generation" (Deut. 5:9). Christians have tried to appropriate both accents, even when unsure just how to relate them.

All these theological pointers have their meaning for the enigma of nature and the mystery of the self. But they give rise to a major theological controversy of the twentieth century. It began with a celebration of biblical monotheism and its desacralization of nature, its denial of the many nature-spirits of animism and the nature-inhabiting gods of polytheism. Theologians rejoiced that humans, in their divinely given dominion, have the right to appropriate nature for their own ends. It is not by accident, they said, that societies influenced by the Bible have led the world in the triumphs of technology and the bending of nature to the human will. In one of the ironies of cultural history, this paean to secularization came to a peak at just the time when events forced a new ecological consciousness on humankind.

Critics quickly arose to blame religion for the reckless human exploitation of nature. Lynn White, Jr.'s, essay of 1967, "The Historical Roots of Our Ecologic Crisis," won almost instant fame. He argued that Western Christianity, "the most anthropocentric religion the world has seen," destroyed pagan animism and "made it possible to exploit nature in a mood of indifference to the feelings of natural objects." He urged a return to the faith of St. Francis of Assisi. A few years later, Arnold Toynbee, once an avowed advocate of Christianity, blamed monotheism and urged a return to a more ancient pantheism, which he claimed "was once universal."[27]

Both sides in this controversy overstate their case. René Dubos finds convincing evidence to conclude:

> All over the globe and at all times in the past, men have pillaged nature and disturbed the ecological equilibrium, usually out of ignorance, but also because they have also been more concerned with immediate advantage than with long-range goals.[28]

Modern Western society has done so more effectively because it developed greater power to do so.

Before the exultant secularists and their critics, William Temple advocated belief in "the sacramental universe": "The whole universe is the expression of [God's] will."[29] Temple's statement is the more impressive because it is not an ad hoc argument designed for the moment, but a fundamental belief. The "sacramental universe" is in tune with Eastern Orthodox belief. The Ecumenical Patriarch Bartholomeus, of Istanbul, has recently said: "The whole universe is a sacrament. The entire cosmos is a burning bush of God's uncreated energies."[30] In American Protestantism, James Nash advocates the doctrine.[31] I'm not quite persuaded. Teaching Temple's book in 1948–1949, I found my students perplexed by the doctrine. Does it treat too lightly the "nasty" side of nature—its extravagant cruelty and waste? Ralph Waldo Emerson, although he adored nature far more than most people, found himself driven to ask: "Must we not suppose somewhere in the universe a slight treachery and derision?"[32]

Is infectious disease an example of that "treachery"? William H. McNeill's groundbreaking book, *Plagues and People*,[33] gives convincing evidence that infectious diseases have been major determinants of history. We have long known that in historic wars, until recently, sickness killed more soldiers than weapons. McNeill amasses evidence from around the world of the power of plagues in the history of nations and empires. In one example, he shows that smallpox was a decisive force in the European conquest of the Americas. Indeed, some Puritans in North America and some Jesuits in South America said that divine providence had used smallpox to clear the way for the newcomers—a doctrine that does nothing to vindicate God or the theological wisdom of the propounders. The devastation of bacilli and viruses, among human beings and animals, refutes any indiscriminate love of nature.

Yet, our undeniable human kinship with nature is impressive. A recent idea, pleasing to some ecologists and New Age nature devotees, is the Gaia hypothesis. Taking its name from the ancient Greek goddess Earth, it argues that the earth is, or is very like, a living organism, regulating nature, atmosphere, and life to maintain an equilibrium. Ironically, its proposer is James Lovelock, who was part of NASA, which is often seen as an example of the human desire to master nature. Although an intriguing alternative to the concept of nature as a blind mechanism or a collection of commodities for human exploitation, it has trouble with the five great extinctions and the history of plagues. Also, it relieves human beings of responsibility, since Gaia will correct our ecological recklessness.[34]

Before the popularity of ecology, Paul Tillich, with his roots in German romanticism, objected to human "intellectual arrogance" and "a domineering attitude toward nature." But he guarded against soft idealization of nature. "Nature is not only glorious; it is also tragic. It is subject to the laws of finitude and destruction. It is suffering and sighing with us." In the sacraments, he found nature participating "in the process of salvation."[35] I wish he had given more attention to plagues and other instances where, if I am right, we have an opportunity and responsibility to do what we can to resist—and fight—hostile forces of nature.

So, I return to my theme of the enigma of nature. I must now speak more directly to the issue of human actions within and upon the processes of nature.

Human Responsibility

Within the mystery and majesty of the whole creation, Christian faith finds a modest human dominion and a responsibility to "till" and "keep" a God-given Eden (Gen. 1:26, 2:15). Human creatures have finite but expanding powers to act upon the given nature. Some uses of that power are a joyful and reverent appreciation of divine gifts. Others are a defiance and blasphemy. How can we distinguish the difference? Two examples of the question have leapt into recent prominence: ecology and genetics.

Ecology

All living species affect their environments, sometimes in symbiosis, sometimes in destructive competition. Bees, gathering food for themselves, pollinate plants to the benefit of humankind and many other living species. Gypsy moths, also seeking food, devastate trees, with no evident advantage to anybody except gypsy moths. Other species, from the tiniest bacteria to the great whales and elephants, act upon their environments without foreseeing consequences. Inanimate processes of nature—balmy breezes and tornadoes, gentle rains and raging floods, earthquakes, volcanoes, meteorites—also affect their surroundings. The human difference is that we do so purposefully as well as unintentionally, often radically and recklessly.

Then come times of accounting. Nature strikes back. Cutting of forests leads to floods. Abuse of the soil exhausts its fertility. Pollution brings disease and death, both locally and terrestrially (as in the "hole" in the layer of protective ozone high above us). Thus, self-interest may bring an awakening of ecological consciousness. Concern for posterity—a more generous but still anthropocentric motive—may do the same.

But more than enlightened self-interest is involved. Something of primal awe before nature persists even in industrialized, high-tech society. The past destruction of the passenger pigeons and the threatened destruction of the spotted owl strike a wide public as wrong. Popular support for the Endangered Species Act has surprised politicians and industrialists. Glimmers of that sensitivity extend even to inanimate nature. The littering of Antarctica and the cluttering of "space" with debris seem somehow wrong to many people who cannot quite say why. To Christian faith they are offenses against God's creation.

This ecological sensitivity is profound, but it raises disturbing questions. Violence and destruction are frequent in nature. The prophetic vision of vegetarian lions and of wolves and lambs feeding peaceably together (Isa. 65:25) is an eschatological vision, not a legislative program. William Blake in "Songs of Innocence" marveled that God had made the little lamb; five years later in "Songs of Experience" he marveled equally at the tiger and asked, "Did he who made the Lamb make thee?"[36]

A syndicated newspaper feature, entitled "Earthweek: A Diary of a Planet," reports each week on earthquakes, volcanic eruptions, tornadoes, droughts and floods, killing hailstorms, epidemics, and (periodically) havoc wrought by El Niño. It never runs short of material. Some of the catastrophes are, at least in part, consequences of human activity. Most are not. Even the sturdiest faith has trouble seeing all these acts as sacraments.

Nature in its heedless destruction annihilates not only individuals but also species. As Tennyson put it,

> . . . She [Nature] cries, "A thousand types are gone:
> I care for nothing, all shall go."[37]

Scientists tell us that, in the great terrestrial catastrophes of the past, something like 80–95 percent of species were destroyed, and that the recovery times ranged from ten to a hundred million years. Throughout earthly history, E. O. Wilson estimates: "Ninety-nine percent of all the species that ever lived are now extinct."[38] Other estimates run as high as 99.999 percent.

Why then should we worry if contemporary society destroys a mere 5 percent? But Wilson warns us: "The sixth great extinction spasm of geological time is upon us," differing from all the others because it comes "grace of mankind."[39] He makes a convincing case for the interrelatedness of many forms of life, for the dependence of human life on insects and microorganisms, for the unintended destruction of species by the careless elimination of their habitats.

I share Wilson's horror at the prospect he describes. I am not quite persuaded by his conclusion: "We should not knowingly allow any species or race to go extinct."[40] I think I would not mourn the extinction of mosquitoes, especially if I lived in a malarial zone, although Wilson can show me that they have an ecological value that I don't see. May I not rejoice in the virtual termination of the smallpox virus? At the moment, samples are preserved in carefully guarded laboratories, and the scheduled date for their extermination has been repeatedly deferred. But they are kept for their possible value in future experimentation—a thoroughly anthropocentric motive.

Acknowledging the very great benefit of bacteria to human life, I could easily do without some: those for tuberculosis, cholera, syphilis, typhoid fever, and tetanus. So far as I can imagine, I would not miss the loss of viruses for measles, mumps, yellow fever, polio, influenza, Ebola, and HIV.

A disembodied spectator might admire the ability of these life forms to mutate and find friendly niches. Influenza and tuberculosis—super-tuberculosis is the new term—despite some human victories over them, return in new forms that baffle us. As a participant in the biosphere, not a spectator, I make my fallible but stubborn judgments: They are enemies.

James Nash, who affirms "the intrinsic value of all God-created being," nevertheless accords a primacy to the human. So he qualifies his love of nature: "[E]ven the deliberate eradication of particular species can be justified to provide vital protection for human health."[41] As examples he proposes the guinea worm and some bacteria and viruses. I agree.

May human beings rightly intervene in natural processes? Yes, we do so inevitably, simply by our existence, also by deliberate purpose. That recognition need not mute the protest against the wanton, arrogant, destructive exploitation of nature so characteristic of our civilization. The evidence mounts that these acts are, in their consequences, disastrous to human values. To Christians they are also irreverent.

Genetics[42]

Of all interventions in natural processes, medical interventions reach most intimately into selfhood. They modify not only our environment but also ourselves. They are very, very old in the human story. Historic medical treatment is partly superstition and pseudoscience. It is partly a folk wisdom that modernity disdains, then sometimes learns to appreciate. Of all medical interventions, genetic manipulation reaches most deeply into human nature. It is not like healing a broken limb or curing an infection. It goes beyond the transplants of kidneys, livers, and hearts. It seeks to change the primal substance of the self—possibly even of persons through all coming generations. People greet it with both eagerness and fear.

Already, genetic interventions are producing effective drugs. Genetic testing guides men and women in decisions about parenthood. Humanity is beginning experimental therapies by genetic treatment of somatic cells to remedy inherited weaknesses or diseases. More radical are the prospects of cloning and of genetic alteration of the germ cells, initially to remove the onslaughts of diseases for generations to come, then possibly to redirect the very structure of human nature.

Ours is the first generation to face the new decisions demanded by the discoveries of DNA and its manipulation. No scriptures of any religion, no writings of ethical philosophers, no laws or constitutions of past governments have ever declared: "You shall, or shall not, mess around with DNA." Not long ago, Nobel laureates in biology Herman Muller and Jacques Monod declared the rearrangement of DNA to be impossible, because no surgery could slice up such minute particles. Then other scientists discovered that "chemical scissors" could do what no scalpels could do. The impossible became a reality.

The ethical challenges are stupendous. Given the history of eugenics, with its futile, prejudiced, often laughable, and often vicious efforts to "improve" human heredity, we had better be wary of new efforts that may be more efficient.

Yet, we do not want to foreclose contributions to human health. Christianity has a long tradition, stemming from the Gospels and extending through history, of concern for healing. And Christian faith, even though it never anticipated recent discoveries in genetics, brings some old convictions to the issues.

Again, we confront the enigma of nature. Christian faith, with its basic belief in the goodness of creation, has reason to favor those therapies that cooperate with nature. When diet and exercise prevent heart attacks, they are preferable to heart surgery. But recognition of the destructiveness of nature sometimes calls for efforts to fight natural processes. There are times to make the most strenuous effort to modify nature.

A Christian ethic might identify four big issues in genetic experimentation. The first is risk. Every day people make risk-benefit calculations. The benefits of driving a car may justify the inevitable risks—although not the risks of reckless driving. The benefits of medicine may justify risks of experimentation, but with some special warnings. Hybridizers reckon that the success of one new plant justifies the failure of hundreds that go on the compost pile. But we cannot say that about experiments on human beings. Geneticists sometimes question tampering with the evolutionary wisdom of millennia, and Christians wonder about intervening in the created order, especially if the intervention affects future generations who have no way of giving consent to risks. So, Christian faith qualifies its prejudice in favor of healing with warnings about risk. But, knowing that once risky medical procedures sometimes become routine—think of heart surgery—it will not rush to dogmatic prohibitions.

A second issue is the purposes of genetic interventions. Often our definitions of health and illness, of normality and abnormality, are social constructions. A dark skin is, in many societies, a social and economic liability. That does not commend genetic treatment to lighten skin color. What needs healing is the social prejudice, not the skin color. Past eugenic practices have often defined good and bad inheritance in ways that are now seen to be vicious and ridiculous. We had better ask whether present definitions are really better.

A third issue is justice. Who will get the benefits of new treatments? Only the wealthy? Only the residents of rich, high-tech societies? There is plenty of evidence that resources put into public health, including such elementary benefits as safe water and air, save more lives than the same resources put into costly, exotic treatments. That does not call for an end to all costly research. Sometimes work on experimental frontiers comes to benefit all humankind. Think again of the abolition of smallpox. But a theological ethic will ask of all medical practice: Whom does it benefit? What does justice require?

A fourth issue is the coming to terms with human finitude, with our essential creatureliness. It is not our privilege to overcome every obstacle, to conquer every foe. The can-do spirit is great—some of the time. It betrays us if it leads to the illusion that every problem has an answer, that the power of science can show us the meaning of life, that hope is a commodity that can be manufactured and marketed. No human conquest delivers a final answer to the mystery of the self and the enigma of nature.

Life is a precious gift. We do well to guard its health. But our lives on this planet are temporary. There are times to resist death. But eventually, for everyone, fighting death is less important than knowing how to die. All these issues call for a venturing ethic. They call for attention by a great variety of people—scientists, artists, theologians, workers and the unemployed, the young and the old. The church may need to go slowly in sweeping pronouncements. That takes some self-control, especially among Christians who know that the church has often been too cautious in opposing crimes of racism and oppression. Excessive caution may be cowardice. It may mean that the speed of technological forces decides major issues before ethical concerns are raised. So the churches should be insistent and impatient in questioning, but not too arrogant in judging. And they should realize that there are situations for an ethic of nuance, just as there are situations for prompt, decisive action.

A Final Word?

Do I have a final word on the mystery of the self and the enigma of nature? No. But for a helpful word I turn to Margaret Mead. The most famous anthropologist of her time, she had a professional interest in the religions of many cultures. Now and then she spoke out of her own faith.

> Was it possible that modern man might forget his relation-ship with the rest of the natural world to such a degree that he separated himself from his own pulse-beat, wrote poetry only in tune with machines, and was irrevocably cut off from his own heart? In their new-found preoccupation with power over the natural world, might men so forget God that they would build a barrier against the wisdom of the past that no one could penetrate?[43]

To those questions, I add the more explicitly theological declara-tion of H. Richard Niebuhr. Writing before the vogue of ecology, he spoke to its issues powerfully. In his "radical monotheism," he con-fessed that God alone is holy. His "Puritan iconoclasm" secularized all places and things, but then turned into a countermovement of the "sanctification of all things."

> Now every day is the day that the Lord has made; every na-tion is a holy people called by him into existence in its place and time and to his glory; every person is sacred, made in his image and likeness; every living thing, on earth, in the heav-ens, and in the waters is his creation and points in its exis-tence toward him; the whole earth is filled with his glory; the infinity of space is his temple where all creation is sum-moned to silence before him.[44]

To that, almost to my regret, I have to add some warning about the hostility of enigmatic nature. But what Richard Niebuhr said is more important than what I add.

Ours is a time for an exploratory ethic, even as it is a time of emer-gency that requires decisive action. I have tried to suggest some pointers toward ways of believing, acting, rejoicing, grieving, and praying—all with awareness of the mystery of the self and the enigma of nature.

NOTES

1. Jacques Monod, *Chance and Necessity* (New York: Vintage Books, 1972; original French edition, 1970).
2. Nicholas Wade, "The Birth of a Notion," *New York Times Book Review* (September 7, 1997), p. 30.
3. William Wordsworth, "Ode: Intimations of Immortality from Recollections of Early Childhood," 1897, Stanza 5 (many editions).
4. Henry Margenau, in *Cosmos, Bios, Theos,* ed. Henry Margenau and Roy Abraham Varghese (LaSalle, Ill.: Open Court, 1992), p. 61. Freeman Dyson, *Disturbing the Universe* (New York: Harper & Row, 1979), p. 250.
5. W. R. Inge, *Outspoken Essays,* 2d ser. (London: Longmans Green, 1932; first published in 1920), p. 166.
6. E. O. Wilson, *The Diversity of Life* (New York: W. W. Norton, 1993), pp. 29ff.
7. Freeman Dyson, "The Scientist as Rebel," *New York Times Book Review* (May 25, 1998), p. 31.
8. Blaise Pascal, *Pensées* (New York: Dutton, Everyman's Library, 1908), fragments 206, 348, 82.
9. "Jedenfalls bin ich 'berzeugt, dass der Alte nich w' rfelt,'" *Briefwechsell,* ed. Albert Einstein, Hedwig Born, and Max Born (Munich: Nymphenburger Verlagshandlung, 1969), pp. 129–130.
10. Aristotle, *Politics,* Book 1, 1256b, 2021 (many editions). Isaac Newton, *Opticks,* based on the 4th ed., London, 1730 (New York: Dover, 1952), Book 3, Part 1, question 28, p. 369.
11. Charles Darwin, "Recapitulation and Conclusion," in *The Origin of Species,* 1859 ed. (London: Penguin Books, 1985), pp. 459–460.
12. Darwin, Letter to J. D. Hooker, July 13, 1856, in *The Correspondence of Charles Darwin* (Cambridge: Cambridge University Press, 1990), 6: 178.
13. Richard Dawkins, *The Blind Watchmaker* (New York: W. W. Norton, 1986), p. 5.
14. John Donne, "Paradoxes," VIII, *The Complete Poetry and Selected Prose of John Donne* (New York: Modern Library, 1952), p. 285.
15. William Wordsworth, "Lines Composed a Few Miles above Tintern Abbey," lines 108–111.
16. Alfred, Lord Tennyson, "In Memoriam," LVI.
17. Thomas H. Huxley, *Evolution and Ethics, and Other Essays* (New York: Appleton, 1903), pp. 81–83.
18. Robert S. Morison, "Darwinism: Foundation for an Ethical System?" *Christianity and Crisis* 20 (August 8, 1960), p. 122.
19. William Herbert Carruth, "Each in His Own Tongue," 1908 (in several old anthologies).
20. Algernon Charles Swinburne, "Hymn of Man," 1871 (many editions).
21. William Schwenck Gilbert, *Princess Ida,* 1884, Act 2 (many editions).
22. "Missionary Hymn," 1819 (in several old hymnals).
23. Francis Bacon, "Of Heresies," 1597. "Of Gardens," 1625. *Novum Organum,* Book I, aphorism 129. All three sayings are preserved in various translations from the Latin and in various editions.
24. George Santayana, *The Life of Reason* (New York: Charles Scribner's Sons, 1905), p. 191.

25. Isaiah 45:7. I am using the King James Version. The RSV and NRSV soften the saying: "I make weal and create woe." In going back to the KJV, I am not expressing a personal preference; I am following eminent Hebraists.

26. William Temple, *Nature, Man, and God* (London: Macmillan, 1949), p. 478.

27. Lynn White, Jr., "The Historical Roots of Our Ecologic Crisis," *Science* 155 (March 10, 1967), pp. 1203–1207 (reprinted in many anthologies). Arnold Toynbee, "The Religious Background of the Present Environmental Crisis," first published in 1972; reprinted in *Ecology and Religion in History,* ed. David and Eileen Spring (New York: Harper & Row, 1974), pp. 137–149.

28. René Dubos, *A God Within* (New York: Charles Scribner's Sons, 1972), p. 161.

29. William Temple, "The Sacramental Universe," in *Nature, Man, and God,* p. 479.

30. Reported in *The Christian Century,* December 3, 1997, pp. 118–119.

31. James Nash, *Loving Nature: Ecological Integrity and Christian Responsibility* (Nashville: Abingdon Press in cooperation with the Churches' Center for Theology and Public Policy, 1991), pp. 112–116.

32. Ralph Waldo Emerson, "Nature," *Essays,* 2d ser., 1844 (many editions).

33. New York: Doubleday, 1977.

34. James Lovelock, *Gaia: A New Look at Life on Earth* (New York: Oxford University Press, 1979; reprinted with a new preface, 1988). Chapter 7, "Gaia and Man: The Problem of Pollution," is the chapter most criticized by ecologists.

35. "Nature Also Mourns for a Lost Good," a sermon in *The Shaking of the Foundations* (New York: Charles Scribner's Sons, 1948). The citations are from pp. 82, 81, 86.

36. William Blake, "The Lamb," 1789; "The Tyger," 1794 (many editions).

37. Alfred, Lord Tennyson, "In Memoriam," LVI (many editions).

38. Wilson, *The Diversity of Life,* p. 344.

39. Ibid., p. 343.

40. Ibid., p. 351.

41. Nash, *Loving Nature,* pp. 173, 189.

42. This very brief discussion of the ethics of genetics relies on my longer treatments in *The New Genetics: Challenges for Science, Faith, and Politics* (Wakefield, R.I.: Moyer Bell, 1996) and in *Human Cloning: Religious Responses,* ed. Ronald Cole-Turner (Cleveland: Pilgrim Press, 1997).

43. Margaret Mead, *Male and Female: A Study of the Sexes in a Changing World* (New York: New American Library, 1955; first published in 1949), p. 19.

44. H. Richard Niebuhr, *Radical Monotheism and Western Culture* (New York: Harper & Brothers, 1960), pp. 52–53.

This chapter was originally published in *Christianity in the 21st Century,* ed. Deborah A. Brown (New York: Crossroad Publishers, 2000), pp. 96–120.

CHAPTER 21

Thomas Aquinas and the New Cosmology: Faith Encounters Science Anew

ADRIAN M. HOFSTETTER, O.P.

Dr. Hofstetter is a Dominican sister and an environmental scientist who gives workshops on Thomas Aquinas and the new cosmology. She is a fellow of the Tennessee Academy of Sciences. She is presently working on a book, *Non-Duality in Science and Religion.*

Why ask Thomas Aquinas for enlightenment about the new cosmology, a subject already controversial among religious women? His misunderstanding of women has caused many feminists to reject him altogether as an authority figure. Yet St. Thomas's great achievement in integrating faith with the most advanced science of his day (despite its pagan source) into a numinous medieval world view is a challenge for any Christian struggling to accept a current cosmology based on modern science.

Few question that the growth and development of modern science and technology have contributed to the global crisis in ecology, sociology, education, economics, religion, and in culture in general that now threatens Western civilization and the entire planet. The intent of this chapter is to bring the enduring work on creation of Thomas Aquinas to bear on some of the troubling aspects of a cosmology based on modern science and to consider the way his science of nature could enrich the creation story as a developing myth to move us to a sustainable future.

Before turning to St. Thomas for help in critiquing the emerging scientific story of the cosmos, I want to acknowledge the positive effect that the new cosmology or universe story has had on religious women. Since awakening to the tragic exploitation of our imperiled earth home, we religious women have made notable responses. Ecology learning centers, wilderness and sacred earth retreats, equinox and solstice celebrations, horticulture and permaculture courses, organic and biodynamic gardens, community-supported agriculture, sustainable farming projects, and land trusts are among the many efforts toward sustainability now found on the properties of religious communities. These are not only hopeful signs of the changes that religious women are making in personal life style, they herald a revolution in consciousness desperately needed if the Western industrialized world is to be diverted from its suicidal course.

Problems with the New Cosmology

Elsewhere I have discussed problems with the new cosmology that have caused divisions among women religious.[1] Of concern to many is the place of God, of a Creator in the scientific account of the origin of the cosmos. To understand this problem we need to consider the mechanical philosophy that has developed over the last few centuries as a legacy from Isaac Newton and René Descartes. Their world as machine stripped the cosmos of life, mind, and consciousness. Their earth, no longer a living organism, became a drab, dead world without color, taste, feeling, beauty, sensibility, or meaning. The scientific method became the road to knowledge with mathematics as its language.

In such a world in which the origin of the cosmos is explained by a few observations, bolstered by an array of assumptions based on mathematical equations, the need for a Creator is questionable. For Stephen Hawking God is needed only to "wind up the clockwork" of this mechanical cosmos "and choose how to start it off."[2] Hawking even thinks he knows "the equations that govern human behavior."[3] With other equations he thinks can provide "understanding of how the big bang created everything in the universe."[4]

Medieval World View

St. Thomas lived in a different world, the thirteenth century, an age of faith, an age in which humans and nature were in close relationship with one another. His profoundly incarnational philosophy and theology[5] reflected an enchanted world, a cosmos in which human beings were at home on a sacred earth provided by a loving Creator. In this world Aquinas taught that theology and science cannot contradict one another. In fact he insisted that you cannot do theology without science. But his Creator God was not dependent on the findings of natural science. To understand the timeless contribution of St. Thomas to the creation of the cosmos, we need some grasp of the difference between his intellectual background and that of cosmologists today.

The liberal arts were foundational to the medieval university. Students and faculty engaged in disciplined debate and rational discourse in their quest to comprehend all of reality. Much controversy at that time surrounded the introduction of the pagan science of Aristotle, which had found its way from Arabic sources into the European university. It was in such a climate, especially at the University of Paris, that Thomas Aquinas could develop his celebrated work on creation.

For St. Thomas the science of nature or philosophy of nature (terms he used interchangeably) is a science distinct from metaphysics and theology. From Greek science he accepted the fact that every change in the physical world requires a preexisting cause, that something in the material world cannot come from nothing. But for Aquinas the fact that God created the world out of nothing was not an act dependent on a physical change. It was not a change from one state of matter to another. We may have physical evidence to date the time the cosmos came to be but not for what caused its creation. Physics alone cannot tell us how matter and energy came to be in the first place. God's act of creating was a metaphysical act, a radical act of bringing the whole cosmos into being and sustaining it in being. The natural sciences can account for change from one material state to another, but not for creation itself. No doubt St. Thomas would accept the big bang cosmology insofar as it explains the time of the origin of the cosmos. But this in no way denies the need for a Creator to bring the cosmos into being from nothing.[6]

So when mathematical physicist Paul Davies concludes that "it is now possible to conceive of a scientific explanation for all of creation,"[7] he is just explaining how matter and physical forces account for changes in the content and course of the cosmos. He does not explain what brought matter and physical forces into being. There would be no cosmos for the modern scientist to contemplate if God had not first given it being. Even Stephen Hawking admits that after finding the one possible unified theory, "just a set of rules and equations," there still remains the question: "What is it that breathes fire into the equations and makes a universe for them to describe?[8]

Neglect of Philosophical Education Today

By comparison to the rich philosophical education in medieval times, today the philosophy of nature, theology, and metaphysics are neglected in the impoverished educational system of the United States.

Our scientists have little or no philosophical or theological background. The reductive scientific method has infiltrated the whole curriculum and causes much of the stupefying education most of us received. It also accounts for the confused myopic thinking and writing among cosmologists. This glaring deficit and neglect in the education of American scientists is responsible for their inability to distinguish the origin of the cosmos from its creation. It is regrettable that there is no reference to any of these disciplines, including the wisdom traditions, in the index of the current popular account of the cosmos, *The Universe Story*.[9]

Cut off from Greek and medieval foundational science, our mechanistic world view, so devoid of life and purpose, leaves us with a physicist like Nobel laureate Steven Weinberg concluding: "The more the universe seems comprehensible, the more it also seems pointless."[10] Philosopher Daniel Dennett finds that "evolution is a mindless, purposeless, algorithmic process."[11] This skepticism and denial of an intelligible world of meaning opens the way for such farfetched cosmological speculation as described by a senior science writer at *Scientific American*.

Much of modern cosmology, particularly those aspects inspired by unified theories of particle physics and other esoteric ideas, is preposterous. Or rather, it is ironic science, science that is not experimentally testable or resolvable even in principle and therefore is not science in the strict sense at all; its primary function is to keep us awestruck before the mystery of the cosmos.[12]

Recovery Needed

The search for wisdom about ultimate realities or metaphysics was a preeminent science for the Greeks and for Aquinas. The appreciation of and recovery of their legacy to the Western world can reroot our thinking in the fertile soil from which modern science arose. Metaphysics is a fundamental science, which "lays the foundation for all the other sciences"[13] and is needed to distinguish the philosophy of nature from mathematics and metaphysics itself.

St. Thomas's science of nature, found in his *Commentaries on the Physics of Aristotle*, offers "a universal scientific knowledge about nature."[14] Its universality is indicated by Robert Hutchins, former president of the University of Chicago: "The Physics of Aristotle, which deals with change and motion in nature, is fundamental to the natural sciences . . . and is equally important to all those who confront change and motion in nature, that is to everybody."[15] In order to recover the nature we have lost through the controlled experimentation and measurements of modern science, we need its reinterpretation within the pre-mathematical and preexperimental science of nature of Aristotle. Only thus can we rediscover a scientific world of common sense, one again intelligible to the human community.

Women scientists offer strong opposition to the "distortion of nature" that results from the metaphysical view of it as a machine.[16] Ruth Hubbard, professor of biology emerita at Harvard, claims there is "selective rendering of nature" by the male-dominated priesthood of scientists. She warns that "As long as the overwhelming majority of scientists are men who are rooted in the ruling class, socially or intellectually (or both) science will supply the 'objective' supports and technical innovations needed to sustain patriarchal, ruling class power."[17]

Elisabet Sahtouris, in her book *Gaia: The Human Journey from Chaos to Cosmos*, also exposes the contradictions evident in the male-dominated mechanical world view of modern science.[18] She claims that seeing Gaia as a mechanism "raises the question of purpose. But purpose is a taboo in scientific descriptions of nature, because God, which Renaissance scientists saw as the Grand Engineer of natural mechanism, is no longer part of scientific explanation. Scientists thus argue a logical contradiction, that nature is mechanical but has no creator and no purpose."[19] She recalls writing shortly after finishing graduate school: "I sometimes think I was awarded a Ph.D. for successfully denying my humanity—behaving mechanically, dissecting nature without feeling or emotion."[20]

Hopes for the Future

A different approach to science is realized in the research of a brilliant woman scientist, Barbara McClintock, Nobel laureate who died in 1992. She integrated the best of modern science with a common sense, relational approach to the world of nature but paid a heavy price among her male colleagues. Their cultural myopia resulted from their inability to understand the subtlety of her deeply perceptive research in corn cytogenetics. Her intimate relationship with the corn plants was evident in her patient looking and hearing "what the material has to say" and letting "it come to" her. Her "feeling for the organism" bolstered this daring challenge to the ruling dogmas of a mechanistic science. Courageously and creatively she chose a natural, common sense, indeed mystical, methodology, which as I have tried elsewhere to demonstrate is our legacy from Aristotle and Aquinas.[21]

Another hope for the recovery of the heritage left us by Greek and medieval science is the 1992 republication of Pitirim Sorokin's classic book, *The Crisis of Our Age*. Sorokin challenges the twentieth century's "veritable blackout in human culture" due to an "outmoded unilateral conception of truth."[22] His remedy is the "re-establishment of an integral and more adequate system of truth and values." He finds this in the great integral cultures of the fifth-century Greece of Plato and Aristotle and in the thirteenth century of Thomas Aquinas and Albert the Great. These eras provided the West with "supreme examples, of embracing in one organic whole divine as well as sensory and dialectic truth."[23] By comparison to Aquinas and other great scholastics, Sorokin characterizes the twentieth century as a time of midget philosophers.[24] Richard Tarnas is another critic of "the philosophy that has dominated our century and our universities," which "resembles nothing so much as a severe obsessive-compulsive sitting on his bed repeatedly tying and untying his shoes because he never quite gets it right—while in the meantime Socrates, Hegel and Aquinas are already high up on their mountain hike, breathing the bracing alpine air, seeing new and unexpected vistas."[25]

Hopes for the future can also be found among the holistic and naturalistic scientists who contributed to the 1996 publication, *New Metaphysical Foundations of Modern Science*.[26] Among them, Arthur Zajonc, a physicist at Amherst College, proposes a metaphysics for the twenty-first century in the neglected works of the poet-scientist Johann Wolfgang von Goethe, who lived almost two hundred years ago, and his able interpreter, the philosopher-scientist Rudolph Steiner, who died in 1925. The philosophy of both of these scientists, like that of Thomas Aquinas, is derived from an intimate communion with nature.

Goethe and Steiner insisted on a new way of seeing. They saw nature in a romantic, holistic way and "the workings of the divine within nature."[27] "Lively engagement with a phenomenon is essential for its understanding because, in Goethe's view, we are changed in the process; we develop faculties adequate to comprehending what is before us."[28] Steiner claims that "because one spirit works both in nature and in man's inner life, man can lift himself to participate in the production of nature."[29] Goethe himself wrote "My own pure, deep, innate and schooled view of things had taught me without fail to see God in Nature, Nature in God and his view was the foundation of my very existence."[30]

Steiner envisions a kinship of his own and Goethe's philosophy of science with that of Aquinas. "In the world outlook of Goethe is to be found what Thomism must become if it is to rise to the highest possibilities of the present time and play a real part in the evolution of (hu)mankind."[31] In the same lecture on St. Thomas in his book, *The Redemption of Thinking,* Steiner sees his own natural science as a revival of Thomism. He insisted that "Modern philosophy must return to Thomas Aquinas and he must be studied—possibly with a few critical explanations—just as he wrote in the thirteenth century."[32]

A Search for an Enriched Cosmology

St. Thomas, like Goethe six hundred years later and Steiner seven hundred years later, would have refused to accept a cosmology based solely on a mechanical and mathematical way of perceiving the cosmos. Whether the cosmos is best understood or interpreted as an organism or as a machine is a metaphysical question. It must be addressed by those who contend that the earth is a living organism while at the same time accepting the thesis that the cosmos can be understood by a mechanistic science explained by mathematical equations alone.

This contradiction presents a challenge to women religious to complement their efforts to manifest and celebrate the wonders of mother earth and all its interdependent inhabitants with a consistent philosophy of nature. Both Goethe and Steiner offer such a philosophy and as contemplative scientists, perhaps mystics, they contribute to a deeply spiritual-oriented cosmology. Barbara McClintock, looking to the East for correctives for the limitations of modern science, claimed to be a "mystic" herself. Certainly St. Thomas, a mystic and a saint, left us a valid philosophy of nature within a framework of faith: "A mistake in our thinking about Nature results in a mistake in our thinking about God." And again, "The opinion is false of those who assert that it makes no difference to the truth of the faith what anyone holds about creatures, so long as one thinks rightly about God. For error about creatures spills over into false opinion about God, and takes people's minds away from God, to whom faith seeks to lead them."[33]

Could the legacy of Thomas Aquinas prepare the way to reconsider the cosmic genesis of Teilhard de Chardin for an enriched twenty-first-century cosmology?[34] Such is proposed by Richard Tarnas, who builds on the cosmic vision of Teilhard as well as that of Jung and Hegel in claiming that the Western mind in its renewed appreciation of mother earth is undergoing an initiatory process into a new paradigm. This transformative initiation, he envisions, is in process within the Judeo-Christian context of personal sin (the shadowside of humans) and the shadow that humans have cast on the earth in the twentieth century producing the "blackout in human culture" to which Sorokin refers. Tarnas sees the momentous feminist revolution as fundamental and crucial to our turning from a path toward extinction to a twenty-first-century vision of humans and other species as part of a cosmos becoming conscious of itself and of a future sustainable world.[35]

Does this vision of a new paradigm for the cosmos fulfill Sorokin's prophetic hopes for the renewal of an integral culture for the West, one built on the legacy of Greek and medieval world views, one that includes the best of the moral, intellectual, and spiritual life of mind and heart? And is the pivotal work of women religious contributing to the ongoing earth and human transformative process at last moving us toward a new creation reminiscent of St. Paul, "the whole created earth groans in all its parts as if in the pangs of childbirth"?[36]

NOTES

1. Adrian M. Hofstetter, O.P., "New or Traditional Earth Spirituality" in *Sisters Today* 69 (Jan. 1997), pp. 15–20.
2. Stephen Hawking, *A Brief History of Time* (New York: Bantam Books, 1988), p. 140.
3. Stephen Hawking, *Black Holes and Baby Universes* (New York: Bantam Books, 1993), p. 144.
4. Ibid., 111.
5. Thomas O'Meara, O.P., *Thomas Aquinas Theologian* (Notre Dame, IN: Notre Dame University Press, 1997), p. 202.
6. William E. Carroll, "Aquinas and the Big Bang" (Iowa: Internet, 1998) http://www.cornell-iowa.edu//science_religion/list.htm.
7. Paul Davies, *God and the New Physics* (New York: Simon & Schuster, 1983), p. viii.
8. Hawking (1988), p. 174.
9. Brian Swimme and Thomas Berry (San Francisco: Harper, 1992).
10. Steven Weinberg, *The First Three Minutes* (New York: Basic Books, 1988), p. 154.
11. Daniel D. Dennett, *Darwin's Dangerous Ideas* (New York: Simon & Schuster, 1995), p. 320.
12. John Horgan, "The End of Cosmology," in *The End of Science* (New York: Broadway Books, 1995), p. 94.
13. *A Synopicon of the Great Books of the Western World*, ed. Robert M. Hutchins (Chicago: Encyclopedia Britannica, 1952), p. 159.
14. Vincent Smith, *The General Science of Nature* (Milwaukee: Bruce Publishing Co., 1958), p. 3.
15. *The Higher Learning in America* (New Haven: Yale University Press, 1986), p. 81.
16. Ruth Hubbard, *The Politics of Women's Biology* (New Brunswick: Rutgers University Press, 1990), p. 15.

17. Hubbard, 18.
18. (New York: Pocket Books, 1989), p. 20.
19. Ibid., 73.
20. Elisabet Sahtouris and Willis W. Harman, *Biology Revisioned* (Berkeley, CA: North Atlantic Books, 1996), p. 20.
21. Adrian M. Hofstetter, "The New Biology: Barbara McClintock and an Emerging Holistic Science," *Teilhard Studies* no. 26 (spring 1992).
22. (New York: One World, 1992), p. 107.
23. Pitirim Sorokin, *The Crisis of Our Age* (New York: One World, 1992), p. 22.
24. Sorokin, p. 216.
25. Richard Tarnas, *The Passion of the Western Mind* (New York: Ballantine Books, 1991), p. 421.
26. Willis Harman with Jane Clark (Sausalito, CA: Institute of Noetic Science, 1994).
27. Jeremy Naydler, *Goethe on Science* (Edinburgh: Floris Books, 1996), p. 48.
28. Arthur Zajonc, "New Wine in What Kind of Wineskins? Metaphysics for the Twenty-First Century," in *New Metaphysical Foundations of Modern Science* (note 26), p. 335.
29. Rudolph Steiner, *Goethe's World View* (New York: Mercury Press, 1985), p. 59.
30. Naydler, 110.
31. Rudolph Steiner, *The Redemption of Thinking: A Study in the Philosophy of Thomas Aquinas* (New York: Anthroposophic Press, 1983), p. 102.
32. Ibid., 113.
33. In Matthew Fox, "Thomas Aquinas, Mystic and Prophet of the Environment," *Creation Spirituality* (July/August 1992), p. 33.
34. Arthur Fabel, "Teilhard 2000: The Vision of a Cosmic Genesis," *Teilhard Studies* no. 36 (spring 1998).
35. Richard Tarnas, "The Great Initiation," *Noetic Sciences Review* no. 47, 25th Anniversary (1998), p. 25ff.
36. St. Paul, Romans 8:22.

This chapter was originally published in *Sisters Today* vol. 71, no. 4 (July 1999), pp. 258–266.

CHAPTER 22

Reformation Sunday, Sermon: Matthew 23:1–12

DAVID E. MEHL

The Reverend Mehl has served Hope United Church of Christ in St. Louis, MO, since 1994. He earned a B.A. at Macalester College, St. Paul, MN, and a M.Div. at Andover Newton Theological School, Newton, MA. He is currently enrolled in the doctor of ministry program at Eden Theological Seminary in St. Louis.

Published in a volume entitled *New Hampshire* in 1923, Robert Frost's poem, "Stopping By Woods on a Snowy Evening," serves as a metaphor for this Reformation Sunday message:

Whose woods these are I think I know.
His house is in the village, though;
He will not see me stopping here
To watch his woods fill up with snow.

My little horse must think it queer
To stop without a farmhouse near
Between the woods and frozen lake
The darkest evening of the year.

He gives his harness bells a shake
To ask if there is some mistake.
The only other sound's the sweep
Of easy wind and downy flake.

The woods are lovely, dark and deep,
But I have promises to keep,
And miles to go before I sleep,
And miles to go before I sleep.

It used to be that on Reformation Sunday Protestants would mark the day with rousing hymns, stirring, often self-righteous sermons, and plenty of patronage to Martin Luther—his courage in the face of Roman Catholic dogmatism and his ninety-five theses hammered to the door of the Schlosskirche in Wittenberg, Germany, on October 31, 1517.

Reformation Sunday over the years became the annual pump-up-the-Protestants day, a line in the sand between Rome and the Reforming Spirit. We were, of course, right, and they were wrong. Reformation Sunday was in part a festival of hubris, a prideful parade of Protestant self-congratulation. With ecumenism at full throttle today, such tribal assemblies seem anachronistic. Evangelical Lutherans and Roman Catholics in our town will gather at the New Cathedral next Sunday to worship together and to sign a covenant of new cooperation, a mutual affirmation of the historic justification by faith. Imagine Lutheran and Catholic bishops side by side in the grand, Romanesque structure on Lindell Boulevard. We've come a long, long way. In increasing quadrants of churchly life, Christians are dialoguing across old, hostile lines, shedding former divisions like so many autumn leaves, sensing there is much more we can do together at the end of the millennium than we could ever accomplish apart.

So what's to say on Reformation Sunday anymore?

There is a new reformation about which to speak this October 31, an exciting dialogue 482 years after the hammering of parchment to the cathedral doors in Wittenberg. This reformation is a deeply religious shift, an important, growing inquiry about God, human life, and the destiny of creation.

More about the future than about the past, this reformation is suggestive as Robert Frost's poem intones: "to stop without a farmhouse near, between the woods and frozen lake, the darkest evening of the year. . . ."

This new reformation is centered in the discourse between science and theology—between liturgy and the lab, if you will—a genuine level of engagement, mutual respect, and sharing. Science and theology are pondering together the deepest divine forests of the cosmos and no one quite knows where the farmhouses are.

And why is this discourse happening? Because at some essential levels, all bets are off on the most tested, trusted, treasured scientific theories, and that has vast implications for us all. Newton's apple may fall from the tree, but newer discoveries in physics suggest a deeper truth, a sub-atomic world of wave and particle that doesn't behave like apples—that doesn't behave like anything we've ever known of before. So, could this then be a glimpse of God, as we sang moments ago in Brian Wren's contemporary hymn, "working night and day, planning all the wonders of creation, setting each equation, genius at play. . . "?

Are there new equations that reveal the genius of God, that therefore invite religion and science to discover a whole new common vocabulary?

These two historically separate disciplines are moving deeper into a lovely, dark woods and there as yet is no map. And how exciting, hopeful, even playful, this all is!

Physicist and theologian Ian Barbour calls this new reformation a trend toward "dialogue," even "integration" of the disciplines and models of science and religion.

Other scientists and theologians look cautiously for a kind of "consonance" or unification of the disciplines where possible and appropriate, and where not, at least mutual respect and humble appreciation for what we can know and what perhaps we cannot ever fully know.

Robert Russell, a UCC physicist and theologian in Berkley, California, believes that, for example, evolutionary theory is a reflection of God at work; the evolutionary universe does not make the Christian faith collapse but rather stimulates discourse and belief in God, the uncovering of God's handiwork, God's "genius at play. . . ."

Theologian Ted Peters declares the magnitude of these close-of-the-century events as a "revolution . . . led by an unpredicted and astounding intellectual trend, namely the re-asking of the God-question within the orbit of scientific discussion about the natural world." No longer needfully separate or adversarial, science and religion are discovering places of mutual meeting to discern "the deeply ingenious nature of God through scientific discovery, the Divine presence in a brave new world of quantum physics, Big Bang and Principle of Indeterminacy, and evolutionary advancement."

As Robert Russell writes: "The universe is more mysterious and more infinite than either science or religion can ever fully disclose, and the urgencies of humankind and the natural environment demand an honest interaction between the discoveries of nature, the empowerment afforded us by appropriate technology, the inherent value of the environment, and the demand that we commit ourselves to a future in which all species can flourish."

This burgeoning revolution requires a new ethic, as science and theology walk together into deeper places of genetic engineering and

scientific discovery; it is far better for the church to be engaged, responsible, encouraging, critiquing, rather than coming up late and con-
demning.

"It is time," trumpets Robert Russell, "that we begin a new, creative interaction between theology and science, an interaction which
honors and respects the integrity of each partner, an interaction in
which convictions are held self-critically and honest engagement is
prized, an interaction which focuses specifically on the most rigorous
theories of mainstream natural science and the most central positions of
mainline theology, an interaction which aims at serving the broader
concerns of the global human and ecological communities. . . ."

It is as Sir John Templeton has suggested, also about humility in
the face of breathtaking change, humility among scientists and theologians, to listen to and learn from one another.

From the biblical vantage point in the Matthew 23 text for this
day, we are witnessing at the close of the century a call to new models
of belief, a renouncement of Pharisee-ism, a joint venture between science and theology in which no one sits at the head table or self-adorns
in the fanciest clothes, but brings to the table humility and awareness
that, like Lutherans and Catholics, science and theology have more to
do together for the sake of the planet and its survival than either discipline can accomplish alone.

It is stopping without a farmhouse near a woods lovely, dark and
deep, and miles to go before we sleep, miles to go before we sleep.

For what we ponder this morning involves the shattering advances in science that touch upon the deepest theological questions we
can ask: Who are we? Who is God? Are we alone in the universe? How
are we to be responsible for what we're discovering? What really matters after all?

Since Luther's hammer, parchment, and nails we have witnessed
a scientific revolution alongside the religious one, particularly pushed
forward during the seventeenth century, if you will, of majestic propor-
tions.

The medieval world-view held that creation was ordered in a unified hierarchy, with every being playing its part; nature served humanity, humanity served God. The social order of things for centuries fit
that world-view; fixed and hierarchical, creation was under our feet,
and we were at the center of the universe—all orbits of things revolving
around us.

The Protestant Reformation did not alter this medieval worldview, even though it turned the church inside out. But by the seven-

teenth century and the rise of modern science, new ways of seeing the world challenged fundamental religious icons. We humans were no longer at the center of the cosmos, and the earth was not really flat. For Galileo's *Dialogue*, published in 1632, and Newton's *Principia*, put to print in 1687, positioned human beings *within* the cosmos but not at the center, and set forth an orderly, deterministic, increasingly knowable universe, built upon observation, experimentation, and mathematics.

Physics was born in this explosive seventeenth century, which overturned Aristotle's way of thinking and which would not be truly challenged in any major way until the twentieth century. And that challenge brings us to this new revolution which re-asks the God-question within the orbit of science.

As Annie Dillard has written:

> Many of us are still living in the universe of Newtonian physics, and fondly imagining that real, hard scientists have no use for these misty ramblings, dealing as scientists do with the measurable and the known. We think that at least the physical causes of physical events are perfectly knowable, and that, as the results of various experiments keep coming in, we gradually roll back the cloud of unknowing. We remove the veils one by one, painstakingly, adding knowledge to knowledge and whisking away veil after veil, until at last we reveal the nub of things, the sparkling equation from whom all blessing flow. . . .

Science has stalked nature as though God can be one day fully known, or that God is no longer necessary for all we need to do in a Newtonian, orderly universe is to improve our microscopes, brain power, and computers and all shall be revealed.

Collect enough data, perfect our instruments, and one day we shall see God, or know the secrets of a godless universe. "Whose woods these are, we think we know. . . ."

Meanwhile religious thinkers and wordsmiths have kept their distance or thrown stones at the scientists' glass houses, uneasy with science's godless tendencies, threatened by science's heady arrogance and relentless pursuit of knowing.

The religious camp wants to hold out for mystery, and the jittery conservatives among us want to say it all came right from the Bible you know, creation in six days, a young earth and people made upright and no room for evolution; for I'm not going to be a monkey's uncle. No, not me. I'm moving to Kansas.

So religion and science—called the "separate majesteria"—have either run separate races or taken pot shots at each other over the generations.

But as Annie Dillard rhapsodizes:

In 1927, Werner Heisenberg pulled out the rug, and our whole understanding of the universe toppled and collapsed. For some reason it has not yet trickled down to the man on the street that some physicists now are a bunch of wild-eyed, raving mystics. For they have perfected their instruments and methods just enough to whisk away the crucial vein, and what stands revealed is the Cheshire cat's grin.

Common sense is out. Like the Pharisees who challenged Jesus, our banquet clothes and prancing about now make us look silly, not smart.

Quantum theory tells us that the world is more strange than we can imagine, holding wave and particle, small and larger world together more and more wonderfully, exquisitely more beautiful and unpredictable than we've ever imagined. And Heisenberg has said, "There is a higher power, not influenced by our wishes, which finally decides and judges. . . ."

So the physicists are becoming mystics. And the theologians are studying quantum mechanics. And there's no farmhouse in sight.

As Heraclitus said, some six centuries before Christ: "Nature is wont to hide herself."

So science and theology approach the "hiddenness" of creation together, the revolution for the new millennium, the re-asking of the God-question, and critiquing in bold ways our understanding of human responsibility; and in so moving together with a blended vocabulary of ethics, may help to save the planet from its own self-destruction.

Jesus came at the Pharisees with new models for God and thus attacked the order of the day; instead of entering into dialogue or searching for common ground, the Pharisees chose to entrap, separate, "one-up" him.

Jesus' argument with these gatekeepers was about the chasm between what they said and how they acted. The Pharisees believed they could command and control adherence to the letter of the law, and in so doing, embody perfect knowing.

Humility, Jesus proclaimed. Humility, rooted in our human searching, our common ground in the cosmos.

Our ongoing reformation approaches differences in ideas and people with a deepening level of humility, whether Protestant, Catholic, or Jew, scientist or theologian.

The old Lutheran book of worship offers a prayer: "Help us to take failure not as a measure of our worth, but as an opportunity for a new start. . . ." Maybe that's the core of our calling, as science and theology humbly come for common cause; as Ted Peters celebrates, "down comes the high wall between church and laboratory . . ." as we embark upon a new century on a very fragile planet earth.

Finally, Robert Frost:

Whose woods these are, I think I know.
His house is in the village though,
He will not see me stopping here
To watch his woods fill up with snow.

My little horse must think it queer
To stop without a farmhouse near,
Between the woods and frozen lake
The darkest evening of the year.

He gives his harness bells a shake
To ask if there is some mistake.
The only other sound's the sweep,
Of easy wind and downy flake.

The woods are lovely, dark and deep,
But I have promises to keep,
And miles to go before I sleep,
And miles to go before I sleep. Amen.

REFERENCES

Annie Dillard, "All Nature Is Touch and Go," pp. 231–233.
Robert Frost, *New Hampshire*, "Stopping By Woods on a Snowy Evening."
The New Century Hymnal of the United Church of Christ, Hymn #11, "Bring Many Names," by Brian Wren.
Ted Peters, *Science and Theology: Toward Consonance*, Boulder, CO: Westview Press, 1999, p. 11.
Robert Russell, "Bridging Science and Religion: Why It Must be Done."

This chapter was originally delivered as a sermon at Hope United Church of Christ, St. Louis, MO, on October 31, 1999.

CHAPTER 23

The Odd Couple: Can Science and Religion Live Together without Driving Each Other Crazy?

MARGARET WERTHEIM

Dr. Margaret Wertheim is the author of *Pythagoras's Trousers*, a history of the relation between physics and religion. She has lectured widely on the subject of science and religion and was the writer and presenter of *Faith and Reason*, a recent PBS special. Her most recent book, *The Pearly Gates of Cyberspace: A History of Space from Dante to the Internet*, has been published by W. W. Norton and Company.

Last June some thirty scientists gathered for a long-anticipated conference in Wheeler Hall, a neoclassical marble edifice on the campus of the University of California at Berkeley. They were an eclectic bunch: astronomers, cosmologists, and physicists (including a Nobel laureate and a leading authority on general relativity) rubbed shoulders with molecular biologists, neuroscientists, and computer scientists. What had drawn the multidisciplinary crowd, and more than three hundred audience members, was the chance to speak publicly about the interaction between science and religion, to talk about how recent developments in their own research fields might be relevant to questions of faith.

The media too were there in force. *The New York Times, The Washington Post, The Wall Street Journal,* and dozens of other major outlets covered the conference, and *Newsweek* delivered the pièce de résistance, a six-page cover story. Radio and television were also in attendance: I reported for PBS. It is no news that God is news—look at any best-seller list—but suddenly the talk about God and science seems to be everywhere.

A few facts: Ten centers devoted to the study of science and religion are now operating in the United States. Together they host an

expanding array of conferences, lectures, and workshops. Around the
country several hundred science-and-religion ("S&R") courses are
taught each year at colleges and universities. Many of them are funded
by the philanthropic might of the John Templeton Foundation, which
is based in Radnor, Pennsylvania, and was founded by the American-
born investment tycoon Sir John Templeton. The foundation sponsored
the Berkeley conference, and it is considering expanding that project
internationally, to the tune of $4 million.

Another Templeton initiative is a $10 million slate of projects for
the theological, social, and scientific study of forgiveness. Projects
funded under that banner include research into cooperative game theory, brain imaging, the onset of AIDS, and primatology. Add to all that
activity a glossy new magazine, *Science and Spirit* (begun with a grant
from the Templeton Foundation), two peer-reviewed journals—*Zygon*
and the soon-to-be-launched *Theology and Science*—plus a veritable tor-
rent of books, and one sees that what is emerging is almost a new academic discipline.

But just what does it mean to study the relations between such
disparate and diverse fields as science and religion? To date, one thing it
has almost universally meant is a focus on Christianity. Although there
have recently been some efforts to reach out to the communities of
other faiths, just about all the major writers in the field so far are practicing Christians. The three books under review here maintain a largely
Christocentric perspective.

Within a Christian context, three questions characterize much
S&R discourse: Can the universe described by science also be seen as
the creation of the Judeo-Christian God? Can that God act within the
scientific universe—and if so, how? Finally, can the Christian story—
with its specific claims about the incarnation of God in the historical
person of Jesus of Nazareth, and its promise of resurrection—continue
to make sense in light of modern science? A corollary to that last question is the issue of purpose: Can the universe described by science be
said to be purposeful, as Christian theology mandates? In the books under review, the short answer to all those questions is yes, though the
authors suggest very different explanations for how and why.

Representing the more orthodox end of the Christian S&R spectrum is John Polkinghorne, an English particle physicist, a past president
and now a fellow of Queens' College, Cambridge, and a current canon
theologian of Liverpool Cathedral. As both a highly respected physicist
and an ordained minister in the Anglican Church, Polkinghorne is one
of the more eminent members of the S&R movement. His new book,

Belief in God in an Age of Science, is a short but succinct encapsulation of his influential views.

For Polkinghorne, the modern scientific understanding of the universe is not merely compatible with the idea of a divine creator; it almost mandates the existence of such a being. Central to Polkinghorne's argument is the so-called anthropic principle. First put forward in 1986 by Polkinghorne's fellow physicists Frank J. Tipler of Tulane University in New Orleans and John D. Barrow of the University of Sussex, Brighton, the anthropic principle proposes that the universe has been specially tailored, or "fine-tuned," to enable the emergence of life. Proponents of the principle ask one to imagine all the physical laws to which the universe might conceivably have been subject, and all the possible values that important physical constants, such as the mass of the proton, might have assumed. Yet, the proponents continue, the laws and constants that happen to hold in our universe are virtually the only ones that could give rise to a universe hospitable to intelligent life. For people who accept the anthropic principle and are also of a theological bent, such fine-tuning is almost surely the deliberate act of a cosmic designer, a Creator who set up the universe so that we (or some life-form like us) would inevitably emerge.

The anthropic principle has received widespread attention not just among religious people, but in secular circles as well. It is based on some rather beguiling features of contemporary physicists' world picture. Consider, for instance, the inverse square law of gravity. The law states that the force between two objects decreases in proportion to the square of the distance between them. In other words, if gravity were even minimally stronger or weaker, stable solar systems could not form. A stronger force of gravity would quickly cause planets to spiral into the sun; a weaker force would allow them to spiral out and drift away. The electromagnetic force is also governed by an inverse square law; if it were any stronger or weaker, stable atoms could not form because electrons would not persist in their orbitals. Thus to proponents of the anthropic principle, it seems that the laws of gravity and electromagnetism, along with many other mathematical relations and physical constants in the world, have been precisely orchestrated to enable atoms and planets—and living systems—to form.

According to Polkinghorne, such a reading of the physical world constitutes a triumphant new natural theology. For him, the new natural theology is different from that of Saint Thomas Aquinas and the eighteenth-century English theologian and philosopher William Paley—who argued, famously, that the mechanism of the eye could be understood only as the creation of an intelligent designer. By contrast, the new natural theology, Polkinghorne says, bases "its arguments not on particular occurrences (the coming-to-be of the eye or of life itself), but on the character of the physical fabric of the world, which is the necessary ground for the possibility of any occurrence." For Polkinghorne, then, the very existence and nature of the physical universe is testimony both to its divine origin and to its inherent cosmic purposefulness.

Yet the anthropic principle suffers from a fundamental flaw. Its proponents assume without question that the mathematical laws and constants applicable to the world around us represent a small subset of the laws and constants that could conceivably exist. As Polkinghorne puts it: "Although we know by direct experience this universe alone, there are many other possible worlds that we can visit with our scientific imaginations." The unacknowledged problem is finding the theoretical grounds to claim that other universes are physically possible. The powers that subscribers to the anthropic principle attribute to the "scientific imagination" are staggering. The basic claim is that if a scientist can, in his or her mind, fiddle with the force of gravity, or the fine-structure constant, or any of the many mathematical parameters found in various equations, and thereby imagine some other universe, then such a universe must ipso facto be a genuinely viable alternative reality. In any other area of human endeavor, such imagining is called fantasy.

In cultures around the world people have imagined a rich assortment of other possible human beings—people with wings, for instance, or people with fins or the private parts of a horse. Yet the fact that I can envision angels, fairies, mermaids, centaurs, and many other fabulous creatures does not make them viable physical realities. The other possible worlds imagined by adherents to the anthropic principle have no greater claim to reality than do any of those creatures. Of course, one can accept anything as a matter of faith, and on that ground I have no quibble with the anthropic principle or its theological extensions. But to suggest that the principle is a sound interpretation of cosmological phenomena is misleading.

The idea that one can pick and choose the mathematical configuration of the universe is based on a quasi-religious Platonistic belief in an a priori realm of mathematical laws that is associated with the "mind of God." Once the supposed realm of infinite potential laws is linked with God, the creation of our specific universe necessarily becomes a conscious, divine act. With that foundation in place, Polkinghorne suggests how God could continue to act in the universe through the stochastic processes of quantum mechanics and the nonpredictive, nonlinear processes now being discovered by complexity scientists.

If you accept Platonism, what emerges from Polkinghorne's book is a coherent picture that demonstrates the powerful consonance that can exist between Christian and scientific world views. But for people who reject a Platonistic interpretation of scientific knowledge—a group that includes not only most philosophers of science but also many scientists—the entire package will fail to convince. Platonism itself is a quasi-religious position. Historically it emerged from a direct association between the integers and the Greek gods, and for most of history it has been sustained by theological underpinnings. The quasi-religiosity of Platonism is a major reason nineteenth-century philosophers of science came up with the alternative position of positivism—which holds that we cannot know the ultimate nature of reality, that all we can know is what our observations and measurements show us. To this day, positivism remains the semiofficial philosophy of the scientific community.

Both Keith Ward and J. Wentzel van Huyssteen want to articulate a more nuanced view of scientific knowledge than Polkinghorne assumes. Van Huyssteen in particular rejects any "foundationalist" vision of the scientific enterprise, or in other words, any claim that some scientific laws or observations are the ultimate truth and are immune to revision or reinterpretation. That philosophical sophistication, however, comes at a price: it seriously complicates both authors' goal of finding a coherent synthesis of Christianity and science. That problem is further compounded by the relatively antifoundationalist view both authors take of religion.

One might think it surprising that theology, of all disciplines, would eschew foundationalism—after all, the idea of God seems the very prototype of the given. But postmodernist thinking has had a great impact on theology for the past half century. And both Ward's and van Huyssteen's books are deeply influenced by the postmodernist desire for pluralism, which translates here into an assertion that the religious systems of other cultures are to be taken seriously. For that reason, both authors must confront questions that Polkinghorne largely ignores.

Ward, who is regius professor of divinity at the University of Oxford, is a relative latecomer to the science-and-religion scene. Much of his long career, which included a stint as a lecturer in mathematical logic, has been spent in the field of comparative religion, and he has written at length on the various ways Buddhists, Christians, Hindus, Jews, and Muslims conceive the world. Ward's widely acclaimed 1996

book, *God, Chance, and Necessity,* defends a theistic and purposeful interpretation of evolution. His new book, *God, Faith, and the New Millennium,*
is the sequel to that work. In it Ward expands his territory, this time
showing how the world view assumed by both the biological and the
physical sciences can be seen as harmonious with the Christian story.

For those who want a general introduction to how Christianity
might fit into the modern scientific world picture, I can think of no better book. Writing in a gentle conversational style, Ward covers all the
major aspects of the Christian world view and shows how they can be
interpreted in light of contemporary science. But there are no literalist
arguments here. Indeed, Ward categorically rejects literalist interpretations of biblical events such as the creation story in Genesis and the vir-
gin birth. Theologically, he says, those stories must be interpreted
metaphorically, and he eloquently describes in each case how one
should do so. Yet in taking that step, he assures Christian readers that
the biblical tales will not lose their religious power. In fact, Ward argues, it is literalism itself that distorts the scriptural messages.

Even for non-Christians Ward's work is valuable. In addition to
his more overtly theological chapters, Ward presents a fine critique of
the strictly reductionist world picture, a philosophy that holds that
everything can be explained by the properties of fundamental constituent parts such as atoms and genes. Given the loudness with which
various proponents of that position have lately been proclaiming their
views, Ward's book is particularly welcome. I happened to be reading it
simultaneously with Harvard University biologist Edward O. Wilson's
recent book *Consilience,* and I could not help thinking what an excellent
antidote Ward provides to that eminent scientist's hubris and epistemic
totalitarianism. (Don't get me wrong: I love the ants and the biophilia; I
just can't stomach the Genes-R-Us approach to human emotions and
culture.) Wilson's attempt to explain everything by an almost puerile
cause-and-effect reductionism is just plain silly.

In a philosophical chapter titled "Breaking out of the Mechanistic
Universe," Ward explains why deterministic reductionism is itself a position of faith—why it cannot be justified by logic alone, as so many of
its champions imply. For causal determinists such as Wilson, who hold
that everything that happens is fully determined by the initial conditions of any system, "it is the laws of physics that make effects follow
from their causes." Determinists, therefore, maintain that everything
that takes place in the universe is ultimately a by-product of physical
laws. But as Ward notes, that view simply raises the question of what
compels the physical world to obey the laws at all. Contrary to the

causative Platonists, who believe the laws themselves have the power, Ward suggests that the mathematical laws physicists discover are "more like descriptions of what actually happens" than they are "mysteriously existing principles that make things happen."

Although such laws may accurately describe how physical action unfolds, Ward stresses that they cannot themselves be causative: those ephemeral equations cannot be the source of physical action. That is a crucial philosophical point, and one too often glossed over by secular Platonists. For Christians, Ward says, the answer to the dilemma is that God is the ultimate source of physical action. He must be seen not just as the creator of the universe, but as the force that sustains the world and everything that happens in it. Whereas nontheists will disagree with that conclusion, it is intellectually honest: one reaches a fundamental philosophical barrier and one makes a leap of faith. As a nontheist myself, I find this argument to be much cleaner than the unacknowledged religiosity of so many causative Platonists, who think that by merely articulating descriptive laws of action and form they have resolved the ontological question.

Much of what is gently implied in Ward's book is explicitly worked through in van Huyssteen's. The latter seeks a "postfoundationalist" synthesis of science and religion, a synthesis that avoids absolutist (and culturally specific) views. For that reason, *Duet or Duel?* is the most difficult of the works under review, and in my view it is perhaps the most important book on science and religion since the 1990 publication of *Religion in an Age of Science*, by the physicist and theologian Ian G. Barbour.

Van Huyssteen, who teaches at Princeton Theological Seminary in New Jersey, is both a philosopher of science and a theologian. But whereas many writers on science and religion have treated postmodernism as the enemy of both, van Huyssteen recognizes that the late twentieth century is an indelibly postmodern milieu. So it is within the basic framework of postmodernism that he attempts to build a bridge between Christianity and science.

The influence of postmodernist thinking on modern theology has been fueled, in large part, by a desire to transcend the religious dogmatism of the past. Crusades are not an option anymore. In the global culture of the twentieth and twenty-first centuries, proponents of all the major world religions have been forced to come to terms with peaceful coexistence. Interfaith dialogue has compelled Christian theologians to take a more pluralistic view of religion, and postmodernism has been an invaluable resource for that enterprise.

But postmodernism also poses a danger for theology. Although individual believers may genuinely value other religious traditions, they must also hold that their own faith gives a true account of reality. And because many religious beliefs are frankly incompatible with one another (Jews and Muslims, for instance, reject the Christian claim that God was incarnated in Jesus), competing claims of religious truth continue to present a major challenge for theology. Van Huyssteen cannot be expected to resolve that dilemma, nor does he. What he does do is point out that it is no longer confined to theology: foundationalist views of scientific knowledge are equally impossible to sustain.

Those views are not likely to win many converts for van Huyssteen among readers of *The Sciences;* even the many theologians who accept some form of religious pluralism seem largely unwilling to countenance any postmodernist assessment of science. In many S&R forums I have attended, postmodernism has been vehemently attacked. Yet I think van Huyssteen is right; it is precisely for its insights about the contextual embedding of *all* knowledge that postmodernist thinking can serve as an important bridge between science and religion.

The current bitterness engendered by the so-called science wars has obscured the fact that postmodernism expresses an essentially reasonable insight: all knowledge is derived within a particular cultural framework and will therefore reflect aspects of that culture. Medieval Europeans, for instance, lived within a Christian-Aristotelian framework, and their cosmology, with its central earth surrounded by ten celestial spheres of increasing metaphysical purity, reflected both Christian and Aristotelian perspectives. Likewise, the Australian Aborigines' understanding of the physical environment reflects their sophisticated philosophy-cum-religion of the Dreamtime.

One of the claims of postmodernists is that modern Western scientific knowledge is also culturally influenced, that it is not purely objective. That does not mean that postmodernists believe scientific knowledge is simply made up; no postmodernist scholar of science of my acquaintance holds such a view. The claim is not that the laws of physics are mere cultural constructs—that, for instance, the inverse square law of gravity could change from one culture to the next. The thesis is rather that the entire world picture described by contemporary physics—such as the view that time is linear or the belief that reality is purely physical—is a culturally specific way of seeing.

Unfortunately, many scientists, as well as many science-and-religion students, have viewed postmodern interpretations of science as inherently threatening. Indeed, I suspect that many scientists would say that if the rapprochement of science and religion demands a postmodernist view of science, then one can live without the rapprochement. Van Huyssteen urges against that fear. In a pluralistic world, he argues, everyone must take a more open stance toward all forms of knowledge, including science. Although that path is necessarily a difficult one—and far more intellectually demanding than foundationalist approaches—it seems to me the only way forward that can avoid a new form of dogmatism. Without such an open-minded perspective, science is in danger of replacing Christianity as the new engine of Western cultural imperialism. For clearly confronting the obstacles facing anyone seeking connections between science and religion in a pluralistic world, *Duet or Duel?* should be mandatory reading for everyone in the field.

After van Huyssteen's sophisticated elucidation of the problem, I was eager to read his proposed resolution. But here I was disappointed. Attempting to break free of foundationalist dogma, he posits that a synthesis of science and religion is to be found in "evolutionary epistemology," a developing field that attempts to understand human rationality in light of biological evolution.

It is a noble goal, but even van Huyssteen does not seem wholly convinced by the potential of the approach. Although he is certainly right that human rationality must be grounded in our biological makeup, he undercuts his proposed solution by stressing—again, rightly, in my view—that our minds are not determined entirely by biology: there must be, he says, a good deal more to rationality than genetic programming and neurological wiring. Beyond the undisputed fact that both religious and scientific thinking emerge from the same neuronal complex (the human brain), van Huyssteen has little to say about how the two forms of knowing relate. Thus his solution does not get one very far along the path to rapprochement. Science and religion remain, if not in conflict, nonetheless separate domains of knowledge.

That shortcoming should not, in my view, be seen as a failure. A genuinely postfoundationalist synthesis of science and religion is something I suspect will be a long time coming. For one thing, such a synthesis would have to address a truly staggering religious pluralism—not just the so-called great world religions, but also the vast diversity of indigenous religions in places such as Australia, Africa, and North America. Why should those radically different frameworks be excluded?

Moreover, philosophers of science are now beginning to claim that many indigenous knowledge systems include a genuine alternative scientific understanding of the world. The Australian philosopher of science Helen Watson-Verran of the University of Melbourne, who has studied the Yolngu Aborigines for the past twelve years, asserts that their understanding of the physical world amounts to a truly scientific system. Similar claims have been made about the Yoruba of Nigeria and the Native American Blackfeet. If that is so, *science* turns out to be a term as multifaceted and problematic as *religion*.

The shadow of Christian foundationalism hangs heavy over the world. It is incumbent upon the science-and-religion movement not to repeat the sins of the past. The question that cannot be avoided is, in any synthesis of science and religion, whose deities and whose cosmologies will be included?

Belief in God in an Age of Science
by John Polkinghorne
Yale University Press, 1998
133 pages; $18.00

God, Faith, and the New Millennium: Christian Belief in an Age of Science
by Keith Ward
Oneworld Publications, 1998
224 pages; $14.95, softcover

Duet or Duel? Theology and Science in a Postmodern World
by J. Wentzel van Huyssteen
Trinity Press International, 1998
182 pages; $16.00, softcover

This chapter was originally published in *The Sciences* (New York Academy of Sciences) vol. 39, no. 2 (March/April 1999), pp. 38–43. ©1999 New York Academy of Sciences. All rights reserved.

CHAPTER 24

What a Piece of Work Is Man: Humanism, Religion, and the New Cosmology

THEODORE ROSZAK

Theodore Roszak is the author of several works that explore the relationship of science and religion, among them *Where the Wasteland Ends*, *The Voice of the Earth*, *The Memoirs of Elizabeth Frankenstein*, and most recently, *The Gendered Atom: Reflections on the Sexual Psychology of Science*. He teaches at California State University, Hayward.

Though they would be the last to admit it, scientists have the same weakness as the rest of us for folklore, by which I mean beliefs that bend the historical truth in order to teach a lesson. Think how often you've come across the story of the Copernican Revolution in astronomy. Before Copernicus, so we're told, the study of the heavens was dominated by human vanity. Popular science writers especially enjoy blaming the geocentric world-view on benighted religious authorities who believed human beings were so important that God placed them at the center of the universe. Only scientists were courageous and clear-eyed enough to overcome such cosmic egocentrism.

For example, in a recent book, *Full House*, Stephen Jay Gould asserts that "We once thought that we lived on the central body of a limited universe until Copernicus, Galileo, and Newton identified the Earth as a tiny satellite to a marginal star." In Gould's eyes, this was the first in a long line of proud scientific achievements, the goal of which was the "successive dethronement of human arrogance from one pillar after another of our cosmic assurance." Similarly, in *The Demon-Haunted World*, the last book he published before his death, Carl Sagan takes up the same cliché. Recounting all the wishfully foolish ideas that science has debunked, he places at the head of the list the notion "that there is such a place as the center of the universe and that the Earth sits in that exalted spot."

No doubt both Gould and Sagan would be shocked to learn that the story they delight so much in telling is pure folklore. If they could find anyone who ever believed that the center of the universe was a privileged and exalted location, they would have found the rare exception. But as with all folklore, the truth is not what matters most. More important is the ethical subtext that clings to the tale, in this case the notion that premodern astronomy was dominated by pride. Scientists want desperately to believe they have more to contribute to our lives than a collection of facts and theories about the natural world; they want to offer us moral guidance as well as clear thinking. They believe that, by dislodging the Earth from the center of the universe, science at one stroke thwarted human self-aggrandizement and called upon mankind to surrender its childish consolations. Like Gould, many scientists would describe themselves as "tough-minded intellectuals," brave souls who can do without the pretensions of cosmic importance that our weak-minded and infantile ancestors needed.

The bravado that attaches to the heliocentric world-view is so precious to modern science that one feels churlish to observe not only that it is wrong, but that it is exactly the reverse of the truth. Where Gould and Sagan find arrogance, they should find meekness if not groveling self-abnegation; and where they credit science with a proper humility, they might do better to detect a certain smug presumption on their own part. Their familiar reading of the Copernican Revolution not only distorts religion, but science as well. In brief, it's bad folklore and ought to be discarded.

Even a cursory survey of intellectual history should be enough to remind us that the geocentric cosmos is neither Christian nor biblical in origin. It was inherited by Western Christendom from Greek astronomers who were the best scientists of their time. The Greeks, of course, did not see the cosmos as "God's universe"; nor did they regard centrality as a "privileged position." In the Ptolemaic system, geocentrism was a matter of naive empiricism. The Earth seemed motionless; the heavenly spheres appeared to move around it. Heliocentrism, in contrast, seemed contrary to observation. After all, if the Earth went around the sun, then one should be able to detect parallax—the apparent movement of any sighted star against the distant heavens. Relying on the naked eye, no one could, not even Copernicus.

Since the goal of ancient astronomy was, like that of subatomic physics today, to "save the appearances," the Greeks sought to find a simple and consistent way to account for the observable data, even if one could not always explain why things were as they seemed to be. In this respect, the Ptolemaic universe not only appealed to everyday experience, but it was practical. It served as the basis for navigation until modern times.

Quite as important as achieving overall empirical consistency, Ptolemaic astronomy was created in obedience to the principles of Aristotelian physics. In Greek physics, the Earth functioned as the gravitational core of the universe. The center was the bottom of Ptolemy's cosmos; that is why heavy things fell "down." Objects containing earth moved toward the place where they "belonged," and indeed they accelerated as they fell because they were jubilantly approaching their proper sphere. This, again, had nothing to do with arrogance. Rather it derived from the qualitative bias of Aristotelian physics. It was assumed that, in a perfect Aristotelian universe, the core of the cosmos would be a solid ball of earthen matter, qualitatively the most ponderous of the four classical elements. Next would come a sphere of pure water, then a sphere of pure air, finally a sphere of pure fire, the latter two elements possessing the buoyant quality of "levity" that one observes in their tendency to lift toward the skies. But ours was clearly not a perfect universe; so in the world we inhabit, the qualities were seen to be intermingled chaotically. Hence, our lives were beset by restless movement, change, decay, and death. All this stood in stark contrast to the superlunary universe, where the fifth element, quintessence, reigned. Quintessence, from which the heavenly bodies were fashioned, was special and totally unearthly; it was weightless, imperishable, and moved perpetually in perfect circles.

These were the teachings of the most rational and empirical scientific thinking of the ancient world. It was a self-consistent and logical system that had nothing to do with privilege or vanity. Greek cosmology stayed admirably free of moral interpretation for a great deal longer than, say, evolutionary biology did in modern times at the hands of Social Darwinists. There were, however, certain ascetic schools of thought in the Greek world that derived a moral lesson from this world-picture. For Pythagorean and Platonic philosophers, heavy matter was at the bottom of the universe metaphorically as well as physically. The body, as a material object, was made from the "lowest" of all substances: hence it was impermanent, perishable, mortal. Moral perfection and epistemological clarity soared high above in a changeless, spiritual realm far beyond the flesh.

Moral teachings like this were not the basis of ancient science; they were a metaphysical overlay that was quite dispensable. But once Christianity entered the picture, natural philosophy took a back seat to theology. Christians, especially of an Augustinian persuasion, readily seized upon these hierarchical distinctions to support their moral code. They eagerly made much of the fact that the Earth was at the "bottom" of the universe, the most distant point from God. In contrast, heaven and the seven orders of angels were at the "top." In their view the lowly Earth was the only fit habitat for human beings who had "fallen," or bottomed-out both morally and physically. Far from being in a privileged position, the human race lived in the cesspool of creation where all the gross, decaying, flawed things in the universe flowed together. That is what it meant to be at the "center." Centrality could be pressed to an even deeper level of degradation. For what, after all, did Christians believe lay at the core of the Earth, deep in its fiery volcanic interior? Hell, filled with all the damned souls that had yielded to the temptations of the flesh. Dante went one step farther. In his *Divine Comedy,* one finds Hell at the center of the universe, and at the center of Hell one finds Satan, frozen into the final icy circle of damnation.

This darkly misanthropic view was carried forward into the Reformation. For example, the seventeenth-century Christian divine John Wilkens believed that "bodies must bee as farre distant in place as in Nobilitie. . . . The Earth is a more ignoble substance than the other Planets, consisting of a more base and vile matter." Calvin was even more emphatic:

> If God had formed us of the stuff of the sun or the stars, or if he had created any other celestial matter out of which man could have been made, then we might have said that our beginning was honorable. . . . But . . . we are all made of mud, and this mud is not just on the hem of our gown, or on the sole of our boots, or in our shoes. We are full of it, we are nothing but mud and filth both inside and outside.

It would take the new science to teach us that even mud, slime, and dirt are wondrous in their complexity and fertility.

We are creatures of "vile matter." That is the true, historical meaning of being at the center of the Ptolemaic universe. Not pride, but guilt. Not privilege, but radical unworthiness. Centrality meant fallenness. For Christian theologians, that cosmological connection served to excoriate human presumption. By the time modern science made its appearance, the war upon human vanity was old business. The new development on the scene, with which science allied itself, was Renaissance humanism. Proudly outspoken humanists dared to court ecclesiastical displeasure by reversing this dark calumny upon the Earth. Pico della Mirandola, arguing for the "dignity of man," was striking a bravely innovative note in Western culture. Shakespeare, caught between two world-views, could turn either into great poetry. Here he is invoking the dour, old cosmology that taught us our lowly place in nature, far below the magnificence of the starry heavens:

> Look how the floor of heaven
> Is thick inlaid with patinas of bright gold;
> There's not the smallest orb which thou beholdst
> But in his motion like an angel sings,
> Still quiring to the young-eyed cherubims.
> Such harmony is in immortal souls;
> But whilst this muddy vesture of decay
> Doth grossly close it in, we cannot hear it.

But then here he is echoing the rising humanistic spirit of his day:

> What a piece of work is man, how noble in reason, how infinite in faculty . . . In action how like an angel! In apprehension how like a god!

The bard's Puritan contemporaries would have rushed to agree with the first passage but they would have cried "blasphemy!" at the impertinence of the second.

Ironically, then, scientists such as Gould and Sagan, in their effort to lower the status of humanity, are unwittingly allying themselves with the misanthropy of premodern theology. But if they wish to score points against their hypothetical religious opposition, they would do better to move in exactly the opposite direction. It is humanistic modern science that has shown us the hidden glories within "base and vile matter" and the astonishing capacity of the human mind, even within its "muddy vesture of decay," to understand nature.

We may also have reached the point where we can dispense with another, closely related scientific cliché, namely that the size of the Earth is a measure of its insignificance. How many times have we heard it said that we live on a infinitesimal planet orbiting around a third-rate star on the edge of a minor galaxy adrift in the infinite void? The Earth may be a mere speck when it comes to size, but what does that have to do with value? If science has taught us anything, it is that physical stature implies nothing regarding significance. The tiniest things in nature, down to the level of the quarks, reveal remarkable complexities worthy of a lifetime of study.

By unjudgingly taking all things great and small into its purview, the science of our day has discovered an extraordinary fact about the "vast impersonal cosmos." We now know that in an expanding or inflating universe, time, size, temperature, and atomic/molecular complexity are intimately related. All these evolve through a unique history. It is only in a universe of a certain age and size that the heavy elements essential to life could ever have come into existence. In a "smaller" universe (meaning in this universe at any time before the most recent several billion years) nucleosynthesis could not yet have taken place, nor would the requisite cooling have occurred. Far from being humiliatingly dwarfed by the size of the cosmos, life on Earth has emerged from a process of stellar evolution that required this much time and this much expansion. At least with respect to the appearance of an inhabited planet, the universe is exactly the "right" size. As John Gribbin and Martin Rees put it, "the conditions in our universe really do seem to be uniquely suitable for life forms like ourselves." Or, to put it more flippantly, but no less accurately: "hydrogen is a light, odorless gas, which, given enough time, turns into people." Meaning that hydrogen could only weave itself into life in a universe just this big, no smaller.

Scientists continue to struggle with the baffling interplay of chance and coincidence in nature, especially when coincidences threaten to add up to the appearance of design. For example, in 1992 the COBE satellite sent back messages that have been called the most important finding in the history of science—"the Holy Grail" of cosmology, as Michael Turner of the University of Chicago termed it. Another member of the COBE team, George Smoot, remarked, "If you're religious, it's like seeing God." COBE was launched to make minute measurements of the cosmic background radiation that is the vibrant relic of the Big Bang. Until COBE, that radiation seemed to be absolutely uniform in all directions, which left cosmologers unable to account for the galactic structure of the cosmos. Where did the galaxies come from in a universe that was formlessly smooth in all directions? COBE discovered that there are irregularities in the background radiation, which the project directors attributed to early cosmic turbulence. From that turbulence came "topological defects" in space; and from the defects "clumps" formed that might have produced the gravitational clustering that transformed primordial matter into galaxies.

"Lumps," "clumps," "defects," "turbulence." These are the words most often used to summarize the results of COBE—curiously lackluster terms to describe the "Holy Grail of cosmology." They are also highly misleading when one realizes that not just any old "irregularity" will do to build a galaxy. It must be the "right kind" of irregularity. No doubt when the process is fully understood, it will be added to the lengthening list of cosmic coincidences that just happen to make the universe a fit home for living, thinking beings.

Words like "lumps" and "clumps" are left over from the agnostic science of the late nineteenth century; they are casually dismissive phrases that are meant to avoid the implication of intelligent structure. But one can use very different images to describe what COBE uncovered. Clumps have also been depicted as gravitational "seeds" from which galaxies sprout like flowers of fire. In any case, when the COBE findings were reported to the world, members of the research team were willing to call their discovery "the handwriting of God," as if their astonishing discovery required some grander rhetoric than science itself could provide.

When Stuart Kauffman titles his book *At Home in the Universe,* or when Hubert Reeves tells us we are the "children of this universe," they are doing no more than drawing metaphorically upon what the best cosmological thought of our time tells us about the place of life in the nature of things. We may no longer be at the center of the universe, but we do inhabit the frontier of unfolding cosmic time. And that makes us, at the very least, participant observers in a universe that would seem to have gone to remarkable pains to make life possible. Reeves, who is among the most moving of the new cosmologers, puts it this way:

> There was this old attitude that . . . people do not belong here, that we are an impossible chance, . . . that we're foreign to this universe. I think what cosmology shows is that this is not true. We are a product of the evolution of the universe. And we are in the same history, in the same evolution as the stars and the frogs. We are all part of the same universe and all part of the evolution which has led to different objects, aspects, beings and in this sense we belong to this universe . . . we are made out of stardust.

Stardust. What would Calvin say had he lived to know that we are indeed created from "the stuff of the sun or the stars"? Would that brighten his dark vision of humanity?

Nothing has greater religious significance in modern science than the service it has done in redeeming nature from the inferior and fallen status to which mainstream religions of the past so often condemned it. The new cosmology and the sciences of complexity have returned us to

that humanistically relevant universe with which modern science began its proud history. There may be hard-headed types in the sciences
who still feel compelled to debunk and belittle, but they are beginning
to look rather like the adversaries Galileo challenged in his famous debate on the new world system. For a variety of reasons ethical, theological, literary, and metaphysical Galileo's foes simply could not let go of
the familiar old Ptolemaic cosmos. So too in our time, scientists who
have taken their stand in life on what Bertrand Russell once called "the
firm foundation of unyielding despair" will no doubt do the same, continuing to speak of our living planet as lost in the stars, adrift in the
void, a result of mere chance, a cosmic absurdity, and so on, and so on.

But the universe no longer seems to be on their side.

This chapter was originally published in *Network: The Scientific and Medical
Network Review* (December 1999), pp. 3–5.